I0817974

Royal
Museum of
Fine Arts
Antwerp

KMSKA

Royal
Museum of
Fine Arts
Antwerp

EDITING
Patrick De Rynck
PHOTOGRAPHY
Karin Borghouts
COORDINATION
Véronique Van Passel

THE FINEST MUSEUM

HANNIBAL

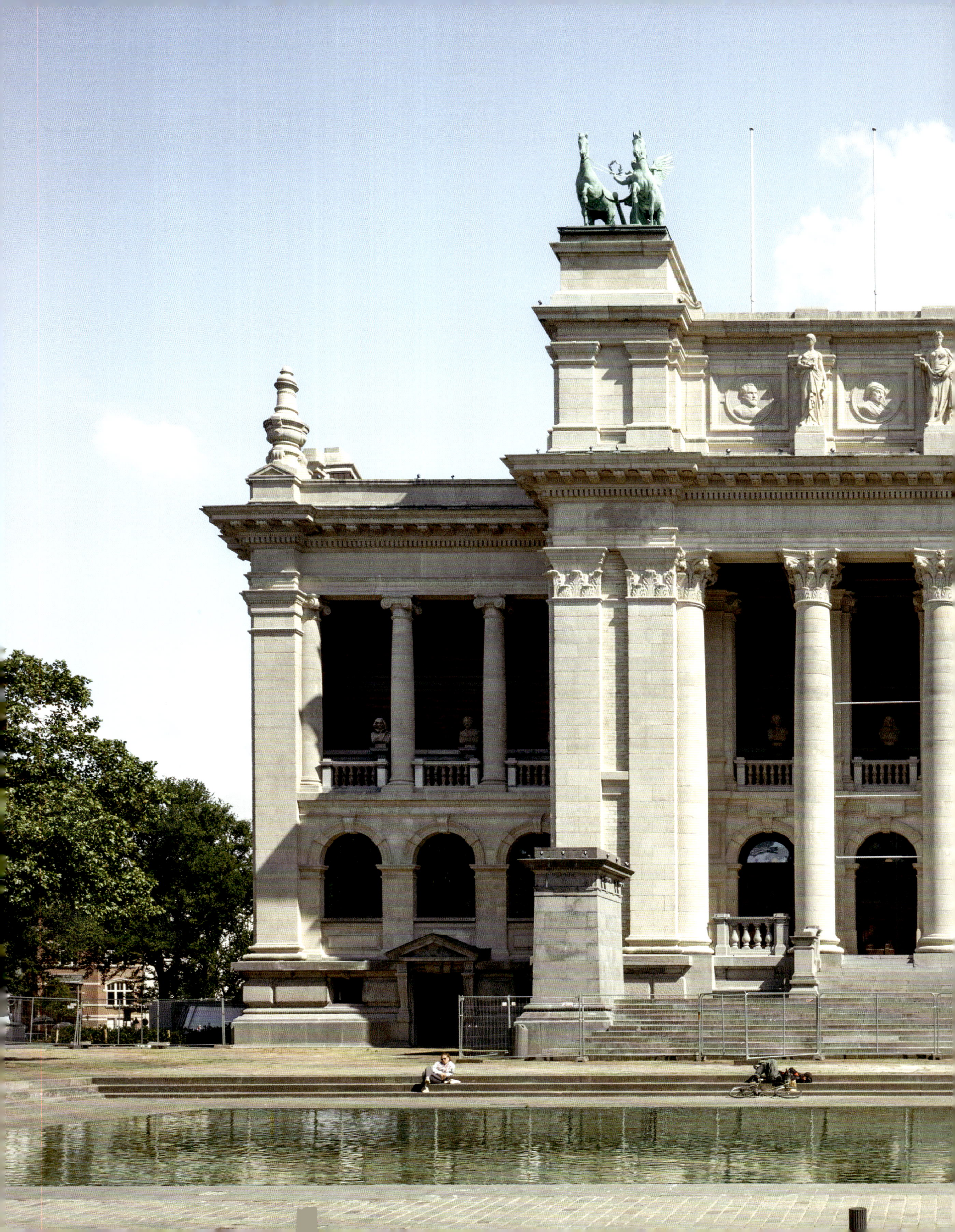

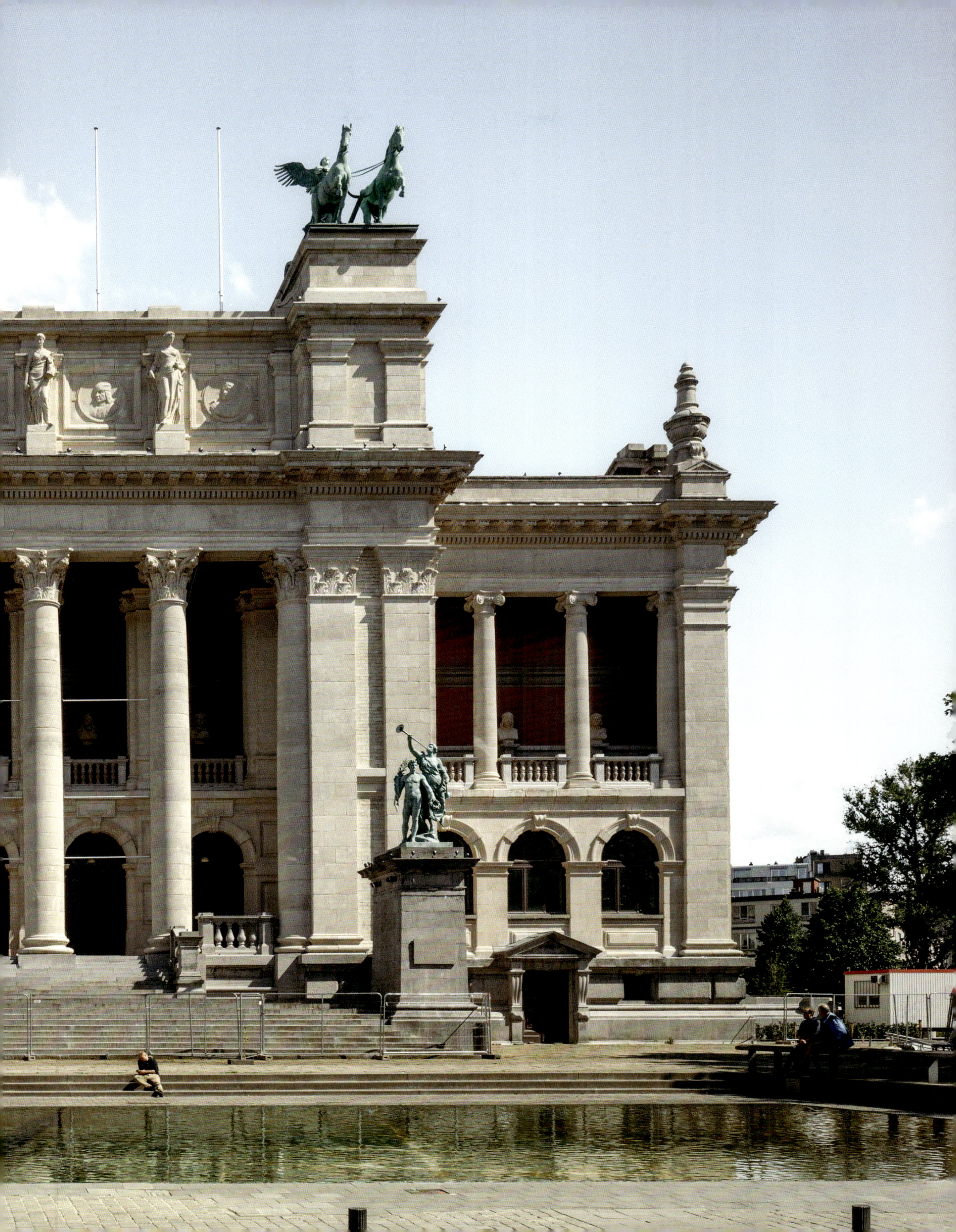

Foreword

Luk Lemmens,
Chair of the Board
of Directors KMSKA vzw

It is with great pride that I write the foreword to this book, which documents the creation process of our *very* fine art museum. After 11 years of construction and renovation, our doors opened to the public once again on 24 September 2022.

This book provides an impression of the energy, enthusiasm, expertise and ideas that so many people have contributed to the new KMSKA. You can feel the love and passion for the museum in everything.

It is my great privilege to be Chair of the Board of Directors at this key moment in time.

The starting signal for the preparation of a masterplan for a new museum came in 2004. That plan was developed by KAAN Architecten from Rotterdam. No fewer than five successive Flemish Ministers of Culture made the necessary resources available. This is how the masterplan was eventually completed in its entirety. Prime Minister Jan Jambon opened the museum with a suitable sense of pride.

It has been an exercise in patience, but also in perseverance. All parties involved deserve praise for this. In particular, I would like to express my gratitude to all the designers and contractors who participated in this enormous project. The entire KMSKA team also has put in a phenomenal effort to finally be able to share "their" museum with you, in all its glory.

Thanks to all these combined forces, the KMSKA is entering a new era. As a truly open house, where everyone is welcome.

Visitors who knew the old museum will hopefully soon feel at home in the new museum too. A beautiful symbiosis has been achieved between the old and the new. Justice has been done to a story that is more than 200 years old, while at the same time we have embarked on a new story.

The new KMSKA will undoubtedly connect with the general public, who were invited to be actively involved in the roll-out of the new concept. Our "finest hundred", an apt name for the KMSKA trial audience, tested everything in advance and gave it their nod of approval.

In the period leading up to the reopening, it was heartwarming to see enthusiasm for the museum growing: in the city of Antwerp, across Flanders, internationally and also, especially, in the business world. It is partly thanks to their support that we were able to realise the book you are holding.

Finally, I would like to thank Patrick De Rynck and everyone who worked on this finest book about The Finest Museum. Photographer Karin Borghouts followed the entire construction period and captured the metamorphosis on film. This book includes a selection of her beautiful photos.

I am convinced that the KMSKA has a bright future ahead of it, as befits the finest museum in the finest city in the country.

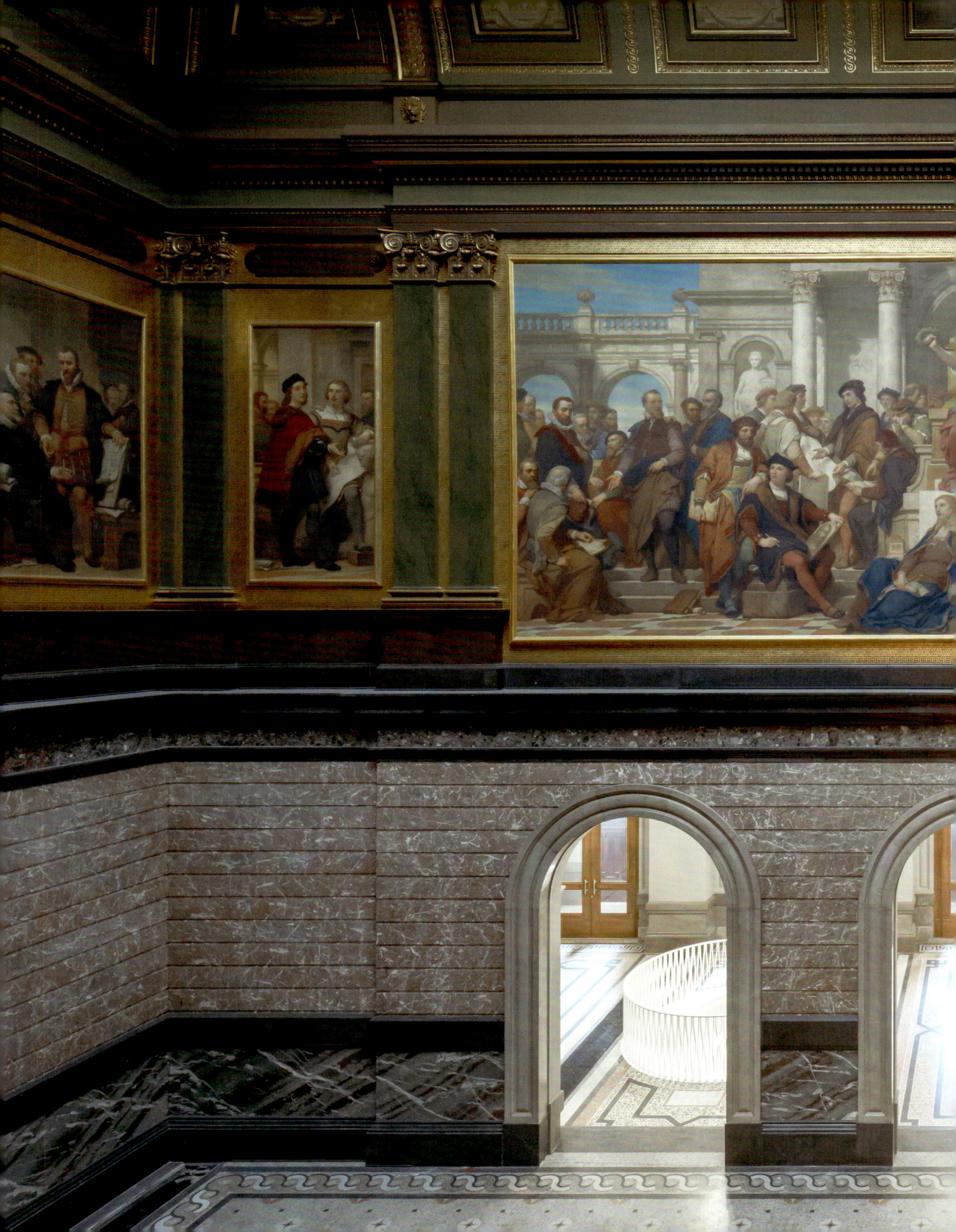

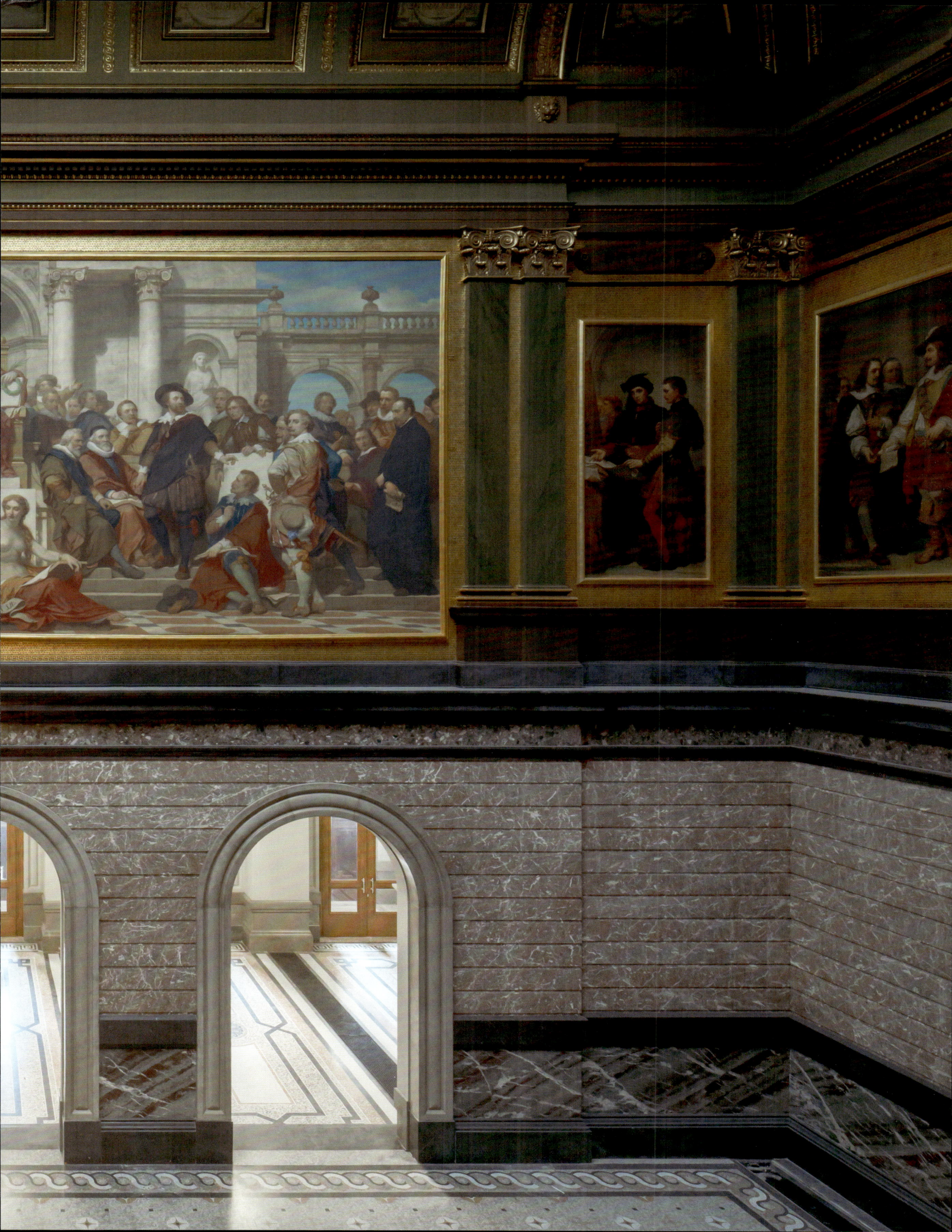

An enterprising museum

Conversation with Carmen Willems,
KMSKA Managing Director

As Director of the KMSKA, Carmen Willems has led the final stage of the museum's metamorphosis. We are, of course, talking about the renovated building and the new museum volume, but also about so much more: the entire museum has been transformed, including the parts behind the scenes. How does she see the KMSKA in the 21st century?

"The most visible metamorphosis is the building itself, there's no getting around it. I am very pleased that the Flemish Government committed itself to such an ambitious masterplan. Having the vision to work with a masterplan was vital. You may have a museum collection with fantastic art, but if you don't have a home for it with a good roof and solid walls, you're nowhere."

"The architect, Dikkie Scipio of KAAN Architecten, created a very ingenious plan using the existing structure of the 19th-century building. It had really become very dilapidated. She made the choice to restore the historic building to its former splendour by removing all later additions. And she then dropped the new structure in, right into the historic patios, as it were. Four legs and a tabletop, as she calls it. She has managed to create two worlds in one structure: the old building is symmetrical, horizontal and offers an enfilade of rooms, while the new building is designed to amaze, and is a mainly vertical entity. Scipio chose to have the new building speak to the old one on equal terms. The two parts shouldn't be in competition with each other. I think she succeeded incredibly well. For this successful integration we've actually already received a significant European prize: the European Award for Architectural Heritage Intervention 2020."

Flexible

If a museum has been closed for a long time, does it mean it's reopening its doors to a different world, especially considering our rapidly changing times? To ask the question is to answer it. Carmen Willems: "I am convinced of it. The world has changed drastically, especially with the added and lasting impact of the coronavirus crisis in 2020–21. There's no denying it. Just think of the rapidly accelerating developments in digital and multimedia. A museum like ours needs to move with the times – and it does. Visitors' expectations are also growing, partly due to competition from novel initiatives appearing in fields approximate to museums. As a contemporary museum, it would be foolish to ignore the fact that people increasingly look at their visit as an 'experience', and that new technologies can help to realise such expectations. So we make good use of them."

"At the same time, our main focus remains firmly on viewing the artworks, and how you can guide, support and inspire people in doing so. This can be done in many ways, but really looking at art always lies at the heart of things. At first glance, the KMSKA's approach may still seem very traditional. Our artworks are our central focus because they deserve all that attention. But visitors will quickly discover that we are inviting them to engage in a dialogue in many different ways and actively encouraging participation."

"I'll tell you about another aspect: when you consider our organisation chart, you can see far-reaching changes. Here too there's been a complete change of structure. We have positions and roles that you'd never have heard of 15 years or so ago – for example, roles relating to participation. All this is necessary if a museum is to keep up with the times. A lot of flexibility is being asked of museum employees."

Silver lining
"Every cloud has a silver lining: the lengthy closure allowed an intensive restoration of the collection's pieces that are on show in the galleries. Our collection is now in top condition, and for works that still need it, there are plans to treat them on site, in the gallery. I know of no other museum that has achieved a programme of this kind and scale in such a short time, and with a collection of this quality. This was possible thanks to our own conservation studio, and also through collaborations with museums abroad. Government support is very important in this regard, but so is private funding. We had to get up to speed very quickly, which was possible partly because of the closure: when the museum is up and running, there are always daily tasks to attend to and you can forget to look after more long-term issues. We were able to fully focus on our role as a cultural enterprise, to meet the expectations currently being made of a large and contemporary museum, and rightly so. We have an obligation to society. The government has a role to play as owner of the collection and of this extraordinary building – it has, accordingly, invested heavily in it. It seems logical to me that a museum should also be able to support its own programming with various sources of income – tickets, concessions, partnerships. Although that remains a major challenge in these uncertain times, I must admit."

"Being a cultural entrepreneur is a mental shift that we have been able to make in recent years, despite the postponements due to the coronavirus pandemic. It's also very interesting to become more enterprising, because you're continually expanding your support base in this way. Partners include you in their communications, for example. In the run-up to the reopening in September 2022, it was great to see how enthusiasm for the museum has grown – which is also a token of hope in these bizarre times."

Visible
Presenting top-notch exhibitions is impossible for a museum nowadays unless it is part of a larger network of museums. Carmen Willems: "If you are closed for a long time and have a collection like ours, it's an excellent opportunity to provide international art loans and thus forge bonds. This has been ongoing since 2011. It's all done by gentleman's agreement, without having to be written down. That's how the sector operates. We are now enjoying the goodwill this generated, in our loan requests for our projects. Another important point is the series of national and international exhibitions, which we largely conceived ourselves, in which we have been able to highlight certain artists in our collection. The KMSKA has remained very visible. We will reap the benefits of that, I'm sure. However, there is also a concern here: networks often rely on personal contacts. How will that evolve, if you see that jobs in the museum world are becoming increasingly volatile, much more so than in the past. How can you then sustainably maintain your network of relationships?"

Up-to-date
A theme that has come to the fore while we were closed is the pursuit of inclusion, diversity and participation: art museums need to appeal to a more diverse audience, be more accessible, allow the population and visitors to be involved… Also, of course, they have their past, and that past is – let's say it – rather masculine, white and elitist. Carmen Willems: "You have to bring about this change, but the essence will always be there in our DNA. You don't have to rid yourself of your past entirely, but of course you can improve your values and bring it up to date. In this respect too, the closure helped us to take the right steps, after much consultation. A lot of thought and effort has gone into encouraging inclusivity and diversifying our offering. Our Artists in Residence programme is one example. When you compare the composition of that group in 2022 with the first one, in 2016, you can see how much more diverse it has become. It's a great change, and it also leads to new crossovers between disciplines. Art museums are also up to this change. I must say that we've been aided in this by the businesses that support us: they too are encouraging inclusion in their own work as businesses, and allow vulnerable people to gain hope through art, to feel awe and to experience that they are part of our shared society."

"It is still a work in progress for a museum like ours – and for all museums. We've come a long way and we shouldn't be ashamed of where we are. Now we're going to find out whether the steps we have taken and the things we are trying out actually work. Ultimately, that's for our visitors to judge."

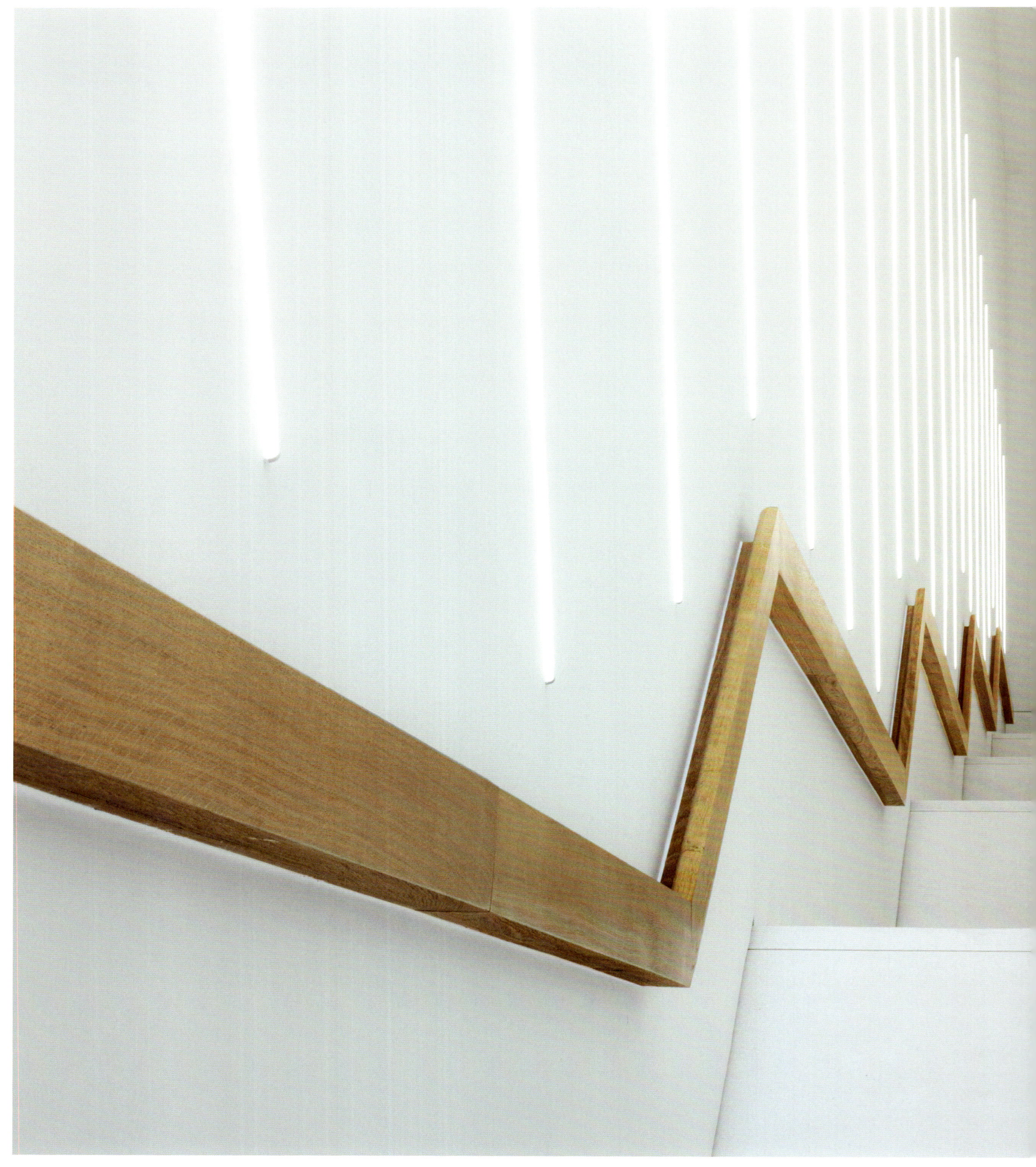

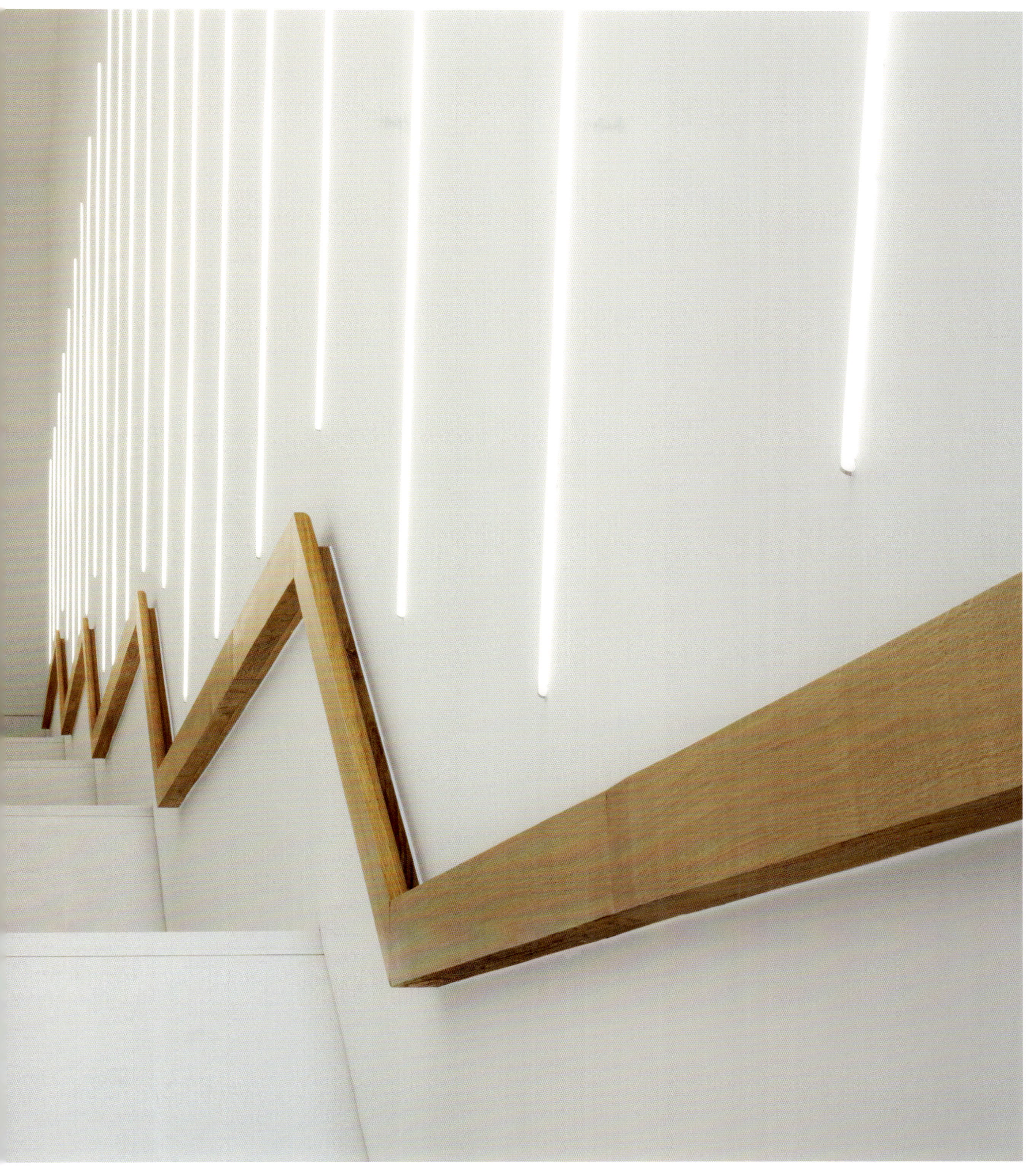

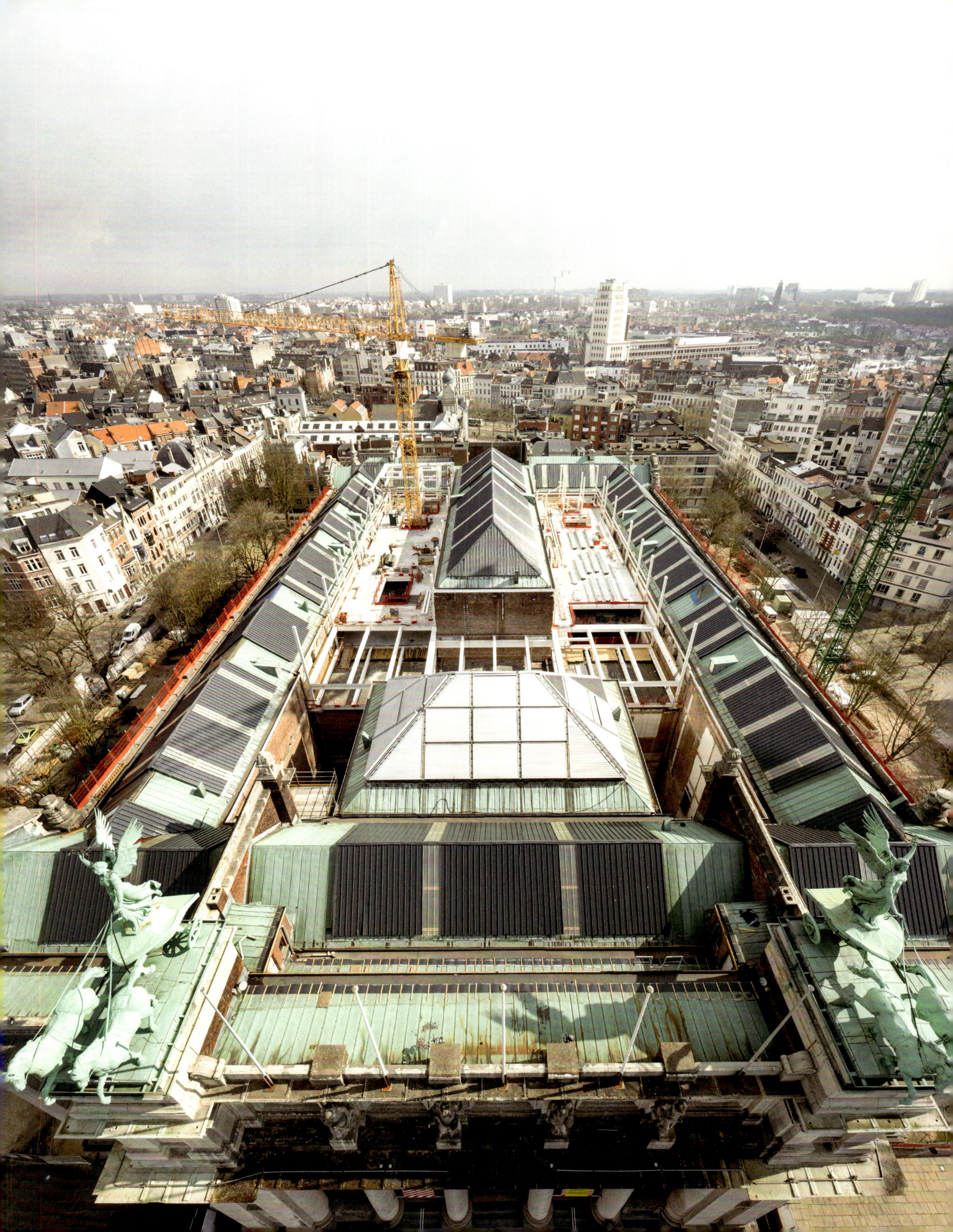

1. A MASTERLY MASTERPLAN

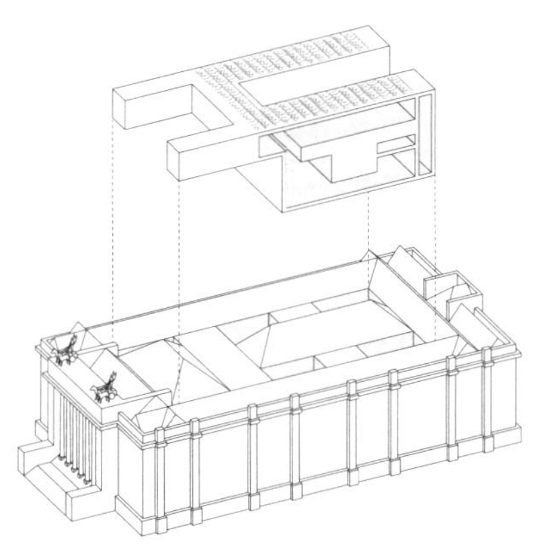

A new, vertical structure was 'dropped' into the existing patio spaces. Two museums in one.

The story of the new KMSKA began on 6 June 2003. That is when Flemish master builder bOb Van Reeth put out an international open call, at the behest of the Flemish government, asking applicants to design a masterplan for the KMSKA. For the first time, the museum building dating from 1890 was going to undergo radical reassessment and expansion. The call yielded 95 proposals, five of which were selected for the next round. The following year, the decision was made: the Dutch firm Claus en Kaan Architecten – now KAAN Architecten – was chosen to further develop the masterplan. In its recommendation, the jury expressed particular appreciation for the concept to 'infill' the existing building; a new 'volume' would be added that would give the museum extra usable floor space without expanding beyond the perimeter of the existing building.

Poor condition

Dikkie Scipio (who we'll be hearing from in these pages) is the only person who has been involved from the beginning to the end. She is the Lead Architect of the masterplan. That means she has worked on this mega project for almost 20 years. In 2004, a phase of researching, designing, discussing, drafting and calculating began; this also involved starting again from scratch, and finally producing a plan that was approved. In November 2011, the renovation proper began, a historic moment for the museum.

In the initial plan, the KMSKA was to remain open during the renovation. Dikkie Scipio discussed this in the autumn of 2012, in the very first issue of the new museum magazine, *ZAAL Z*: "What we did not know at the time was that the building was in a much worse condition than had been expected. Large amounts of asbestos were found and the climate-control system had to be replaced in its entirety, so we were forced to include as a requirement in the masterplan that the museum would have to close after all. That was a major setback, of course, both financially and for the staff, who quite naturally wanted the museum to stay open."

Two worlds

The big idea behind the masterplan did not change. Dikkie Scipio, again in 2012: "The basic concept is that we want to restore the 19th-century museum and its characteristic enfilade as much as possible. The quality of the monumental building's interior is defined by the route that visitors follow through the galleries, like a promenade through a park. But over the years, this historic route had been completely disrupted by various newly added functions. The twofold nature of building and collection was important to me from the start; the building is an intrinsic part of the collection, and vice versa. We have concealed the new extension in a vertical museum in the four courtyards with a large gallery on top. The new museum will not be visible from the old museum. They will actually be two completely different worlds housed within one building. The new vertical museum will overawe through its experience of space. You will be focused on the art and the airiness, not on the materiality. In the old museum, we are returning the stately historic galleries to their original colours. Here the materials are more important. They give you different ways to view the art. That interaction is interesting."

The masterplan in short: offering a new and additional spatial experience as well as restoring the grandeur and eminence of the 19th-century building, inside and out. Combining verticality with horizontality. And what's more: maintaining an unchanged exterior elevation on all sides. In the underlying concept, the building, the garden and the surrounding neighbourhood all come together as one whole. Another crucial element of the masterplan was the restoration and renovation of the façade, which was realised by PERSPECTIV architecten.

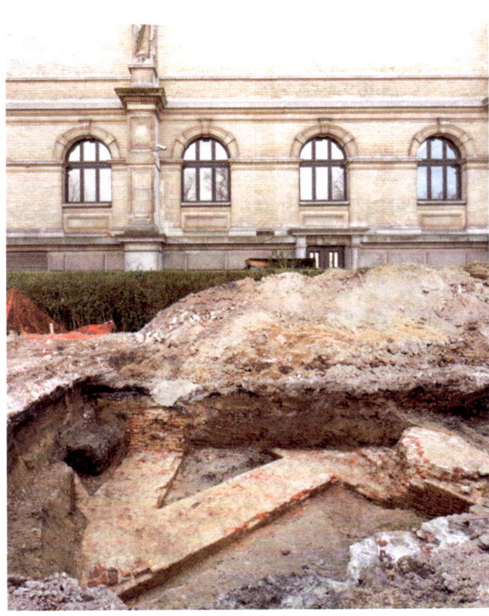

The archaeological remains of the citadel of Alva were documented during the renovation works.

Stacks of history

For Dikkie Scipio, KMSKA's ties to the neighbourhood, connection with the city and role in history all play a very important role: "The 19th-century building claims its place in the city. This is unmistakeably the treasury of Antwerp, its treasure trove of art. The building stands in the city with a clear sense of pride. Everything surrounding it shares in that pride. I would like people to enter into a dialogue with their environment again. We have forgotten how." As for the history of the place: "It is bizarre that the museum is standing on the ruins of a citadel, which was built to subjugate Antwerp. The city tore down the citadel in 1874, as it was not a monument anyone wanted to cherish. It's insane to think that a temple to art has risen in a place of so much oppression and combat – so much history stacked on top of history."

Closely intertwined

Back to the new/old museum. In which the 'old' and the 'new' world very deliberately do not crossover into each other. Dikkie Scipio: "As an architect, you can choose to display your design very visibly, or to delay the amazement. I believe in the delayed moment, in many layers that slowly reveal themselves. That way, the visitor is drawn to places that have no functionality whatsoever. The spacious quality is a pure gift. Then there are little curves and doors everywhere in the design that introduce humour and playfulness. This invites the visitor to really engage with the building."

And yet the two parts of the renovated KMSKA are also closely intertwined. This is not a monument on to which an extension has been added: "The new and the old need each other: they rely on each other and support each other, functionally, technically and materially. In the new part, for example, there are two technical towers, which provide air-conditioning, heating and the necessary cooling for the whole building."

A long-term project

Dikkie Scipio: "Our basic concept was powerful and had widespread support. At the same time, we were able to adapt it as new developments emerged during the many years of the project. This often happens, in many different ways. We were able to improve the concept, but always within the existing framework and in line with the basic premises of the masterplan. One example of something that changed gradually is the public facilities. We redesigned them. The restaurant, shop and reception area are more generous than originally planned. This came about because of advancing insights into what public comfort should be in a museum. The library's reading room is also more prominent now. But it all remained within the zone we had designated from the start, at the front of the building."

DIKKIE SCIPIO: THE BEAUTY WE ARE CAPABLE OF

"As an architect, you don't want to be fashionable. You have a social responsibility, especially with projects of this scale. Your building must be capable of keeping step with changing times. For me, that is the ultimate form of sustainability."

"The original design is a revelation of high standard quality, and I hope we've made that visible again. By adding something new, the building continues to evolve. So that all that knowledge and that beautiful collection can grow towards the future. It's great to be able to do that with a building."

"Making something that has the same level of impact, but does not diminish the strength of the old building: that's what our intention was. To let the old and the new play together. People will naturally have a preference for one or the other. But the new part gives the museum ways of dealing with the collection that are different, without in any way implying there is anything wrong with the old. It's all about mutual respect."

"The museum is more than a house in which art is stored, it is also a place that says something about who we are. About what we are capable of as humans. When you open a newspaper, you almost feel like cowering in a corner from shame. It helps us to sometimes see what beauty we are – also and equally – capable of."

"I think that is what's so fantastic about all those people who made their contributions here, with all their knowledge and expertise. You may be the initiator, but it's all the people involved who believe in your ideas who make it a success. Ultimately, this project is owned by many people."

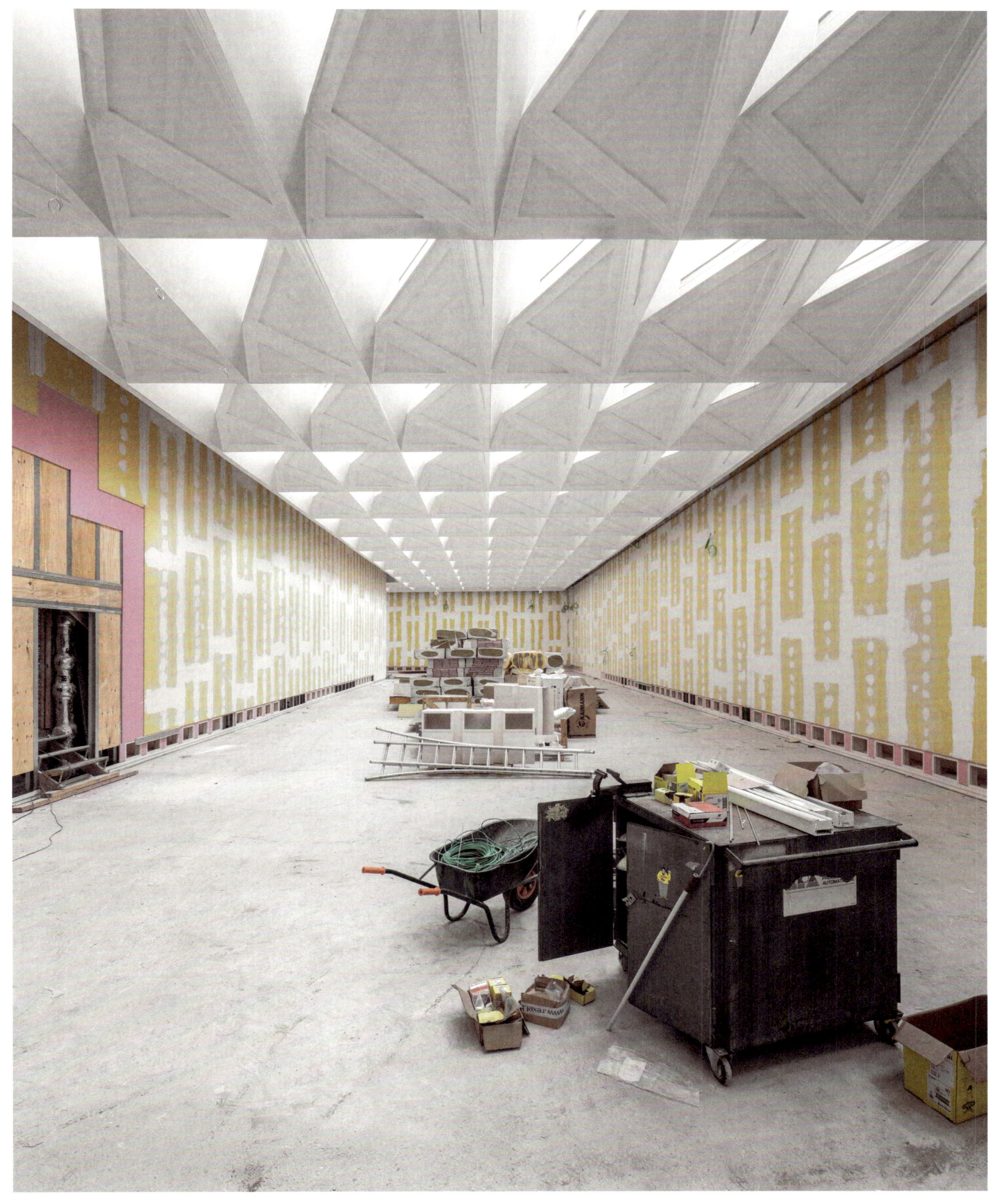

The new Colour gallery on the top floor, the so-called 'tabletop'.

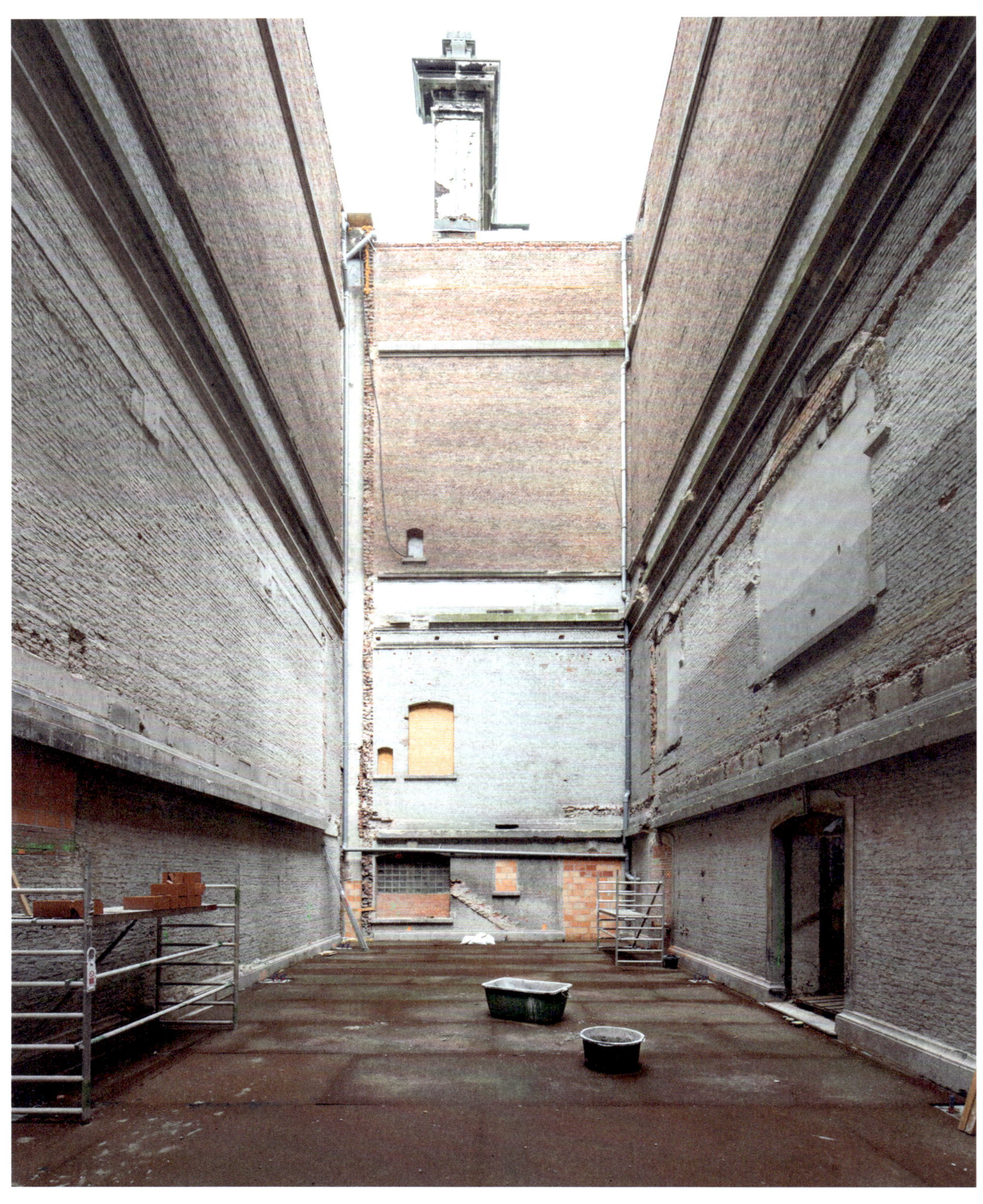

The patios were cleared out to make space for the new vertical museum.

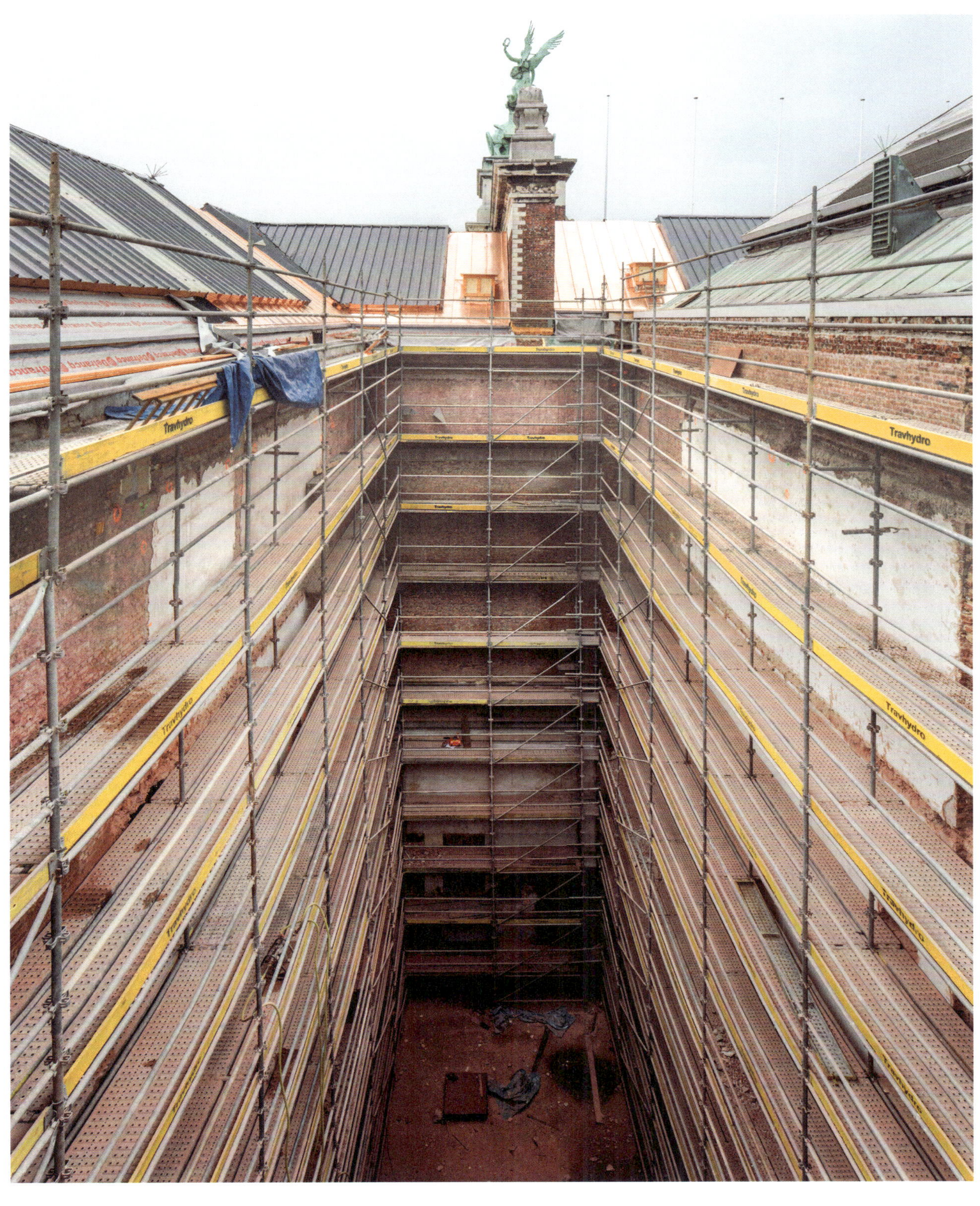
Travhydro
Travhydro
Travhydro
Travhydro

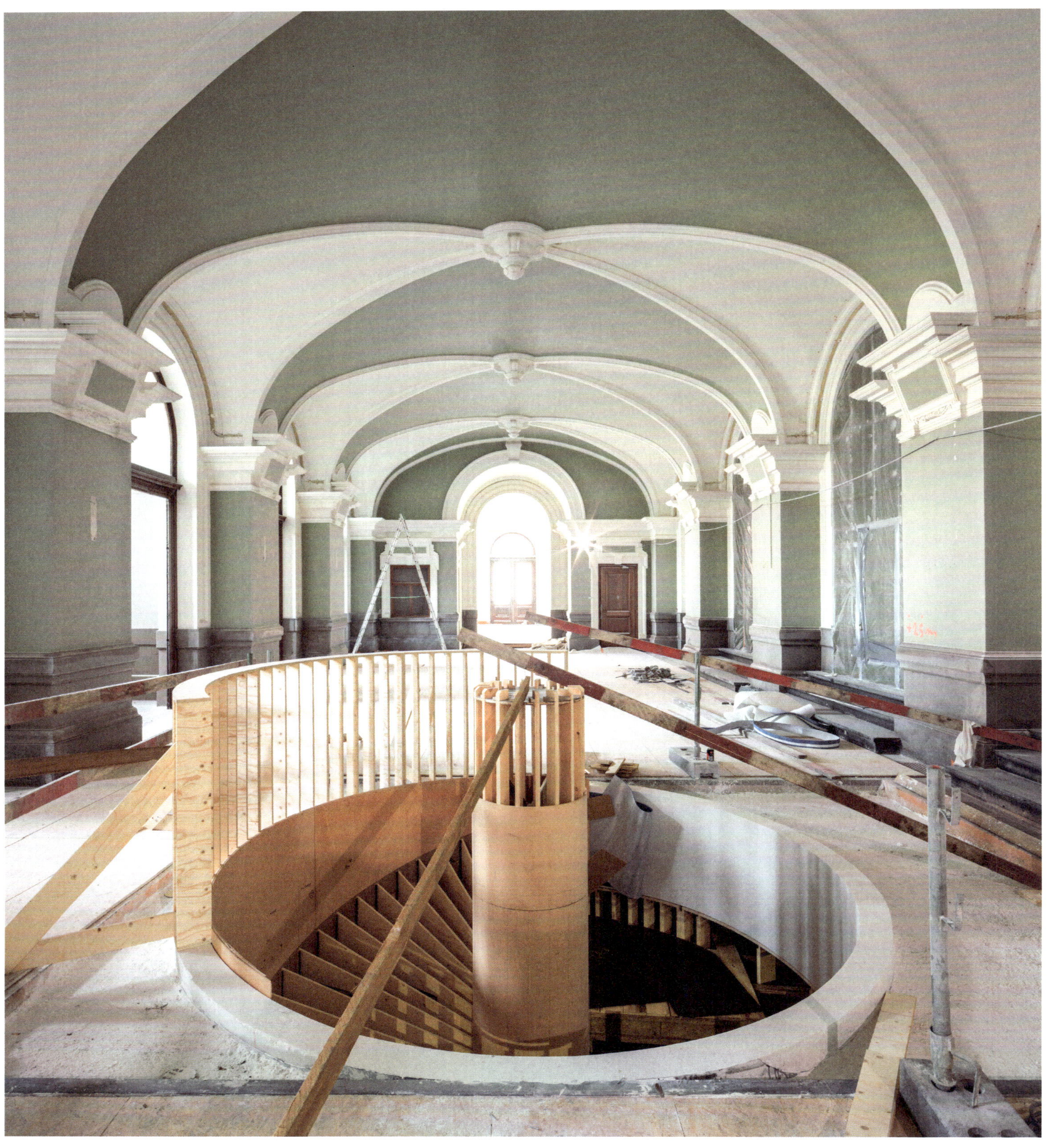

The concrete winding staircase in the entrance hall was cast in one piece.

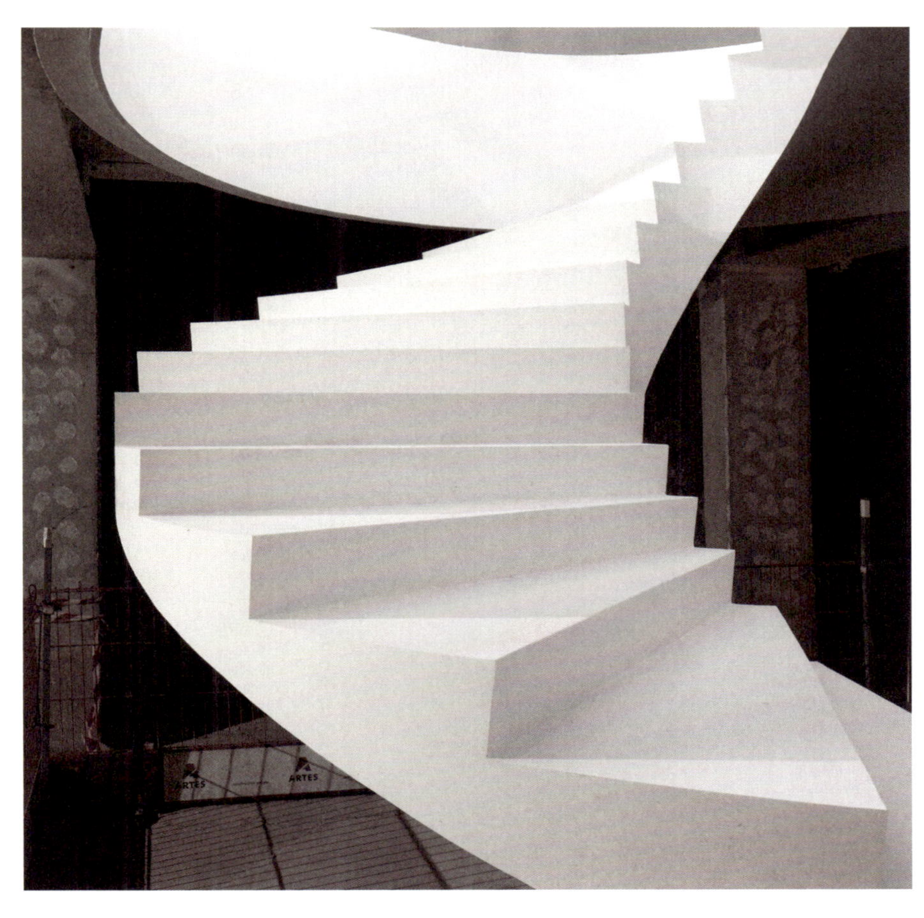

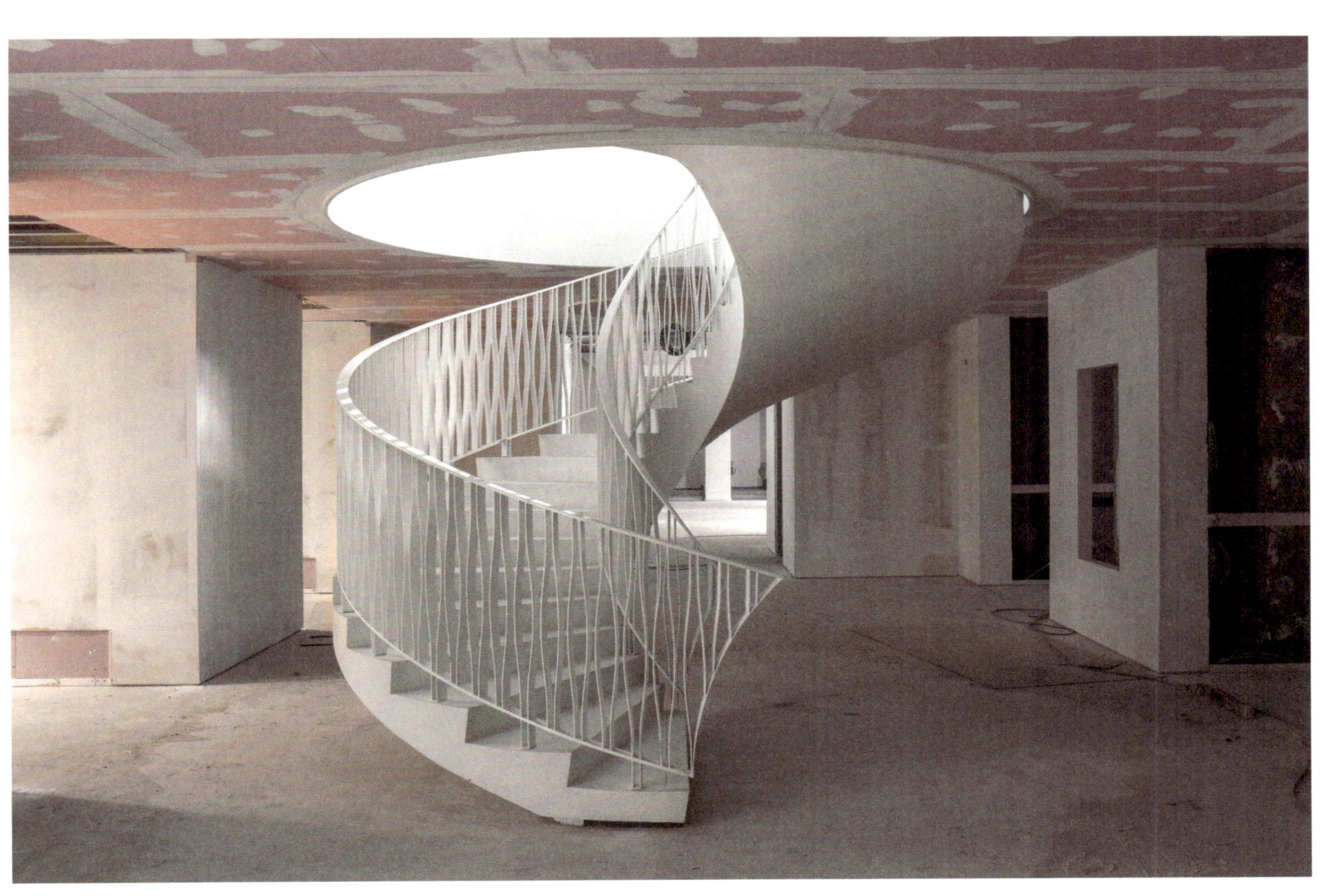

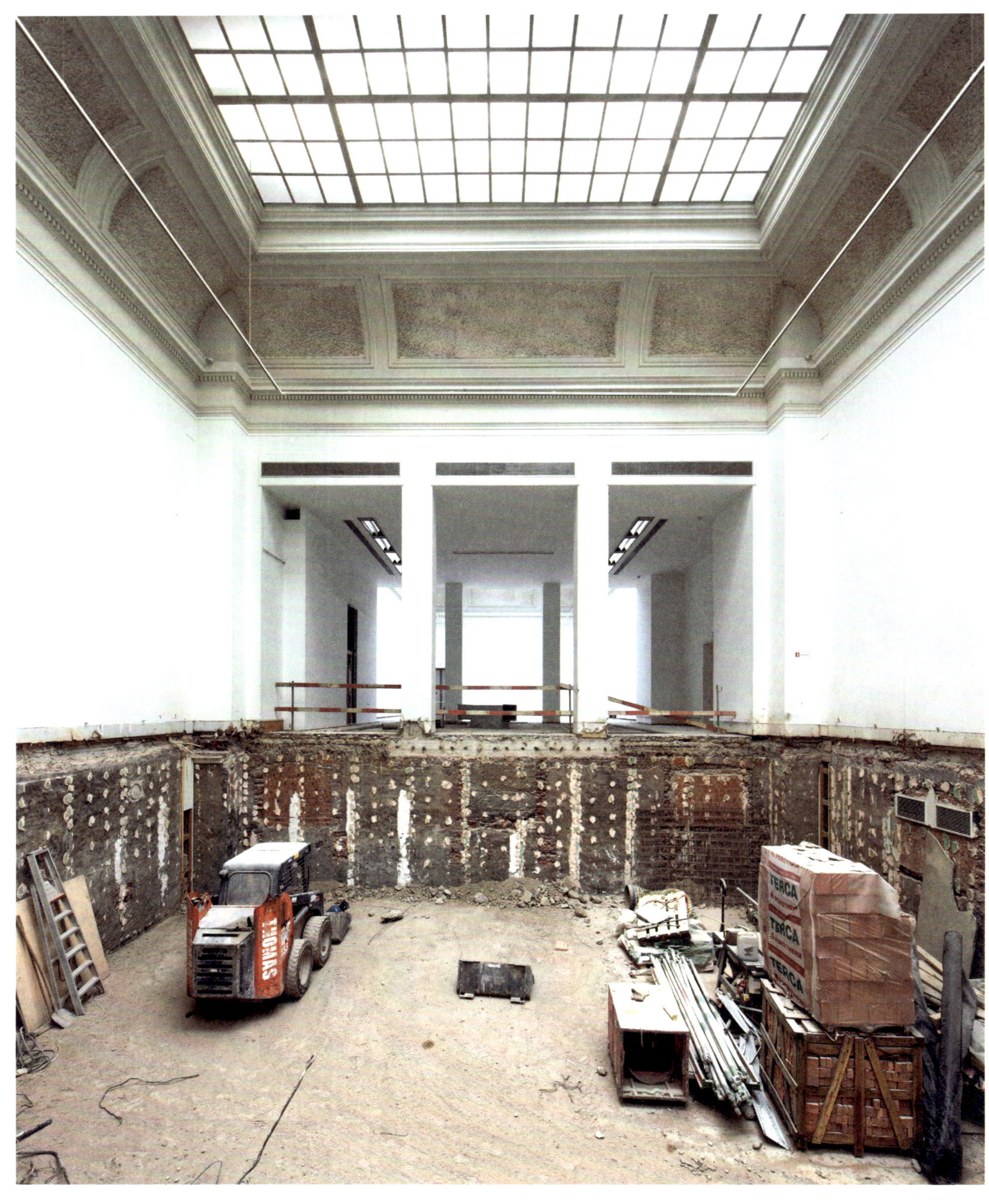

One of the patios during demolition.

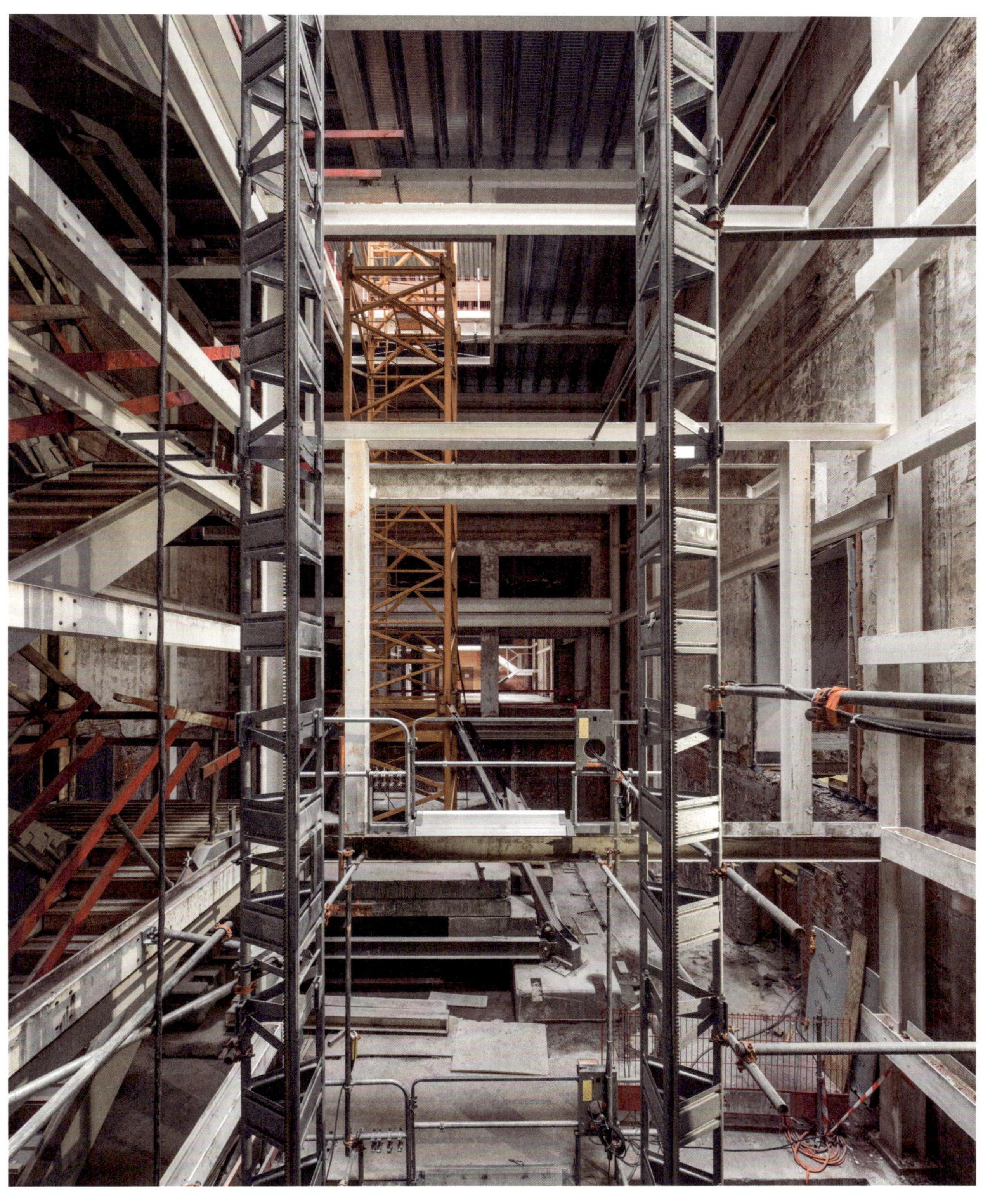

To form the new museum volume, a steel structure weighing 1,000,000 kilogrammes was put in place.

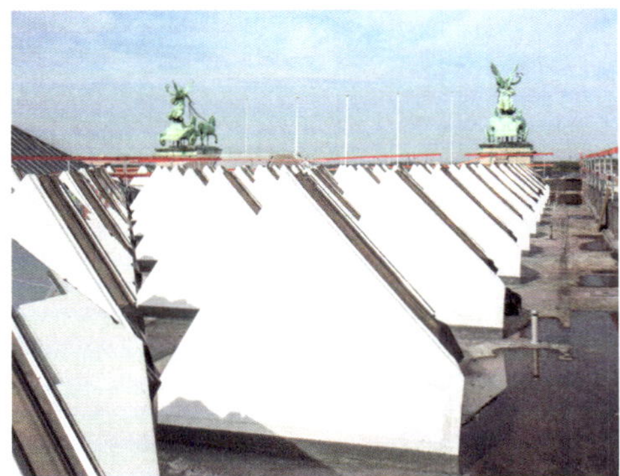

198 white skylights capture the daylight.

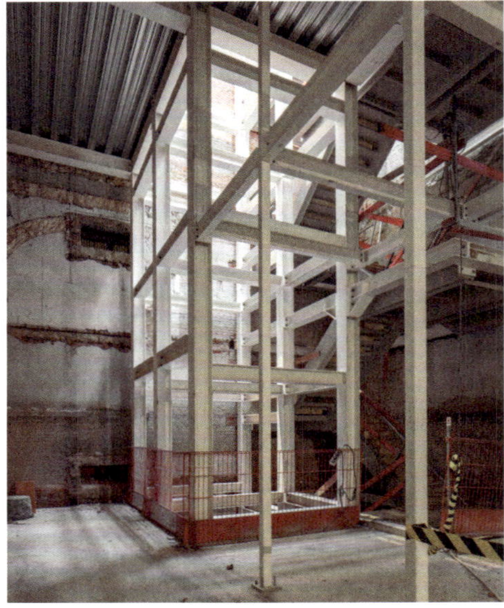

Steel construction of one of the voids.

What are the special, perhaps even unique, aspects of the KMSKA project, when viewed through the lens of the contractor of the masterplan? Director of Works Thomas Musters and his colleague Tom Meirte, both from Artes, know everything there is to know about it. Both were responsible, alongside a large team, for the complete renovation.

Starting in 2011, Artes Roegiers took care of the first phase: demolition, removal of asbestos and outdated installations, clearing the patio spaces and building a new storage depot. From late 2014 on, Artes Roegiers and Artes Woudenberg were jointly responsible for phase two: the realisation of the public area at the front of the historic building, the restoration of the historic halls, the new conservation studio, the installation of the newest technological systems and, of course, the construction of the new museum volume, which fills the demolished patios while remaining separate from the existing building. Realising these plans involved building a new foundation (with 147 piles) and placing a steel structure (weighing a million kilogrammes) on top of it, to form the new museum volume.

Invisible

Thomas Musters: “That’s a very special aspect right there: the steel construction of the new museum. This is new construction we’re talking about, but here we have combined it with the restoration and renovation of an existing building. That is complex enough to start with, and in the case of a museum such as the KMSKA you need to involve a wide range of specialised disciplines. To tackle this challenge, we formed a multidisciplinary building group with sister companies Artes Roegiers and Artes Woudenberg. And don’t forget, this was also simply an enormous building site.”

“The two volumes are separate from each other, that’s true, but then again not entirely. Just think of the technical systems that needed to be able to enter the historic building from the new building, and which we also had to install in such a way that they’re hidden from the public. Technology is right behind all the thin wall constructions, but the visitor won’t notice a thing. Installing the technical systems was not a simple job, let’s put it that way.”

“In terms of logistics and planning, this was a kind of ‘group artwork’ for us. For example, the restoration of the ceilings in the historic halls was done by a succession of specialists. Our own restorers, plasterers and casters, as well as various other technicians, steelworkers and glaziers – all were involved.”

Stunning architecture

Tom Meirte: “If I may highlight a few more features, the 198 white skylight elements on the roof are amazing. They’re angled towards the north to catch the daylight, which is distributed across all the floors of the new museum via four voids, 23 metres high. The triangular skylights were prefabricated in moulds and then assembled on site. There was not the slightest room for error in the placement. The alignment had to be perfect, which took some first-class craftsmanship. Or look at the high-gloss cast floors – an architect’s dream. But to be able to construct them flawlessly, the substrate and the climate – temperature and humidity – have to be perfect. That’s no mean feat on a construction site where so many workers are walking around every day.”

“We’re talking about some very distinguished architecture here, with a high level of attention to detail: a lot of items were custom-made for this project. The architects knew exactly what they wanted. That wasn’t always easy to execute, but the results make the imagination soar. The new winding staircase made of white concrete in the entrance hall is a beautiful example; it was cast in one piece.”

A EUROPEAN PRIZE

In 2021, KAAN Architecten and the KMSKA won the European Award for Architectural Heritage Intervention, in the Intervention in Built Heritage category. This biennial prize shines a light on first-rate heritage interventions, and there were almost 300 candidates that year. The award was accompanied by this jury statement:

"The Royal Museum of Fine Arts (KMSKA) in Antwerp was designed as a 'daylight museum' in the 19th century but underwent many ill-considered modifications over the decades. This recent intervention has revived the old grandeur of the museum by combining a thorough renovation of the historic building with a contemporary extension that is concealed within the existing structure. The original dark pink, green and red colour scheme, plasterwork ceiling ornamentation and tall columns were re-established in the 19th-century exhibition galleries. Meanwhile, the new vertical museum arose as an autonomous entity, filling the four original patios. Wherever the new extension 'cuts through' the solid mass of the monumental museum, subtle marble inlay pieces have been applied. The vertical museum offers a route full of surprises, with bright white exhibition galleries, hidden spaces, long staircases, sweeping sightlines and a range of varying degrees of daylight. These contrasting and at the same time dialoguing entities sit side by side, as two different worlds in one building. They are both exciting and both exist to serve the art."

The biannual European Award for Architectural Heritage Intervention is organised with the support of the Association of Architects for the Defence and Intervention in Architectural Heritage (AADIPA) and the Architects' Association of Catalonia (COAC). The competition celebrates successful heritage projects. One of the award-winners preceding the KMSKA is the new Rijksmuseum in Amsterdam.

The mouldings from the Rubens Gallery were carefully stored and later fitted back in place like pieces of a puzzle.

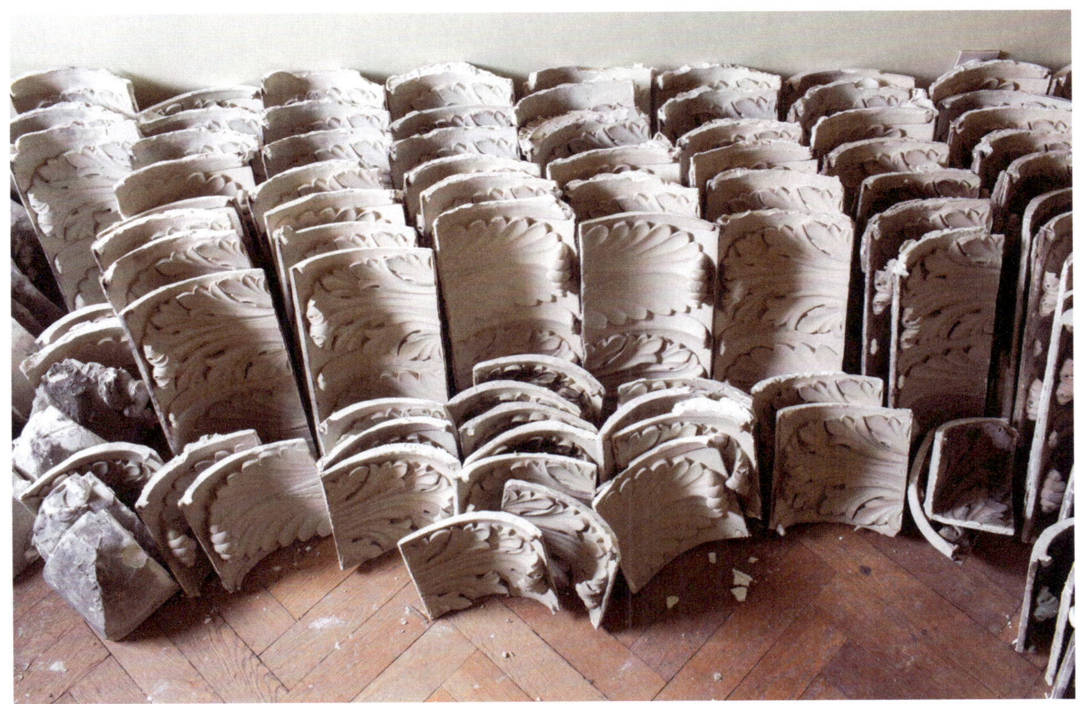

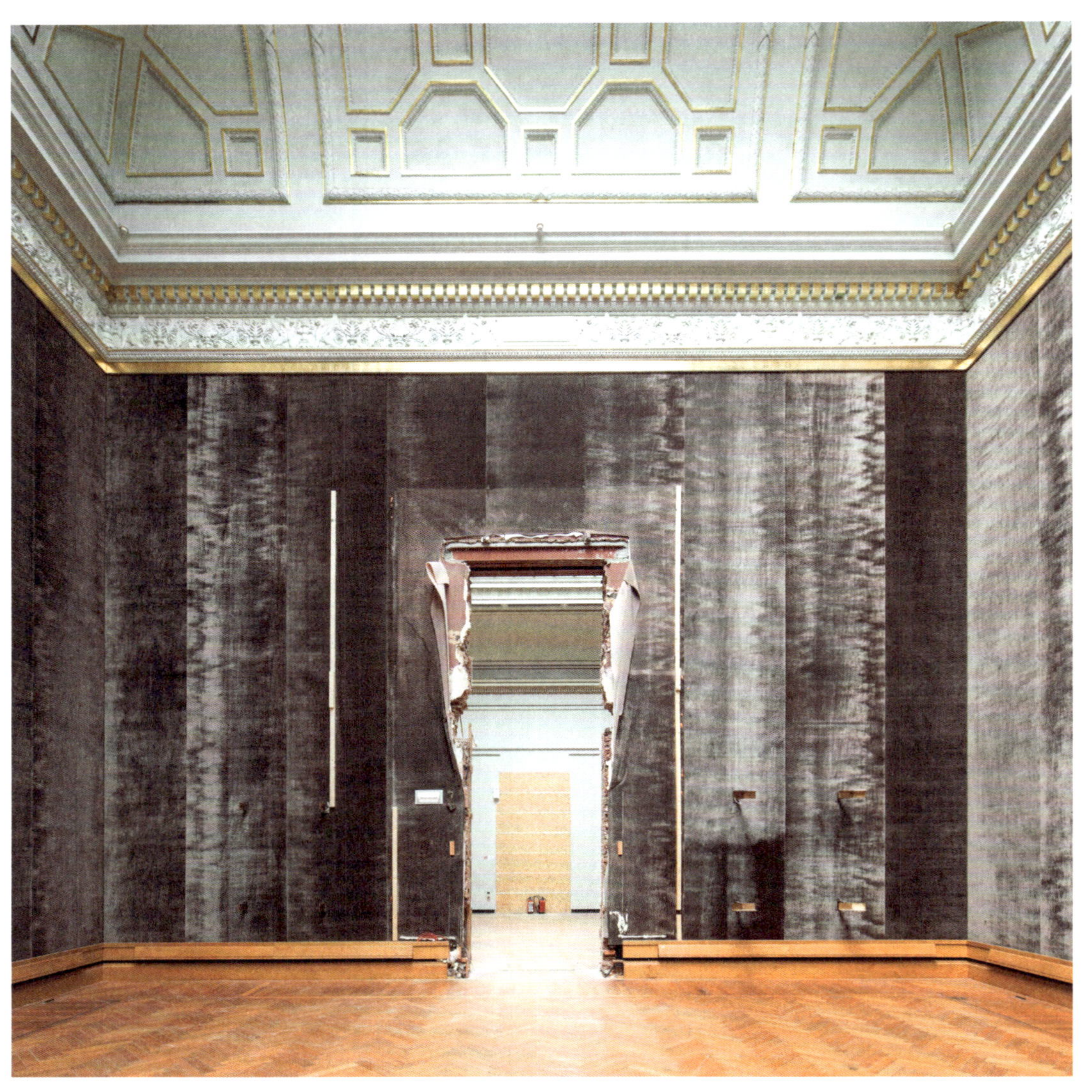

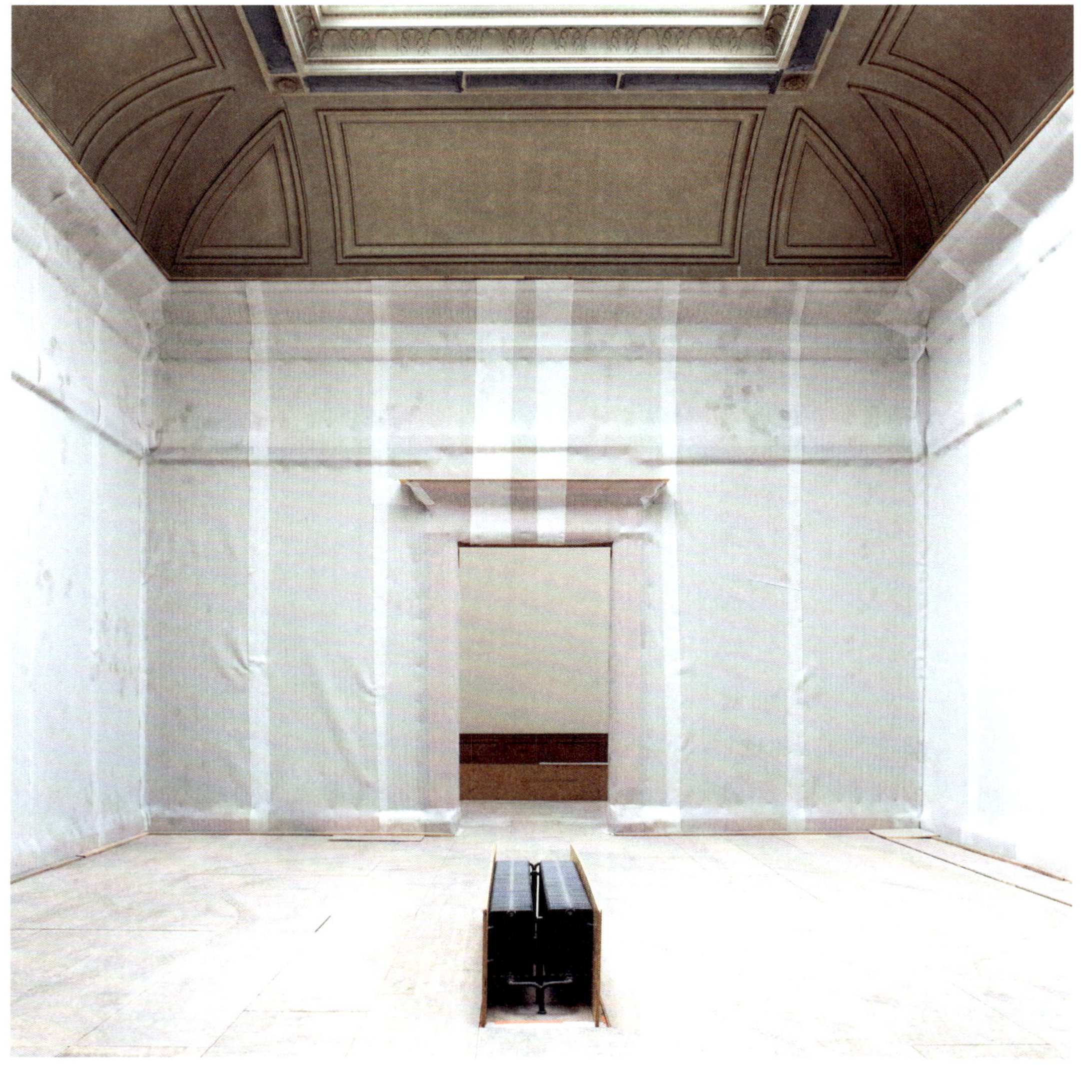

Some doorways needed to be enlarged to allow for the removal of monumental artworks.

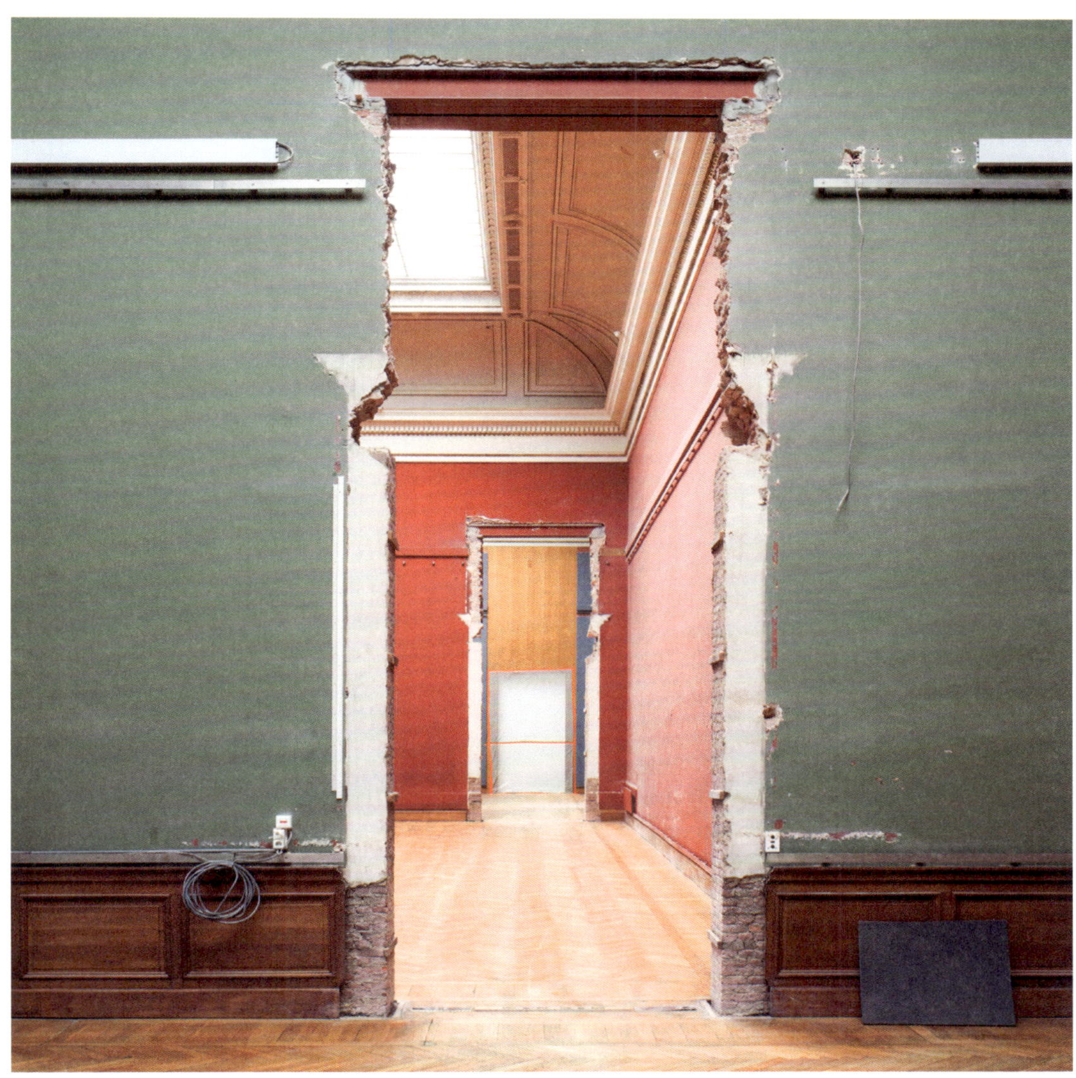

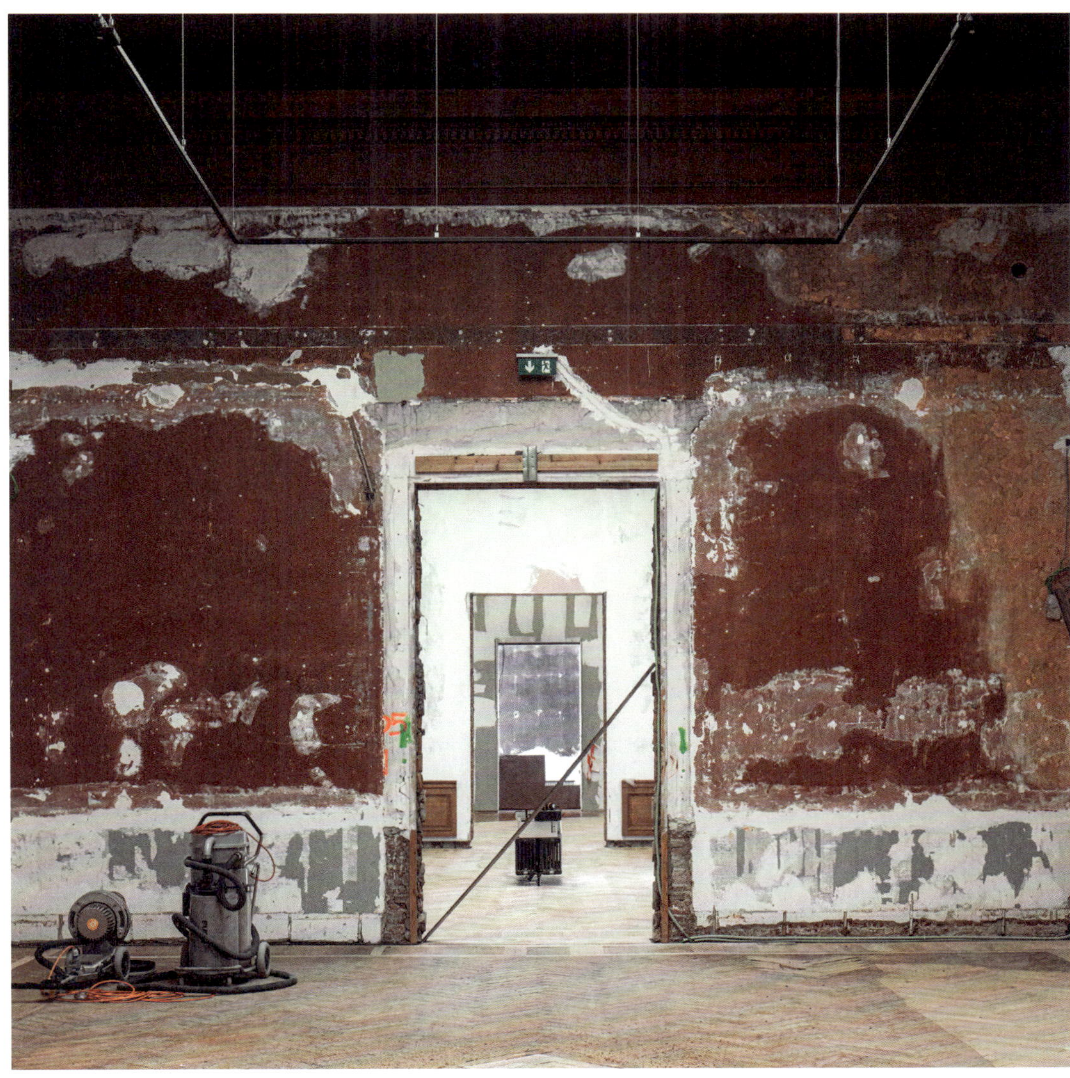

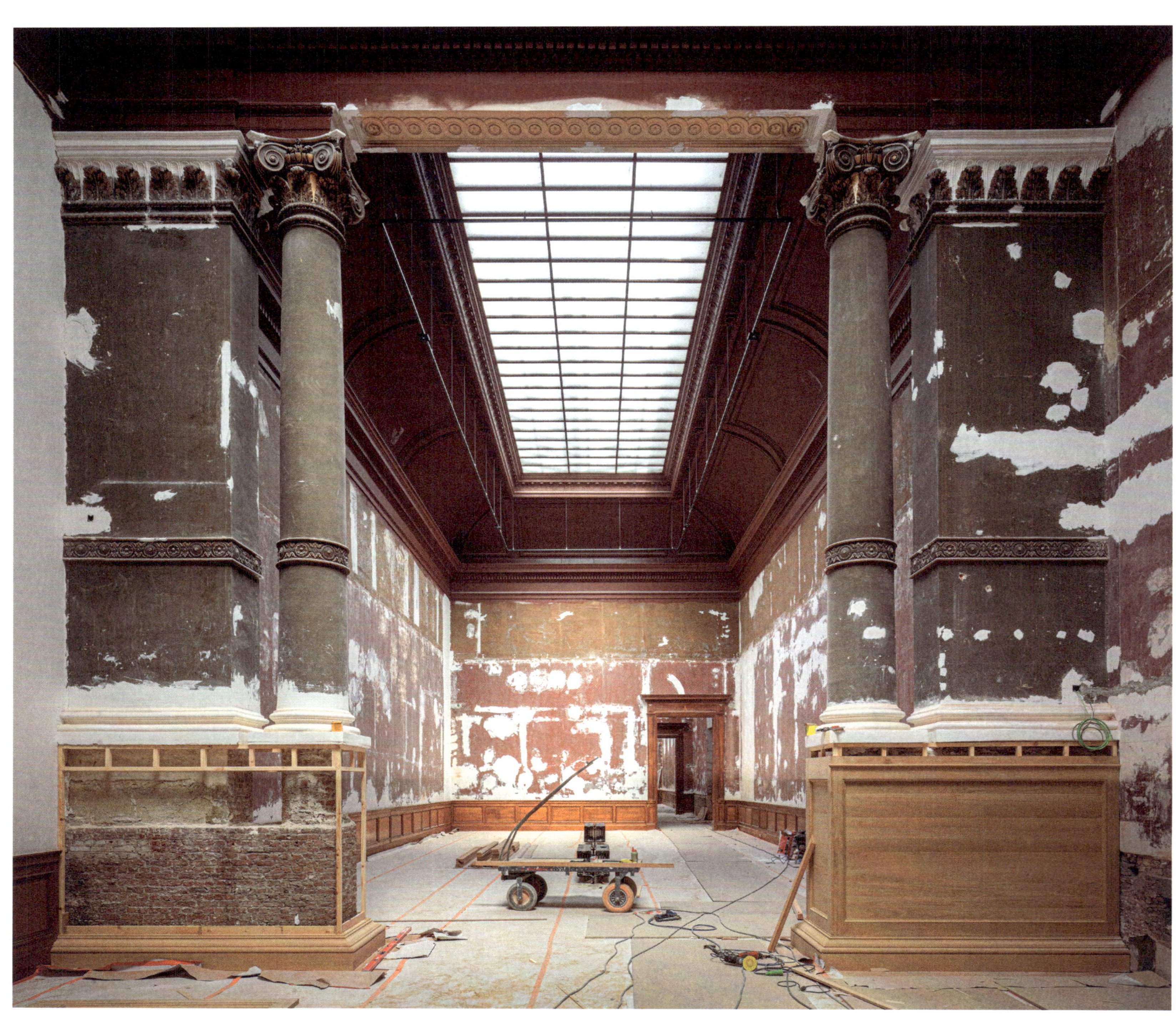

Ornamental columns were discovered behind false walls.

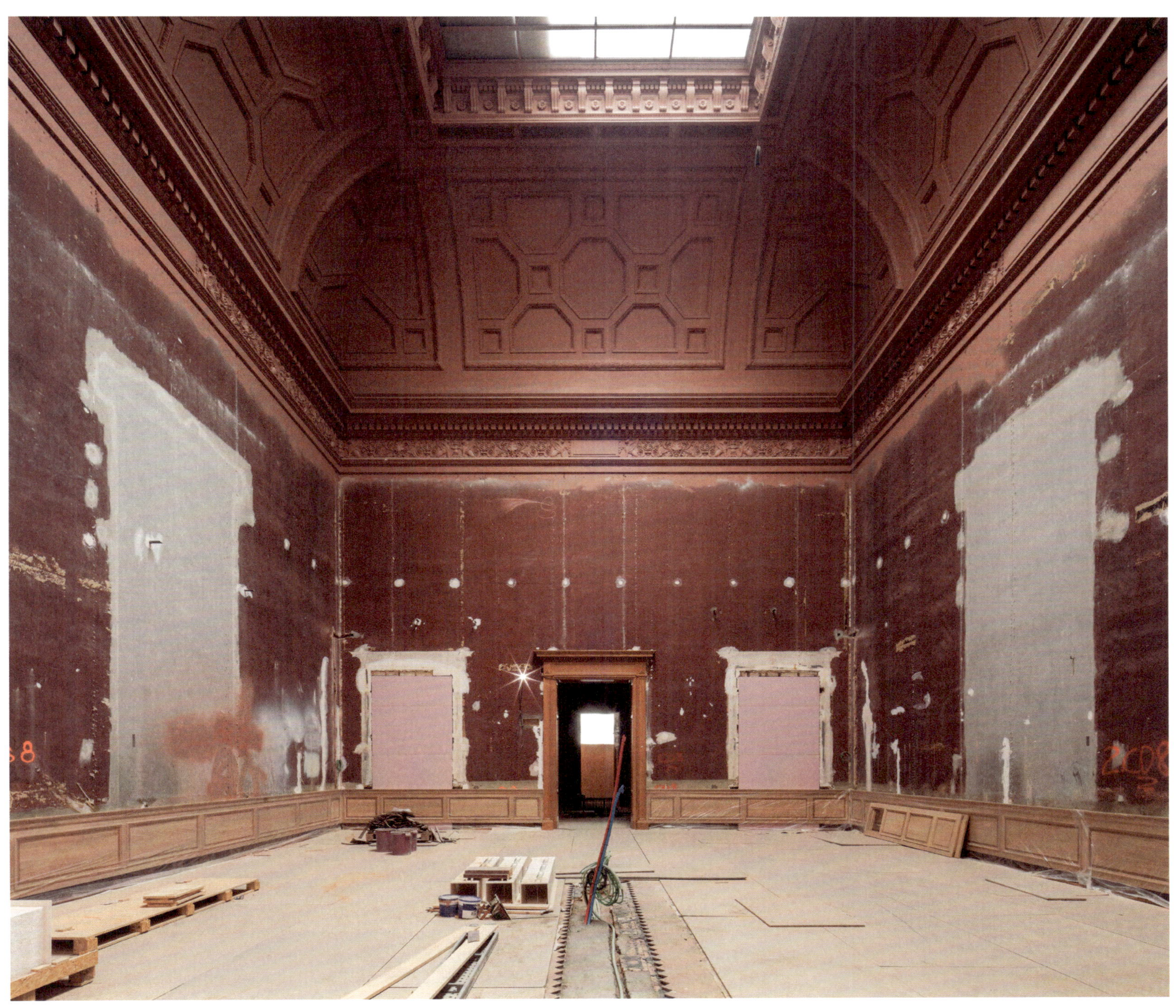

The two doorways to the Jordaens Gallery were replaced by one central doorway, returning it to its original state.

2.

RECOVERED GRANDEUR: THE RENOVATION OF THE HISTORIC MUSEUM

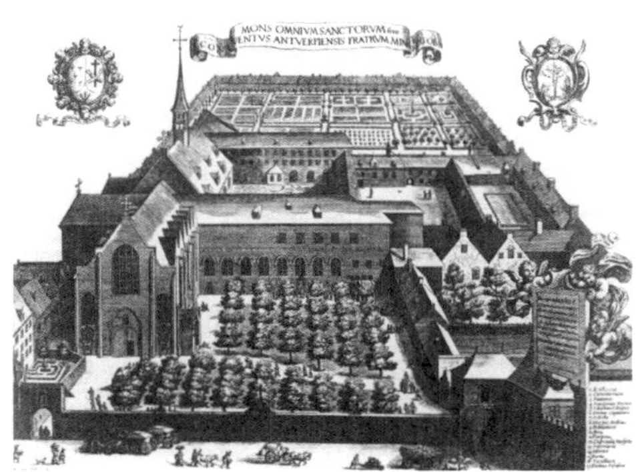

The museum, founded by imperial decree in 1810, was located in the former Recollects Convent.

We know it's a concern of visitors who knew all the ins and outs of 'their' museum: will we still recognise 'our' favourite venue after the massive and endless renovation and construction project has been completed? Will we still feel at home? To which the KMSKA confidently says, yes! But, of course, these visitors will also be surprised when they encounter the new elements. We walked through the historic building with collection researcher Siska Beele. She knows the countless nooks and crannies behind the many magnificent doors, like no other. And she knows the history of the complex.

To the South!

Starting in 1810 – the year in which the museum was created by an imperial decree from Napoleon – what we now know as the KMSKA was housed in the Royal Academy, the old Recollects Convent on Mutsaardstraat (formerly Mutsaertstraat). The city of Antwerp decided to build a new home for the museum in 1873. The location was pinpointed in 1875 and it also became clear that the state would lend its support to the construction. Leopold de Wael was mayor of Antwerp at the time. One of the motivations for the new building was a fire in August 1873, which threatened to destroy the Academy Museum. The South district ('t Zuid) was chosen as the new site: after the razing of the infamous citadel of Alva, space had become available there to build a new city district as well as modern port infrastructure. The museum was given a central place in the ambitious building plans for 'the South'. How exactly central is immediately visible when you look at the neighbourhood on a map or from the sky.

Two still quite young architects – Jean-Jacques Winders and Frans Van Dijk – won the architectural competition in 1879 and were commissioned to work together to achieve a compromise of their two plans. The duo went on study trips to gather inspiration from other museums, in the Netherlands and Germany. The Alte Pinakothek in Munich made a particular impression with its classical temple splendour. Construction started in 1884 and six years later, on 11 August 1890, the new museum was ceremoniously inaugurated. The commemorative plaque in the entrance hall bears testimony to the occasion.

The old masters and modern masters were allocated 23 painting galleries on the top floor, each designated a letter. The scenography was typical for art museums of the time: paintings hung in rows next to and above one another, covering the walls from top to bottom, without much consideration for size, colour or theme. One distinction was that the old and modern masters were hung separately from one another. The galleries on the ground floor – two longitudinal, two transverse – were used for sculptures, engravings and... photographs of paintings by the world-famous local hero, Rubens.

Call for expansion

1925. The building soon became too small for the collection it was intended to house. To solve the problem, architect Van Dijk designed an extension with two side wings – but his proposal was rejected. Instead, the four patios were covered and converted into large galleries. The long galleries became smaller museum halls, and all the rooms on the upper floor were redecorated. These changes, made in 1927, Rubens' 350th birthday, lasted until 2011. The style of presentation also became more modern: fewer works were hung in each

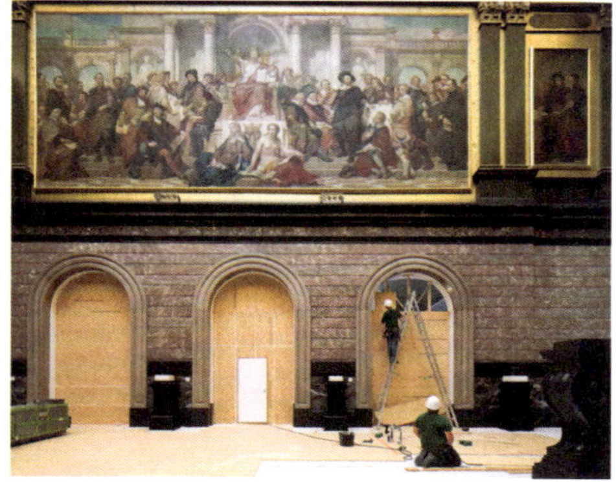

The De Keyserzaal was provided with a new gable roof but not renovated. The space was sealed and pressurised to keep it free of dust.

room and they were kept at eye level, art-historical and aesthetic criteria were brought to bear, and old and modern works were exhibited on two different floors.

The director at the time, Cornette, pointed out that the expanded space "in the near future will no longer be sufficient to accommodate the new works appropriately". His call for expansion was repeated frequently by his successors – after the modernisation following the Rubens Year of 1977 (when record visitor numbers topped 625,000), and after the renovation marking the museum's 100th anniversary in 1990. It was 2003 when the Flemish state architect issued the open call that led to the new KMSKA masterplan. That year also saw the publication of 'The Museum Book', which, after a summary of everything that had been achieved in the meantime (climate control, storage depot, fire protection, office spaces and so on), contains the following circumspect phrase: "Necessary changes do not always turn out to be improvements." And: "We are still awaiting a suitable solution for the required infrastructure (restoration, workshops for children)." That solution has now finally been found.

De Keyser and Rubens

Feeling at home starts at the point where one enters the museum. After the new entrance area with all its mod cons, for many the KMSKA's true entrance is still the De Keyserzaal, which was always intended as an overture, as the ringing first chord of the symphony that follows. A museum today would call it a 'wow space', a space that impresses and welcomes at the same time.

The De Keyserzaal is one of the few places in the new KMSKA where nothing has changed during the renovation, apart from the new glass gable roof. The 39 paintings – a proud parade that tells the story of the Antwerp painting school and celebrates its famous members – did not need restoration either; that had already happened in 1999. The hall itself contains almost every type of Belgian marble. And it's worth remembering that Nicaise De Keyser designed the entire series of paintings for the old museum on Mutsaardstraat (1862–1872). As director of the academy, he was also curator of the Antwerp Academy Museum. His work in the gallery named after him is a kind of visual aperitif to what is the highlight of the museum: the Rubens Gallery, dedicated to the local hero – and world-famous star – Peter Paul Rubens.

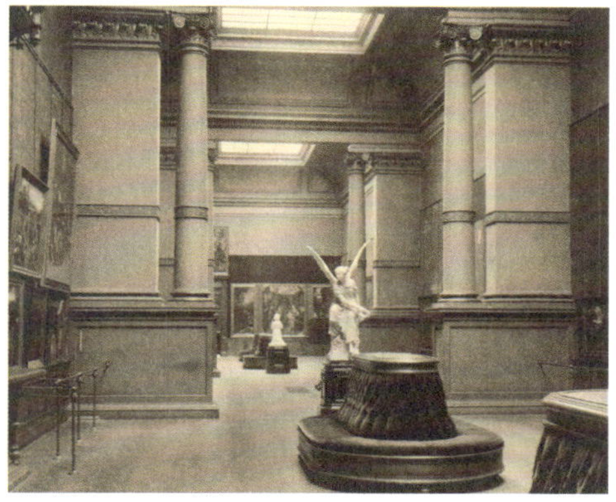

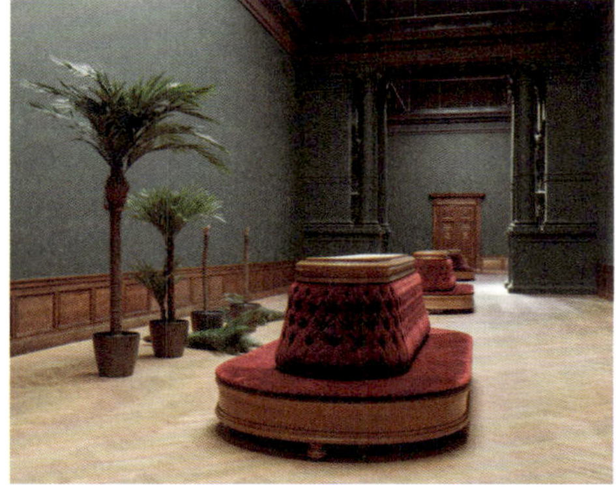

The iconic red velvet benches have been restored.

Pompeiian red and olive green

In the De Keyserzaal, you can choose between going to the first floor or up the stairs to explore the top floor. In the latter case, in the fabled Rubens Gallery – which has retained its name and purpose –you will encounter the bulk of the recent renovation work in the historic museum: the restoration of the original 1890 design. This showcase gallery has walls in antique red, and gilded decoration on the ceiling. The other rooms are painted in Pompeiian red and olive green. The historic panelling has been restored – replaced if necessary, but always faithfully copying the original (much of the woodwork had been removed in the past in a push for modernisation). The familiar, even iconic seating, is still there: the old benches were retained if possible and newly copied if necessary. (They still hide the radiator heating too.) The same goes for the impressive doors in the old museum, the panelling, the parquet floors and so on.

The pedestrian route through the renovated old museum is as flawless as when it was conceived: symmetrical, easy to follow, with good sightlines and surprising perspectives. Quite a few spaces had been repurposed over the decades – as a restoration studio, storage depot, office space, warehouse – which led to a lack of clarity and a sometimes labyrinthine experience for visitors. In the first phase of the masterplan, all the additions were removed, the original route was restored with the same sightlines as in 1890 and, as a bonus, original, forgotten columns reappeared unexpectedly from behind false walls. Everything looks 'pure' again too, because the new technical installations are invisible to those who do not try too hard to find them. Here, they have been built into the ceilings. You have to remember that the KMSKA always was a daylight museum, since its very inception. It was only in 1976 – not until 1976! – that artificial light was added. Before then, the museum sometimes closed at 3pm on a winter's day.

Space!

The renovation has finally solved a problem that the KMSKA had been struggling with for decades: a shortage of space. The new KMSKA now has 11 galleries for temporary exhibitions in the 19th-century museum, totalling a generous 1,500 square metres and alternating pleasingly between larger and smaller spaces. The rooms are located on the first floor and are easily accessible for all visitors. They are organised as an enfilade of spaces adjacent to the new museum volume, with daylight entering through the windows of the outer façade. This creates an entire floor that, depending on the type of exhibition,

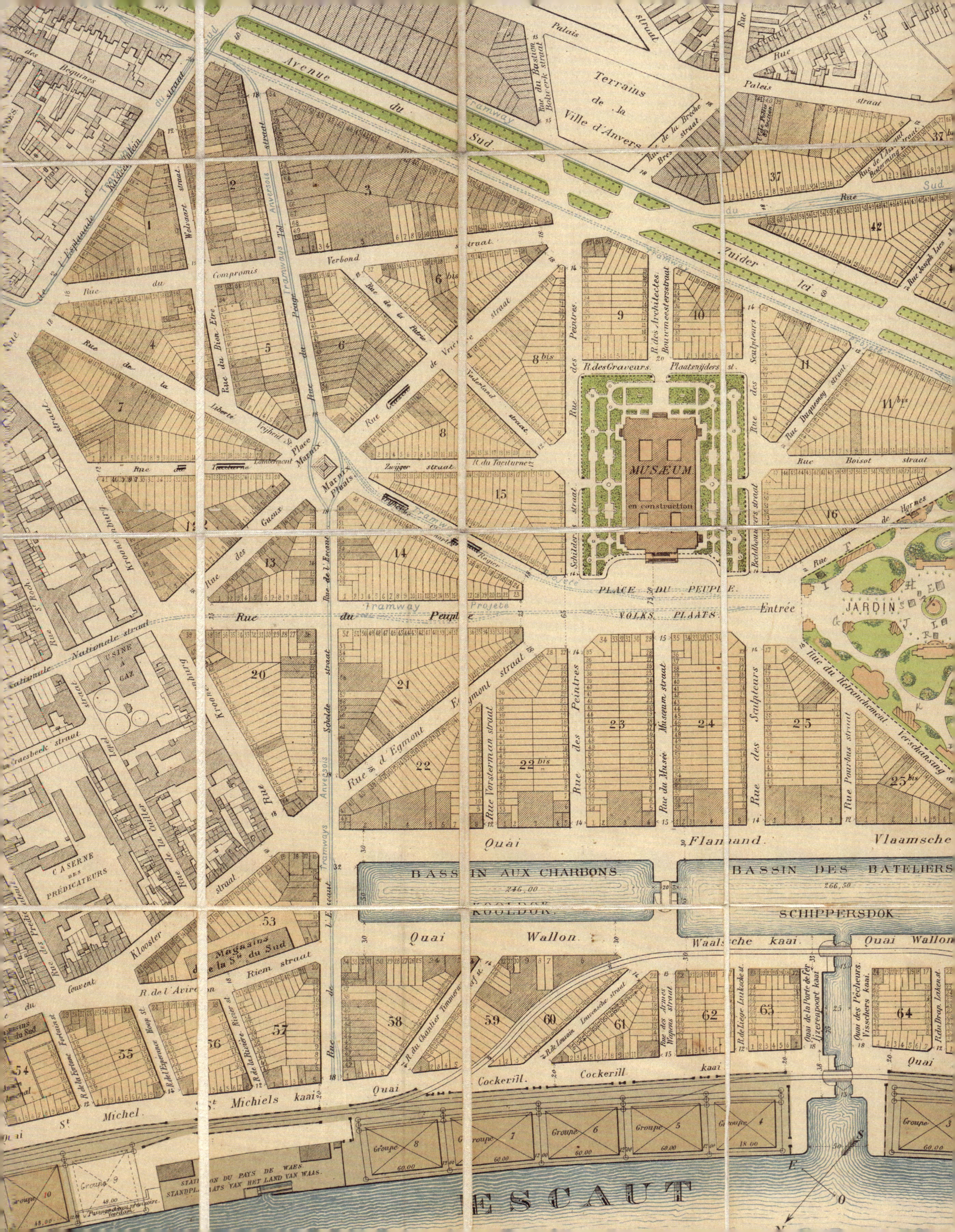

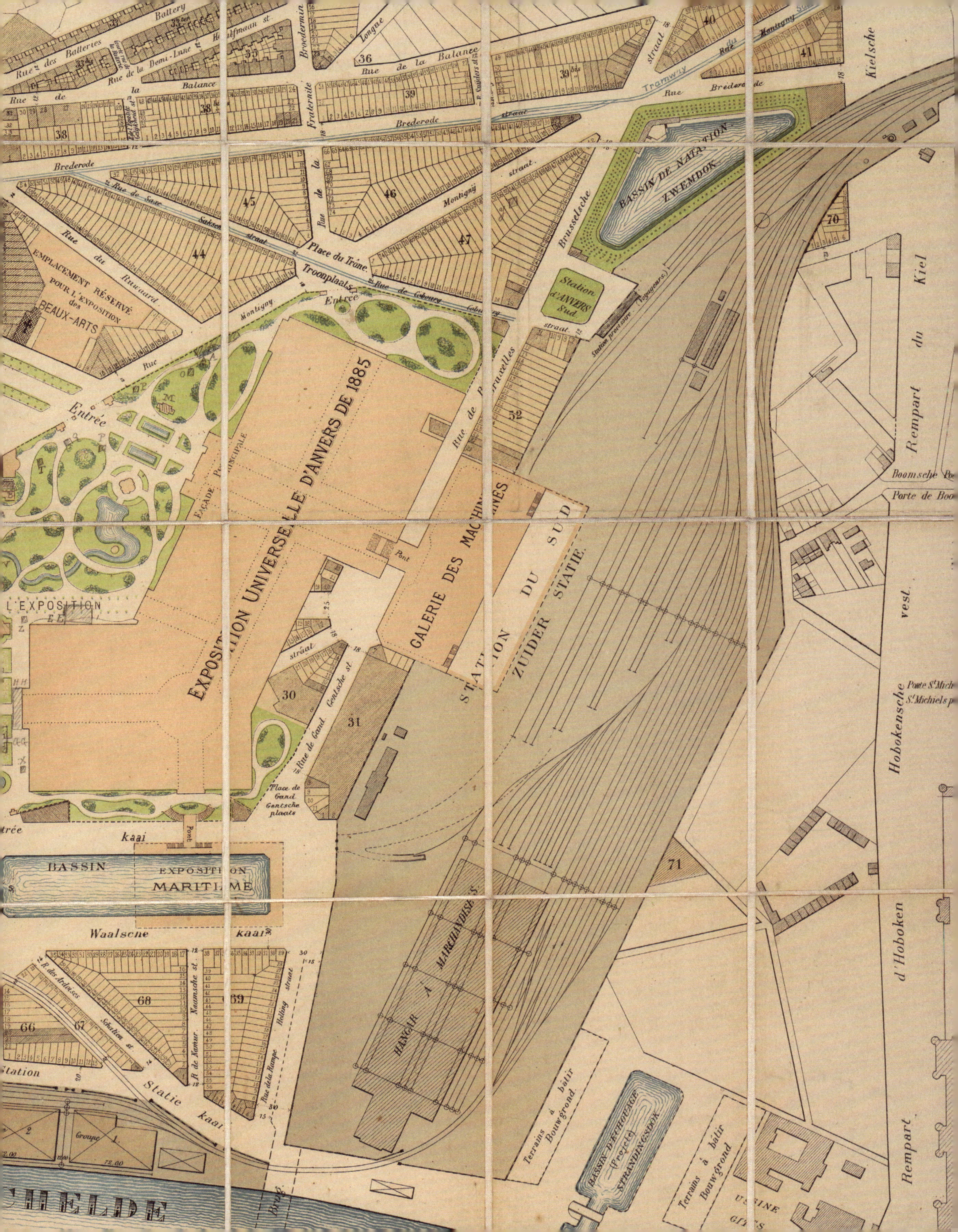

Rue des Batteries
Rue de la Demi-Lune
Rue de la Balance
Bréderode
Rue de Saxe
Saksen straat
Place du Trône
Troonplaats
Rue de Cobourg
Montigny straat
Brusselsche
BASSIN DE NATATION
ZWEMDOK
Station d'ANVERS Sud
Tramway
Rue Bréderode
Kielsche
Rempart du Kiel
Boomsche Po
Porte de Boo
EMPLACEMENT RÉSERVÉ POUR L'EXPOSITION des BEAUX-ARTS
Rue du Ruwaard
Entrée
EXPOSITION UNIVERSELLE D'ANVERS DE 1885
FAÇADE PRINCIPALE
GALERIE DES MACHINES
STATION DU SUD
ZUIDER STATIE
Rue de Bruxelles
L'EXPOSITION
Pont
Rue de Gand
Gentsche st.
Place de Gand
Gentsche plaats
Hobokensche vest
Porte St Michel
St Michiels p.
kaai
BASSIN
EXPOSITION MARITIME
Waalsche kaai
R. des Ardoises
Schaliën st.
R. de Namur
Namsche st.
Rue de la Rampe
Helling straat
Statie kaai
Station
Groupe 1
HANGAR À MARCHANDISES
Terrains à bâtir
Bouwgrond
BASSIN D'ÉCHOUAGE (Projeté)
STRANDINGSDOK
USINE
Rempart d'Hoboken
Rempart

pp. 34–35: The museum, the museum garden and the surrounding neighbourhood were all designed as one integral entity in the 19th century.

can be used in whole or in part. And without having to remove part of the permanent collection, as was often the case in the past. A pivoting wall in the rear gallery can act as a partition. The new museum volume also provides space for temporary exhibitions, but of a very special kind: a print cabinet in a room with subdued lighting to display works on paper, which will rotate regularly.

Postscript

It's only when you leave the old museum that you notice a tiny part of the old museum that has become completely redundant and now looks a bit forlorn: the old, wood-panelled and somewhat claustrophobic ticket office. The days of yore are definitely past.

Photographs of the upper galleries from around 1925. In some places, the walls are covered with paintings all the way up to the cornices.

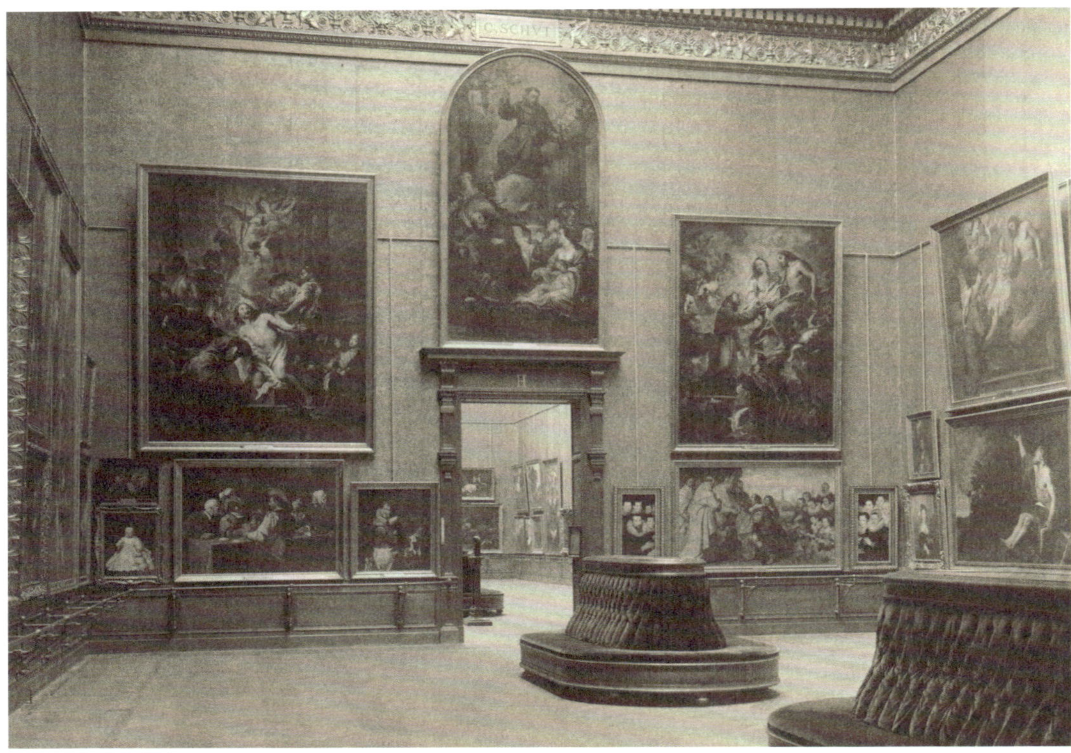

In 1927 the four patios were covered. That was the first and last expansion of the KMSKA until 2011.

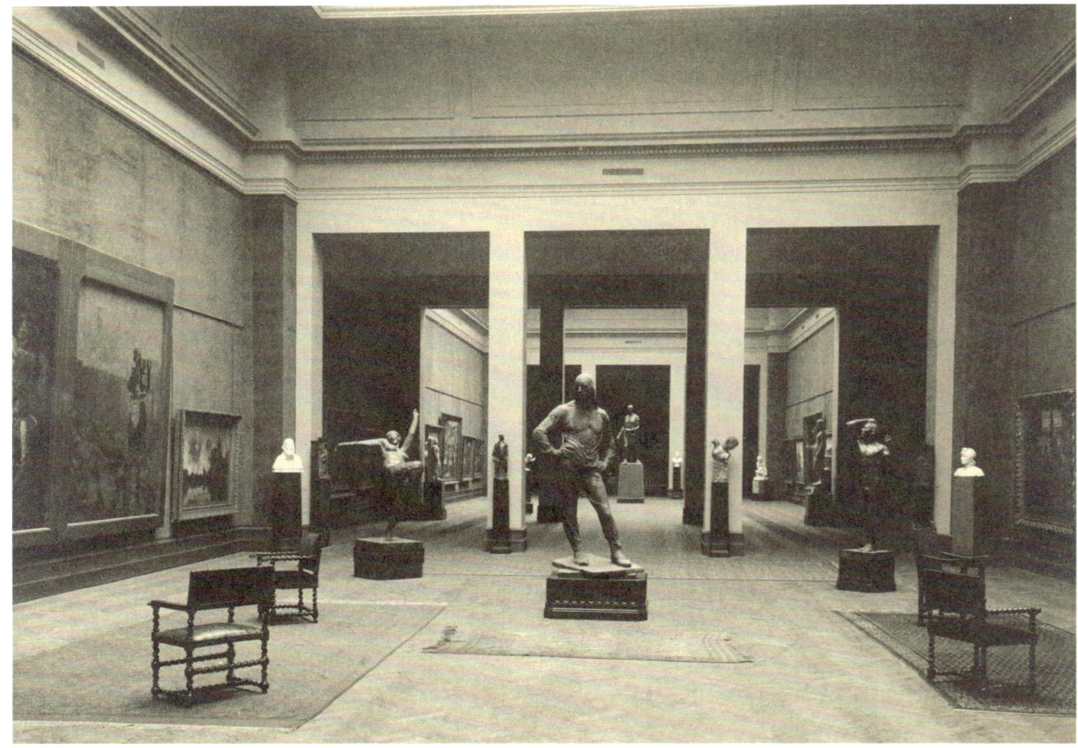

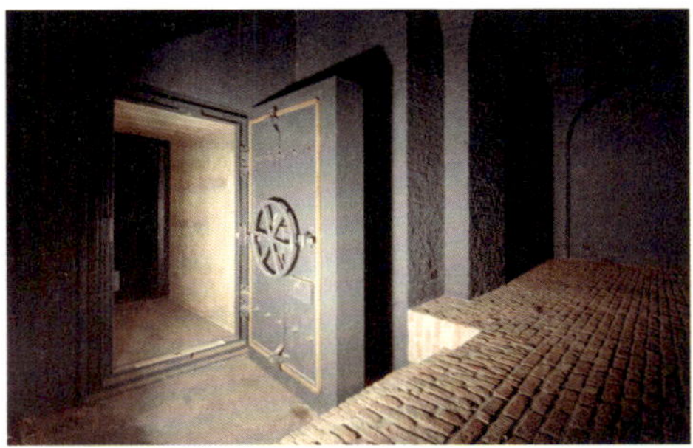

The door of the nuclear vault.

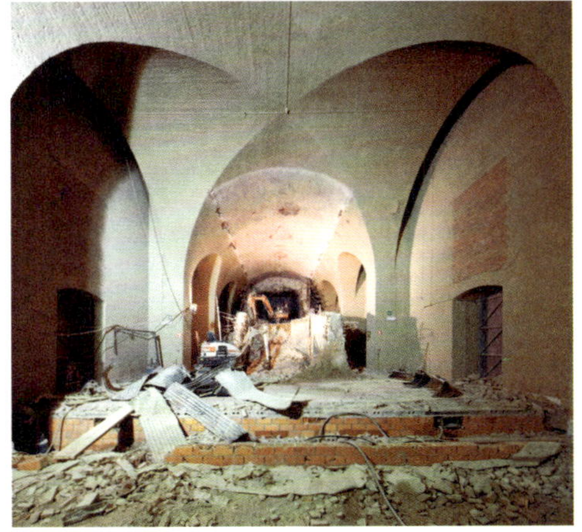

It took two mini-diggers three months to pulverise the nuclear vault in the bombproof shelter with pneumatic hammers.

There are many dangers that a museum and its collections may face, including the possibility of war, and the bombing and looting that follows. This has been demonstrated countless times, and in various places, in the 21st century alone. The KMSKA has shielded itself against this danger from the start. Quite literally.

From cellar to vault

At the end of the 19th century, architects Winders and Van Dijk were already taking this kind of disaster scenario into account when designing the KMSKA. A space under the central upper galleries of the museum was described in the 1877 competition as follows: a bombproof room to house at a minimum the most precious paintings of the museum in times of war. The result was a solid brick construction, 47 metres long, 11 metres wide and 8.5 metres high. The "bombproof cellar" – a slightly odd name for a structure that is actually located on the ground floor – was a fact.

Twenty-four years after its opening, the moment they had prepared for arrived with World War I. The museum closed, the galleries were emptied and the bombproof cellar was filled with artworks. That scene was played out again at the beginning of World War II. Colossal paintings by Rubens, among others – *The Adoration of the Magi* weighs more than 600 kilos – were hoisted down through hatches and along narrow gullies. That system is still in use today.

At the end of World War II, in Japan, the world got to know the atomic bomb. A new era with a new threat had dawned. And a new concern for the KMSKA: in the early 1950s, at the beginning of the Cold War, the Ministry of the Interior decided that a concrete nuclear shelter should be built at the back of the bombproof cellar. In 1952, the nuclear vault was finished. Dimensions: 21 metres long, 5.5 metres wide and about 9 metres high. The ceiling was an average of 1.5 metres thick.

Demolition

One of the first actions of the KMSKA masterplan in 2012 was the construction of a new storage for works of art. Right inside the museum itself. In fact, actually inside the bombproof cellar of yesteryear, where the nuclear vault was still located. The demolition of the vault was a herculean task for the company responsible, Alceco. The idea of using explosives for the job was eventually abandoned because it was too risky; the reinforcement of the vault was simply too strong. If this had been possible, the matter would have been resolved in a matter of seconds.

Instead, the work had to be done manually. Just to create a way in, the floor of a museum gallery had to be removed, and it was then still a daunting challenge to smash a passage through a one-metre thick masonry wall. Two mini diggers with pneumatic hammers – 'mini' because larger machines were too big for the narrow width – then spent three months crushing 1,350 tonnes of (highly reinforced) concrete and 81 tonnes of steel. Conveniently, it created a heap of rubble at least four metres high; the claws of mini diggers can only reach as high as five metres... and four plus five is nine, handily reaching the top of the vault.

On 7 June 2012, removal of the vault was complete. The construction of the new storage depot could begin.

pp. 38–39: The bombproof shelter has made way for what was to become the new storage depot.

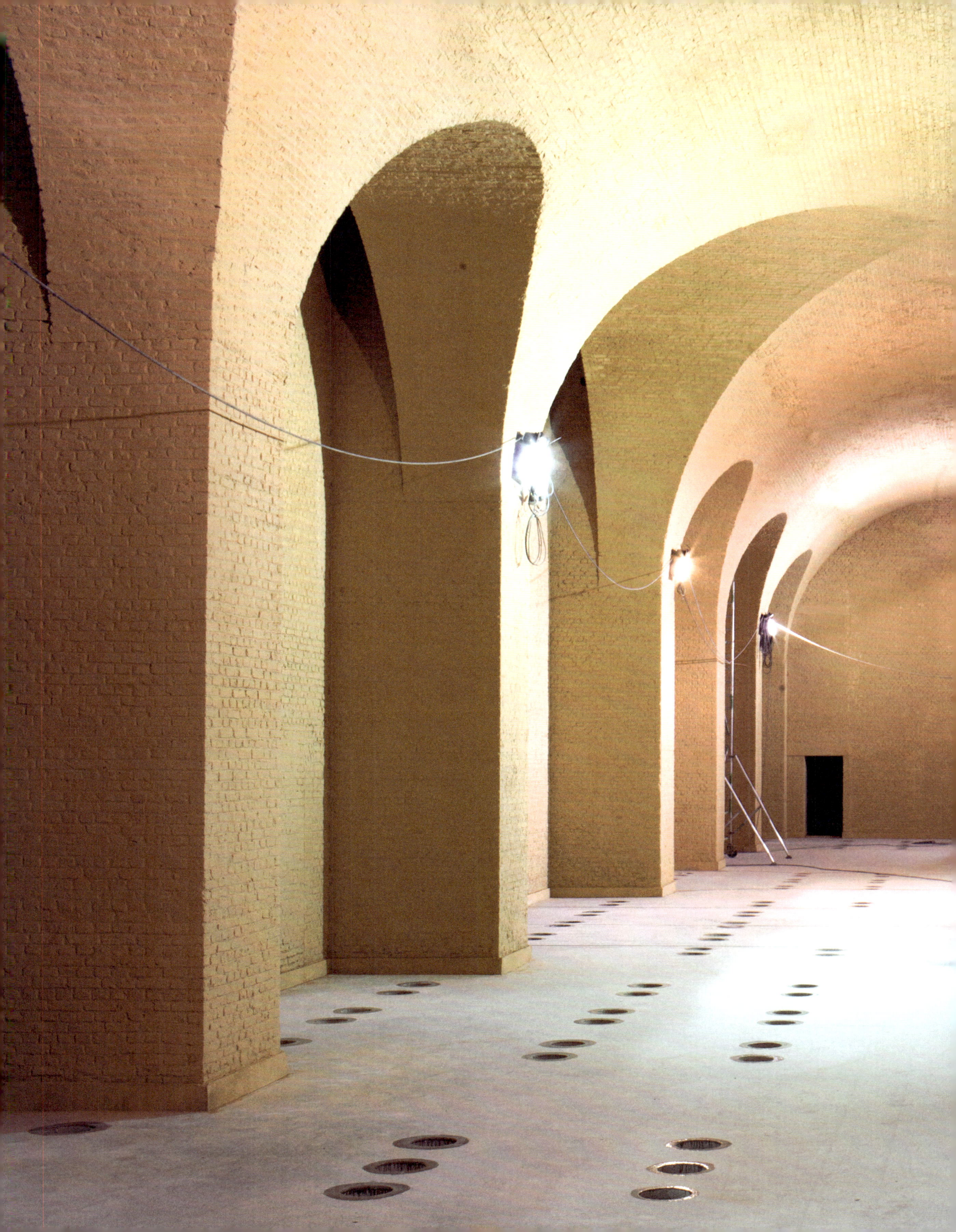

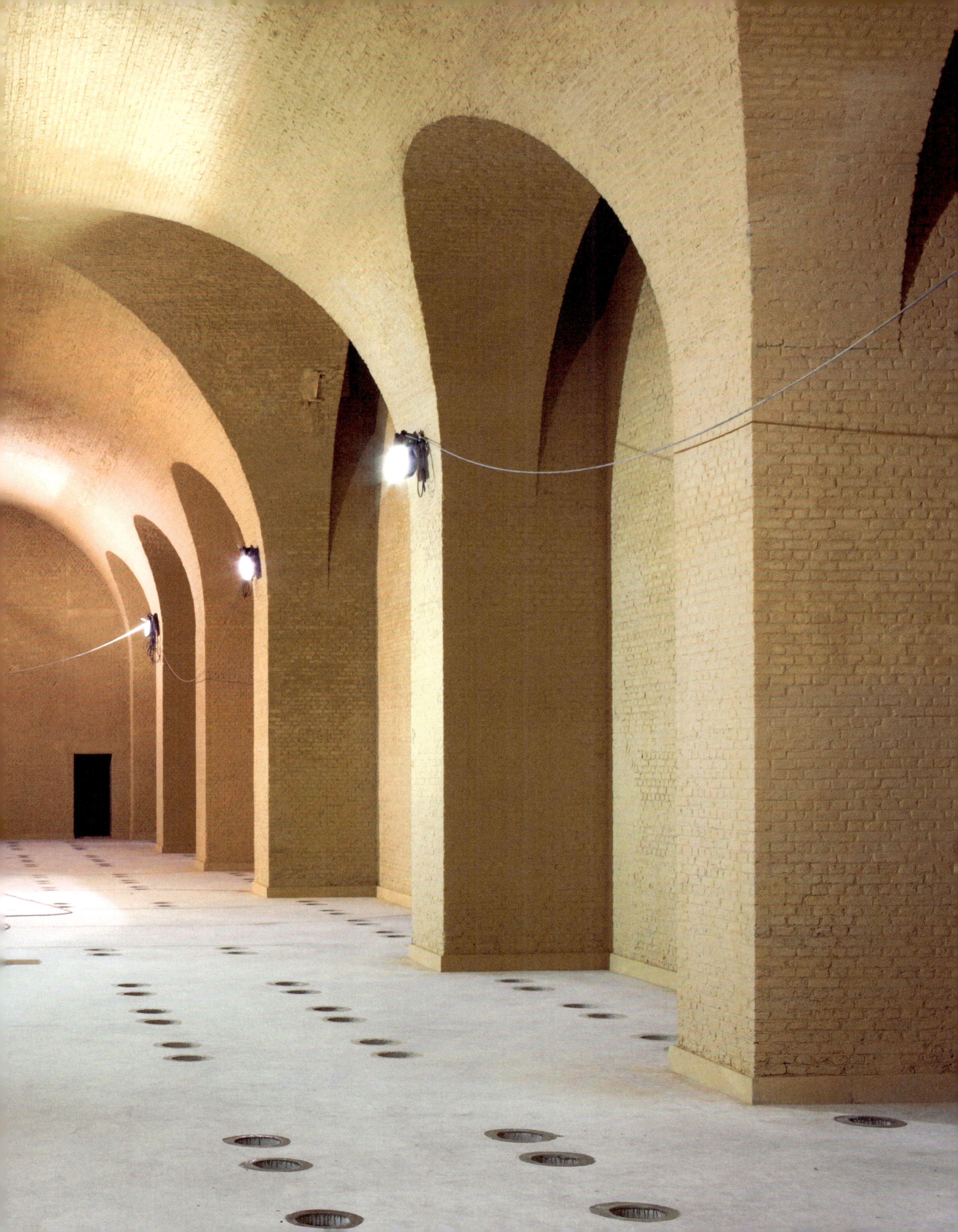

NOT ALL THAT GLITTERS IS GOLD: THE GILDED DECORATION

The 1880s. The museum is under construction. Architects Winders and Van Dijk are planning two grand halls at the heart of the complex; they could be called Galleries of Honour. Large altarpieces will be exhibited here, and it's no accident that they are works by three of Antwerp's greatest artists: Rubens, Van Dyck and Jordaens. The galleries are named after them. The works that are to hang in these galleries are the finest pieces from the collection at the time – and still are today. Most of them come from the churches and monasteries of Antwerp.

The museum archive preserves correspondence between the two architects about the two galleries, in which they describe in great detail the colours they will use to finish them. It is clear these halls must be imbued with a majestic quality. For the walls, their choice fell on antique red, with pale brown hues for the upper walls, "*pour obtenir une harmonie complète de l'ensemble*" ('to create perfect harmony for the whole').

The finishing touch, the shining pinnacle of their work, is to be applied to the mouldings: gold leaf! Once again creating perfect harmony for the whole, they decide. Or at least the illusion of gold leaf. in their search for gold leaf, Winders and Van Dijk encounter the problem of finance. Other roads need to be travelled in pursuit of a comparable effect but with cheaper, more frugal materials. They request samples from museums in Berlin, among others. Finally, they decide to apply silver leaf with gold varnish. As we learn from their letters.

However, in the course of the restoration programme, the microscopes of the Royal Institute for Cultural Heritage (KIK-IRPA) revealed a rather different story: the "gilded decoration" is actually a non-oxidising metal foil with a layer of varnish on top! The architects did not, in fact, carry out the plans so exhaustively debated in their letters.

For the restoration of this pseudo-gold decoration, the decision was made to return to the original plan, in consultation with the Flanders Heritage Agency and the restorers of Altri Tempi: it was done with a combination of aluminium and pigmented varnish. All that glitters is... still not gold!

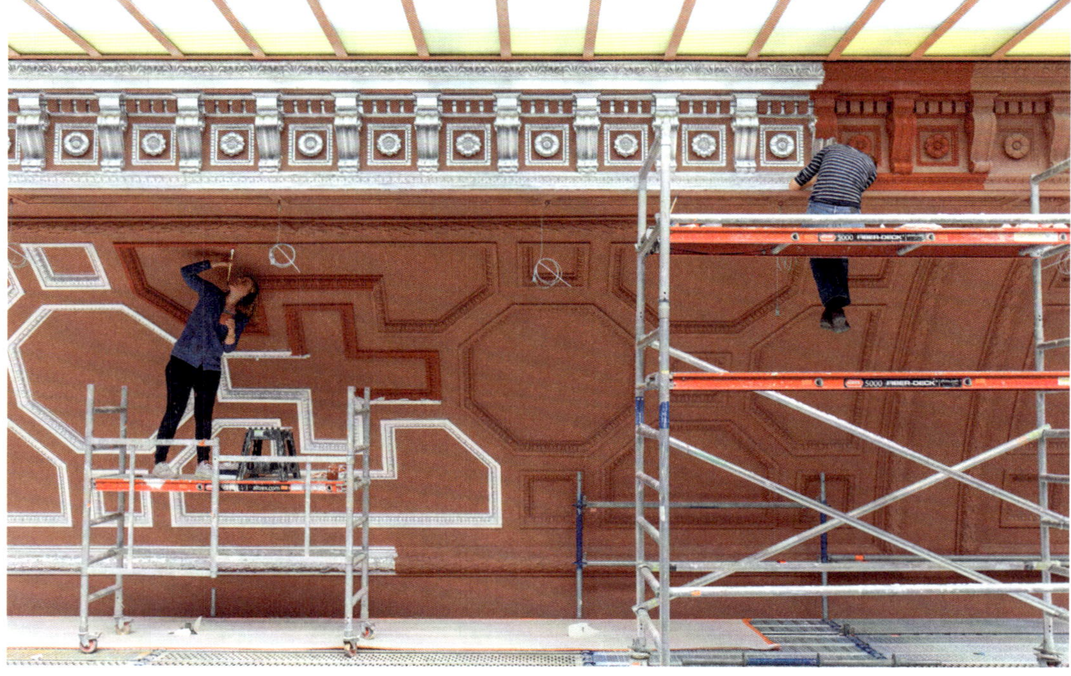

New gilding on the ceiling ornamentation of the Rubens, Jordaens and Van Dyck galleries.

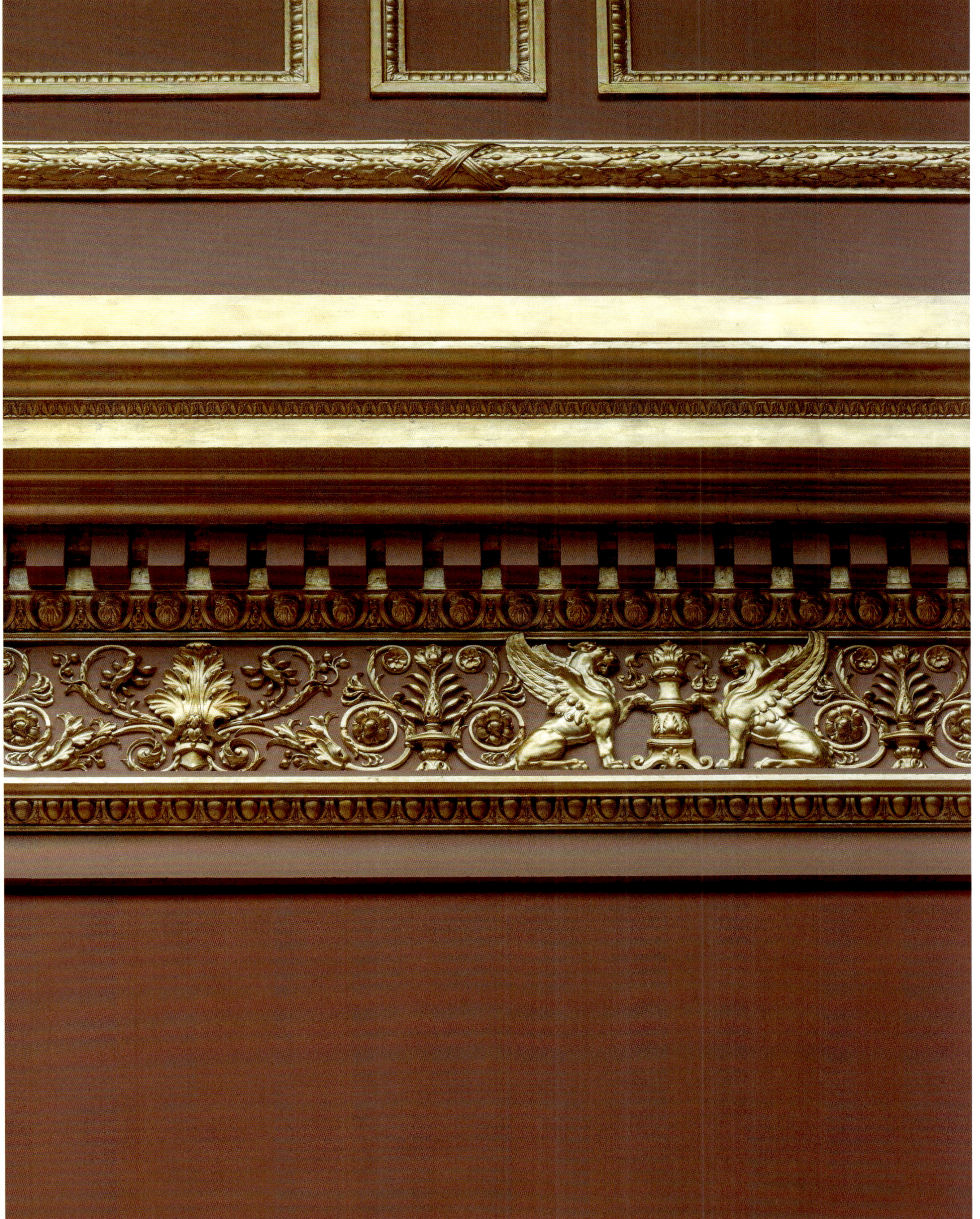

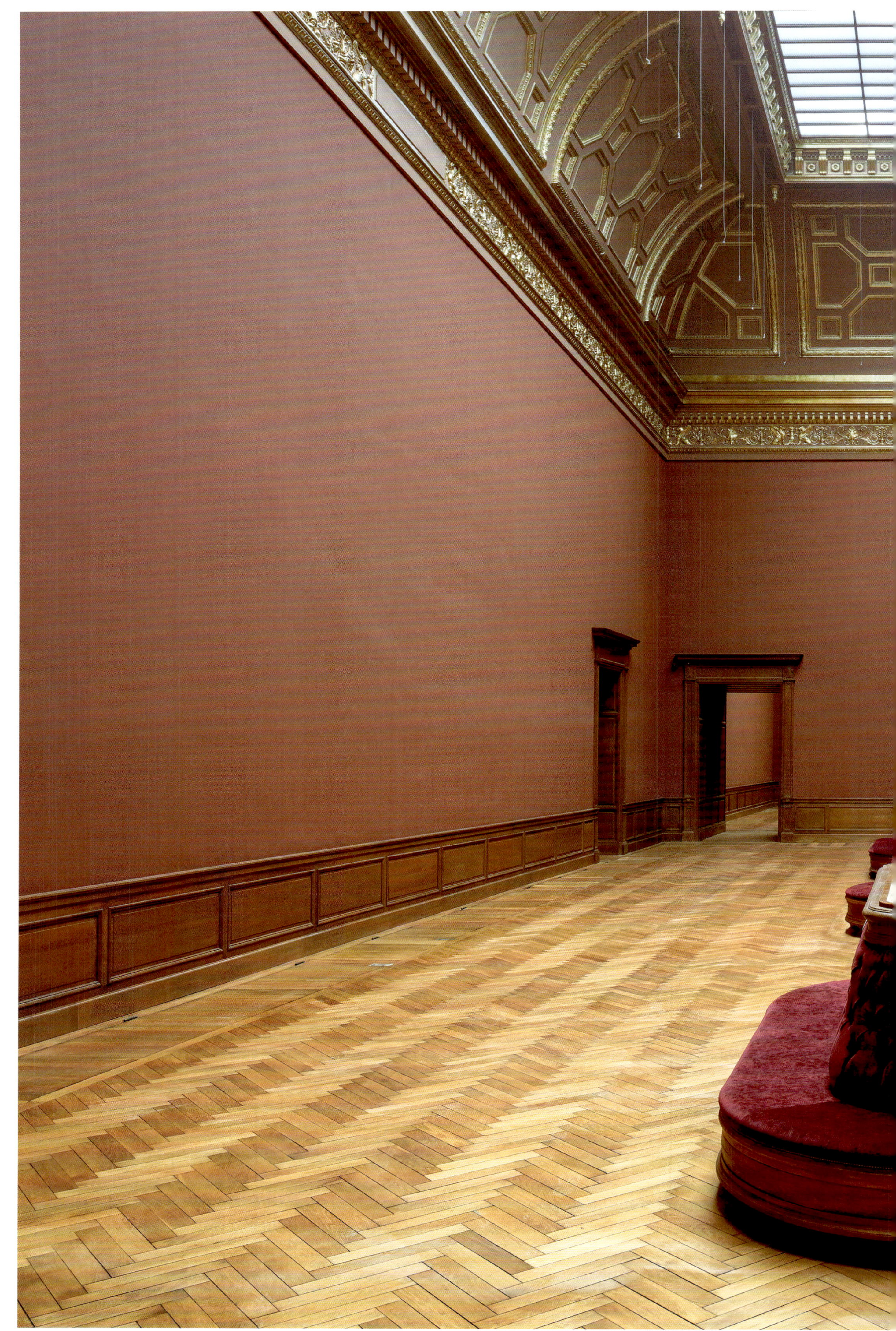

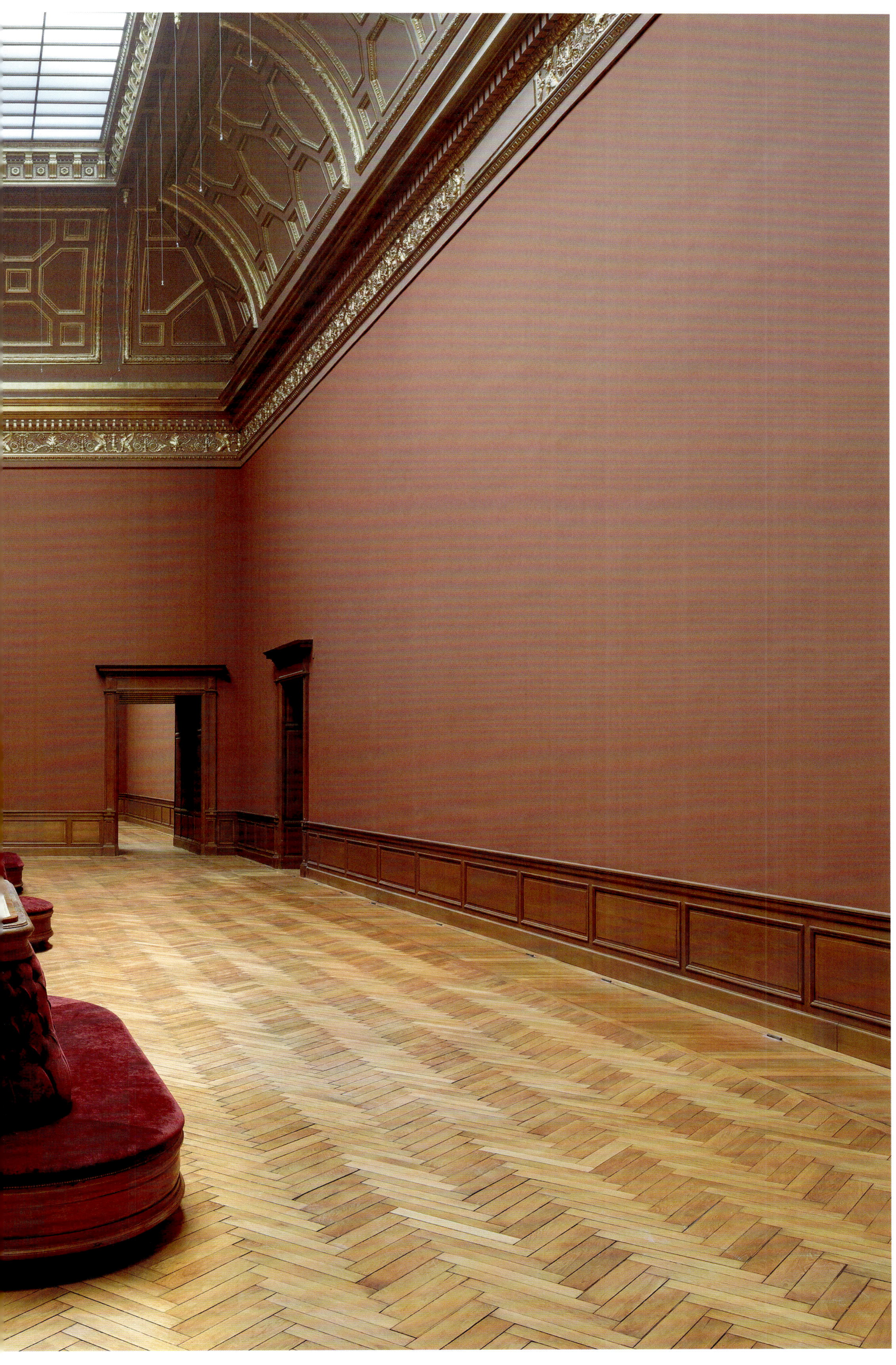

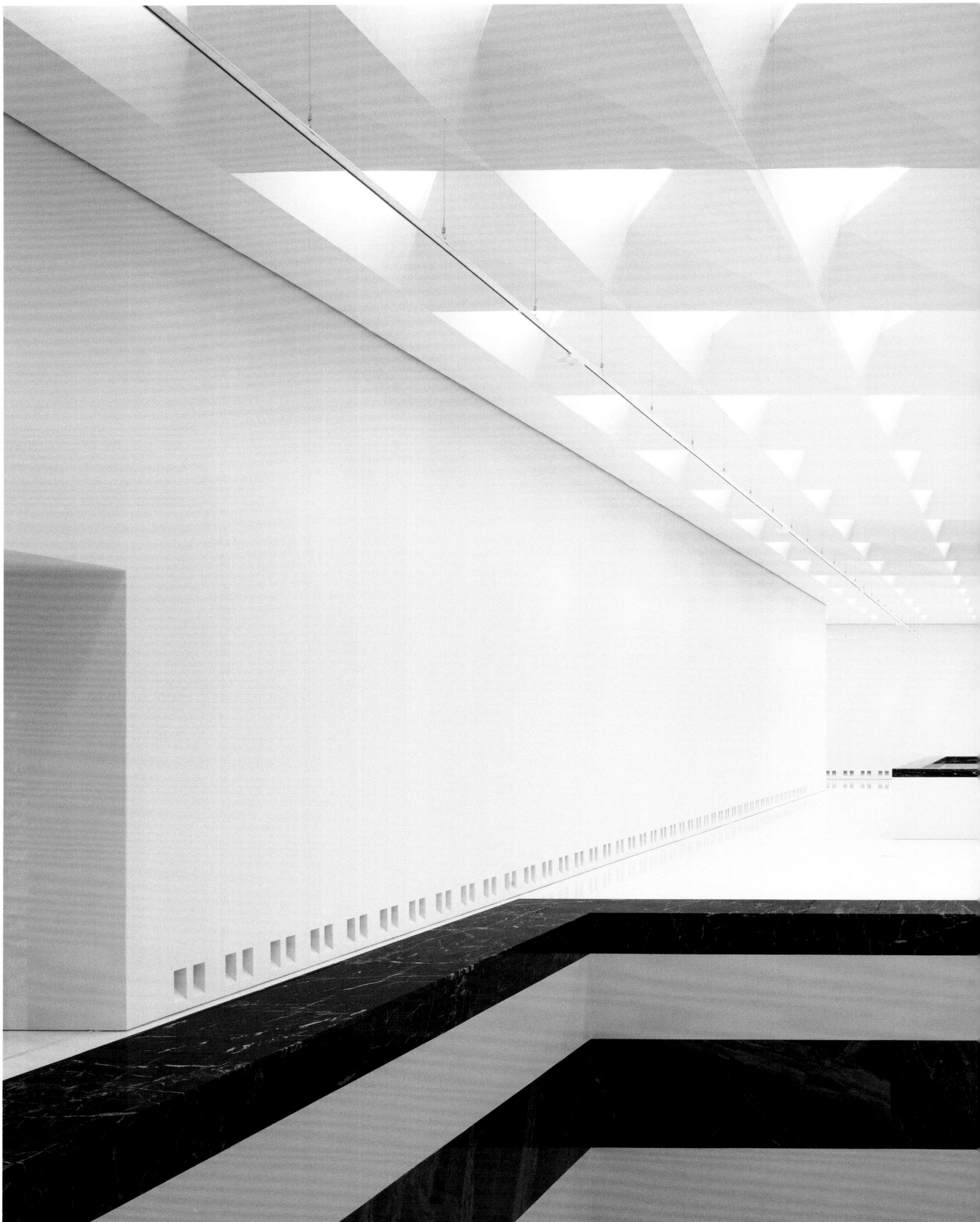

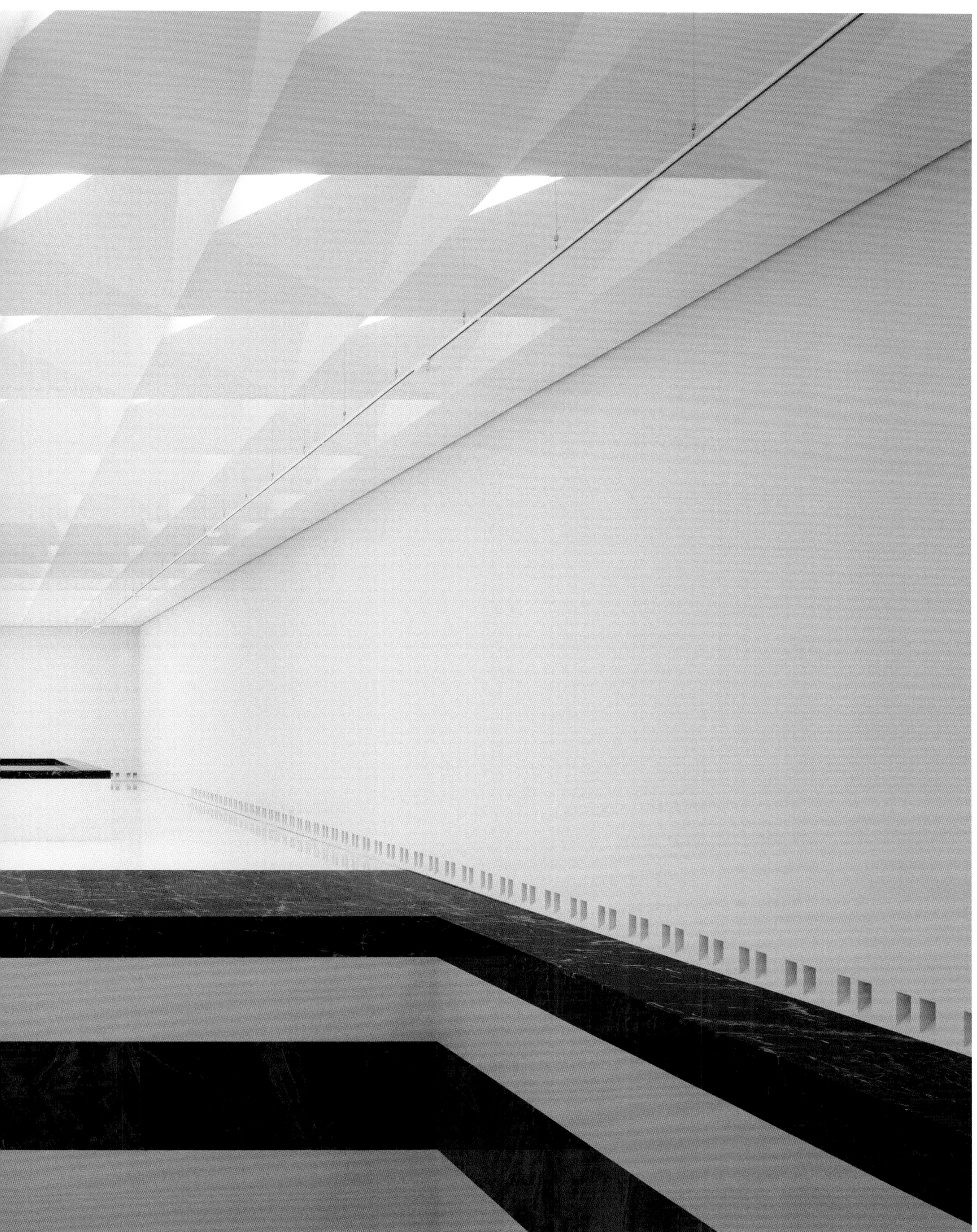

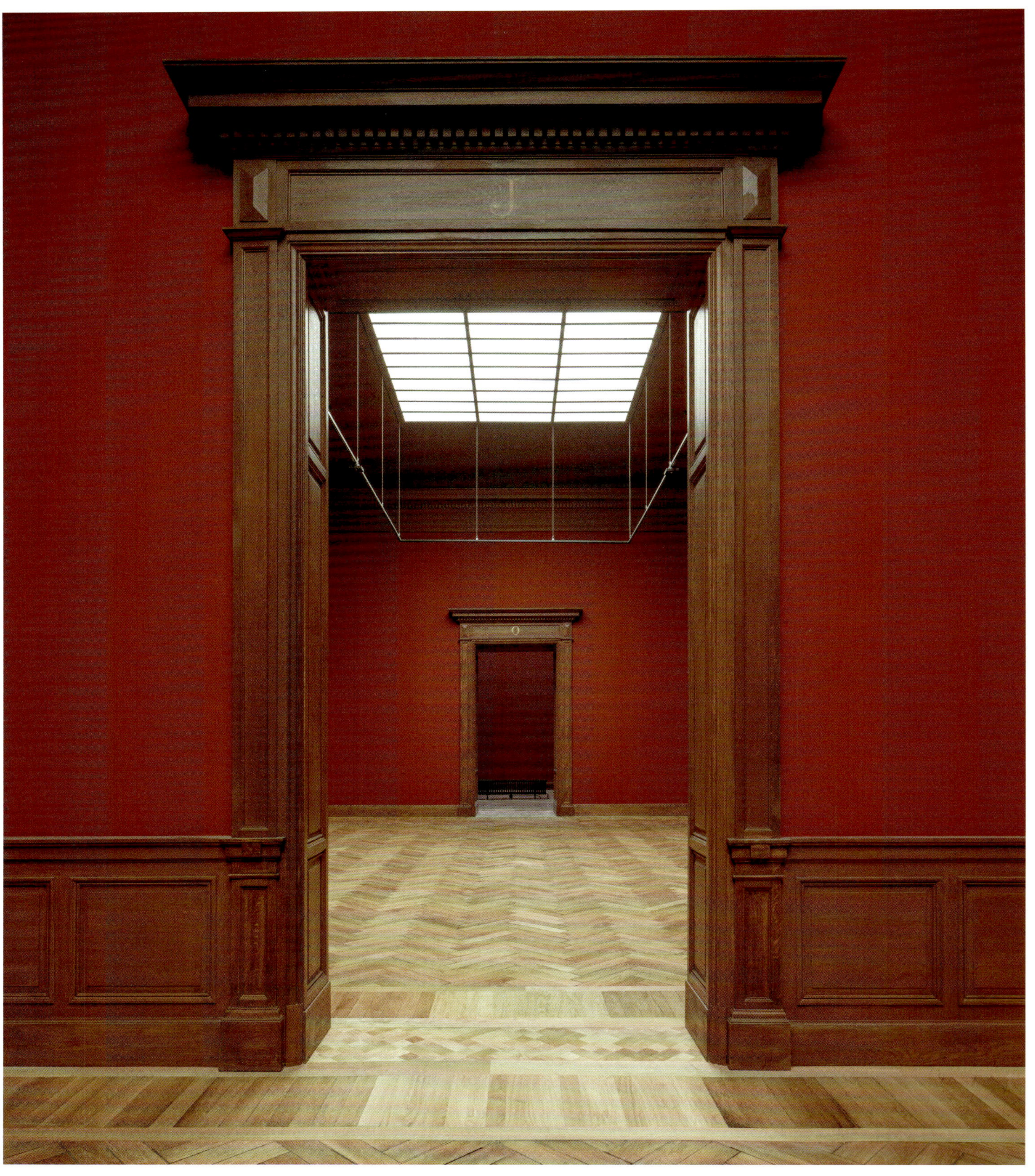

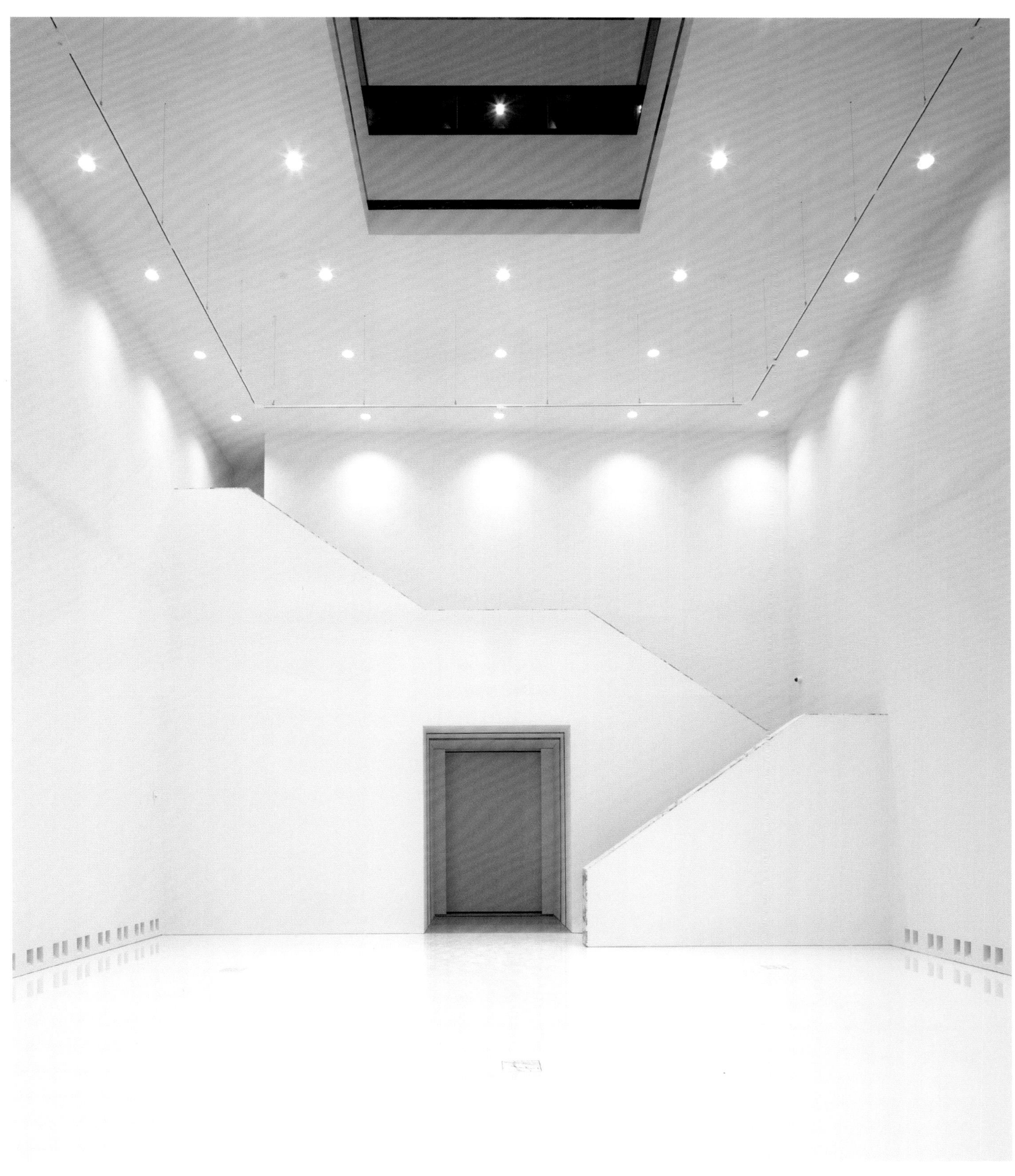

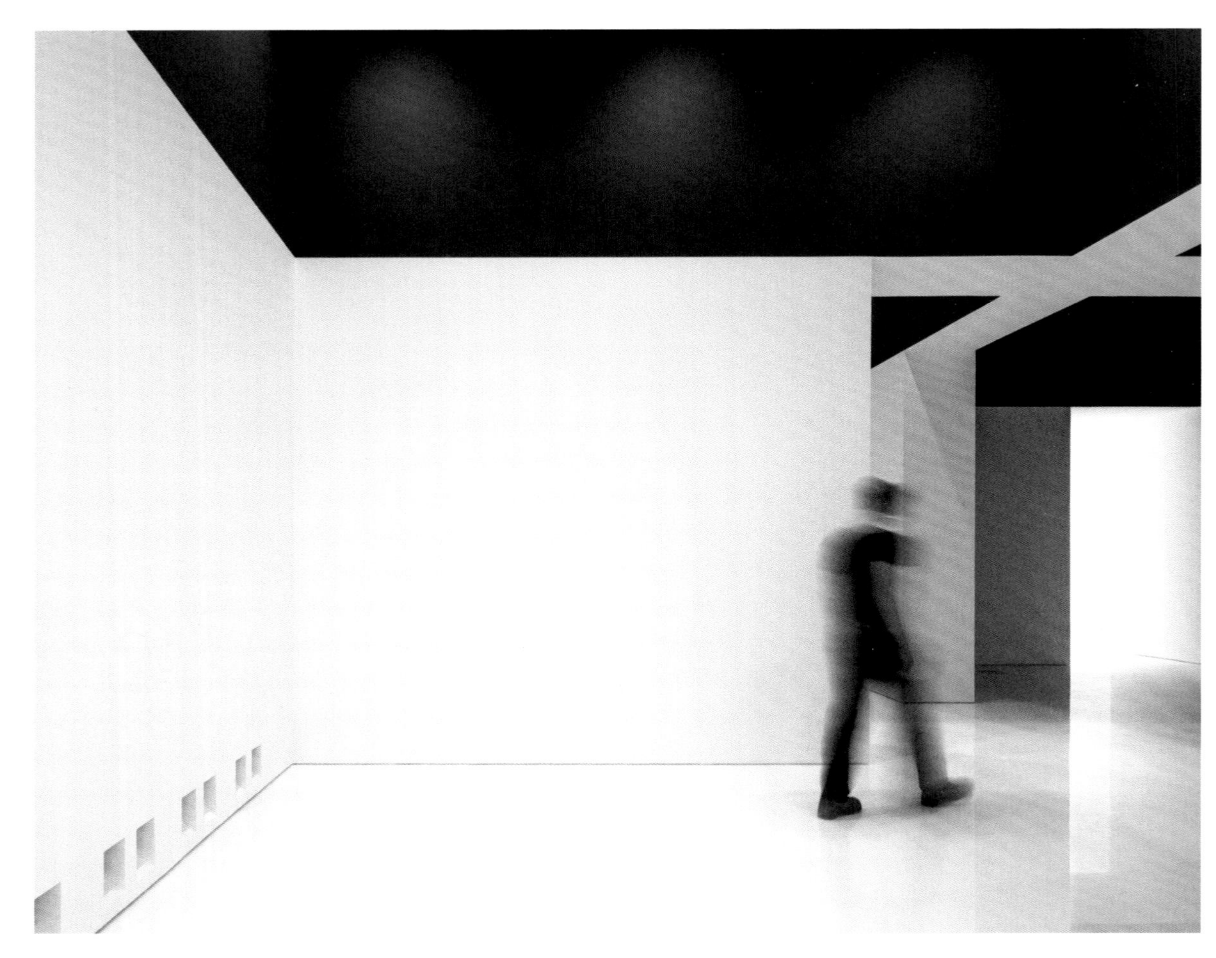

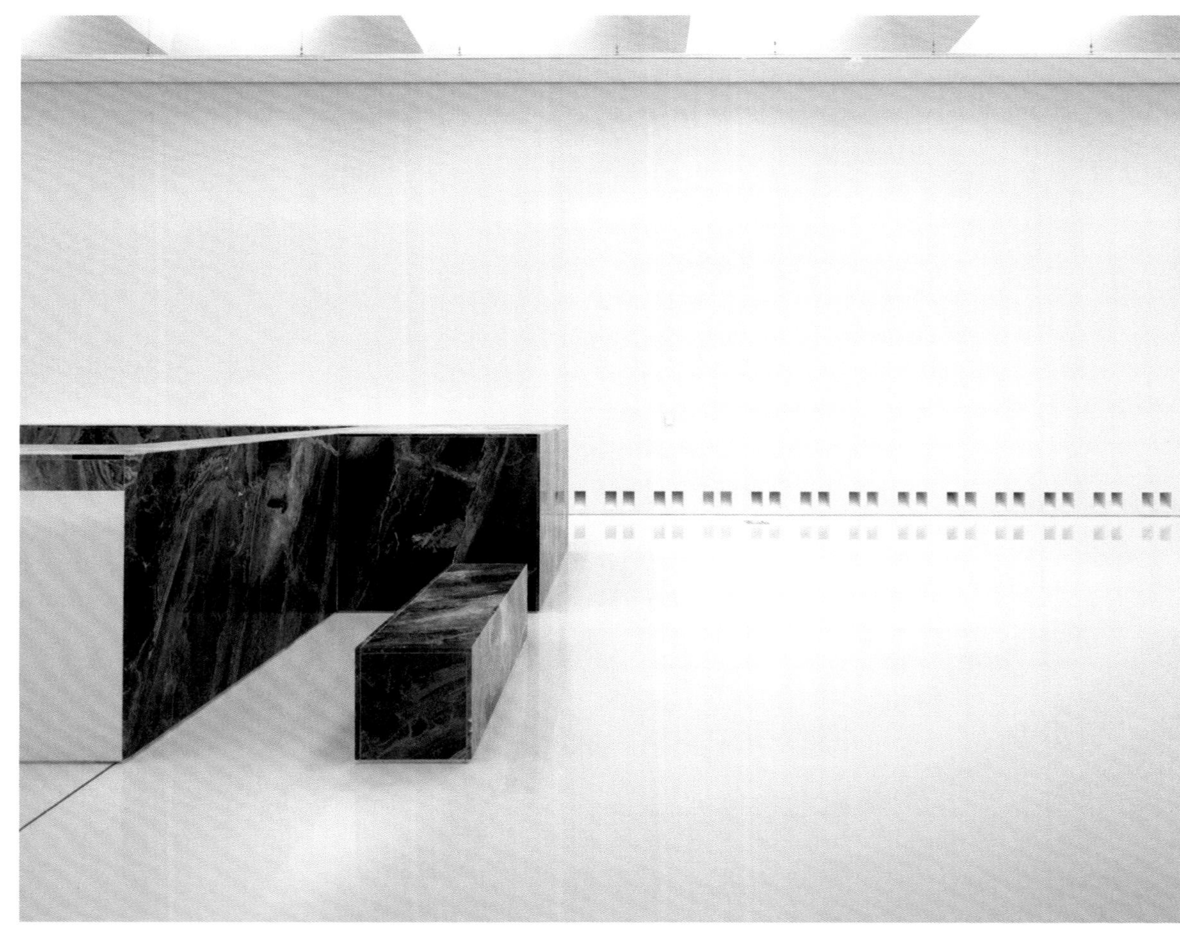

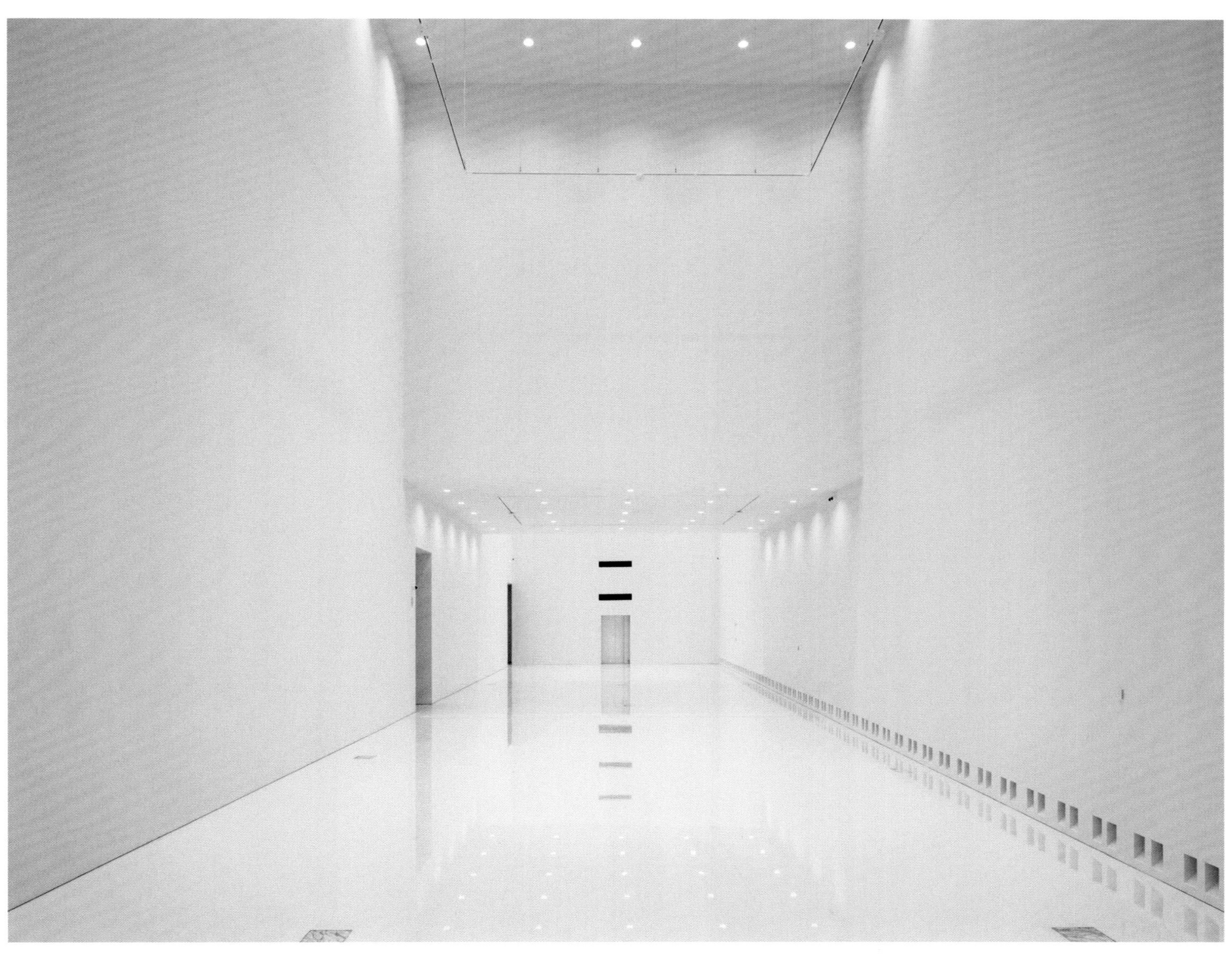

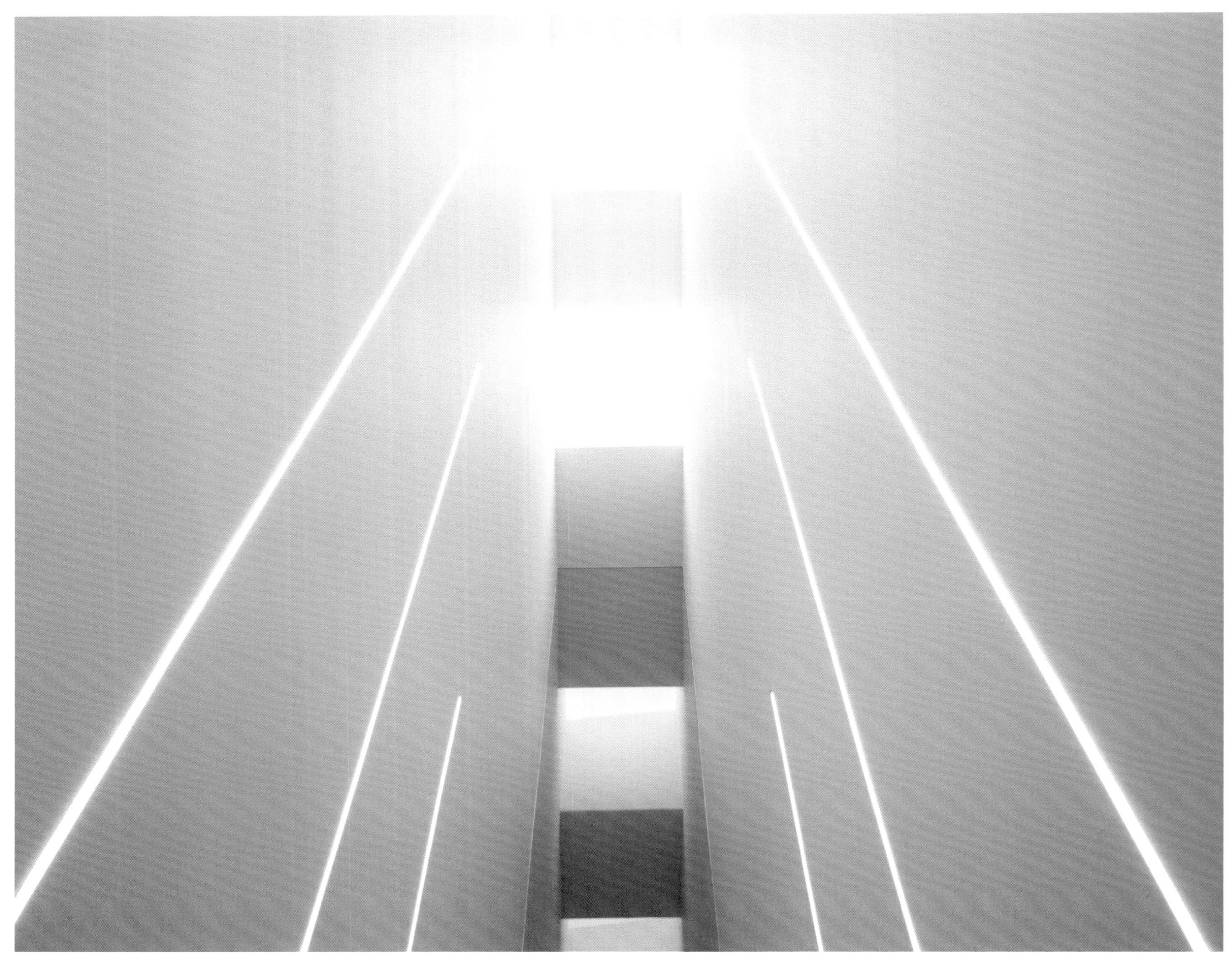

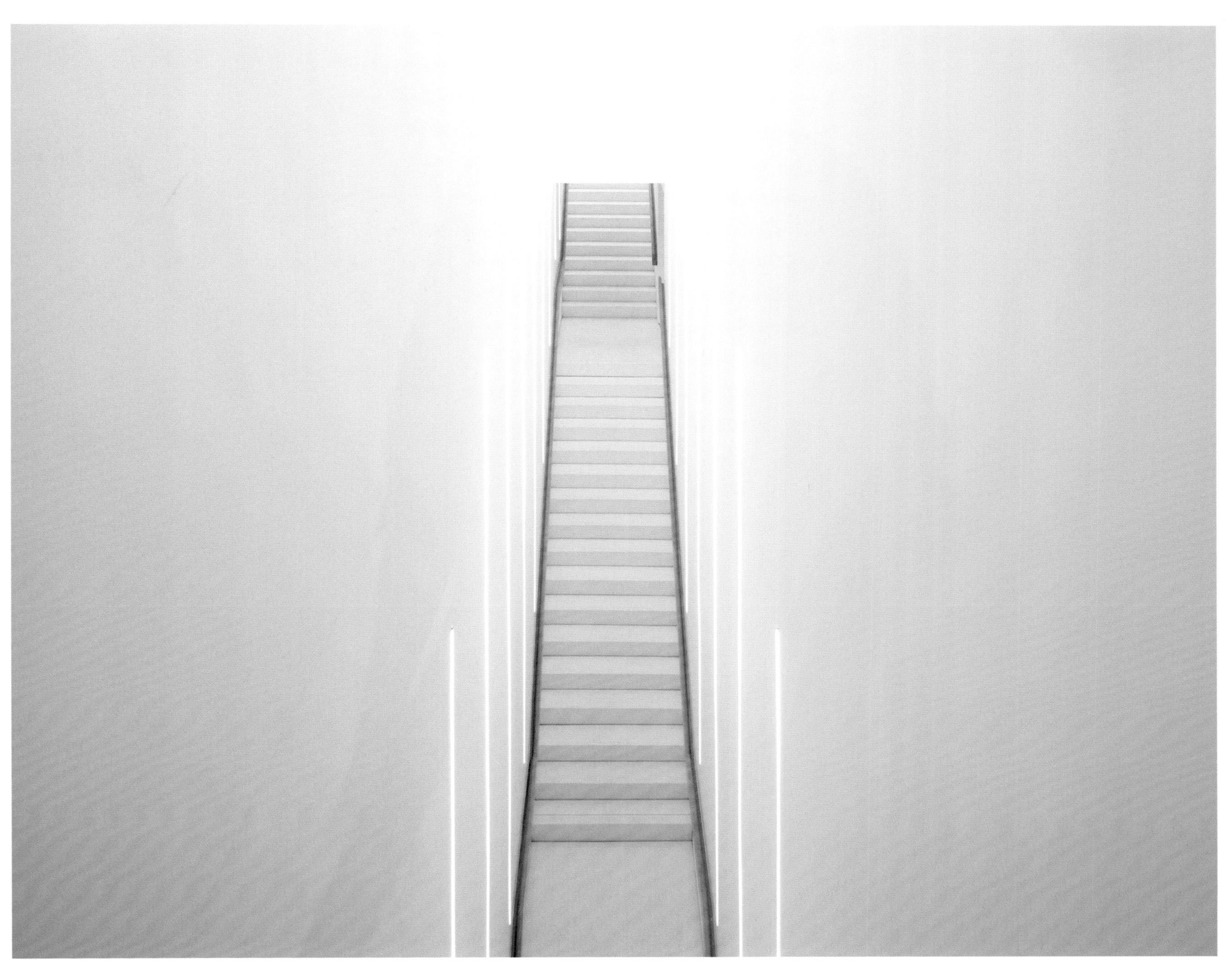

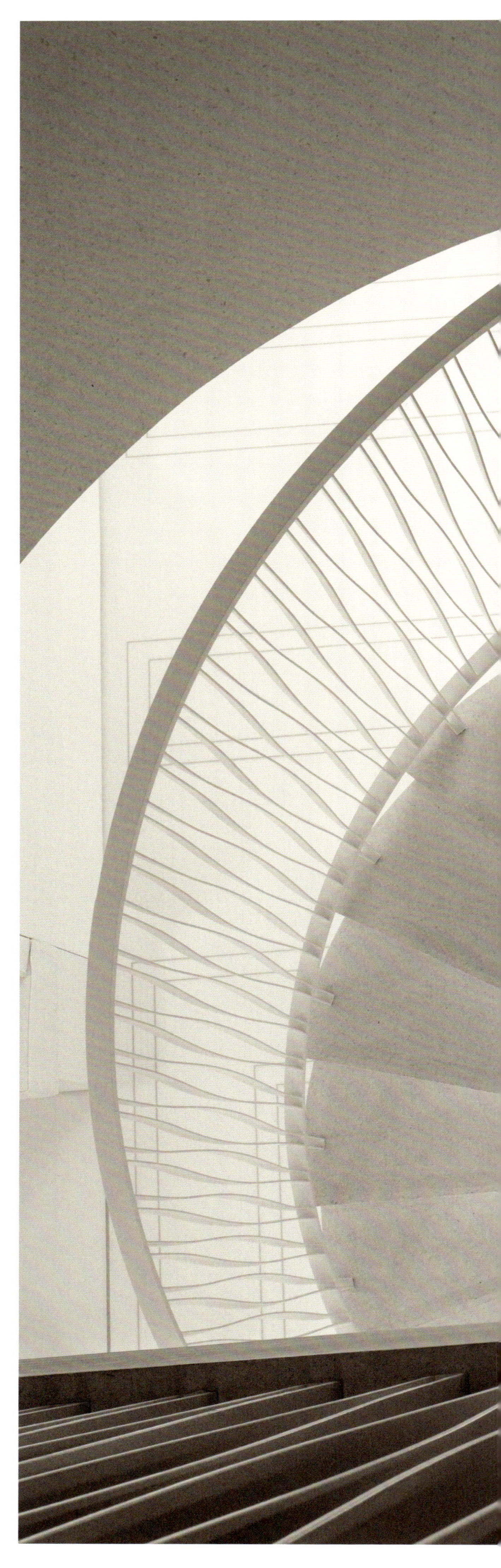

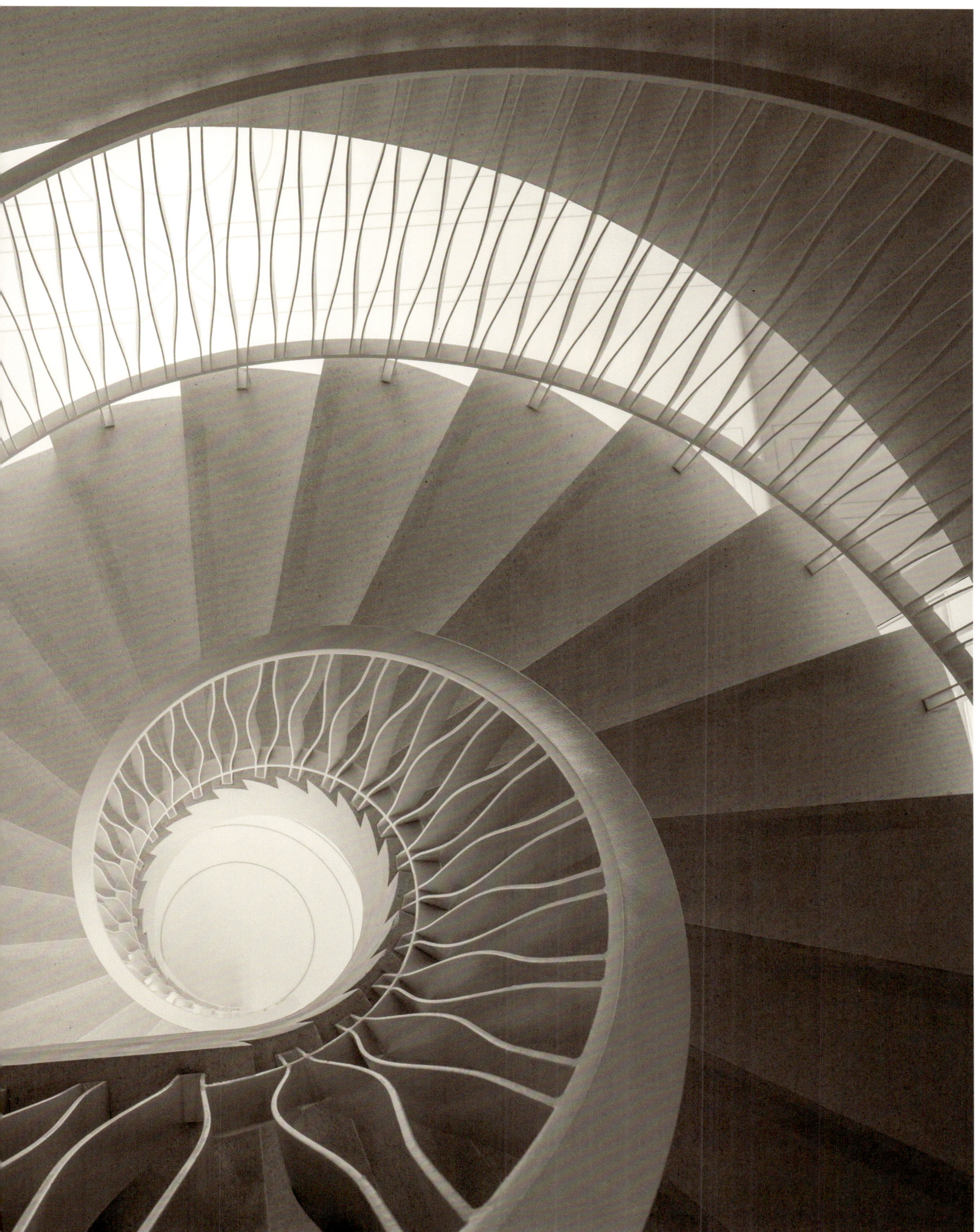

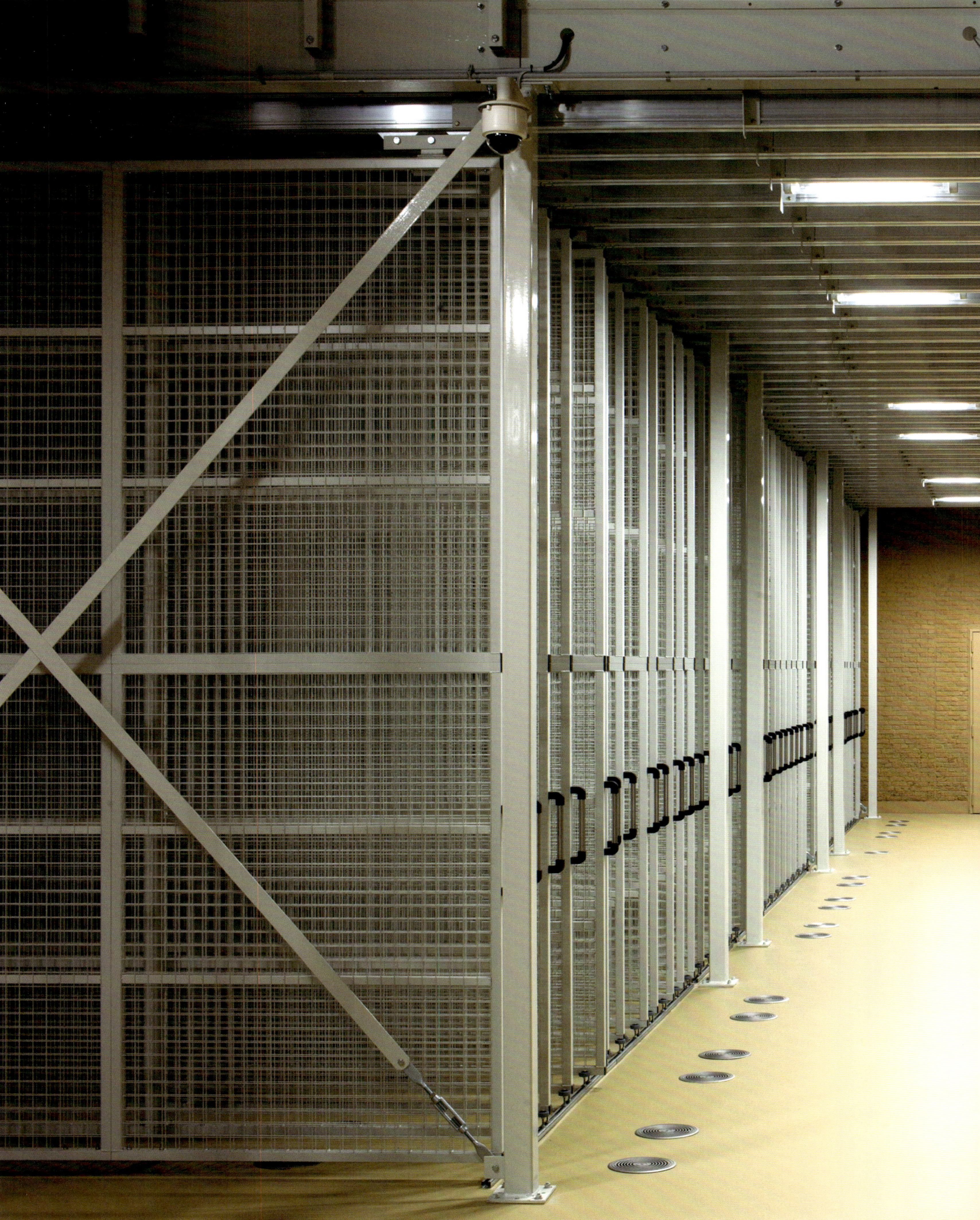

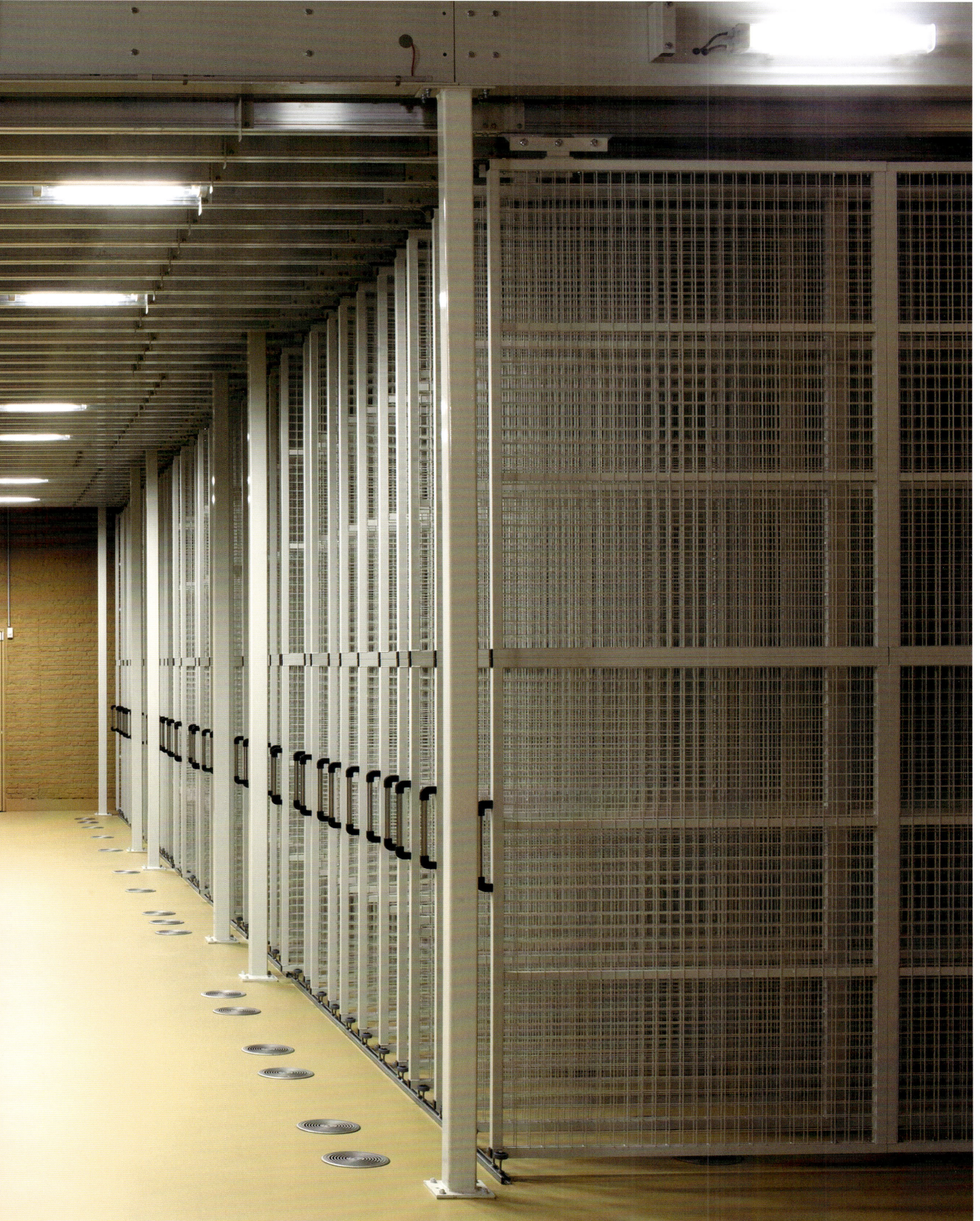

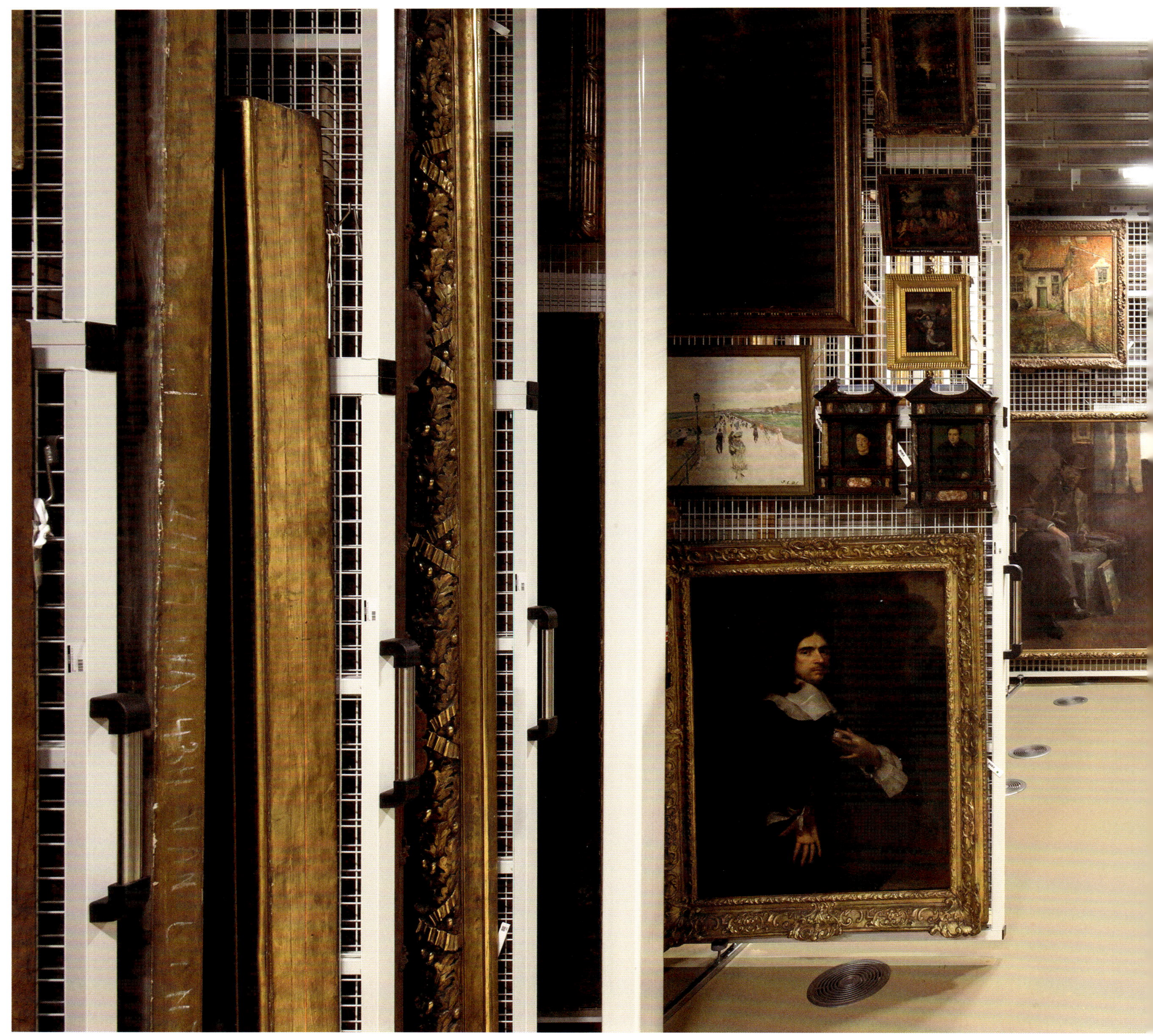

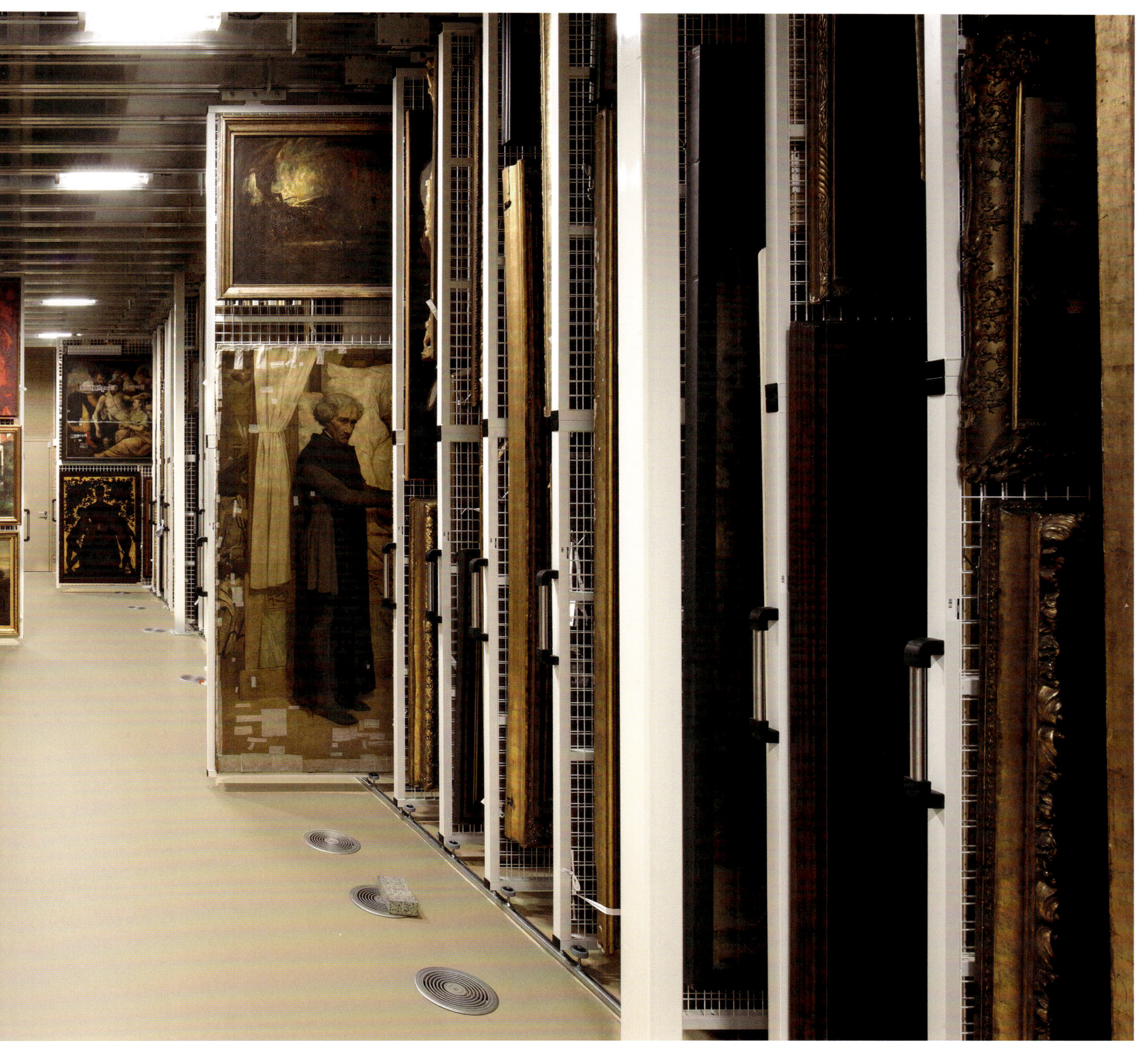

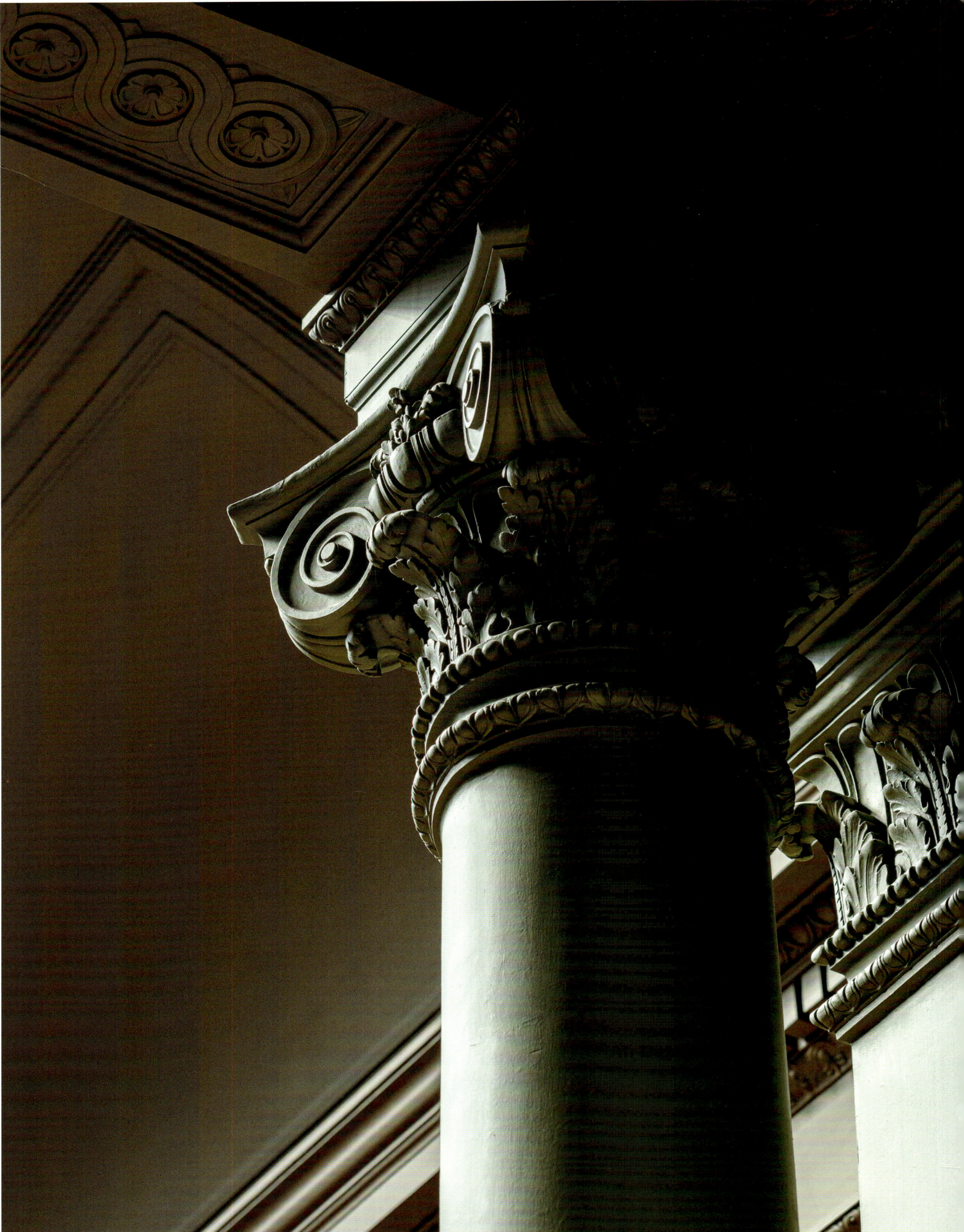

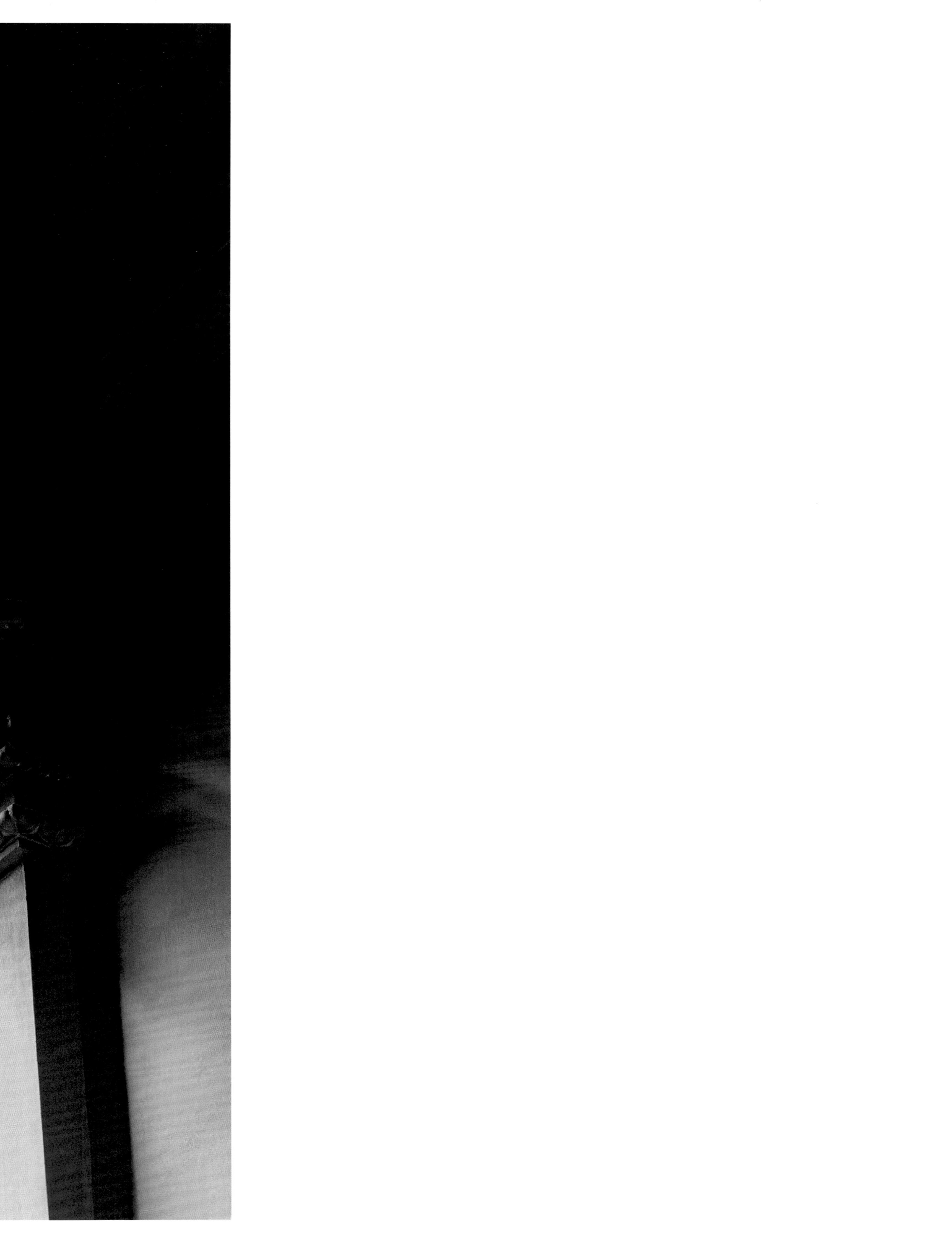

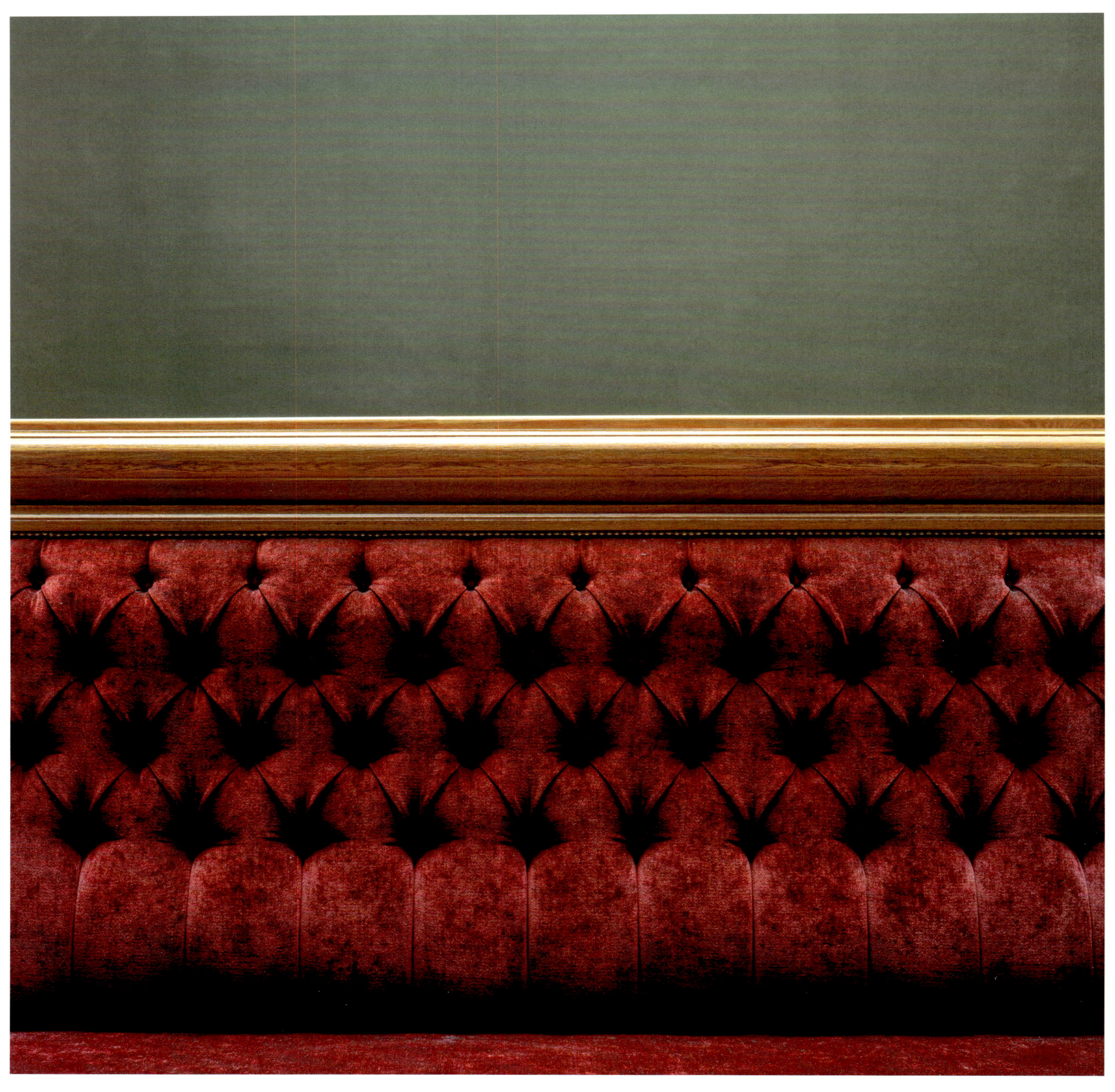

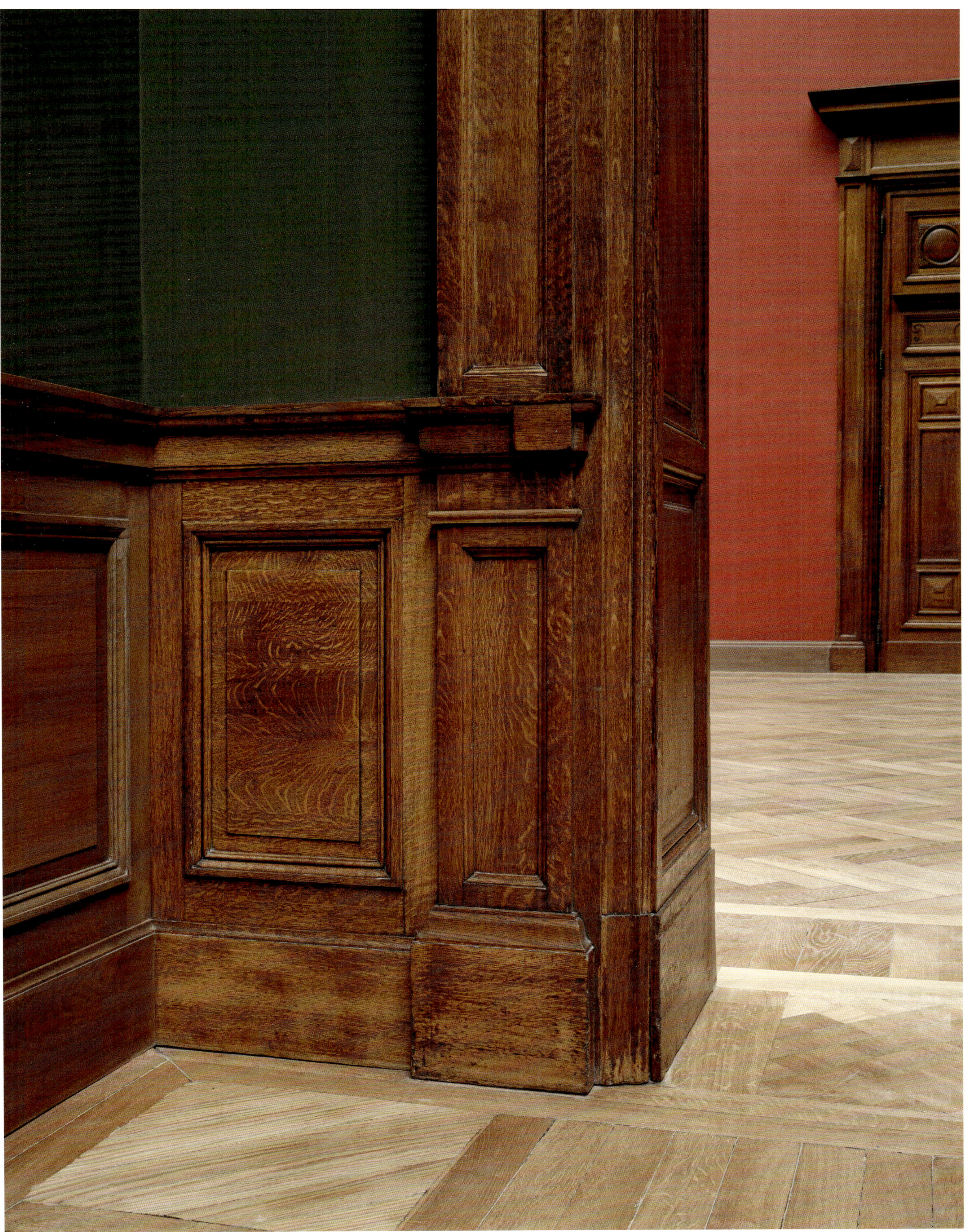

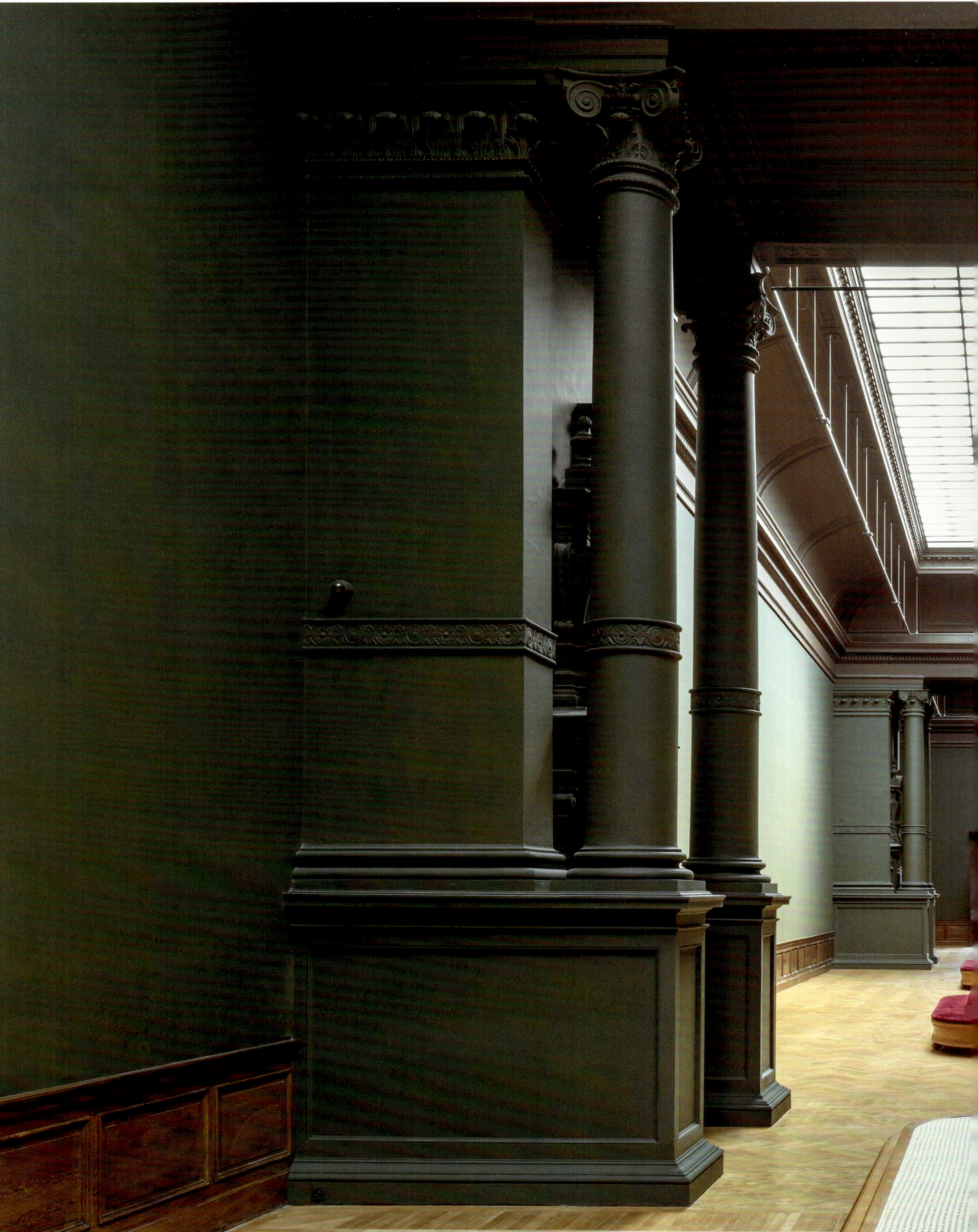

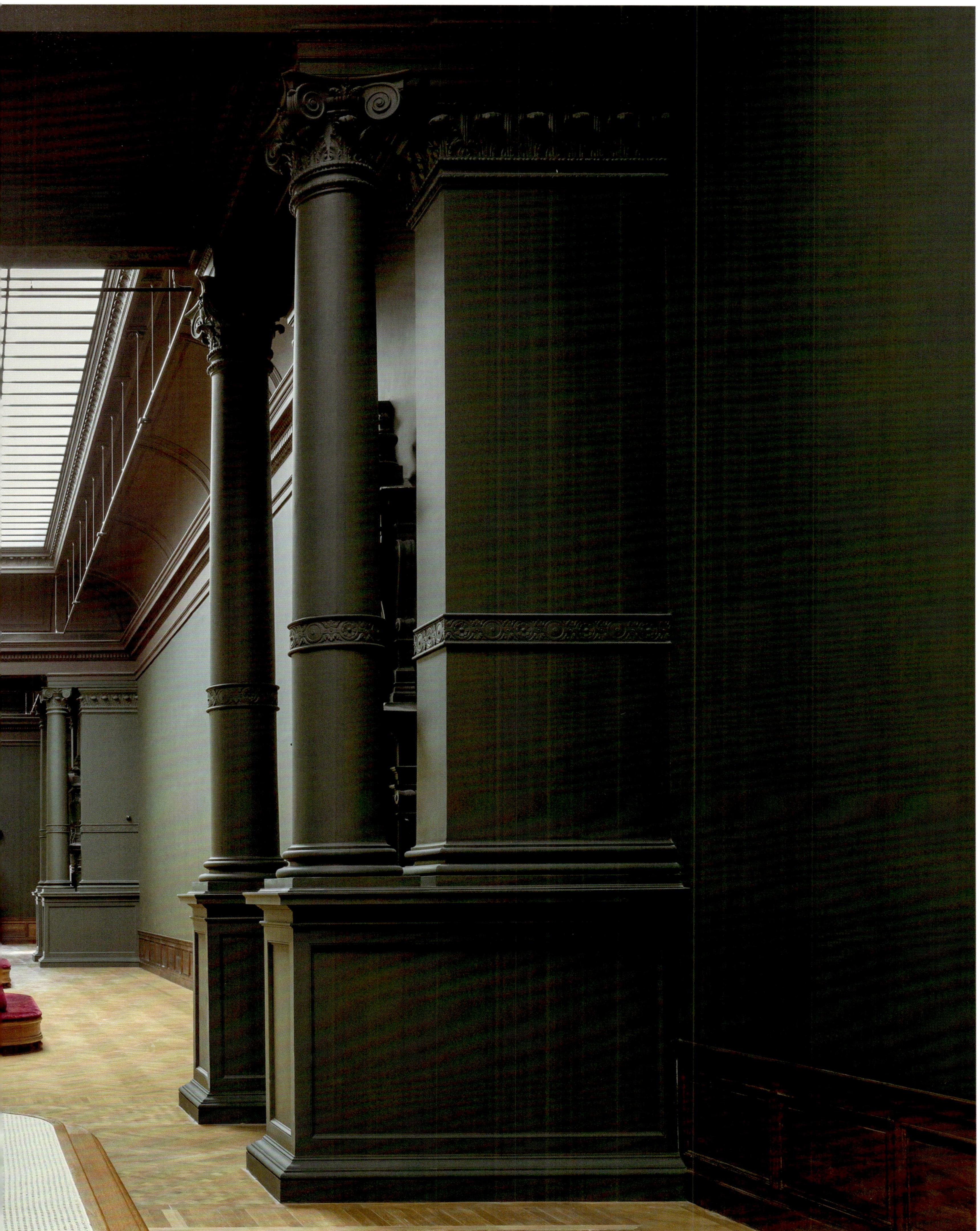

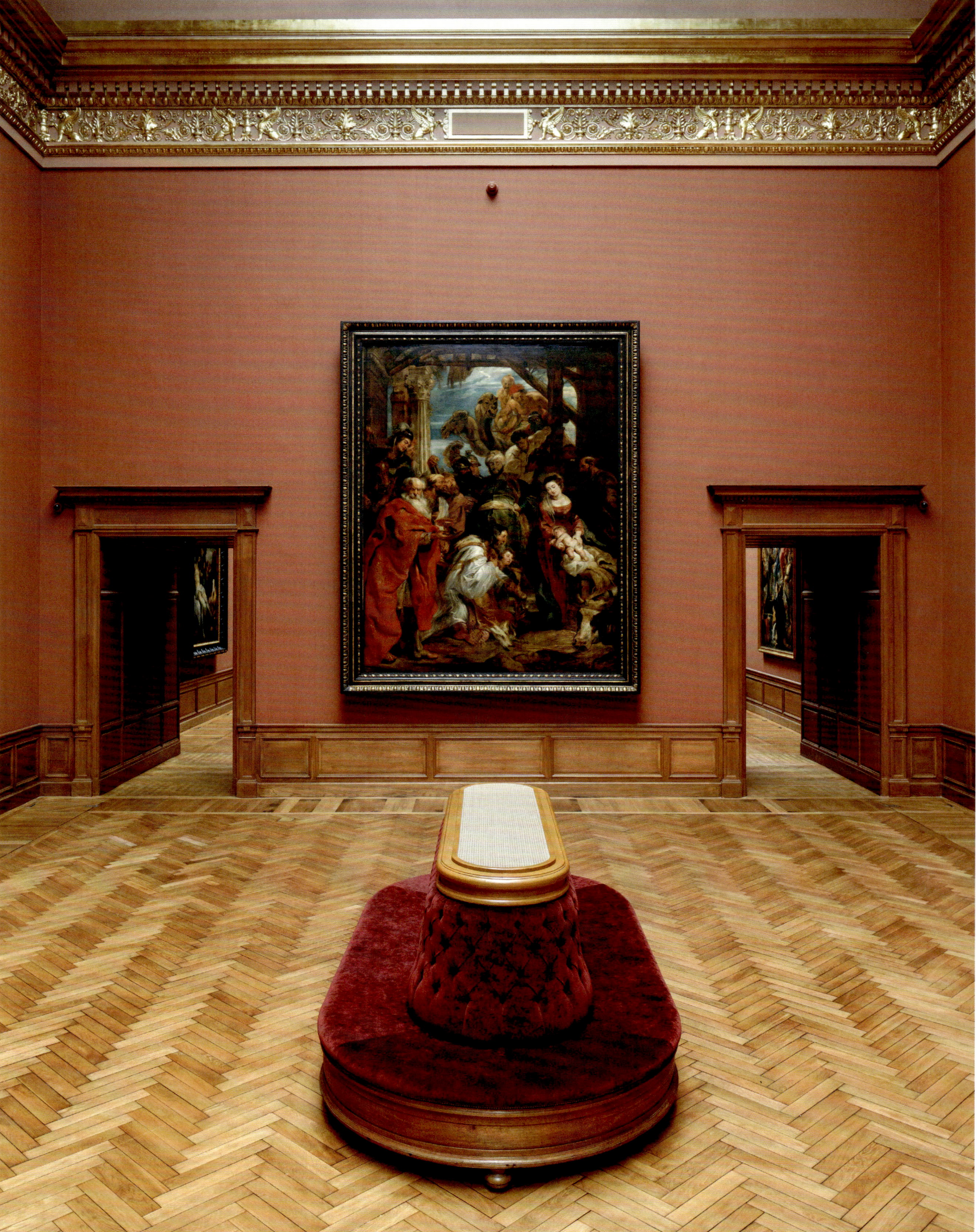

3. THE GROWTH OF THE COLLECTION

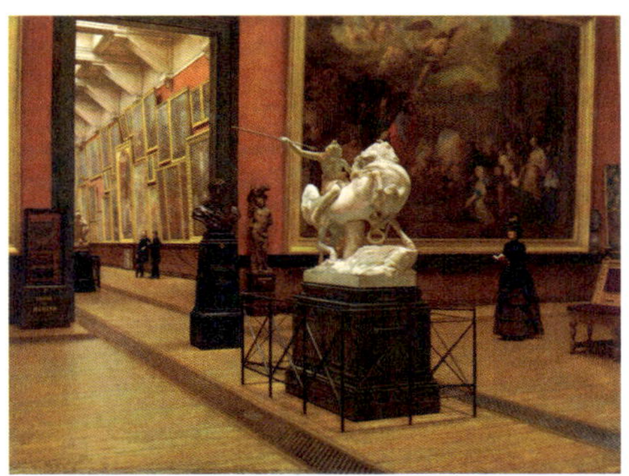

This painting by Henri Van Dyck from 1886 shows two galleries from the former museum of the academy on Mutsaardstraat. *Interior of the Academy Museum*, oil on canvas, 88.5 × 115.5 cm, inv. 1141.

The collection: that's the main game for a museum, its reason of existence. How has the KMSKA collection grown? What are the key moments across the decades of our existence? Here is a brief overview.

1810 – The early years
When Napoleon created the museum by imperial decree in 1810, the collection already totalled 223 works of art. They were, for the most part, religious paintings and portraits from the 16th and 17th centuries, and included work by Antwerp greats such as Rubens, Van Dyck and Cornelis de Vos. The collection consisted primarily of works that had belonged to the Antwerp Guild of St Luke, the 15th-century guild from which the Antwerp Academy had emerged in 1663. Some pieces came from demolished or repurposed churches, monasteries and public buildings.

By 1815, the collection had grown to 241 works of art. This included just under 20 works that were returned to the Academy's Museum from their temporary exile in France after the defeat of Napoleon. Shortly after, King William I bestowed upon the museum the only work by Titian that can be found in a public Belgian collection.

1841 – The legacy of knight Van Ertborn
In 1841, the museum acquired 144 works in one fell swoop. Florent van Ertborn, a knight, mayor of Antwerp and a member of the museum's special committee, saw it as his responsibility to provide inspiring examples, especially of old masters' paintings, to the Academy students in 'their' museum. His legacy, which is very high quality, mainly contains works from before the baroque era, with Flemish and European Primitives as its chief focus. It also includes 'foreign' pieces, such as Jean Fouquet's *Madonna* and the oldest works in the collection: four panels by Simone Martini from c. 1340. This was when the KMSKA collection achieved European stature.

1851 – The inauguration of the Museum of the Academicians
The Museum van de Academiekers (Museum of the Academicians) was founded in 1851. A new academic corps was established alongside it: an honorary club of tutors from the Antwerp Academy and academies in other countries, membership by invitation only. It existed until 1936. The members were artists themselves and it was a founding principle that, on admittance to the corps, the museum receive a representative work by and a portrait of each member: a self-portrait or a portrait by a third party. Many of these artworks have ended up in the KMSKA collection, which means that it can now exhibit a large number of works by important artists from the 19th century, from Flanders and beyond.

1859 – The bequest of Baroness Adelaïde Vanden Hecke-Baut de Rasmon
Baroness Adelaïde Vanden Hecke-Baut de Rasmon left 41 works to the museum, including a number of Dutch paintings (mainly, but not all, genre pieces) from the Dutch Golden Age (17th century) and several works by Flemish masters: landscapes, portraits, interiors, cityscapes. These were a valuable addition to the collection, which up to this point had focused primarily on religious art.

1864 – The founding of Artibus Patriae
In 1864, the society Artibus Patriae (meaning 'for the arts of the fatherland') was founded in Antwerp. Officially, it was called Maatschappij tot Aanvulling van het Museum van Antwerpen (Society for the Development of the Antwerp Museum), advertising its purpose to help enrich the museum's collection. Members included historians, wealthy citizens, artists and also art collectors. The society existed for exactly 100 years and greatly influenced the collection policy, especially in the first half of the 20th century. During its lifetime, it donated more than 270 works to the museum, demonstrating a strong preference for art from the 17th and 19th centuries.

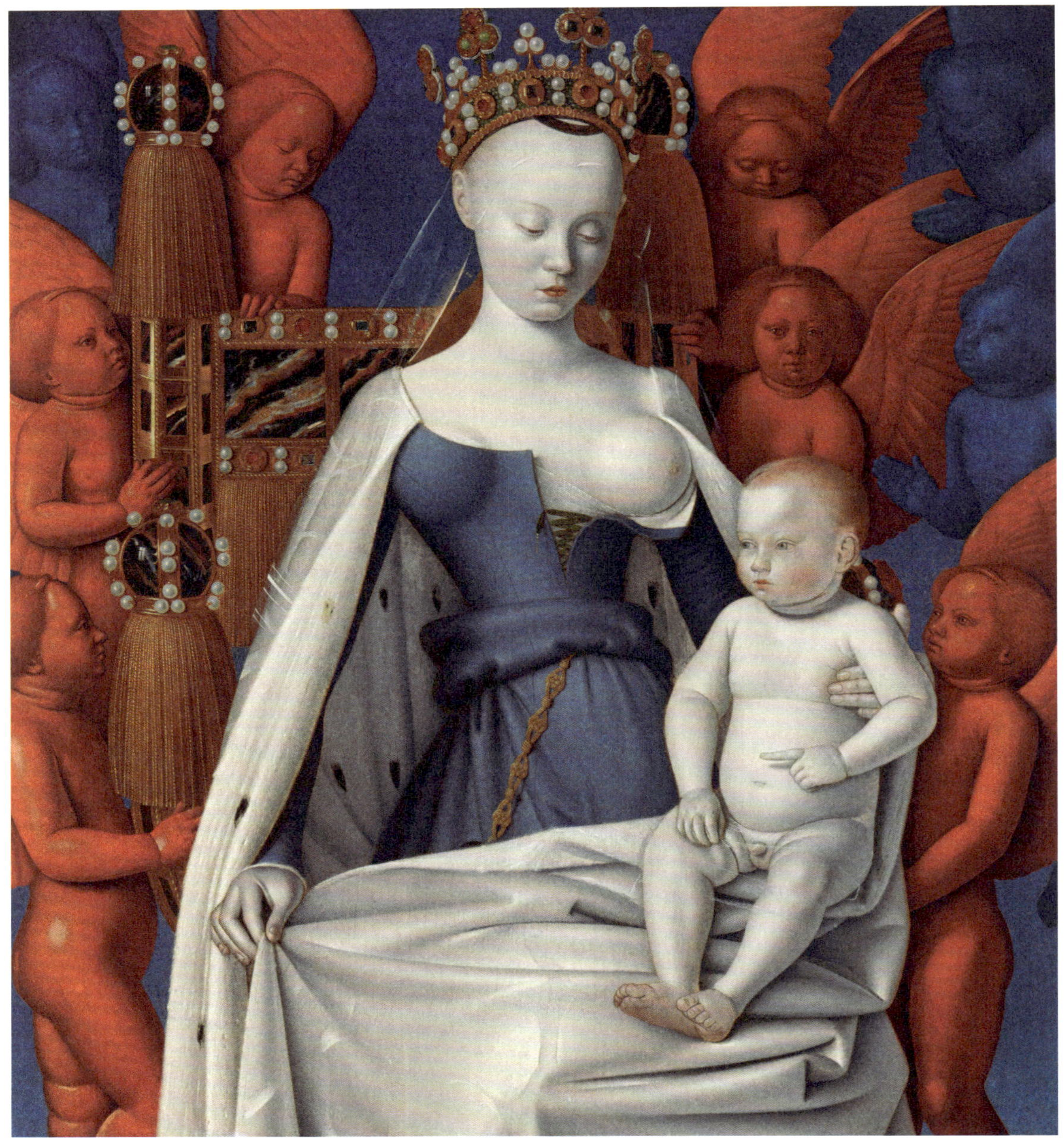

In 1841, Knight Florent van Ertborn bequeathed no less than 144 works of art from the 14th to the 16th centuries, including this work by Jean Fouquet, *Madonna Surrounded by Seraphim and Cherubim*, c. 1450, oil on panel, 94.5 × 85.5 cm, inv. 132.

Rembrandt Bugatti, *Begging Elephant*, c. 1908, bronze, including pedestal: 19 × 10 × 25.5 cm; pedestal: 5.5 × 9 × 9 cm, inv. 2334. Jacqueline Van den Bergh donated this little sculpture in 1937. The elephant who was the model for the statue was also called Jacqueline.

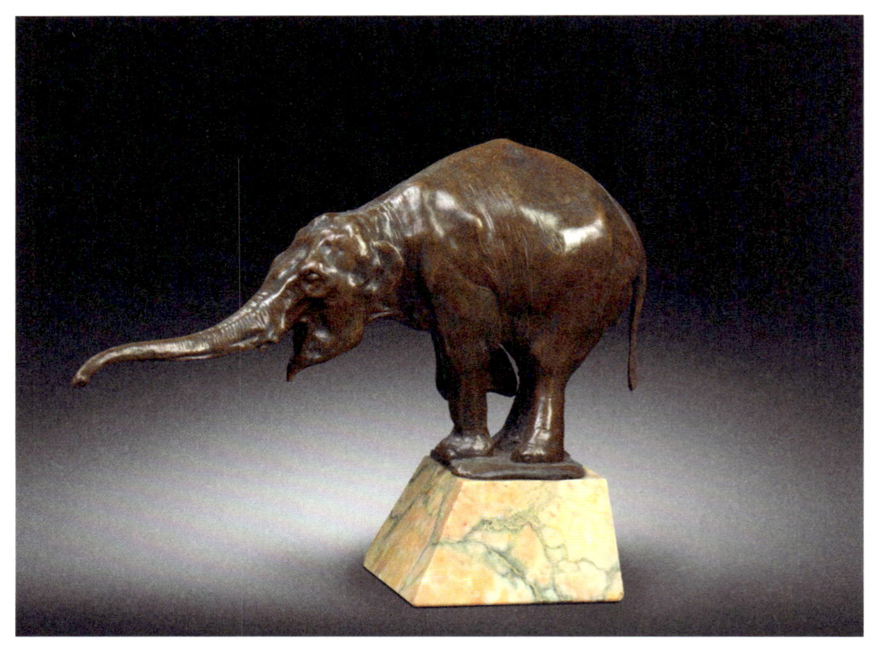

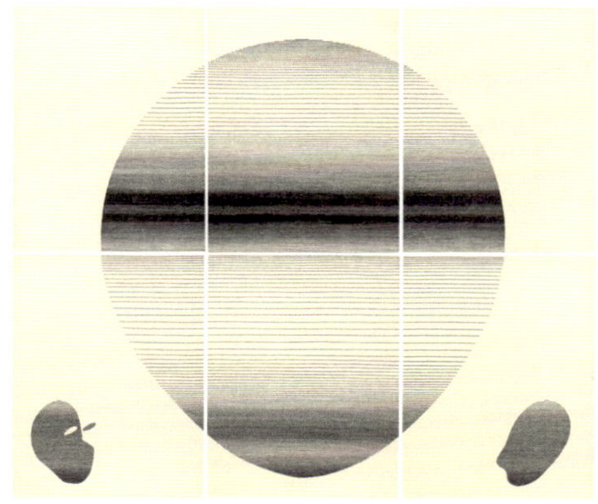

Michel Seuphor, *Prajna paramita avec donateurs*, 1964, ink on paper, 134 × 153 cm, inv. 4032/1–6. Donation of the Berckelaers Indivision Gift, 2021.

Number of works in the collection	approx. 5,882 Triptychs and sketch-books are counted as single works. If they weren't, the total would be 9,118 items.
Number of paintings	2,330
Number of sculptures	722
Works on paper	1,961
Rubens prints	714
Number of donated works	approx. 2,340
Number of purchased works	approx. 1,905

From the 1870s – Acquisitions

From around 1860, the Academy Museum itself gradually began to purchase works, reaching a buying crescendo in the 1870s. The museum made these acquisitions with grants from the city and government, and was especially active at the triennial salons of contemporary art organised by the Koninklijke Maatschappij tot Aanmoediging der Schone Kunsten (Royal Society for the Promotion of Fine Arts). The boom in the 1870s was undoubtedly related to the plans for the new museum in the South district, called 't Zuid. When this was finally completed in 1890, the number of donations also rose considerably, a trend that continued up to World War II. In 1928, the museum became a state institution. After another boom in the 1950s – including the procurement of a notable number of contemporary Italian artists – acquisitions started to ebb in the decades that followed.

1902 – Oscar Nottebohm's first donation

In 1902, Oscar Nottebohm (1865–1935), a descendant of a German trading family that had settled in Antwerp in the early 19th century, gave a painting to the museum, the first of a long series of donations. He eventually gifted the museum a total of 30 prestigious works, mainly depicting mythological scenes and genre scenes, his favourite genres. Nottebohm, who was also a member of Artibus Patriae, wanted to fill gaps in the collection where the 16th and 17th centuries were concerned. Upon his death, he bequeathed the museum a monetary donation as well as valuable art books and catalogues.

1905 – The establishment of Kunst van Heden

The Kunst van Heden (Art of the Present) association was founded at the home of Louis Franck. Until after World War II, this group of citizens, art lovers and artists joined forces, at exhibitions, salons and in publications, to promote artists who in their view were not receiving enough recognition. Thanks to and at the instigation of Kunst van Heden, numerous legacies and donations were left to the museum. In the role of intermediary, Kunst van Heden is therefore responsible for the largest 'collection' of modern art donations. The Franck family deserves a special mention in this regard, in particular François Franck, who donated 43 paintings in the period 1920–30. It's partly thanks to Kunst van Heden that the KMSKA's Ensor collection has been able to flourish.

Ongoing – Donations

With the exception of the two world wars, when only seven donations were made between 1914 and 1918 and 14 between 1940 and 1945, the stream of gifts and legacies from 1840 to 1940 was fairly stable. After World War II, a downward trend ensued in both donations and legacies.

1948–1973 – Walther Vanbeselaere, art collector for the state

During his long regime as curator of the museum, Walther Vanbeselaere's primary aim was to bring together a comprehensive overview of Flemish modern art in 'his' museum. He strove to compose ensembles of the artists he considered key figures in various generations of artists, such as Henri De Braekeleer, Constant Permeke, Frits Van den Berghe and Gustave De Smet. But he also had a keen eye for the international context of his time. Vanbeselaere supplemented the KMSKA collection with work by artists such as Edgar Degas, Hans Hartung, Karel Appel, Ben Nicholson and Giacomo Manzù.

1989 – The legacy of Dr Ludo van Bogaert-Sheid

The KMSKA already owned a considerable collection of works by Rik Wouters when, in 1989, Dr Ludo van Bogaert-Sheid, an eminent neurologist, donated 59 works by Wouters, including 13 paintings, 39 works on paper and eight sculptures. The donation had already been notarised in 1974. It is a key moment in the acquisition history of the KMSKA.

2018 – The bequest of Mrs Gilberte Ghesquière

Thanks to the generous donation of 136 works by Mrs Gilberte Ghesquière, a number of great names from the 20th century have entered the KMSKA collection, including Pablo Gargallo, Jacques Lipchitz and Jean-Michel Basquiat.

2021 – The Berckelaers Indivision Gift 2021

Five grandchildren of Fernand Berckelaers – the artist known as Michel Seuphor – with the support of family friend Agnes Caers, donated 57 "gap drawings" with horizontal lines. With this important addition to the collection of modern art, they wish to raise the profile of Seuphor's art in his native city and country.

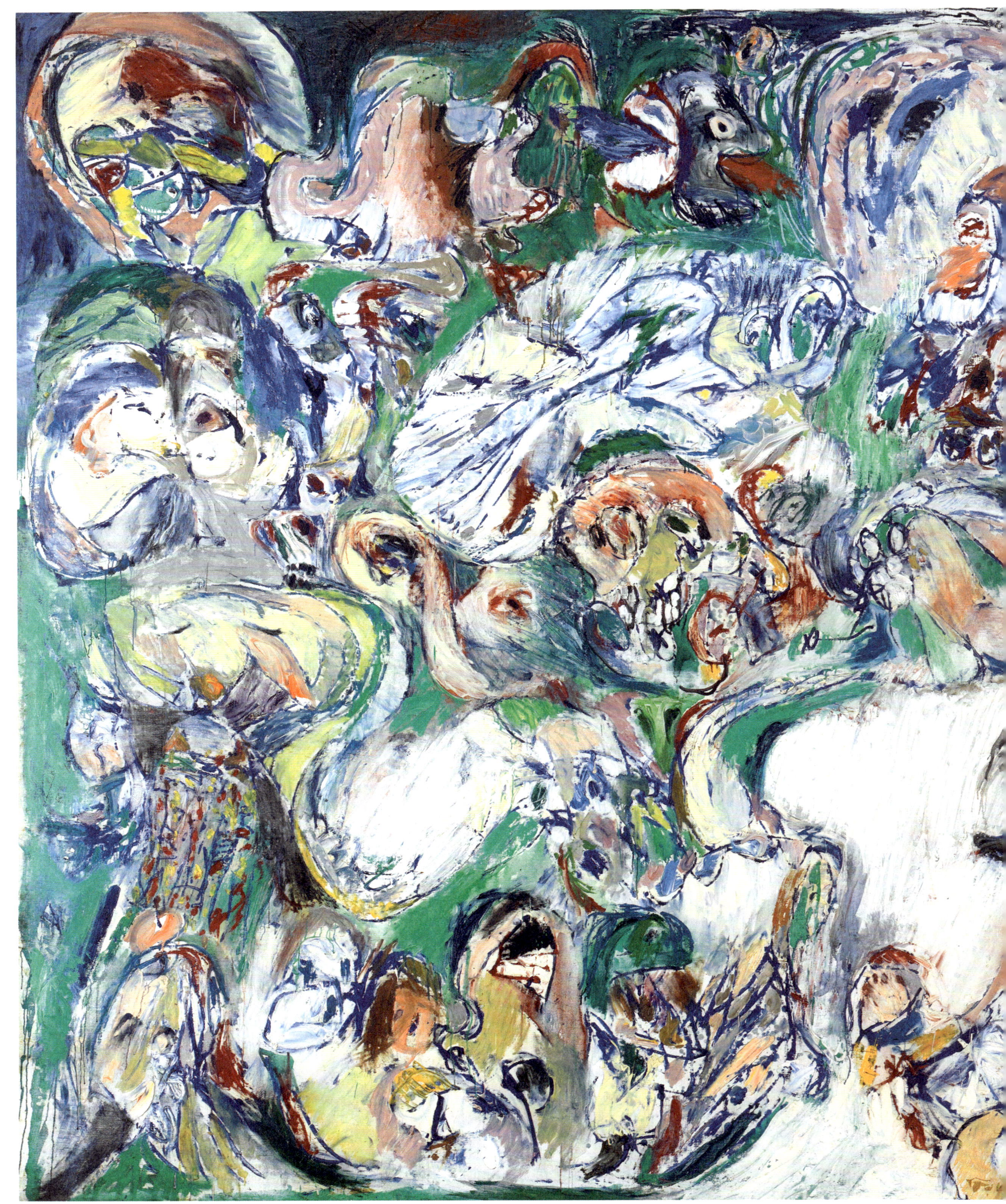

Pierre Alechinsky, *The Last Day*, (1964), oil on canvas, 330 × 500 cm (within frame), inv. 3039. Bought from the artist, 1968.

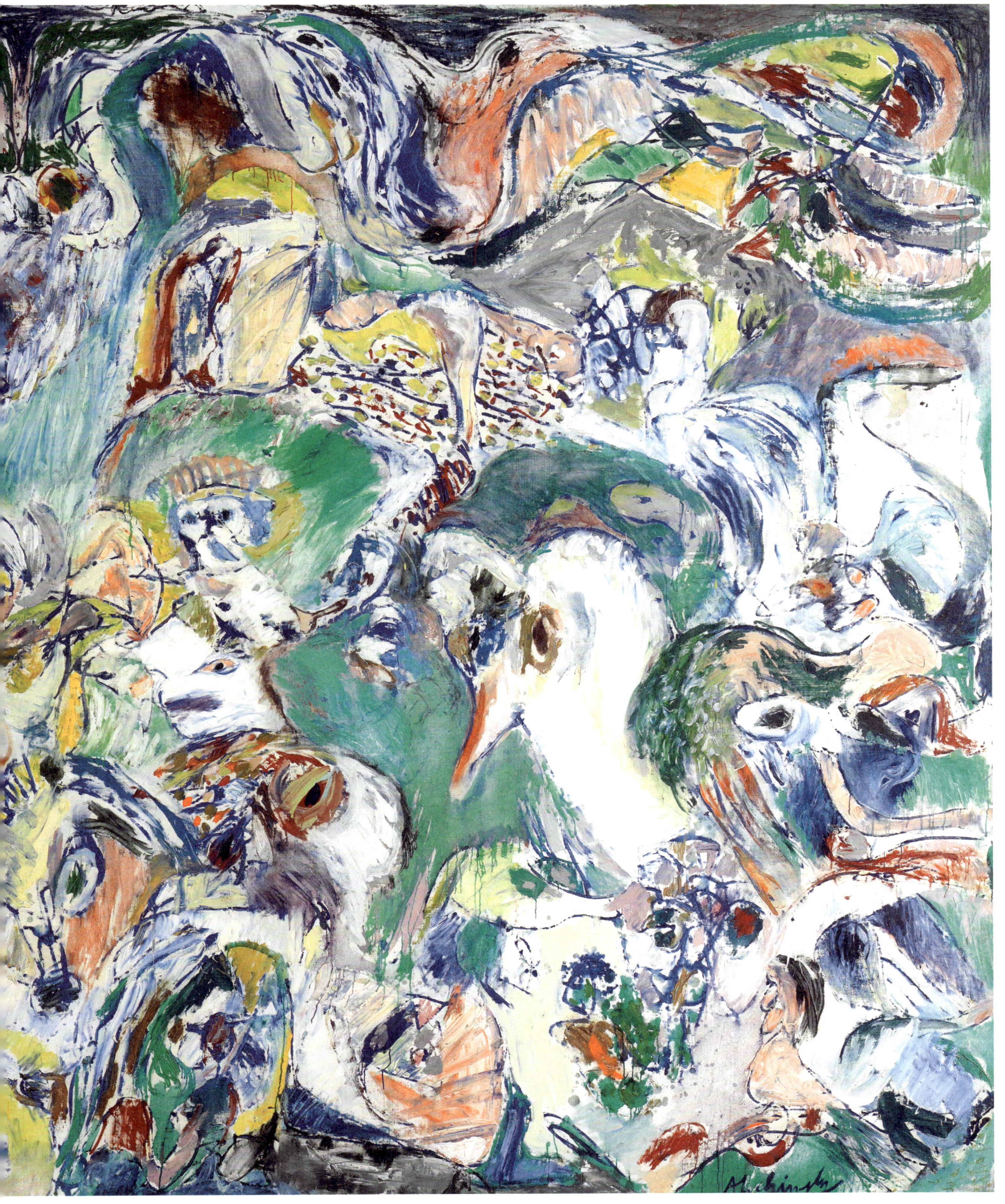

GENEROUS BENEFACTORS

The KMSKA collection contains a similar number of donated or bequeathed works and purchased works. As such, the role and impact of donors and testators on the collection is significant. This is a pattern that was set from the start, when Knight Florent van Ertborn made his pivotal donation in 1841.

A more recent example is the collection of works by the Antwerp modernist Jules Schmalzigaug, who died young in 1917, and who has recently – and deservedly – started attracting attention. The KMSKA owns 51 of his works. This collection came about in stages: Schmalzigaug's brother, Walter Malgaud, first donated seven works in 1928. After that, things remained fairly quiet for almost a century, until in 2015 the collector Maurice Verbaet sold 18 works by Schmalzigaug to the KMSKA and donated 17 etchings to the KMSKA. Three years later, Gilberte Ghesquière bequeathed the museum another nine works by Schmalzigaug.

In many cases, benefactors have been closely involved with the museum and its work. A good example is the Franck family, in particular François Franck, who not only enriched the collection but also improved the entire museum organisation. François and his brother Louis encouraged their extensive network of contacts to support the museum and donate artworks. It's mainly thanks to donors like these that work by living artists entered the museum in the 20th century. After all, the purchase of work by living artists is a very delicate affair. This is how the Ensor collection and the collection of paintings by the Latem artists started out.

The motives of donors are varied. For example, Florent van Ertborn thought that his collection could (among other things) provide the students at the Academy with some fine examples of art. Families of artists sometimes hoped to get their relative's work into the collection and especially into the museum galleries – always a tricky path to navigate for a museum. Connoisseurs of the collection sought to fill gaps: good examples are Oscar Nottebohm and the members of the Artibus Patriae association. Other donors were focused mainly on one artist, and moved by a sense that after their death, their favourite deserved a place in a museum of standing; the important donation from Dr Ludo van Bogaert-Sheid, consisting mainly of works by Rik Wouters, falls into this category.

This is clearly a win-win situation. The museum benefits from the donations – especially at times when the purchase of many types of art is an extremely expensive undertaking – as do the benefactors for various reasons. Their works are well cared for in the museum and become part of a splendid collection with international allure. And join the bequests of the many donors who preceded them.

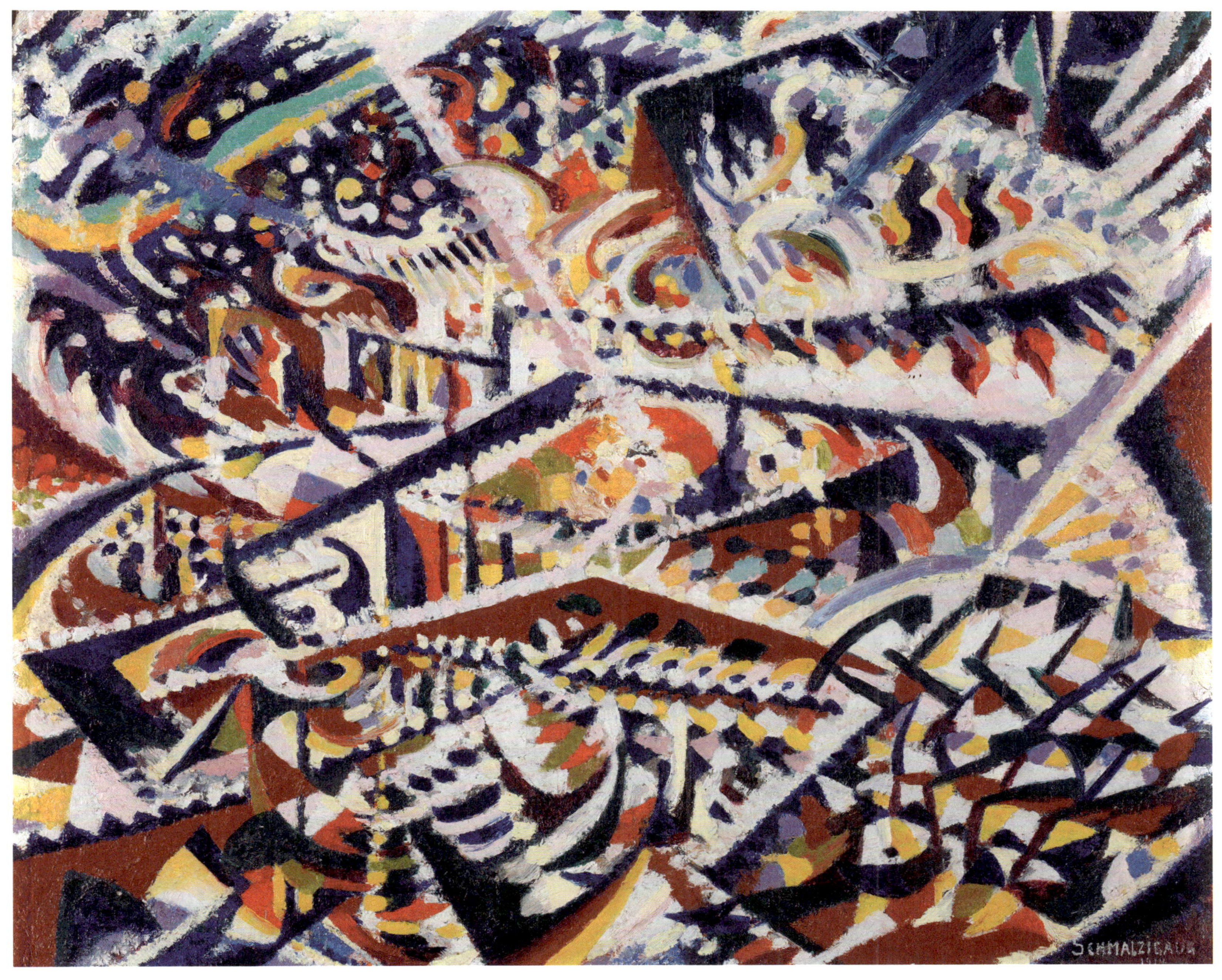

Jules Schmalzigaug, *Light + Mirrors and Crowd: interior of a Popular Ballroom in Antwerp*, 1914, oil on canvas, 52.5 × 64 cm (within frame), inv. 2100bis. Donated to the museum by Walter Malgaud, brother of the artist, 1928.

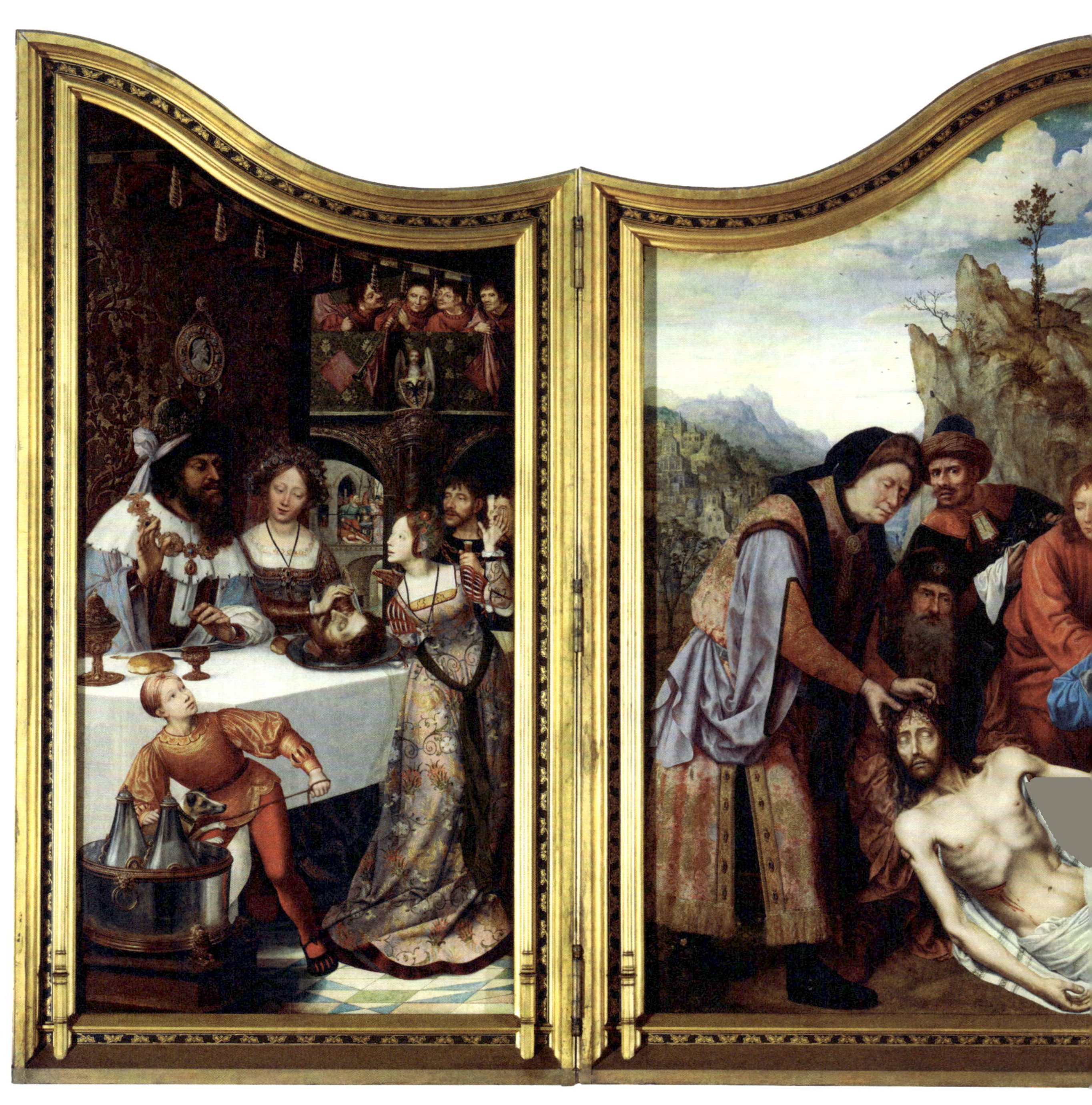

Miraculously (still) in Antwerp

Quinten Massys, *Altarpiece of the Joiners' Guild*, (1511), oil on wood, 260 × 263 cm (central panel) (within frame), 260 × 123.5 cm (side panels), inv. 245–249

In the year 1497, the Antwerp joiners seceded from the coopers and set up their own trade guild. Ten or so years later, they commissioned a large triptych from Antwerp's leading artist of the time, Quinten Massys, for their altar in the church now known as the Cathedral of Our Lady. Two of the main figures in the triptych are John the Baptist and John the Evangelist, the patron saints of the joiners' guild. Massys's work served as an altarpiece on the site for which it was intended for a good 20 years.

But then came a turbulent period in the life of this particular work of art. In 1533, it narrowly escaped a raging fire that reduced large parts of the cathedral's interior to ashes. Later, so the story goes, both Philip II of Spain and Elizabeth I of England offered large amounts of money for the triptych. But in vain. In 1566, all hell broke loose, when a wave of iconoclasm swept the continent and a great deal of religious art was smashed to smithereens. Painter-writer Karel van Mander recorded that Massys's triptych was brought to a place of safety. When the Calvinist city council of Antwerp ordered the sale of all

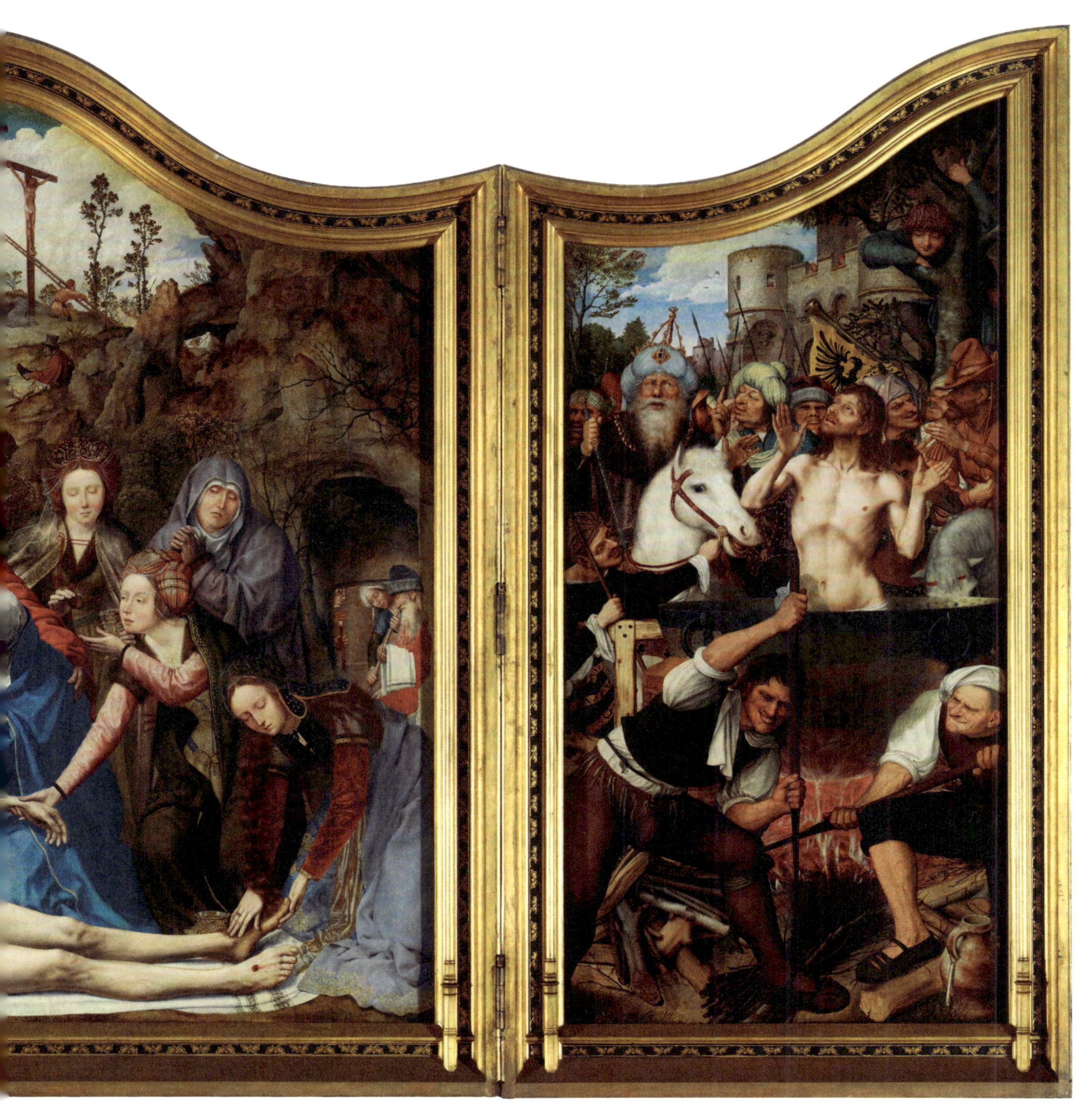

ecclesiastical art in 1581, the city magistrate purchased Massys's altarpiece on the advice of artist Maerten de Vos. It was displayed in the town hall's Statenkamer (State chamber) for seven years.

There, painter Michiel Coxcie altered the triptych's format to rectangular by adding a sky and coats of arms. Hans Vredeman de Vries provided the work with a perspective decoration on the border all the way around. Around 1600, Karel van Mander wrote that it was already becoming difficult to see exactly how many horse's heads Massys had painted. In 1650, the work was viewed as being in a pitiful condition. As a consequence, it has undergone numerous restorations in its lifetime.

Back to 1589 – when Antwerp again belonged to the Catholic Spanish Empire – Massys's altarpiece was returned to the cathedral, where it stayed for more than 200 peaceful years. The rest of the story is similar to that of several other works in the KMSKA's collection. In 1798, during the French occupation, the painting was moved to the Ecole Centrale, in the former abbey of the Carmelite Sisters. In 1802, as part of the collection of the Academy of Fine Arts, it moved to the Antwerp Handelsbeurs, and in 1811 to the former Recollects Convent, where the 'old' KMSKA was housed until 1890.

Royal gift

Titian, *Pope Alexander VI Presenting Bishop Jacopo Pesaro to Saint Peter*, (1503–1506), oil on canvas, 147.8 × 188.7 cm, inv. 357

This work by the young Titian – the only one we know of in a Belgian public collection – was a royal gift. King William I, monarch of the Netherlands and Belgium from 1815 to 1830, bought many works of art and was also a patron to artists. He and his wife, Wilhelmina of Prussia, took advice on this subject from the mayor of Antwerp, Florent van Ertborn, who held and still holds great importance for the KMSKA through his generous donation in 1841.

Much of what William I acquired eventually made its way into public collections. This Titian, for example. He purchased the work in 1823, along with 16 other paintings, at an auction of the collection of a Danish diplomat, Count Edmund Bourke. Robert Fagel was William I's front man for the purchase. The king donated most of the Bourke paintings to the Rijksmuseum in Amsterdam and the Royal Cabinet in The Hague. Two works ended up in Antwerp: a piece by David Teniers II and this Titian.

Titian painted the canvas before 1510, as a commission for Jacopo Pesaro – the kneeling bishop depicted in the picture. Pesaro was commander of the papal fleet and had recaptured the island of Santa Maura (now Lefkas in Greece) from the Turks in 1502. Presumably, he wanted the work to hang in his Venetian palazzo as a reminder of his victory. It was in Venice that none other than Anthony van Dyck recorded seeing this Titian, then part of Count Wildman's collection, in 1623. In 1639, it was part of the collection of the English King Charles I in London's Whitehall Palace. In 1651, it was sold to Thomas Bagley "of Harrison". At the end of the 17th century, the painting ended up in the San Pascual convent in Madrid, from where it passed, via another stopover, to Edmund Bourke. During all these relocations, the work was repainted several times, acquired layers of dirt, suffered damage, received new layers of varnish and was restored according to standards different from those of today.

At the beginning of the 21st century, it was restored again, with meticulous care, and housed in its current frame.

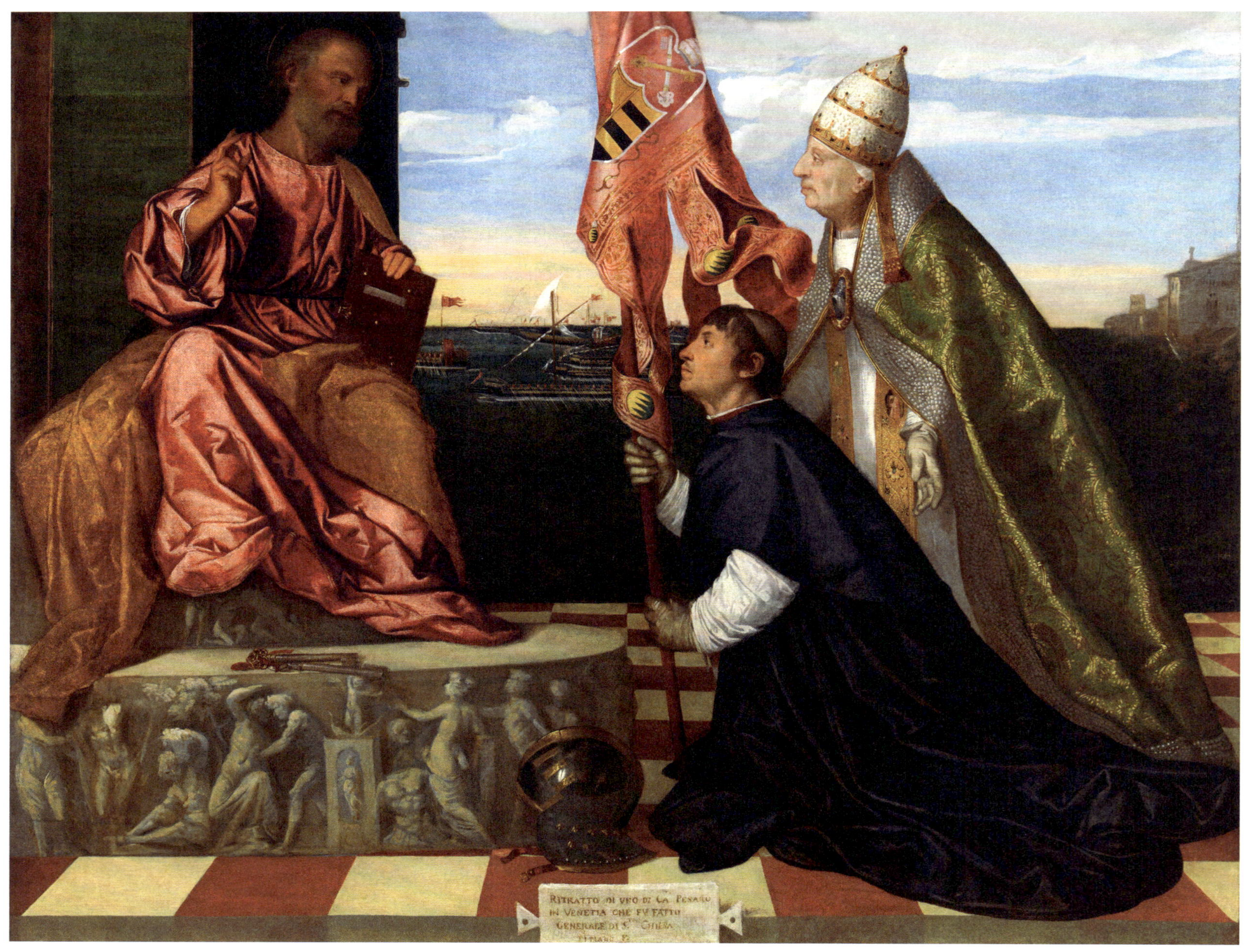

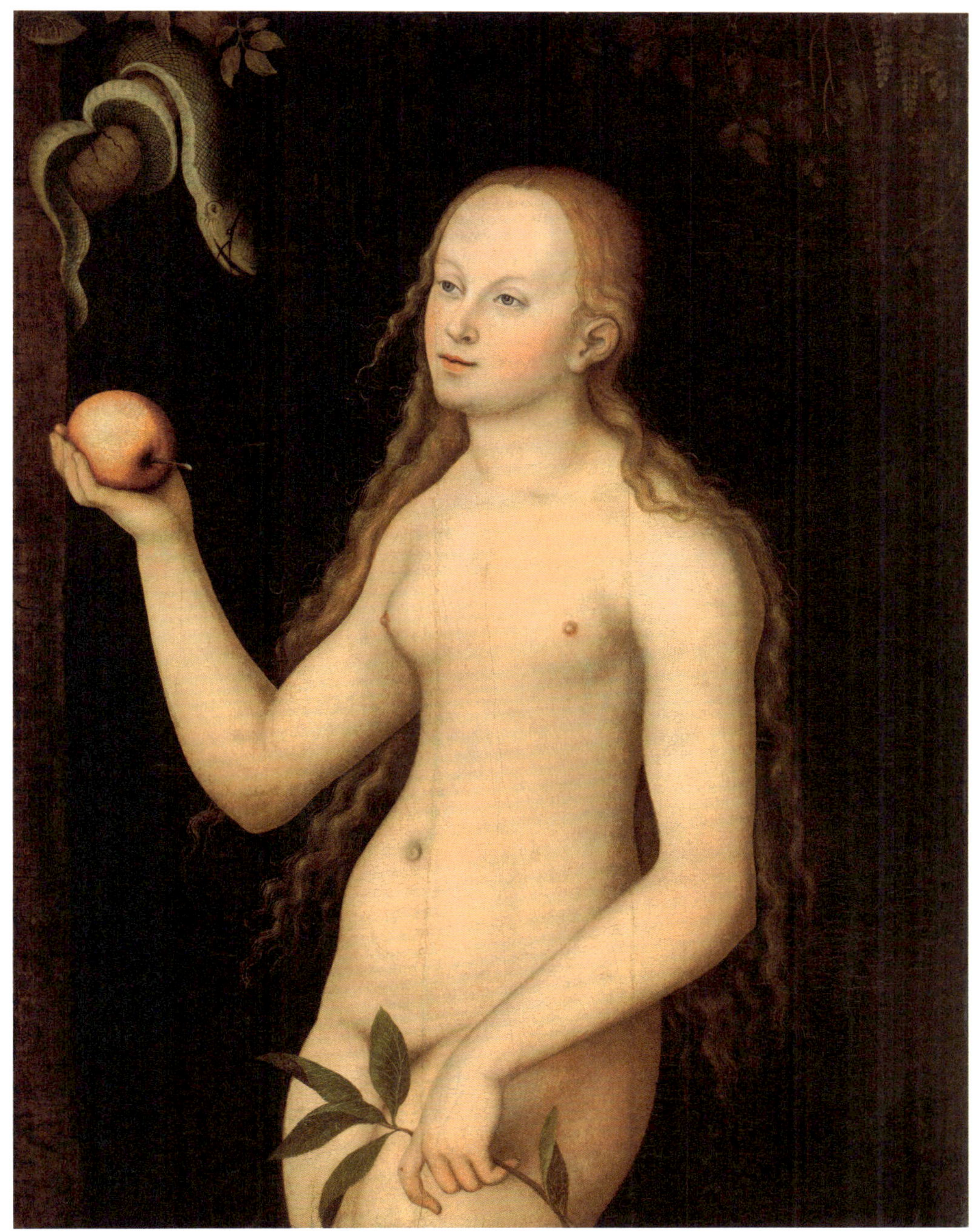

Hermann Göring's Eva

Lucas Cranach the Elder,
Eve, (1528–1530), oil on wood,
86 × 65 cm (within frame),
inv. 5048

Female nudes became the trademark of 16th-century German artist Lucas Cranach the Elder and his son, Lucas Cranach the Younger, who was happy to imitate his father's work. The wealthy Cranachs ran an atelier where successful compositions were copied. Such as this *Eve*. This panel may have been shortened at the bottom, since Cranach usually painted Eve (and also Adam) at full length.

At the start of the World War II, Cranach's *Eve* returned to Germany. Brussels art dealer Le Roy sold it to the Mühlmann Department in The Hague, which in turn sold it, in December 1940, to Hermann Göring. After the invasion of Poland in 1939, Göring had appointed the art historian Kajetan Mühlmann as his "special representative for the safeguarding of art treasures" – including in the Netherlands, where he set up the Mühlmann Department.

Göring kept Cranach's work with him in his fancy residence in northern Brandenburg, Carinhall – named after his late Swedish wife, Carin von Kantzow. There were at least 1,500 paintings and sculptures and about 170 tapestries at Carinhall. The lion's share of this collection was looted art.

In 1943, part of the collection was moved for safety to the Altaussee salt mine in southern Austria. Göring transferred another part by train to tunnel bunkers in Berchtesgaden in January 1945. It was there that the American Monuments, Fine Arts & Archives programme found *Eve* and transferred the work, recorded as number 785, to the Central Collecting Point in Munich.

Eve was finally "restituted" to the Belgium Department of Economic Recovery and released to the KMSKA in 1951. In 2022, approximately 2,800 works of art stolen from Belgium by the Nazis have still not been returned to their rightful owners.

Coda: The KMSKA also owns a small panel (38.5 x 25 cm) by Lucas Cranach the Elder, depicting Eve and Adam. It comes from the 1841 legacy of Knight Florent van Ertborn.

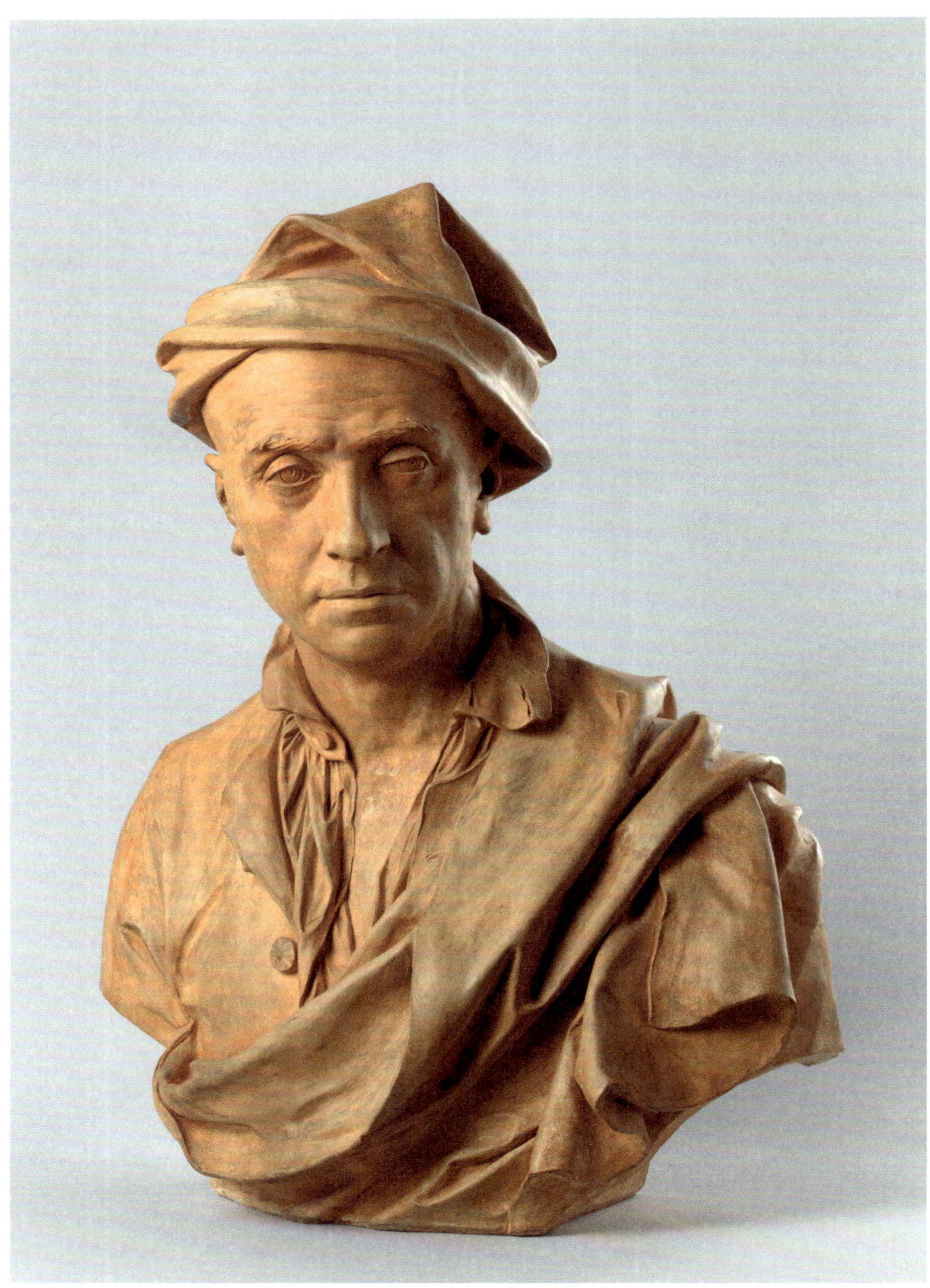

Friends torn apart

John Michael Rysbrack,
Self Portrait, (c. 1735),
terracotta, 60.5 × 49 × 26 cm,
inv. IB00.079

We only know what the sculptor John Michael Rysbrack looked like thanks to a painted portrait of him by John Vanderbank (National Portrait Gallery, London). And also thanks to this vivid, finely detailed terracotta bust, undoubtedly a finished work (not a preparatory study). The maker signed his 3D self-portrait on the inside. Born in Antwerp, Johannes Michael Rijsbrack moved to London in his twenties, where he achieved great fame and became a key figure in English sculpture.

At the Yale Center for British Art In New Haven, US, there is a very similar terracotta bust, also by Rysbrack and also signed (and this time dated: 1727). It is a portrait of Antwerp painter Peter Tillemans. He also emigrated to London. Rysbrack and Tillemans must have known each other. The two artists are both sculpted in the same casual pose, mirror images of each other.

We know that the first buyer of the two pendants, Cox Macro, was an art collector and patron of both Tillemans and Rysbrack. Macro bought the 1727 bust of Tillemans in the year in which the painter died: 1734. He immediately commissioned a bust of Rysbrack himself. A letter from Rysbrack, dated 4 March 1735, shows that Macro needed to exercise patience – which shows that Rysbrack did not finish his self-portrait bust until after that date. Although Tillemans' bust was already seven years old by then, Rysbrack made his self-portrait match that of his colleague and friend who had passed away.

The two busts were displayed in an alcove in the stairwell of Macro's rural home in Norton, Suffolk, in England. They remained together until 1912, when a distant descendant of Macro sold them to Norwich art dealer Levine for a mere £10. Tillemans' bust ended up in New Haven via various dealers, and was long thought to be Rysbrack's self-portrait. The real self-portrait passed into the hands of the Antwerp collector Charles Van Herck via the Kreglinger auction of 1953. In 1996, Van Herck's heirs sold his 123 terracotta works to the King Baudouin Foundation. The Foundation donated them to the KMSKA in 2000, on a long-term loan.

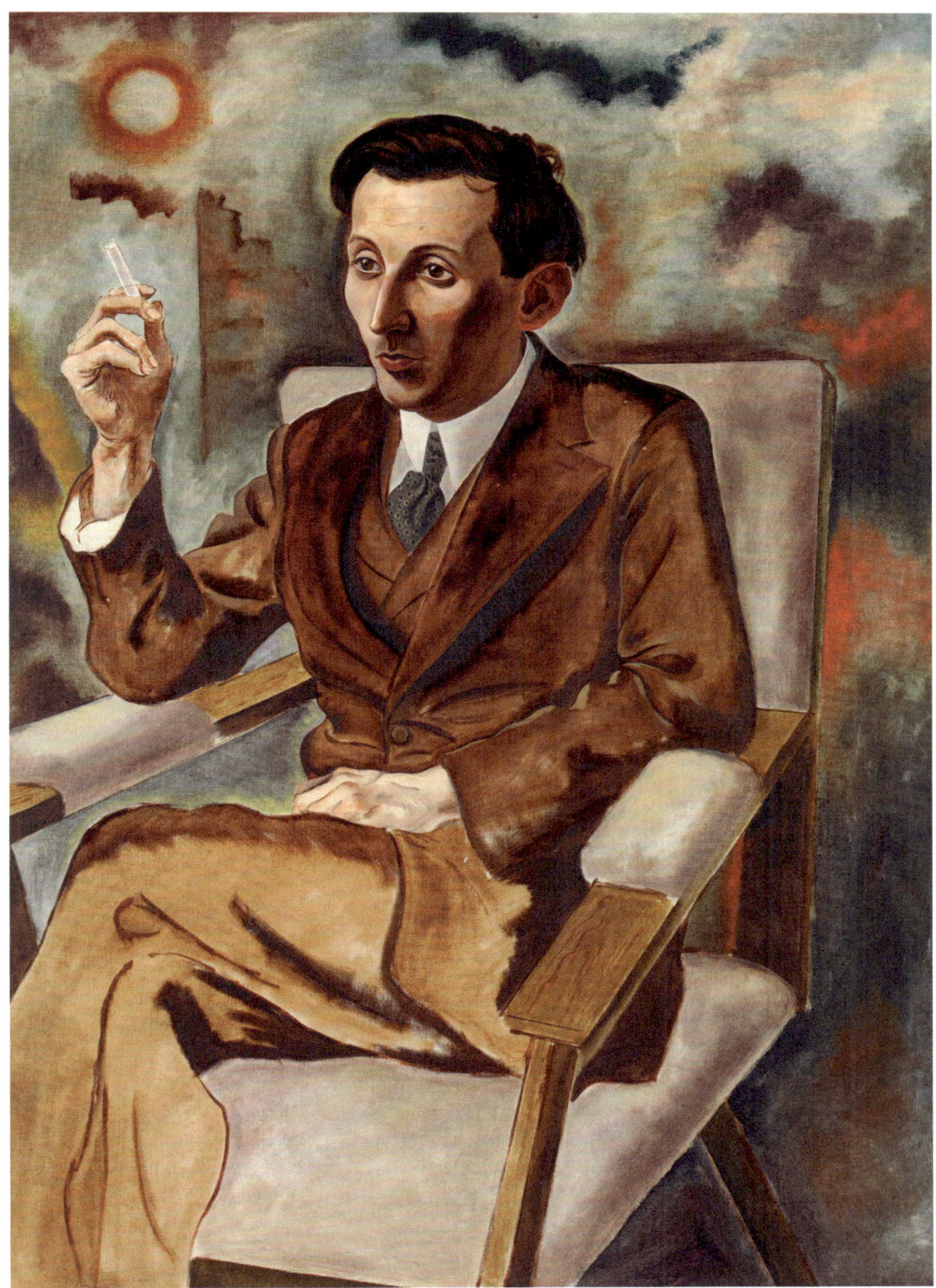

“Degenerate” writer portrait

George Grosz, *The Writer Walter Mehring*, 1926, oil on canvas, 110 × 79.5 cm (within frame), inv. 2454

At the beginning of June 1939, KMSKA Chief Curator Arthur H. Cornette received a letter from Switzerland. Art dealer Theodor Fischer is asking whether he has received the illustrated auction catalogue of 125 modern paintings and sculptures from German museums. The sale is scheduled for 30 June in Lucerne. It includes works by 39 modern masters, including Vincent van Gogh and Pablo Picasso. They have been removed from museums because, according to the Nazi ideologues, they are “degenerate” or immoral. In other words, avant-garde and experimental. Since 1937, more than 16,500 works of art had been given this label and then auctioned, sold or destroyed.

The auction in Lucerne was met with fierce objections. The US called for a boycott, because they supposed this spectacle was only meant to raise foreign currency for the German treasury and to buy weapons. “Lying propaganda!” Fischer retorted. The German government has nothing to do with it, he said. The proceeds will go to museums to purchase new artworks. Collectors and art dealers in particular showed interest in the auction, museums hardly at all. Nevertheless, three Belgian institutions made their way to Lucerne: the Musée des Beaux-Arts of Liège and the two Royal Museums of Fine Arts, of Brussels and Antwerp. The Belgian delegation viewed this as an opportunity to buy top-class modernist works – and save them at the same time.

And that is how 16 of the 85 allocated lots ended up in Belgium, four of them in Antwerp: works by Lovis Corinth, George Grosz, Karl Hofer and Jules Pascin. This quartet places the Flemish modernists in the museum’s collection within a European perspective. Financially, the purchase is providential. The portrait of writer Walter Mehring by Grosz – both *Kulturbolsjevists* (“cultural Bolsheviks”) according to the Nazi regime – is Antwerp’s least expensive acquisition: 280 Swiss francs. Gustave Pauli, director of the Hamburger Kunsthalle, had bought it in 1928 for his museum’s modern department. It remained there until 21 August 1937, when it was removed to the Nazi storage depot at Schloss Niederschönhausen in Berlin. Where it stayed – until it turned up as lot number 43 at the auction in Lucerne.

After four centuries of art history, you would expect researchers to start running out of things to say about the work of Peter Paul Rubens – but nothing could be further from the truth. Art historians are still diligently studying the artist's catalogue raisonné, which encompasses many thousands of works. Traditionally, art-history research focuses on iconography, the visual language of the paintings. The mythological, biblical and historical narratives depicted by the scholarly Rubens are often complex and frequently misunderstood. Centuries later, some works are even given new titles. It's only since the late 20th century that researchers have begun the material-technical study of Rubens' paintings and to research the creative process that preceded the works of art.

The KMSKA has in its care a famous collection of 27 Rubens paintings and nearly 700 engravings reproducing the artist's compositions. It's true that the collection is not representative of his amazingly diverse output, but with a number of undisputed masterpieces it does occupy a leading position. For a long time, Rubens' panels and canvases at the KMSKA slumbered under thick layers of yellowed varnish that made them difficult to 'read', and to research. A turning point came when the museum established a new conservation studio and embarked on an accelerated campaign to improve the condition of the collection pieces. Starting in 2000, the smaller Rubens works were all given restoration treatments that brought the master's richly varied colour palette to the fore again. *The Prodigal Son, The Holy Family with the Parrot*, the oil sketches for *The Arch of the Mint*, the Rockox triptych and the Michielsen triptych were all restored in 2019. *Venus Frigida* was restored at the Kunsthistorisches Museum, Vienna in 2016, and the portrait of *Jan Gaspard Gevartius* and *The Holy Trinity* were treated at the Getty Conservation Institute, Los Angeles in 2021–22. As part of these restorations, the condition of each painting was documented. This was done with the help of ultraviolet and infrared refraction, with X-rays, and by taking samples. In collaboration with the University of Antwerp, the artworks were also examined using state-of-the-art techniques that provide information about the materials used (FTIR, SEM EDX) and about ageing due to environmental factors (MA-XRPD).

As well as the research undertaken in the course of the restorations, a Getty-funded Rubens Research Project was established in 2007. This aims to screen the KMSKA's entire Rubens collection in order to learn more about the creation process and painting techniques, working towards an online research catalogue. Some of the art-historical and material-technical research were made available online in editions of the *Rubensbulletin* between 2008 and 2014. As the closure of the KMSKA caused an interruption to the project, so the reopening in 2022 marks the restart of the research. The KMSKA is actively collaborating with academic and museum partners at home and abroad on the project. The museum hopes to complete this research by 2027, the year in which we will commemorate Rubens' 450th birthday.

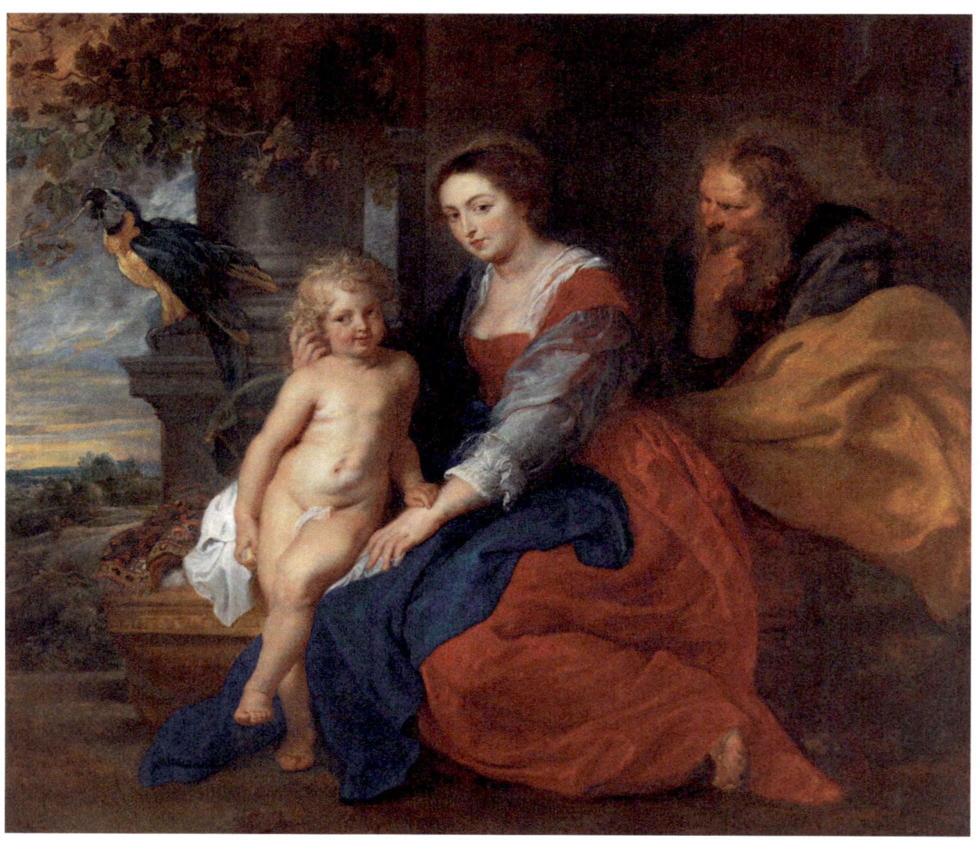

Peter Paul Rubens, *The Holy Family with the Parrot*, 1614–1633, oil on panel, 164 × 190 cm, inv. 312

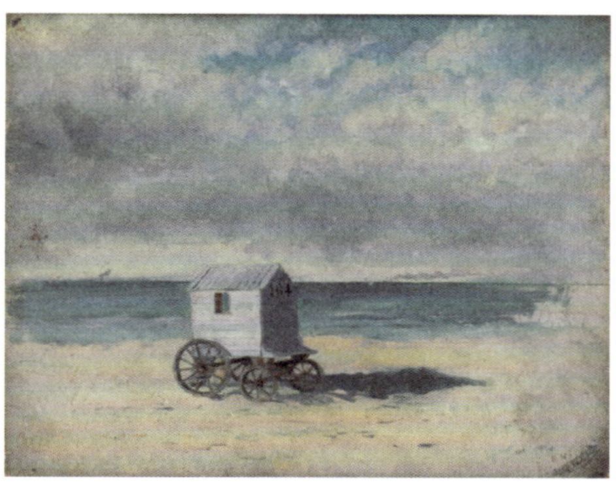

James Ensor, *Bathing Hut on the Beach*, 1876, oil on cardboard, 17.5 × 22.5 cm, inv. 2972

With 39 paintings and more than 600 drawings, the KMSKA has the largest collection of work by James Ensor in the world. The museum aims not only to cherish and exhibit this collection, but also to be the leading reference centre for research on the oeuvre of this Belgian modernist. James Ensor (1860–1949) is famed for his paintings of masks, macabre scenes with skeletons, and satirical works depicting crowds of people.

Game changer

In 2013, the Ensor Research Project was established within the warm embrace of the KMSKA. Mapping out the artist's creation process using state-of-the-art technology, the project is investigating how Ensor made his works.

Ensor was chosen partly because the KMSKA has a veritable gold mine of his paintings, drawings and etchings, but also because he's one of the most important Belgian artists of modern times – a linchpin, an innovator, a game changer. As the end of the 19th century approached, he switched from a naturalistic representation of reality to works in which he started to freely use light, colour and form. Ensor was in good company, alongside other innovators such as Vincent van Gogh, Paul Gauguin and Edvard Munch. He never ventured into the field of abstraction, but experimented constantly and explored all the new paths that art took in the 20th century, without doggedly pursuing one direction.

State-of-the-art

The Ensor Research Project combines classical stylistic and art-historical research of letters, manuscripts, sources, preliminary studies and designs with high-tech, material-technical research. The project is led by Dr Herwig Todts, KMSKA Conservator of Ensor and Modern Art, and Annelies Rios-Casier, a PhD student researcher (conservation and restoration master) at the KMSKA and the University of Antwerp (UA).

Ensor's paintings are examined using classic technologies including ultraviolet, infrared and X-ray. These provide information about, respectively, the varnish layer, the charcoal underdrawings and any paint containing heavy metals, such as lead white. In addition, UA has two state-of-the-art scanners to thoroughly examine the paint layers. These macro-XRF and macro-XRPD scanners provide new information about overpaints and paint pigments.

"This is not a project that an art historian can do alone," explains Todts. "The material-technical findings must be interpreted by a specialist, one who also knows what it's like to work with paint and canvas. Initially, I was working with Karen Bonne, now with Annelies Rios-Casier. We're combining our research results to come to a conclusion."

Mapping Ensor

What have they learned so far? Research has shown that the young Ensor did indeed paint his *Bathing Hut on the Beach* (1876) on the beach: grains of sand can be found in the paint. Also, it's been argued for a long time that Ensor used very poor quality material. *Christ's Entry Into Brussels in 1889* (1888), for example, is said to have been painted with the kind of paint used on walls. This turns out to be completely wrong: on the contrary, Ensor used expensive and precious paints that he bought from, among others, Blockx, a company that also supplied Monet.

The researchers have found that in his early academic period, Ensor was still building up his paintings in a very classical style with different layers of paint. When he started making his mask paintings, he stopped using this technique: he began to put colours next to each other and used pure, unmixed paint. He borrowed this approach from the Impressionists after having seen works by Monet and Renoir in 1886.

The Ensor Research Project aims, first of all, to map the Ensor paintings in the KMSKA collection, then those in the Mu.ZEE Ostend collection and preferably all important public and private collections in the Benelux, as completely as possible. For her PhD dissertation, Annelies Rios-Casier is researching whether a number of findings are confirmed in 12 key works, including *The Intrigue* (KMSKA), *Christ's Entry into Brussels in 1889* (J. Paul Getty Museum, Los Angeles), *Still life in the Studio* (Neue Pinakothek, Munich) and *Skeletons in the Studio* (National Gallery Canada, Ottawa).

One of the cornerstones of the KMSKA and its operations is the museum library. The research and cultural heritage library is a paradise for anyone seeking information on objects from the collection and its artists, or about fine art from the Low Countries and Europe in general. On paper and in digital form.

The KMSKA library story begins in 1904, when the curator at the time, Pol de Mont, started actively acquiring books and other publications. He embarked on this project with a view to writing the first collection catalogue. In 1916, the first mention of a library catalogue appears – initially as index cards arranged in alphabetical sequence. Over time, the book collection continued to grow, distributed over various departments of the museum.

Like the museum collection, the museum library has received frequent donations and bequests in the course of its existence, with Oscar Nottebohm's bequest from 1936 as a notable high point. It comprises 2,300 publications, including 1,737 auction catalogues, some of them containing handwritten notes with sale prices and the names of buyers. Such catalogues are a particularly important resource for people looking to write the life story of a work of art.

The KMSKA library got its own reading room and storage depot in 1949, by which time it was already in possession of more than 10,000 bound volumes. From that point on, external users were also welcomed. city architect André Fivez was responsible for designing the new reading room – he created a functional, contemporary interior, spacious and light. A few years later, the most illustrious librarian of the KMSKA was appointed: author Maurice Gilliams. The following decades were a time of continuous expansion for the library, and from the 1990s, the digital revolution started here too.

In the new KMSKA, the library occupies pride of place at the front of the building. The reading room is a high and large hall spanning two floors, with three windows and two large, suspended LED aureoles lighting the space. The lower level is furnished with solid oak bookcases, encompassing 271 metres of shelving: here you can find magazines, reference works, catalogues and books about the artists in the collection and about seven centuries of Low Countries art. That era is the focus of the museum's art collection and of the library's acquisition policy.

At the time of reopening, the library had approximately 95,000 publications. Here too, digitisation has really covered a lot of ground, even accelerating during the years of closure. Ingrid De Pourcq, Head of the library: "The library collections were being kept in an external depot in Antwerp. Partly because of this, we shifted our physical services more and more to digital services. Working with teams from the library and the archives, we are committed to providing as much digital access as possible, for our curators and collection researchers as well as for external users. We're always asking ourselves: do we have this information in digital form already, or can we digitise it, is it possible to provide it in that form? For the user, it means faster service and home delivery."

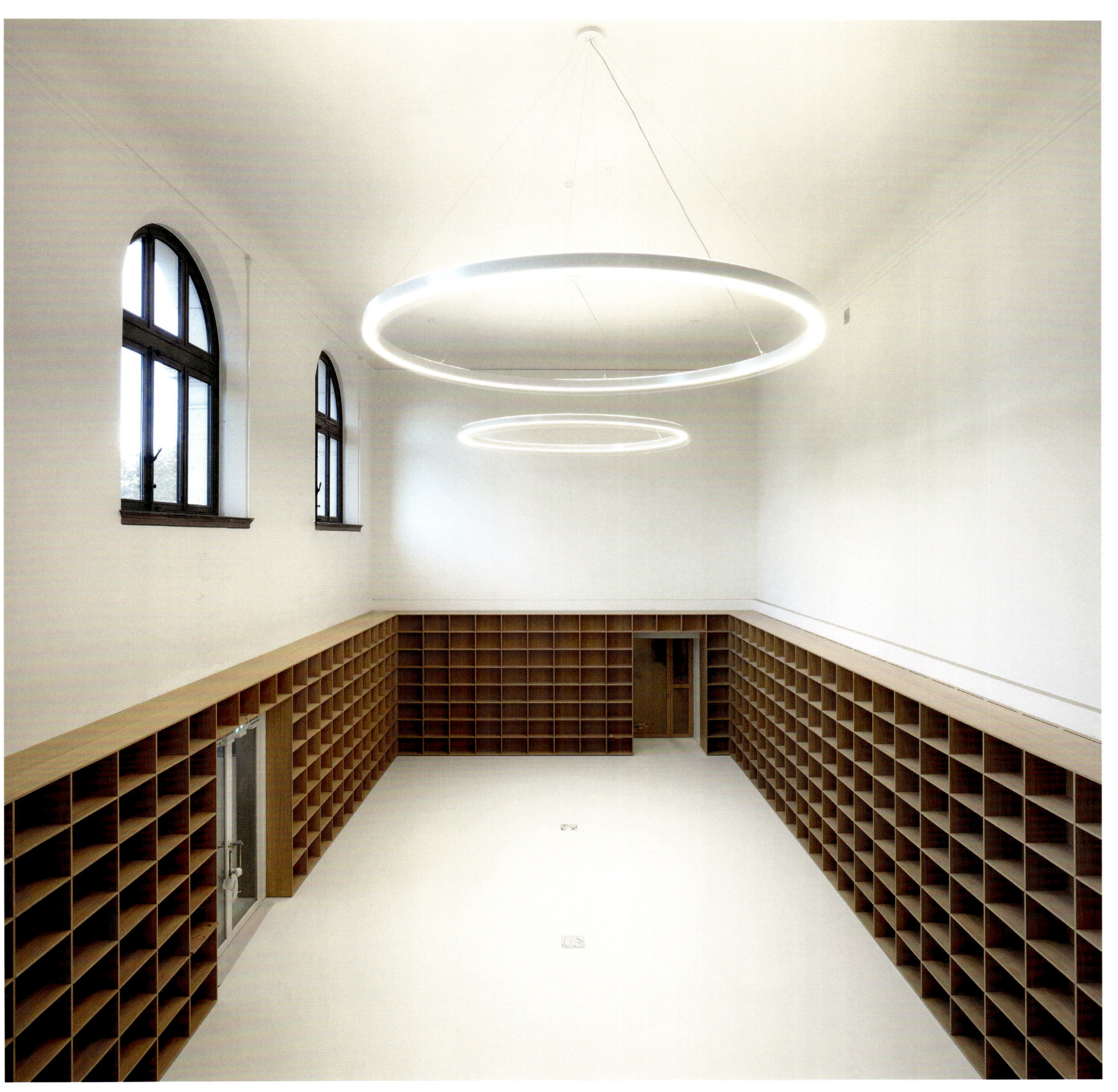

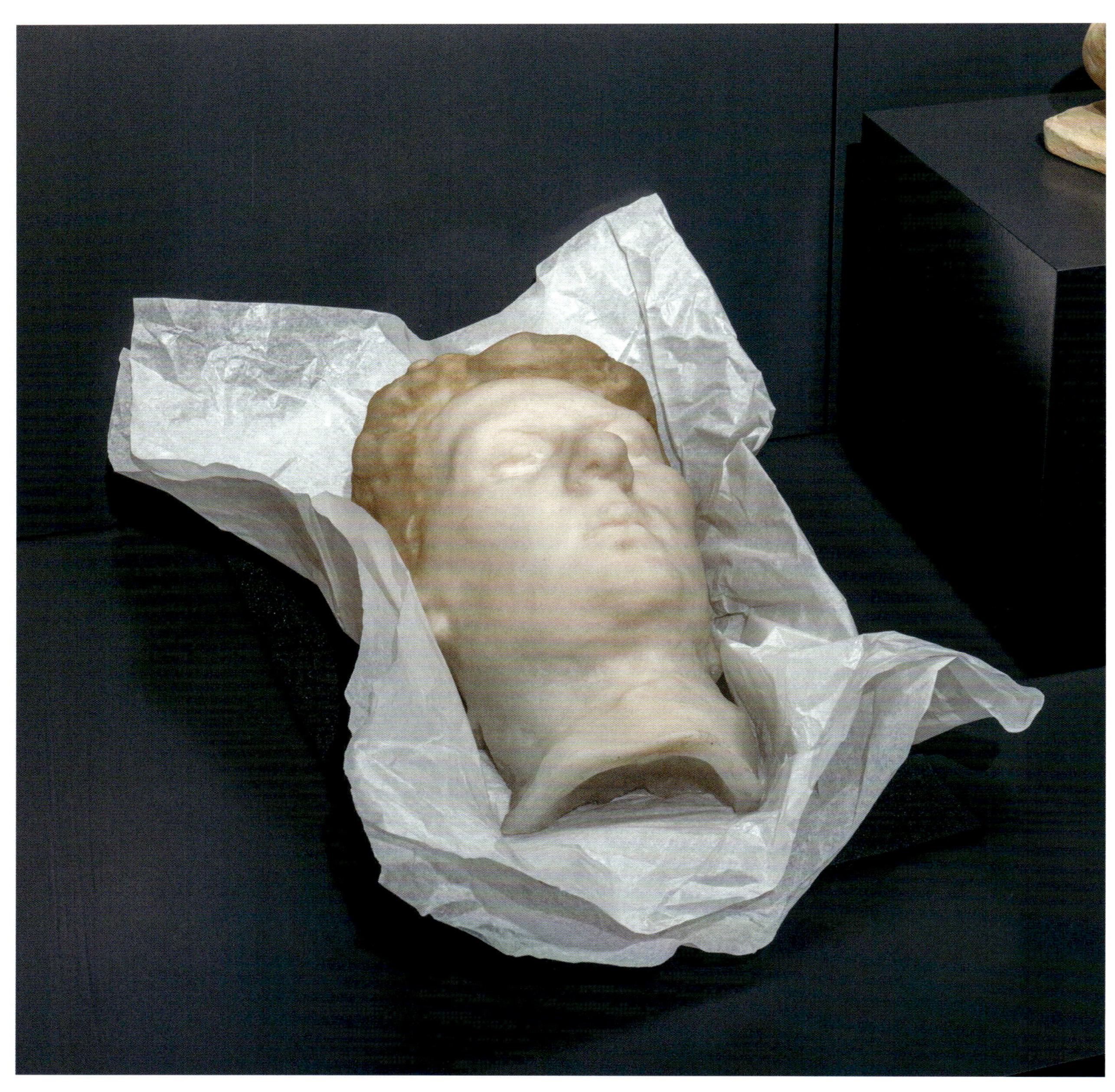

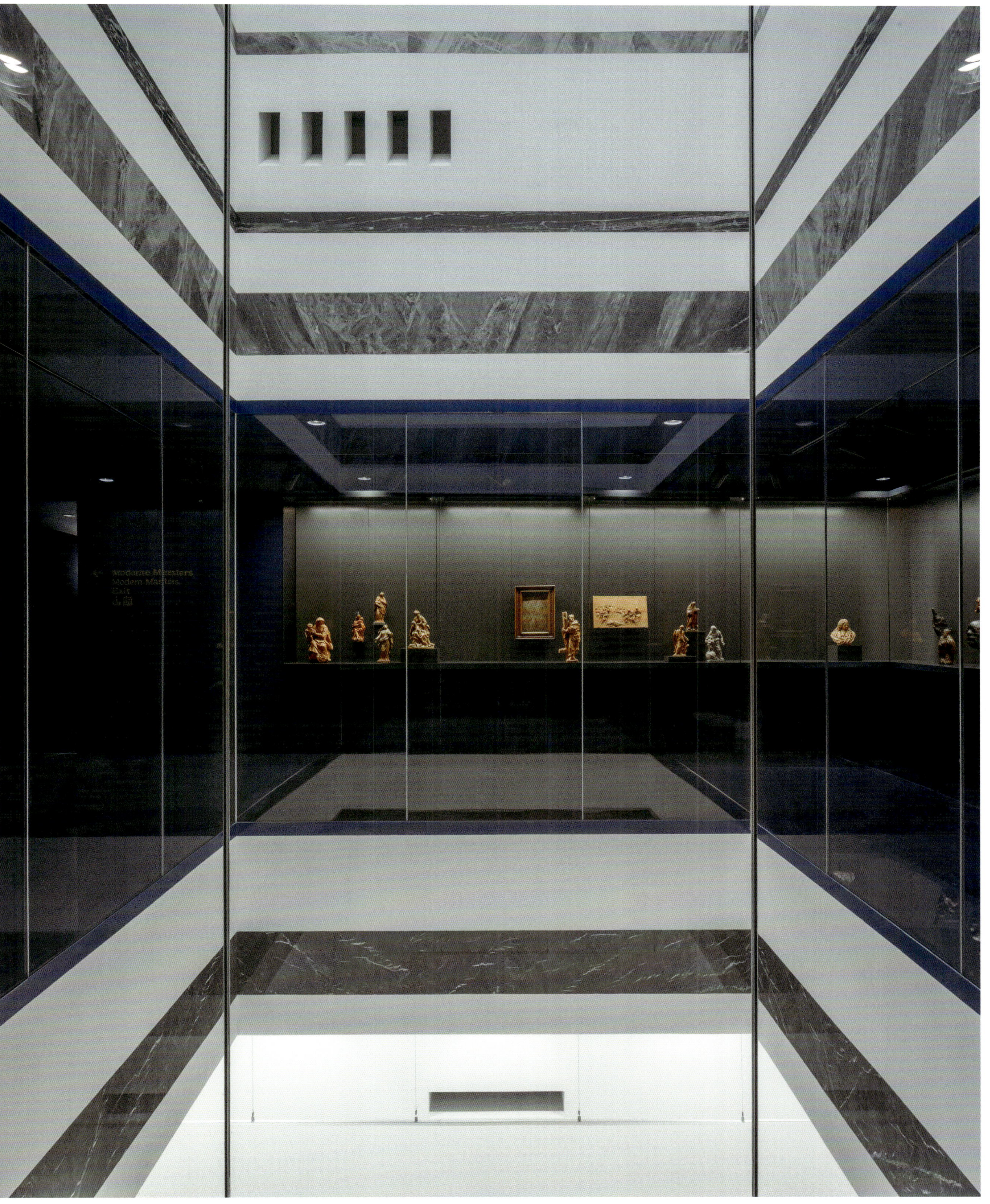
Moderne Meesters
Modern Masters
Exit

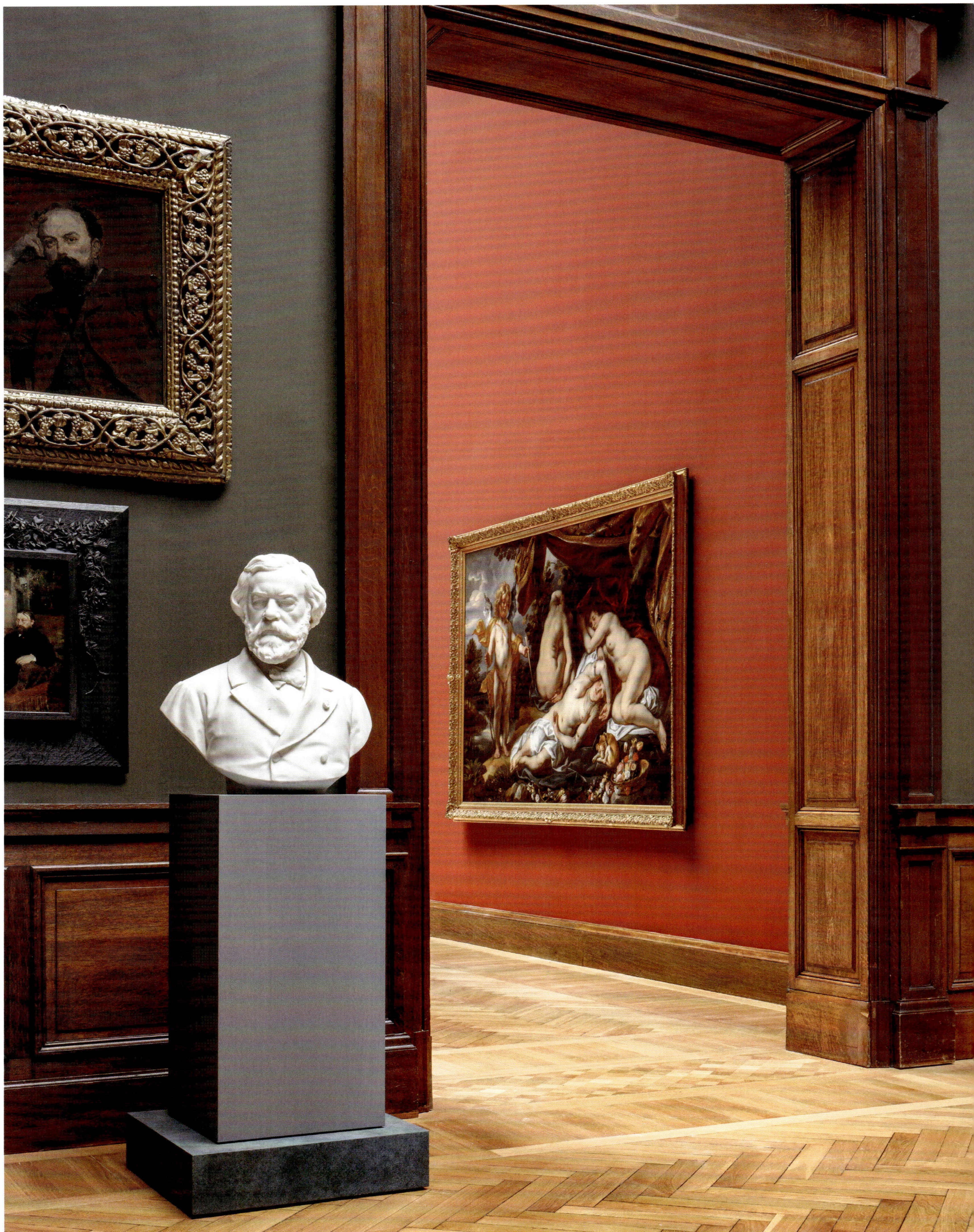

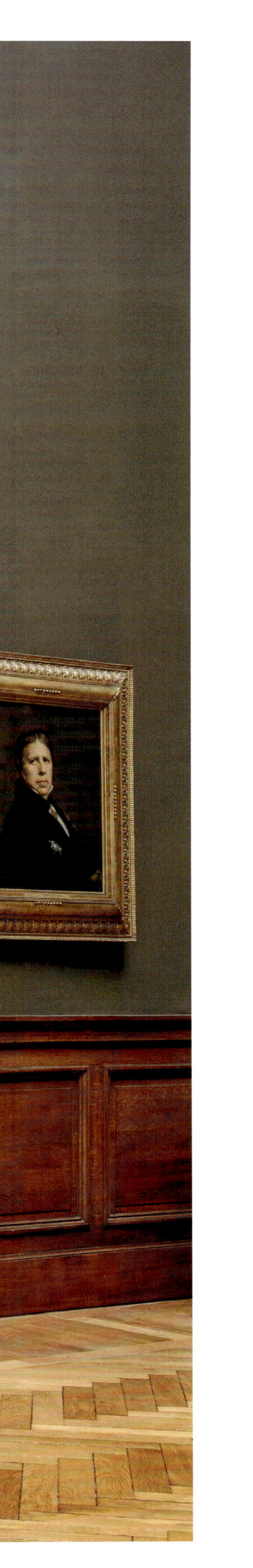

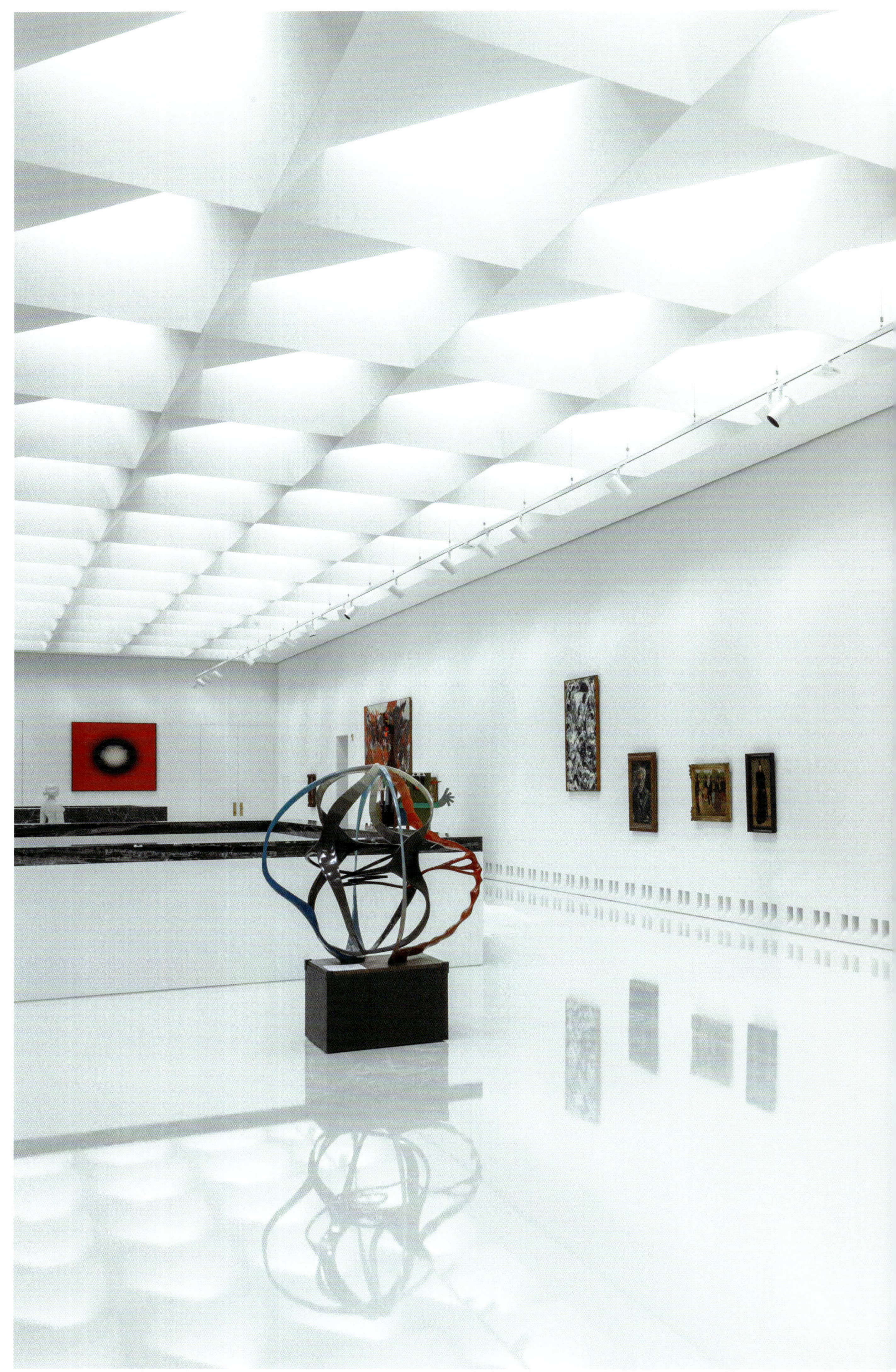

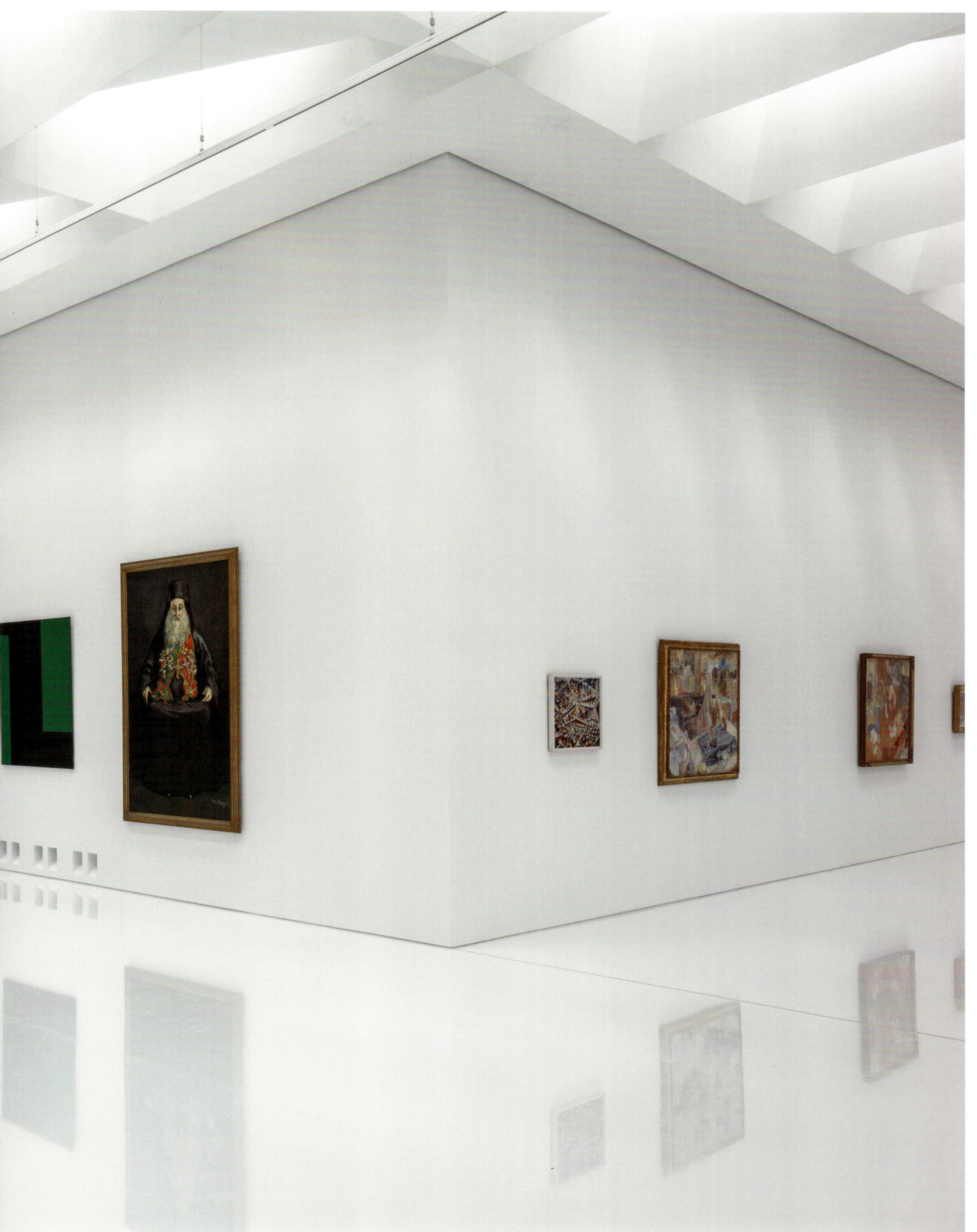

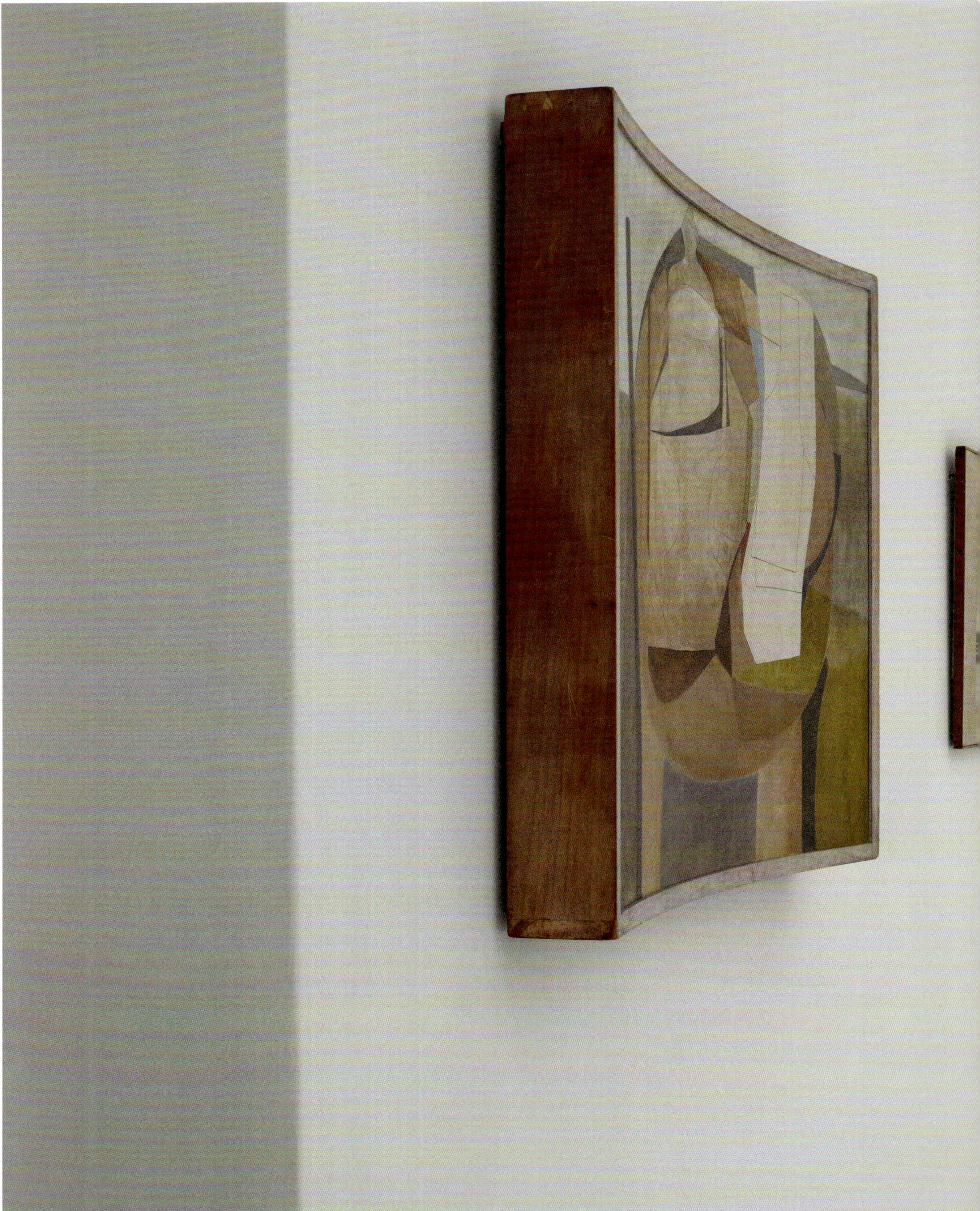

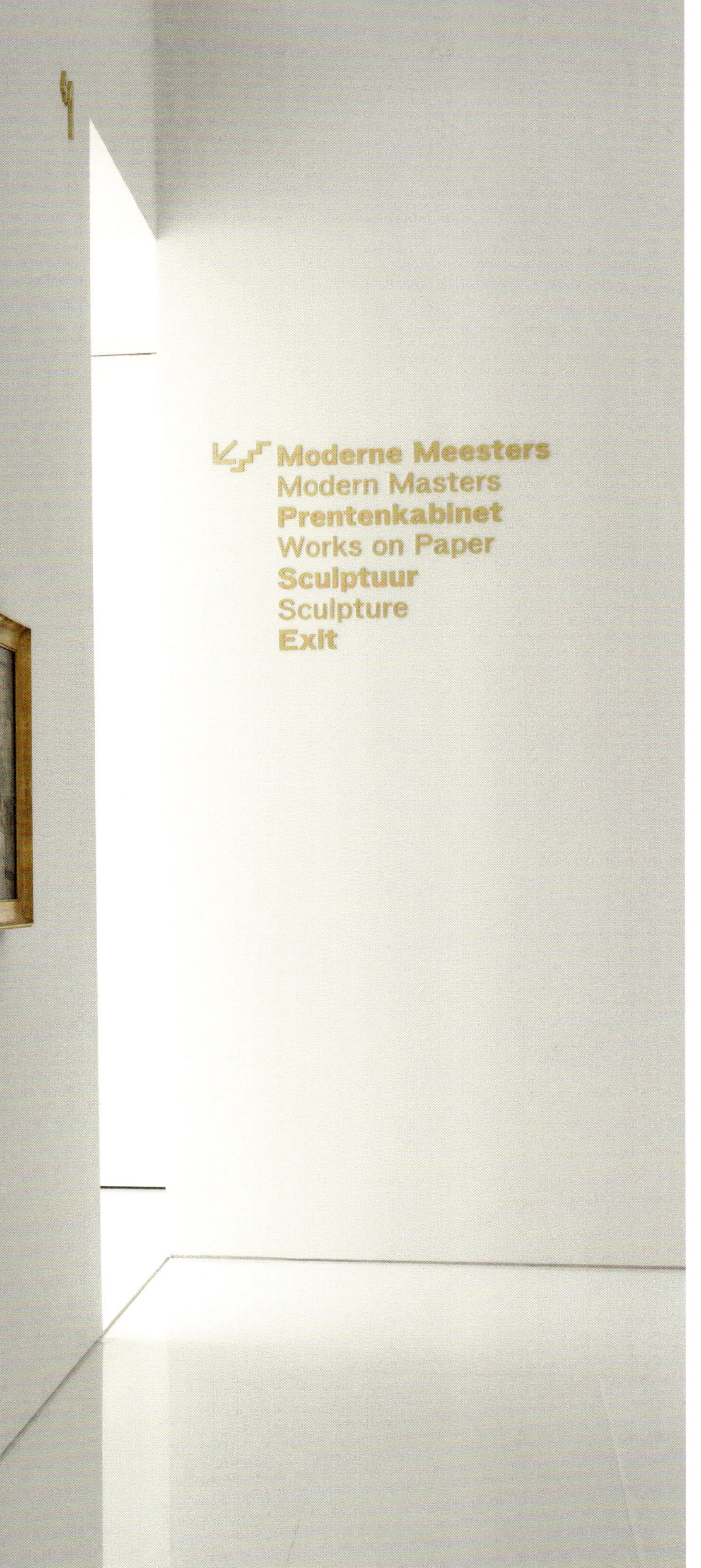
Moderne Meesters
Modern Masters
Prentenkabinet
Works on Paper
Sculptuur
Sculpture
Exit

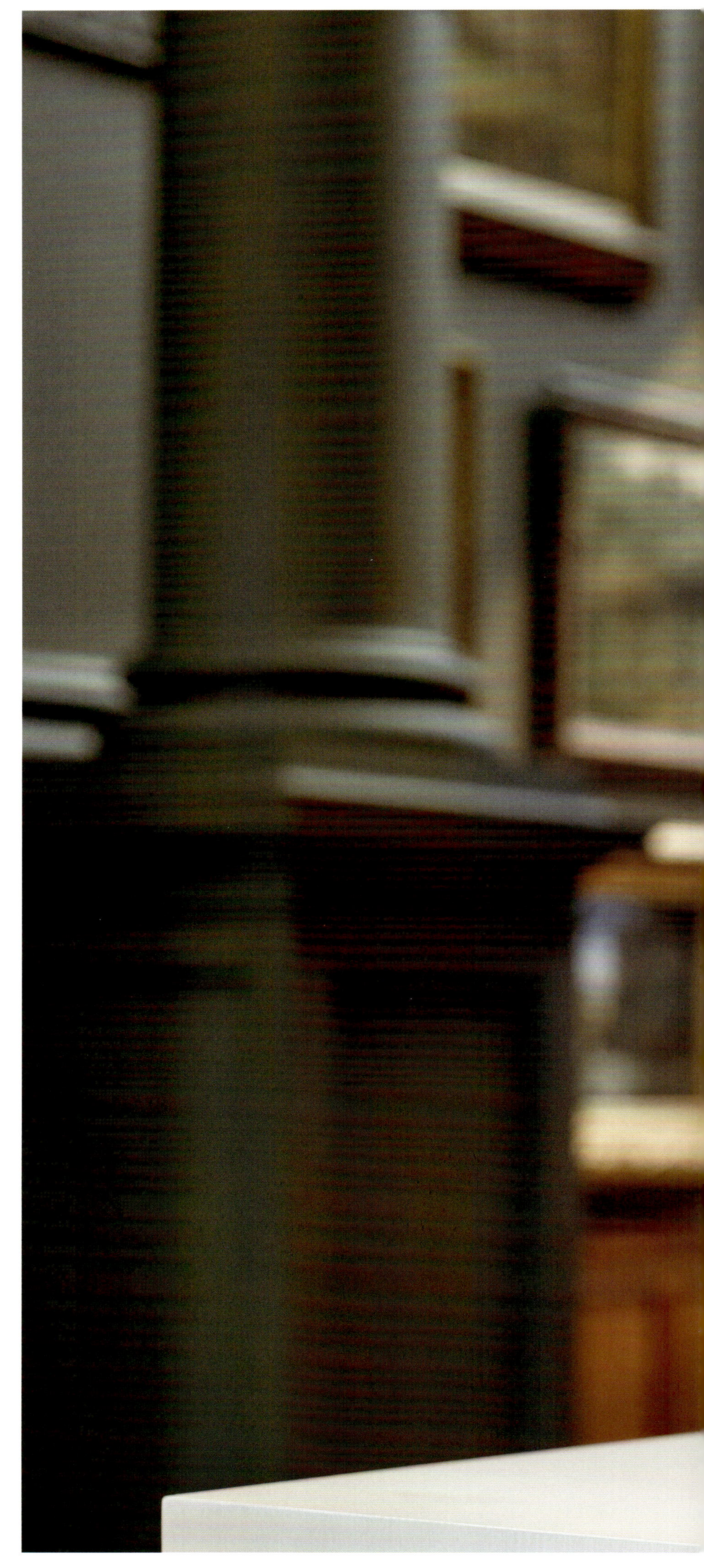

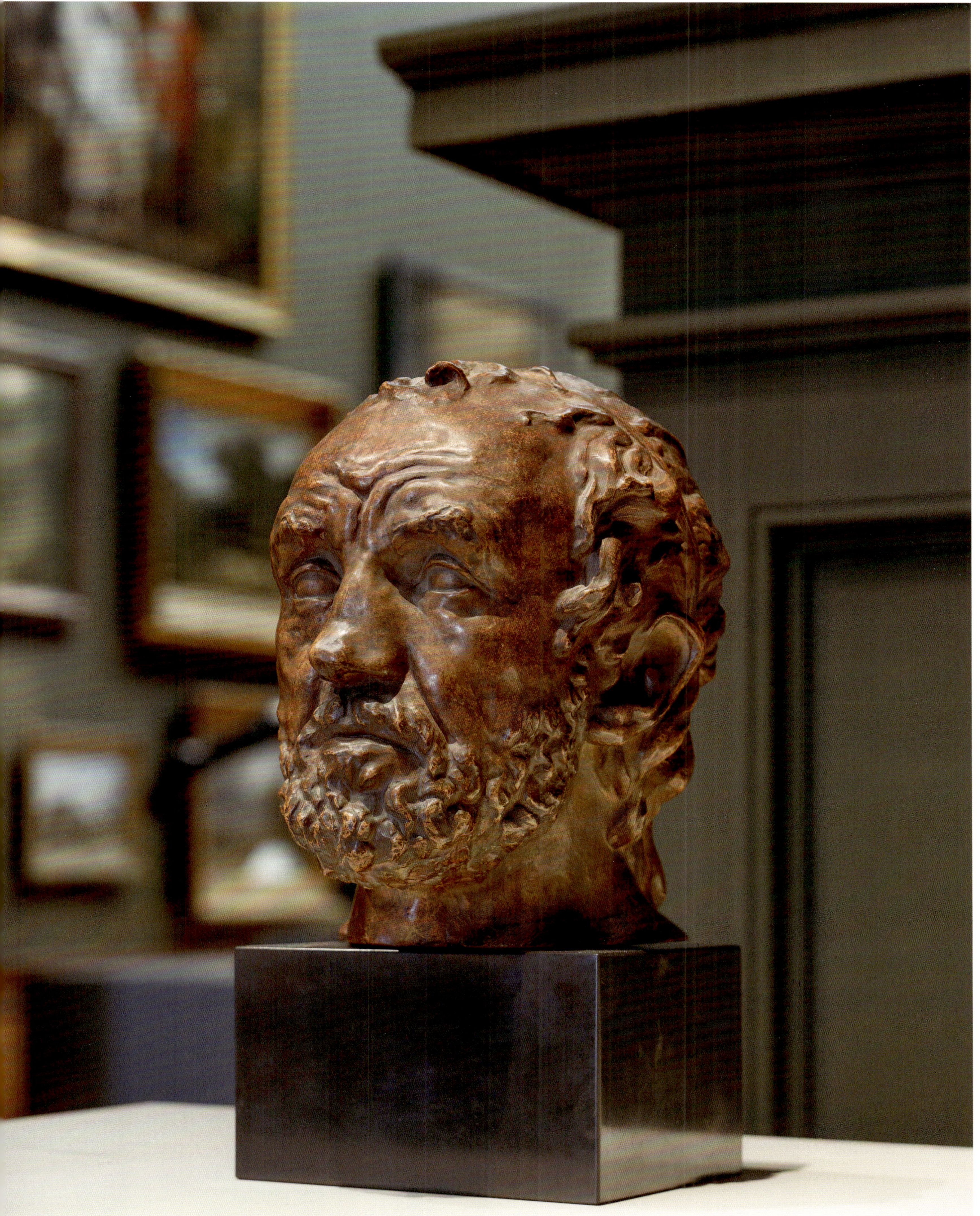

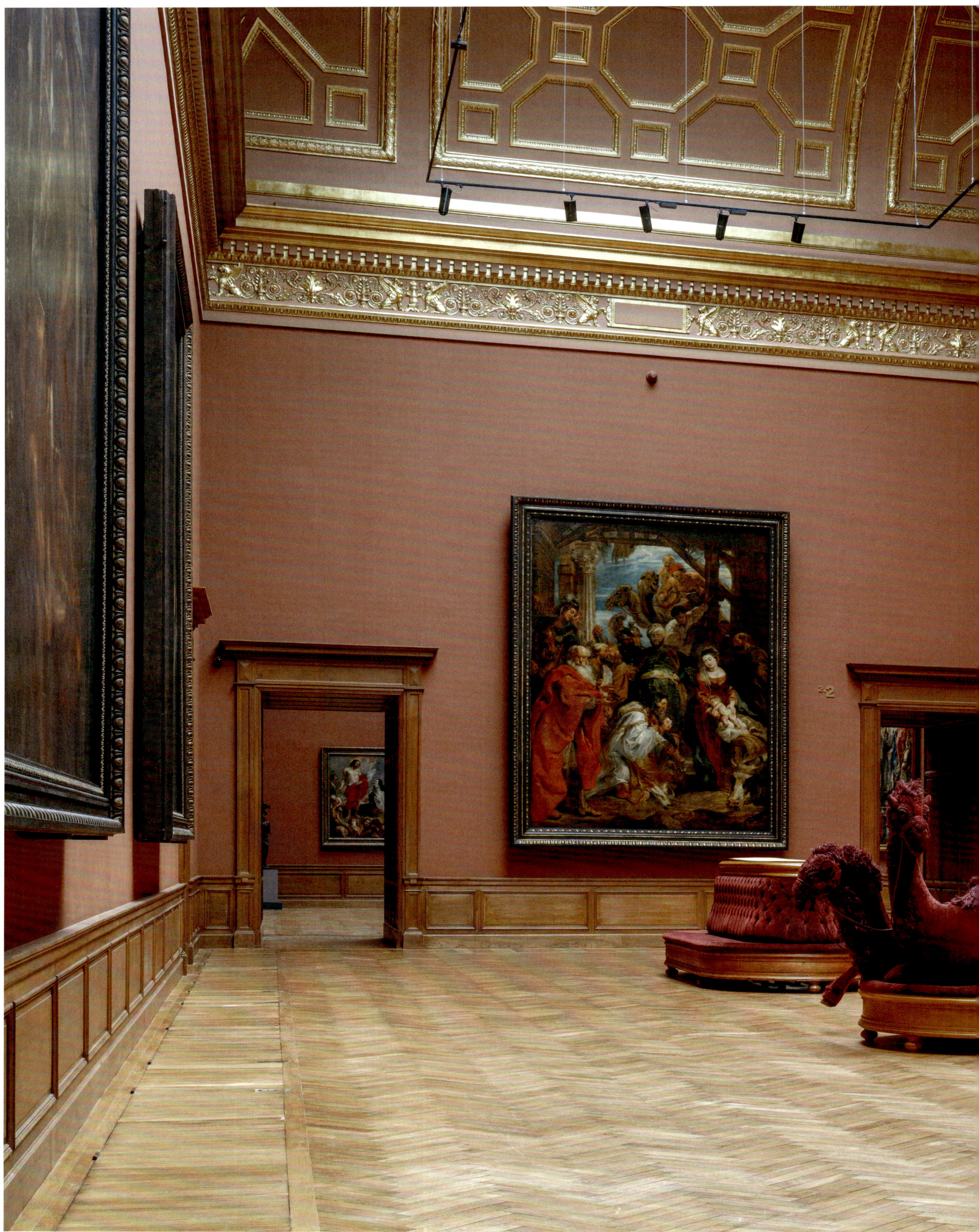

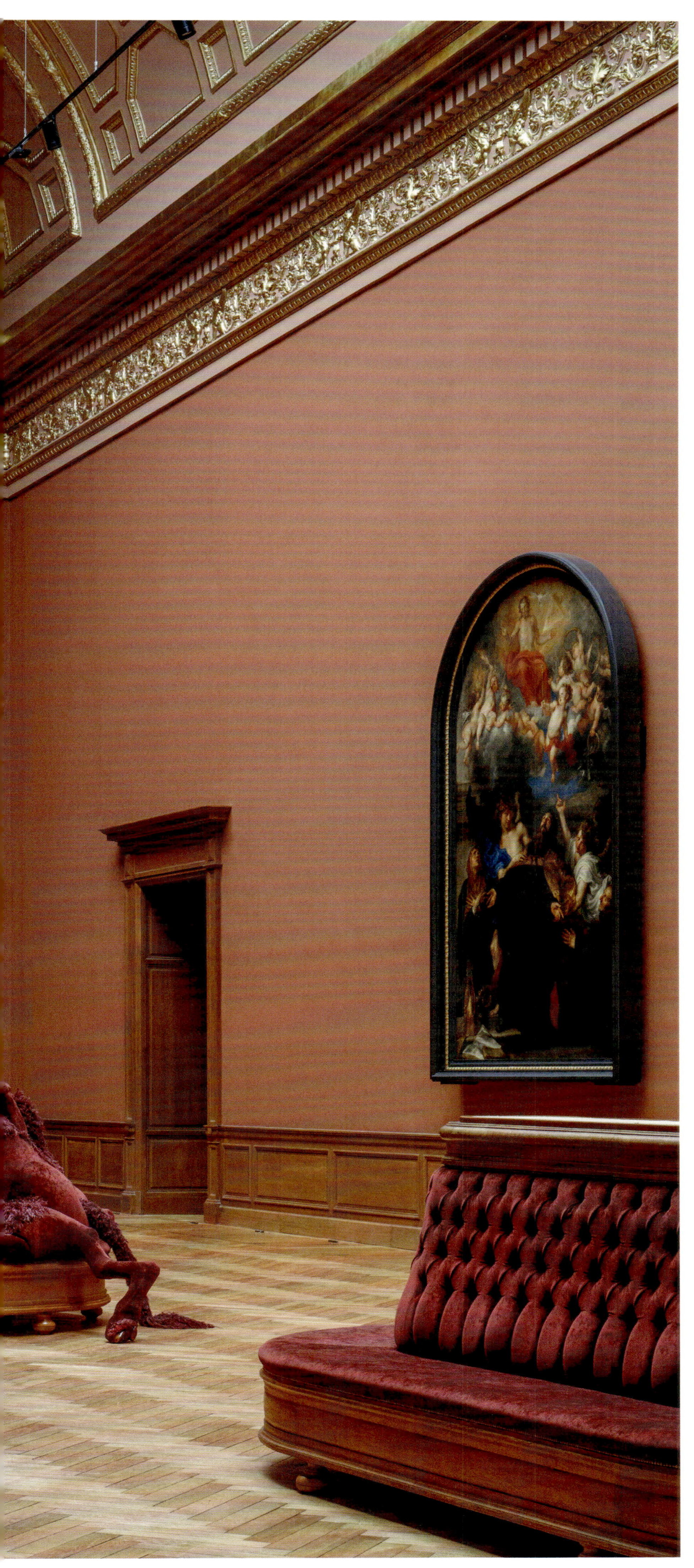

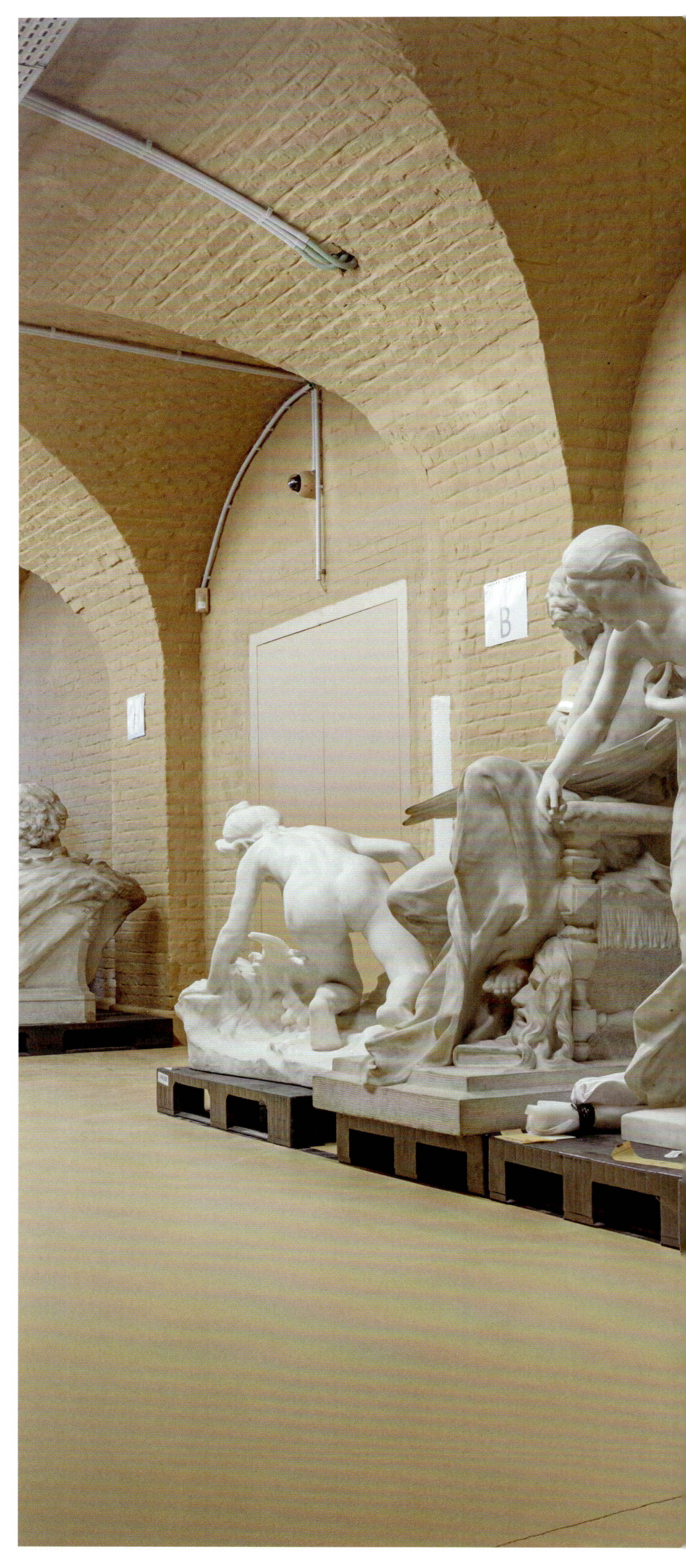
B

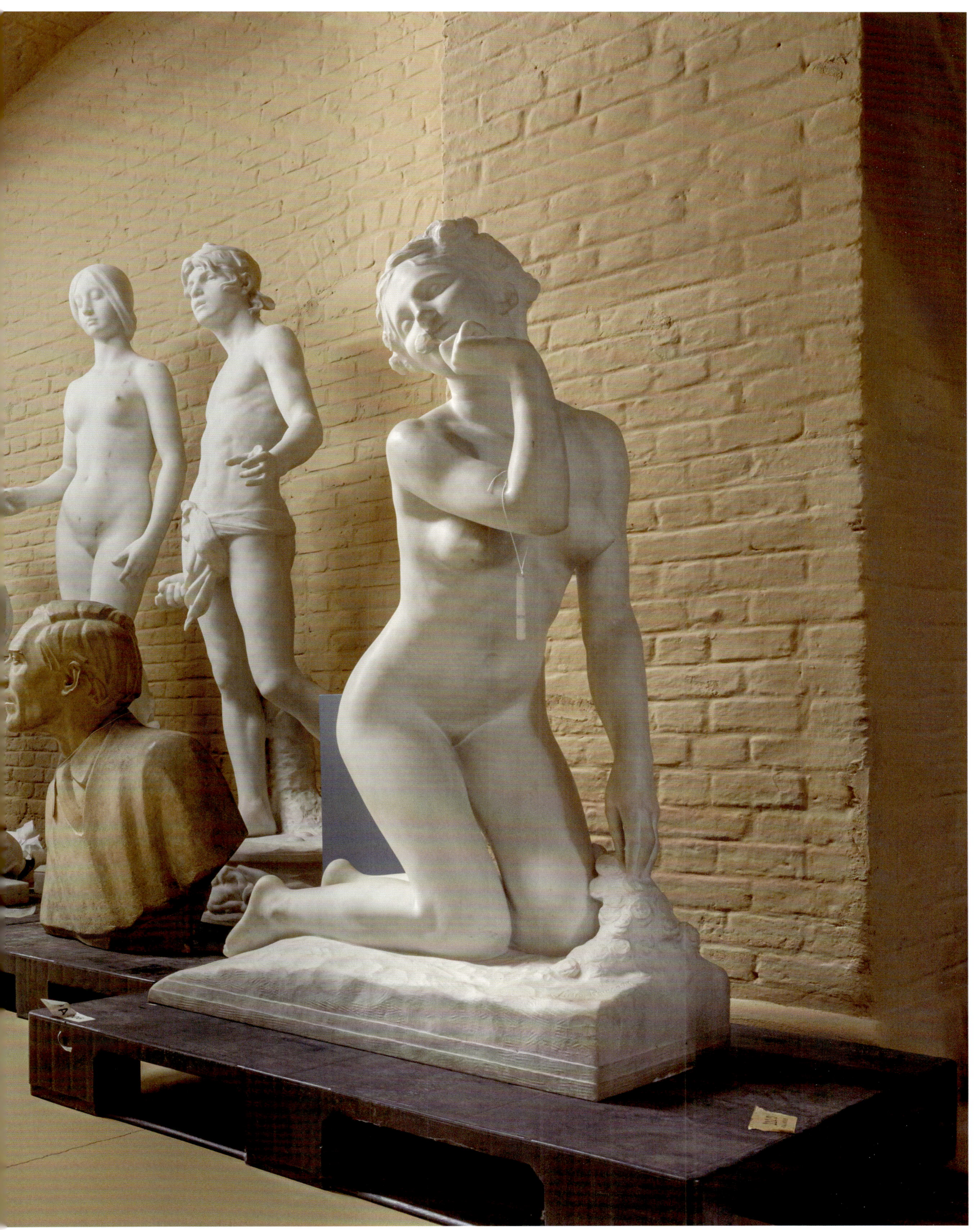

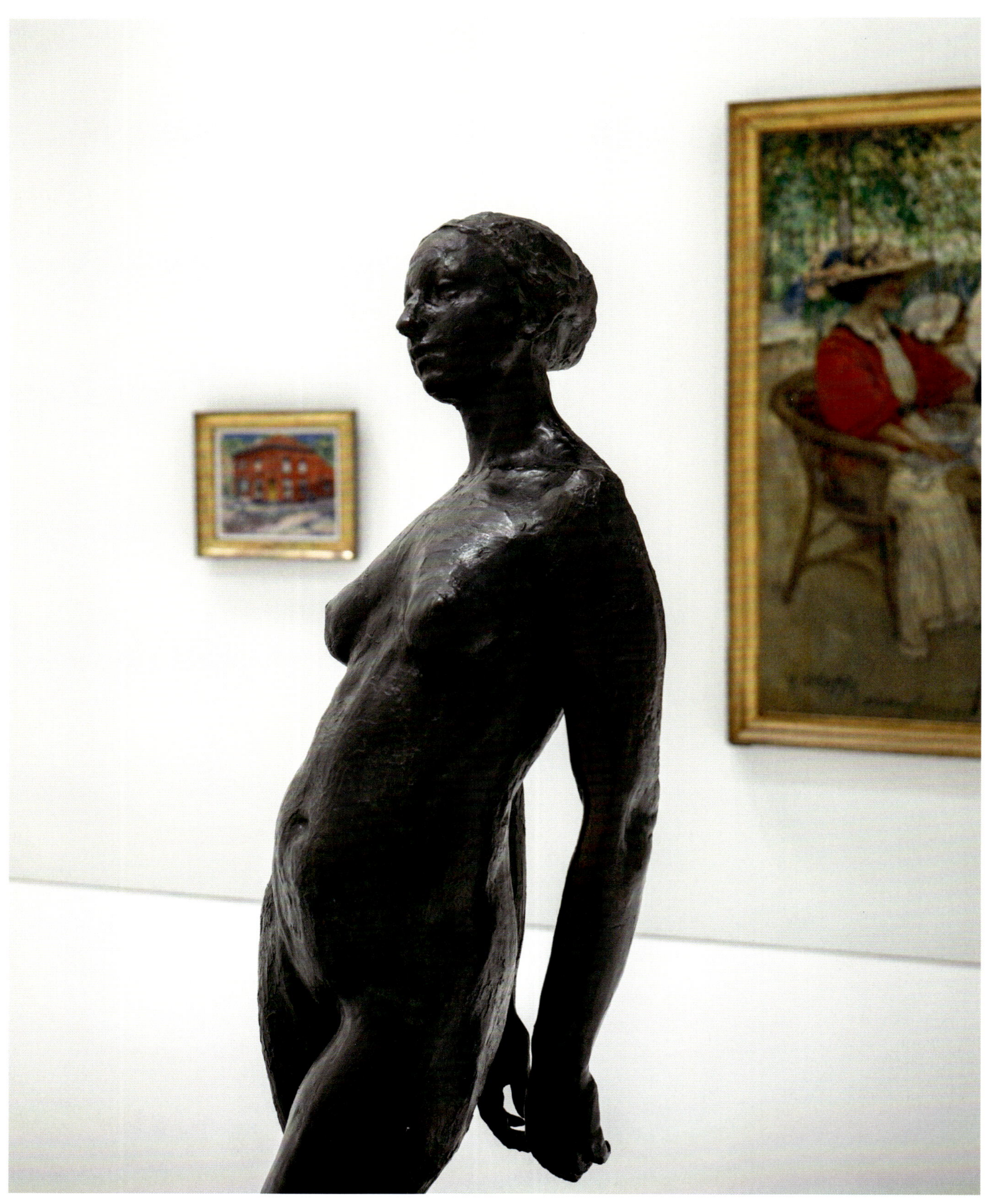

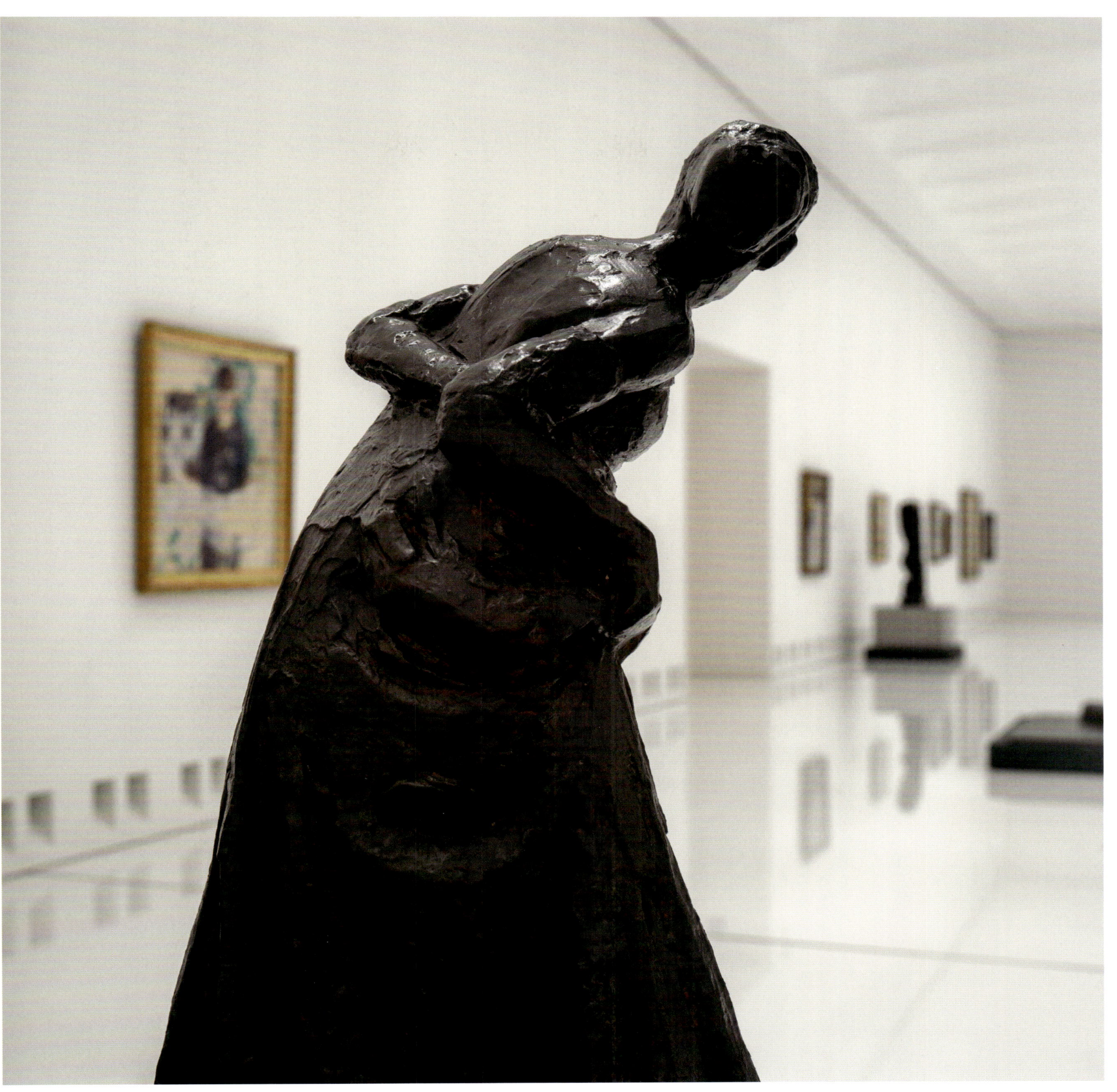

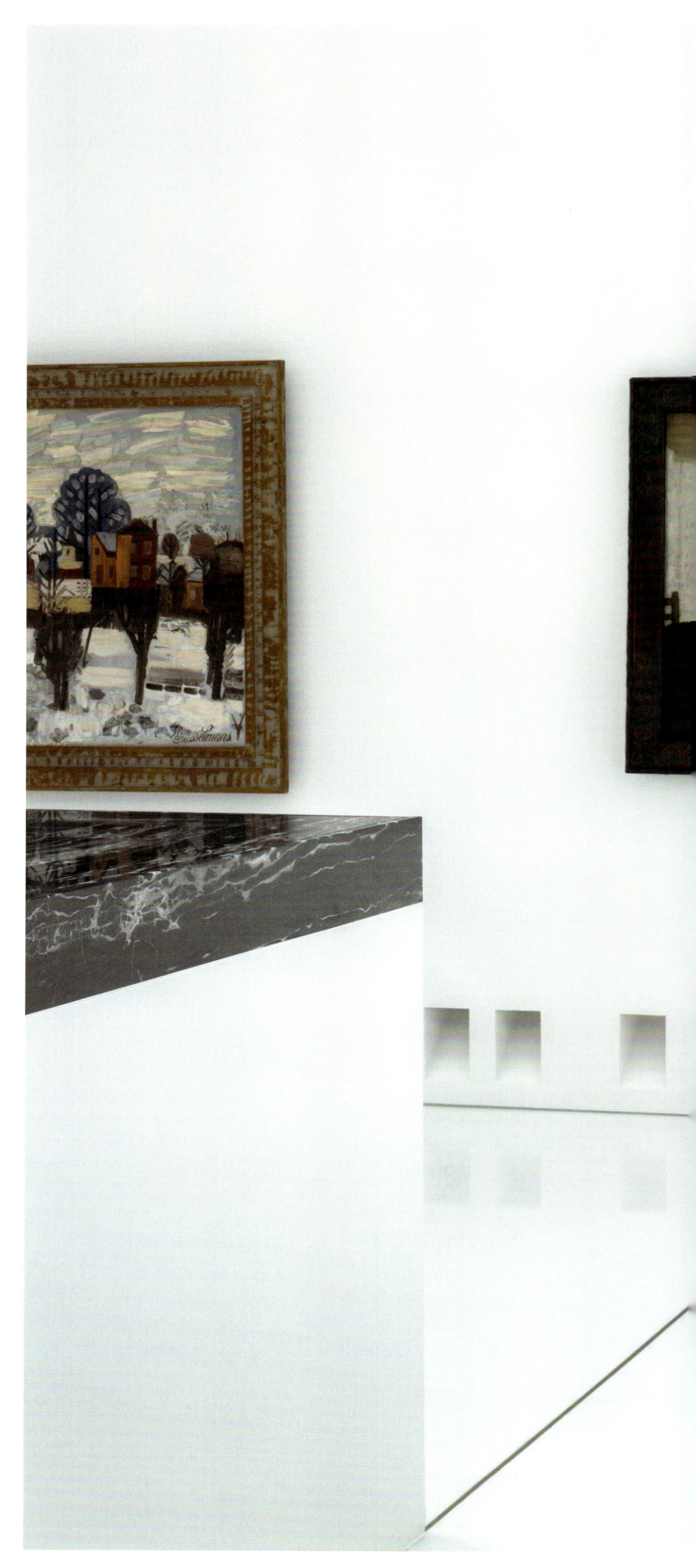

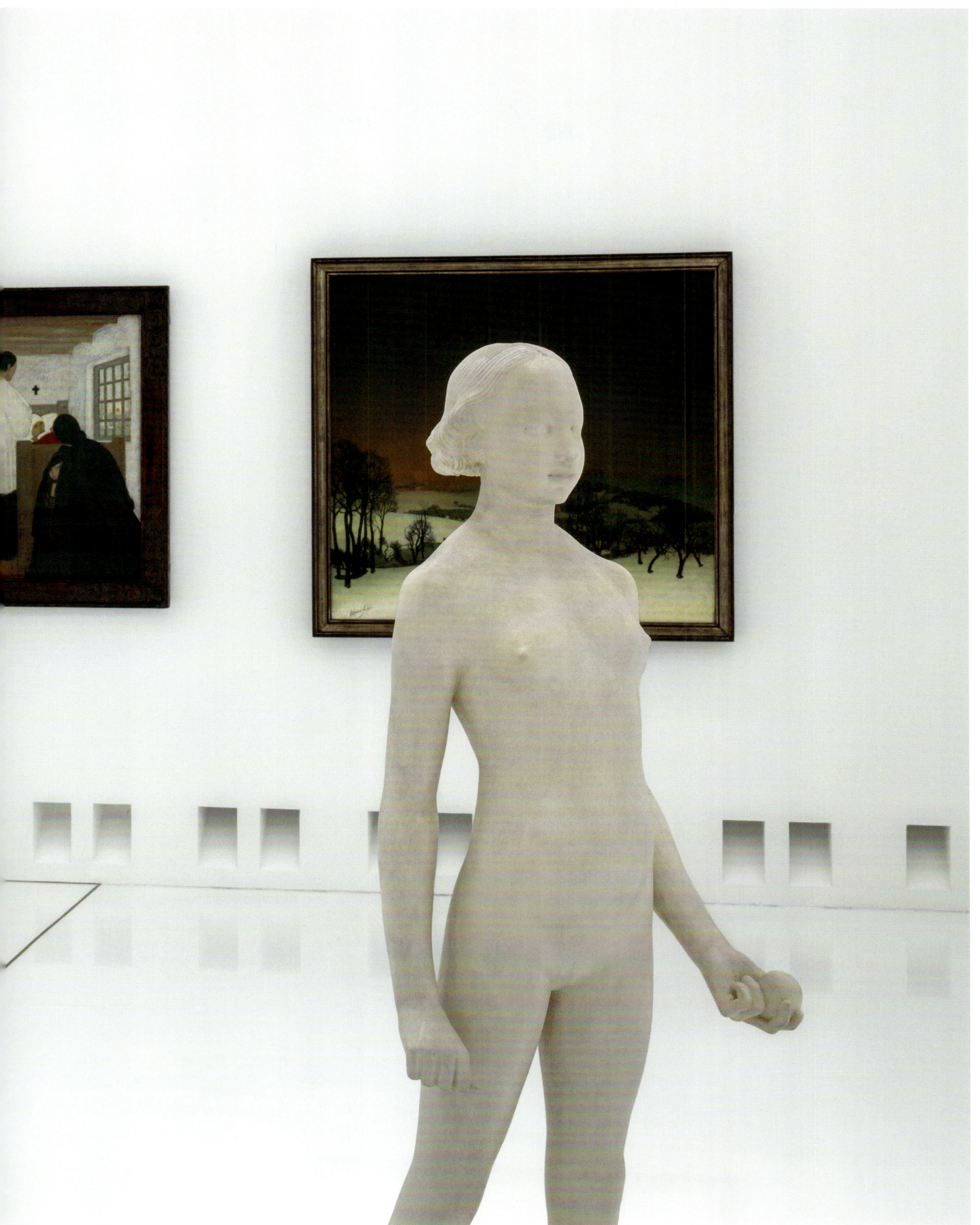

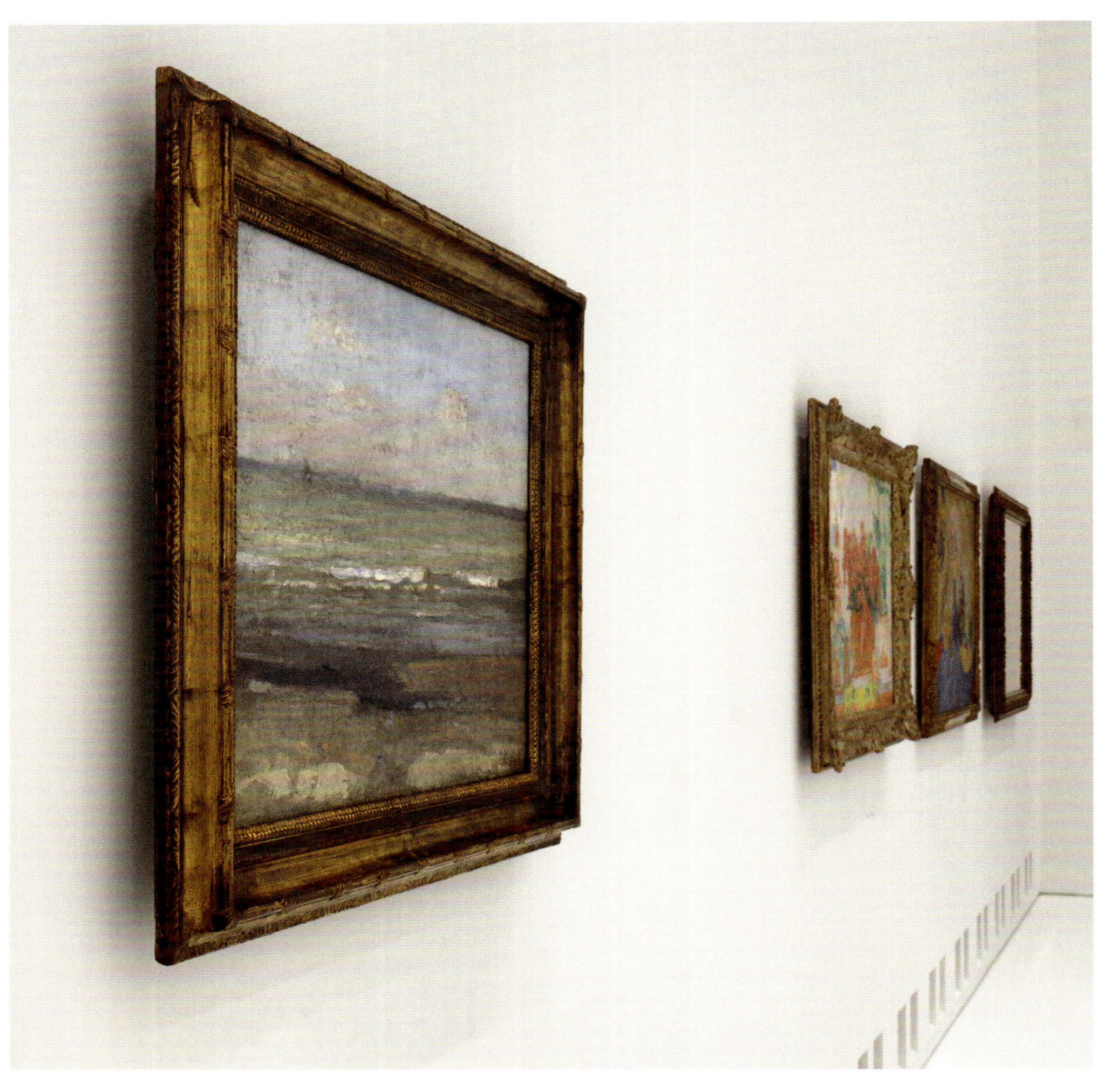

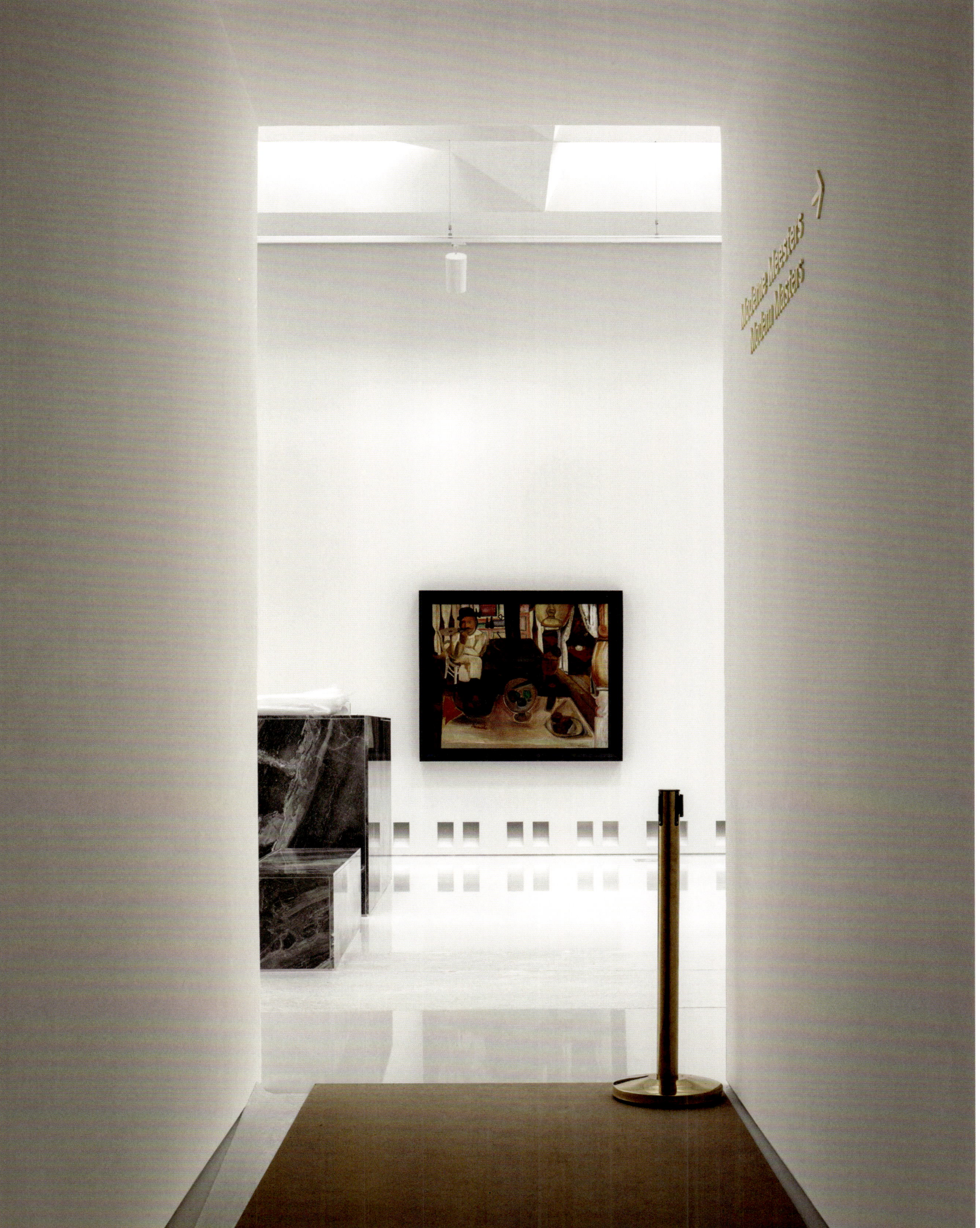
Moderne Meesters
Modern Masters

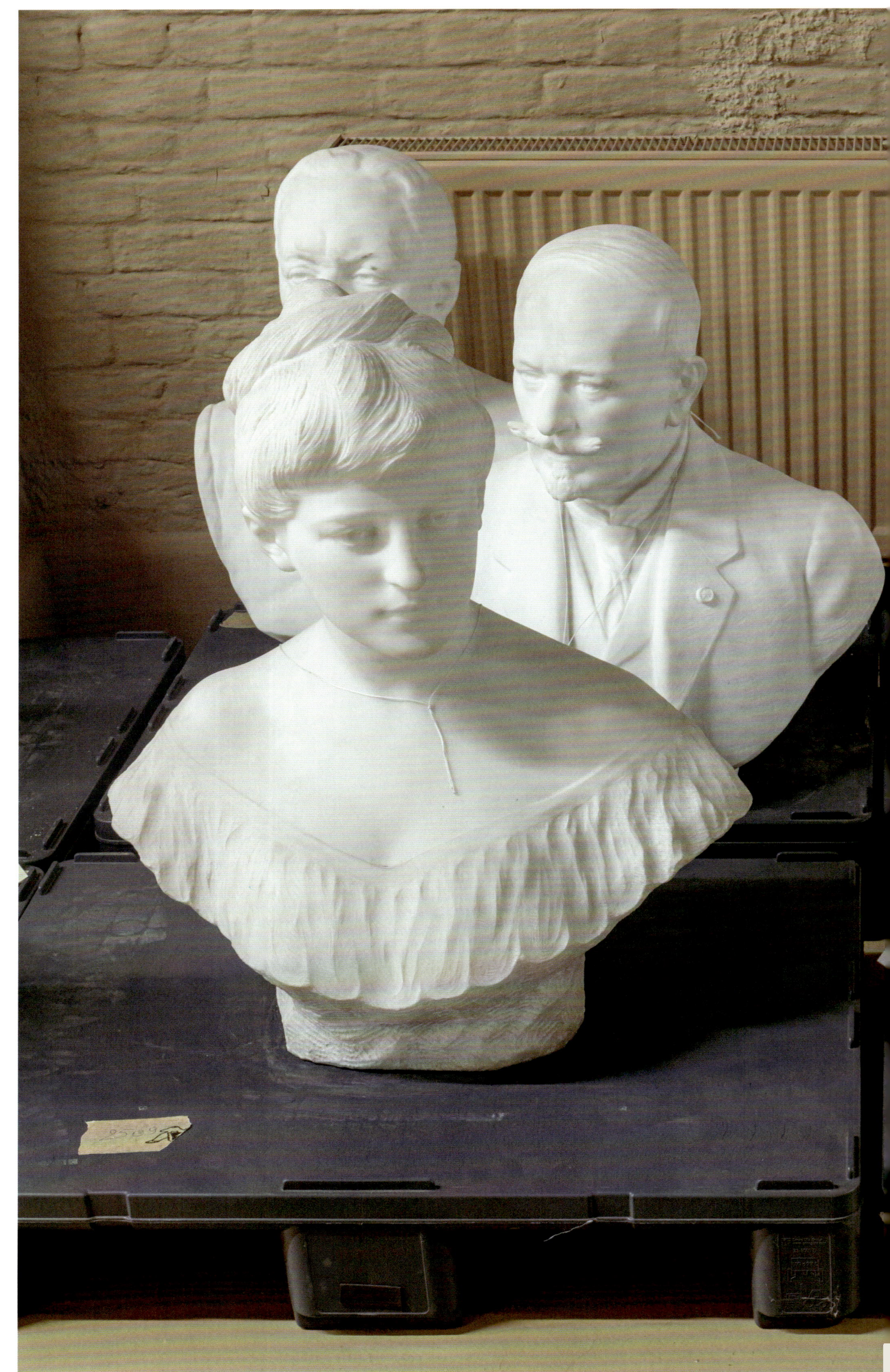

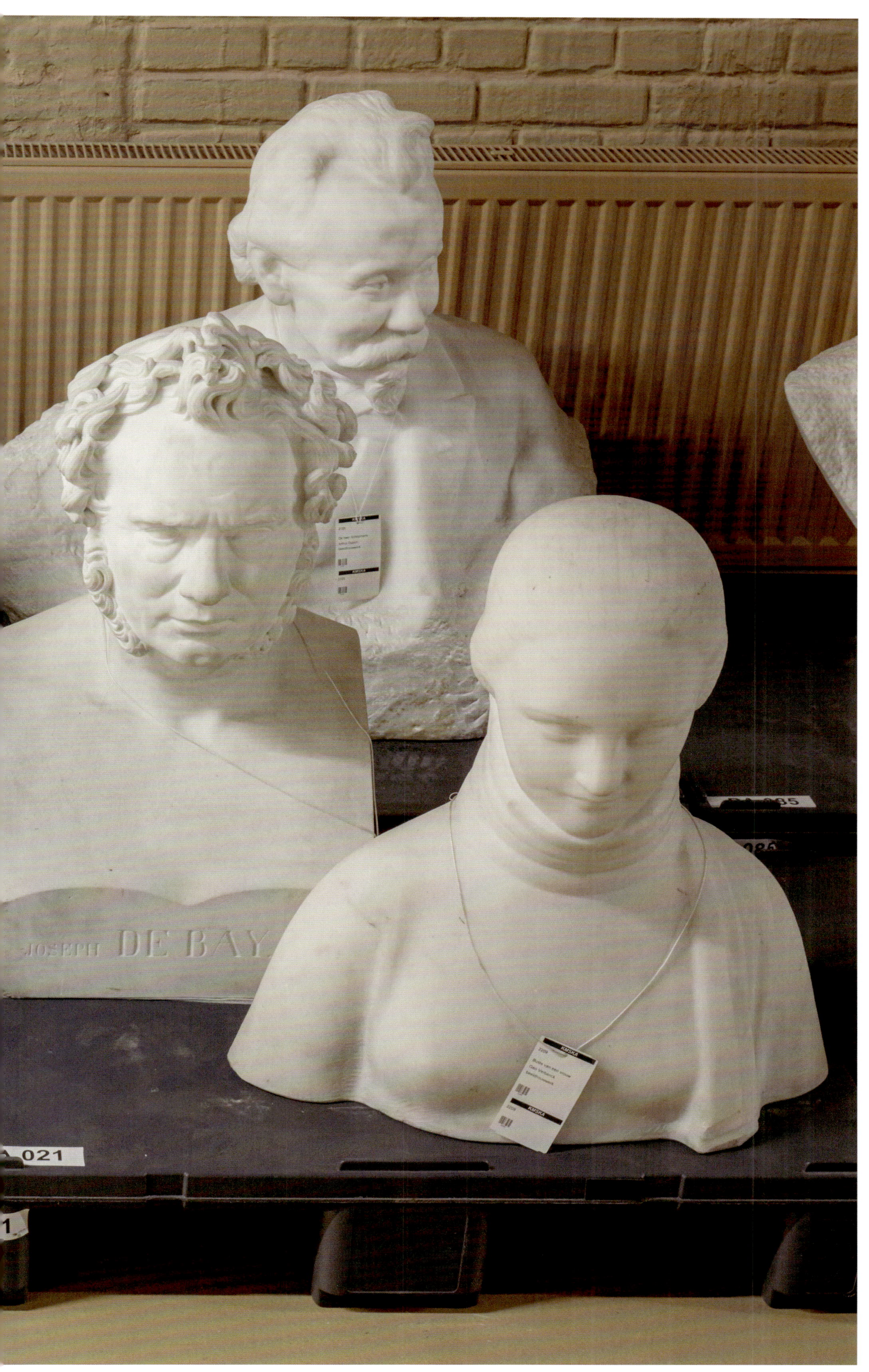
JOSEPH DE BAY

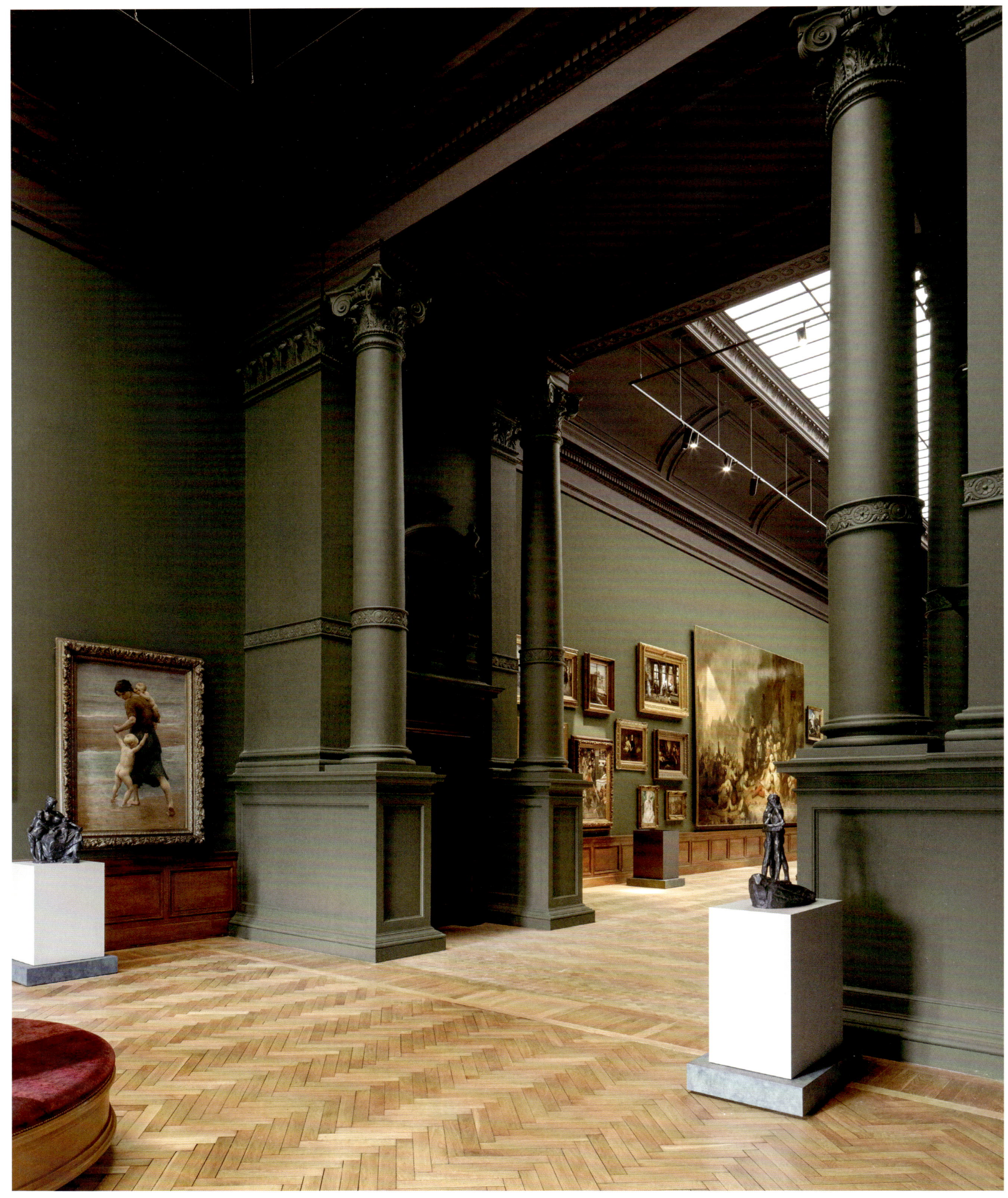

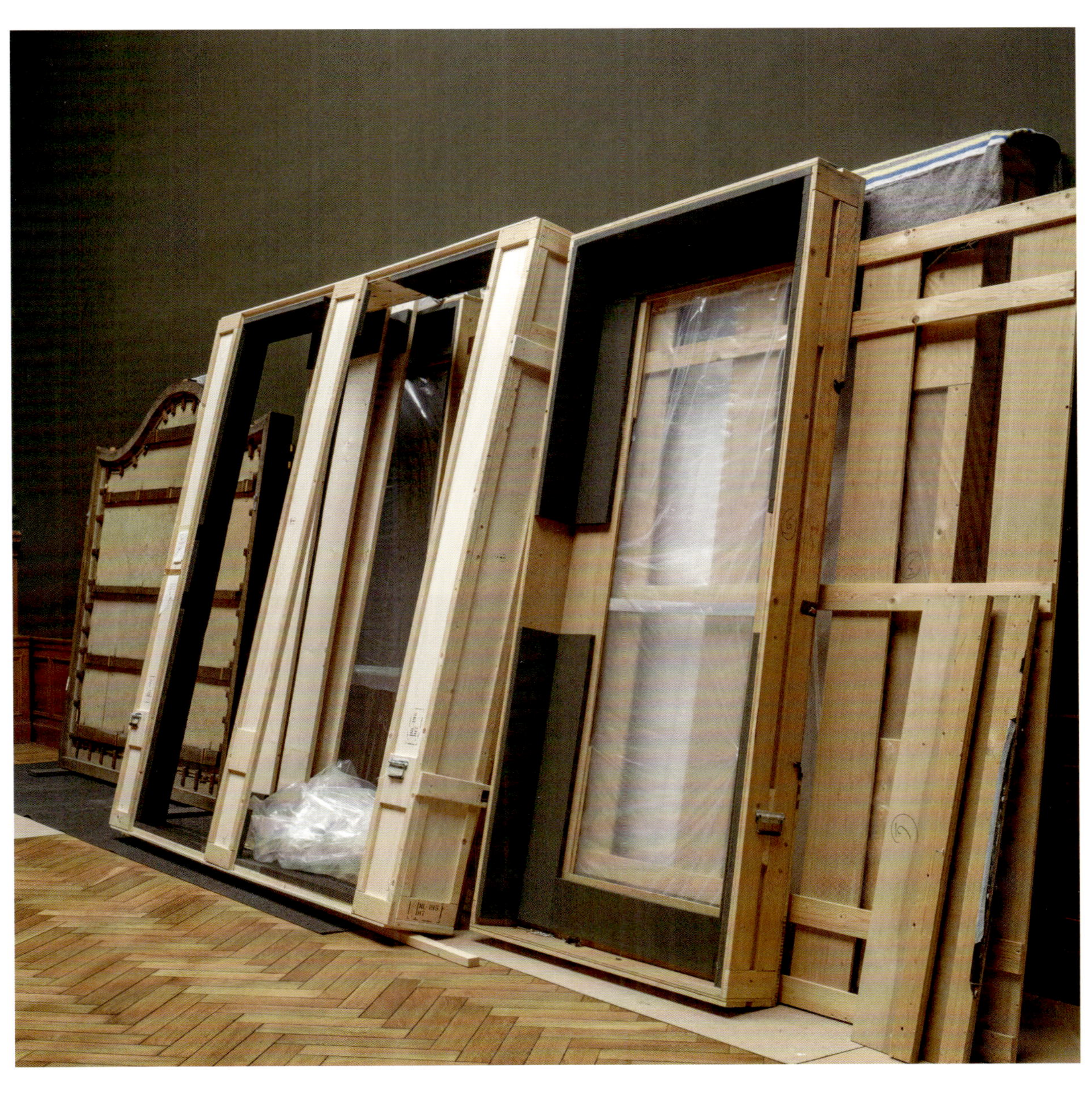

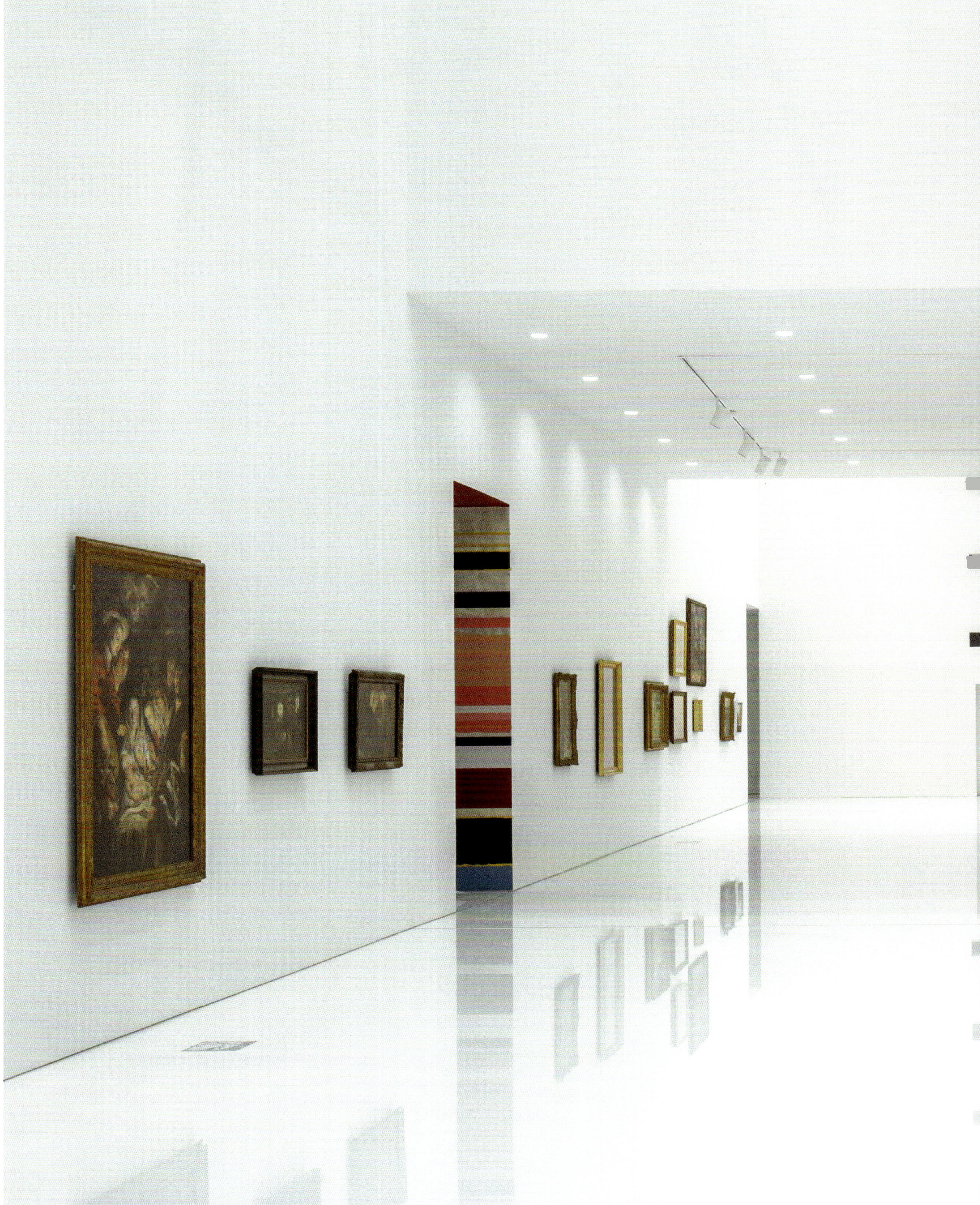

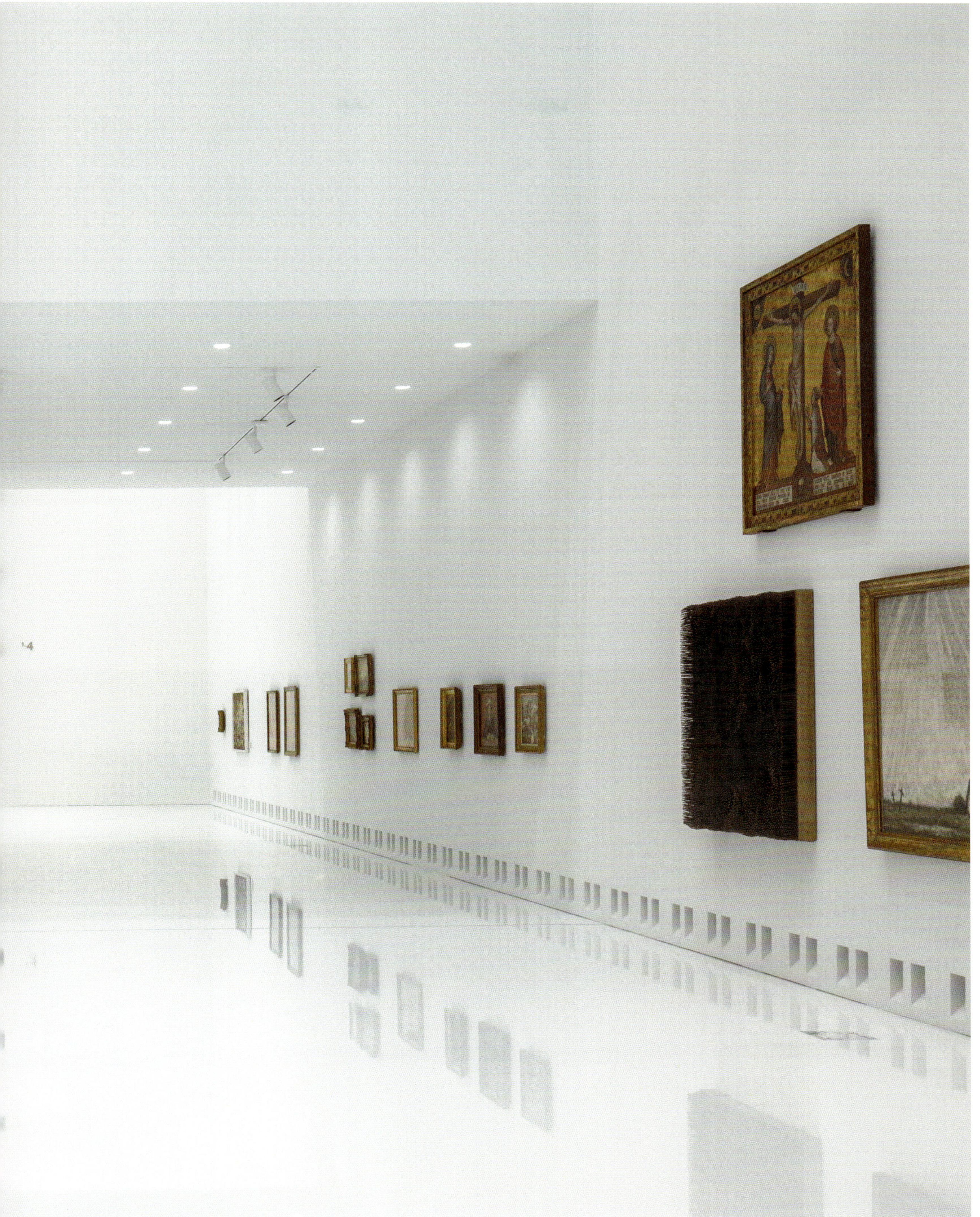

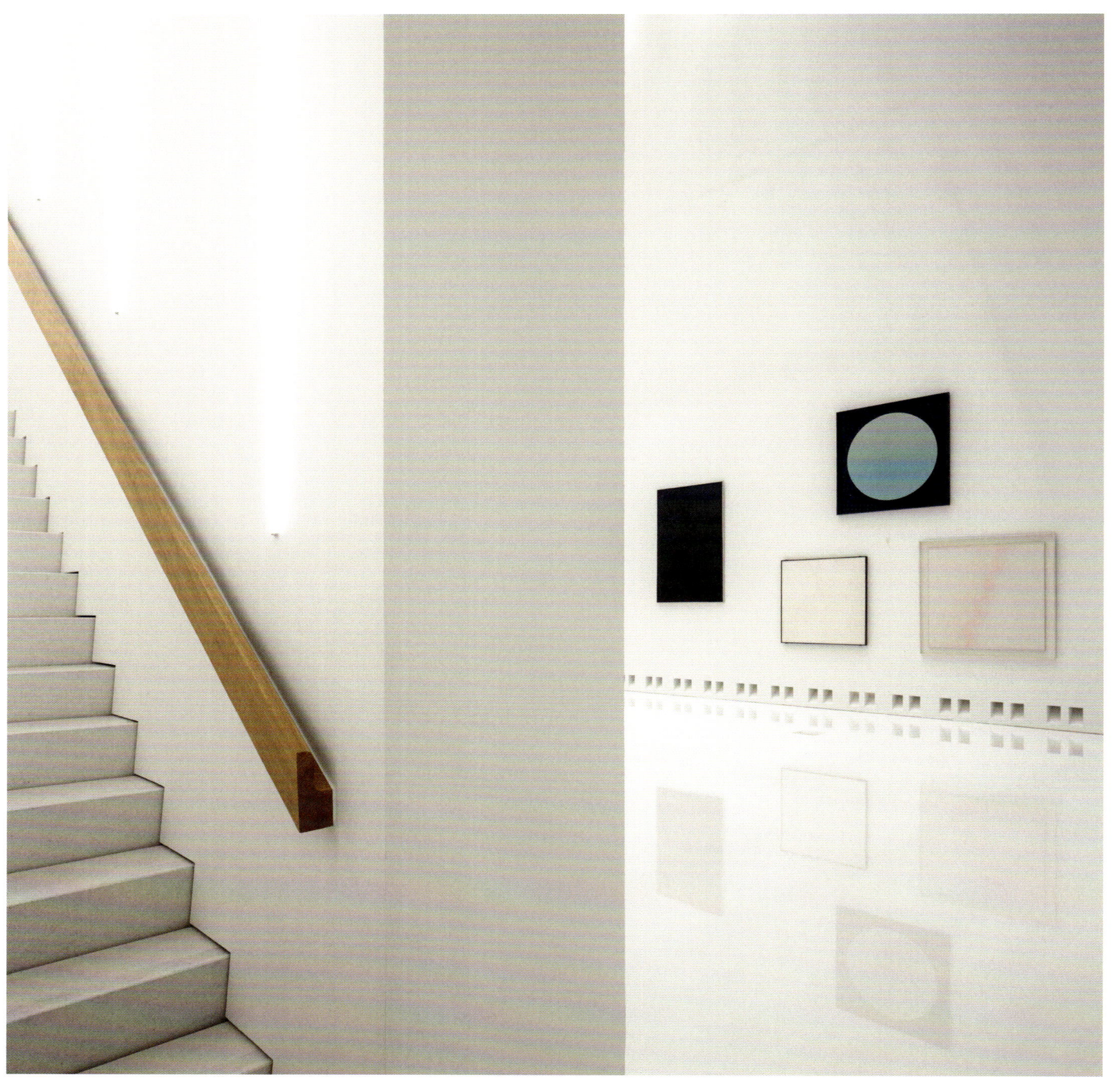

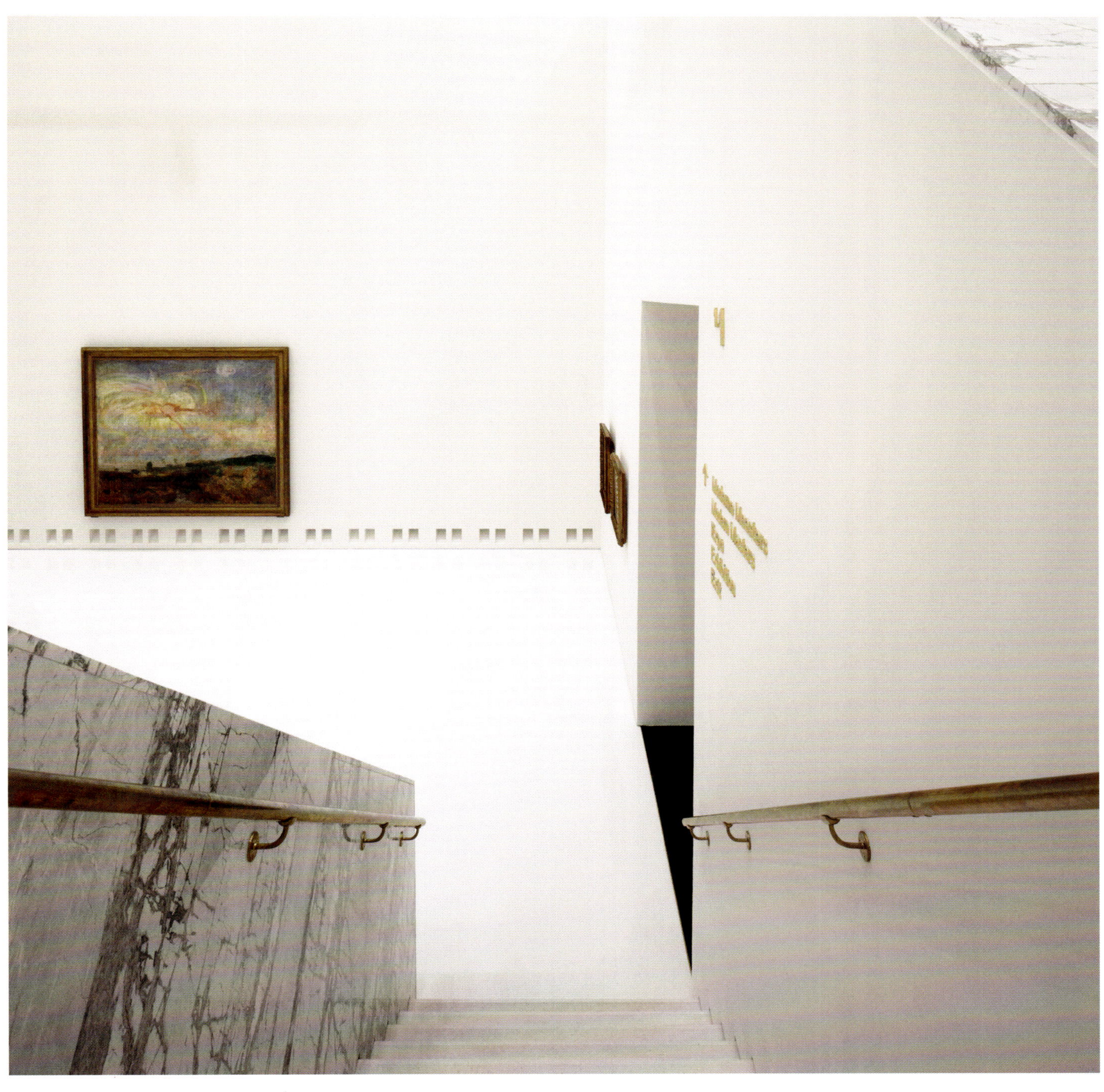

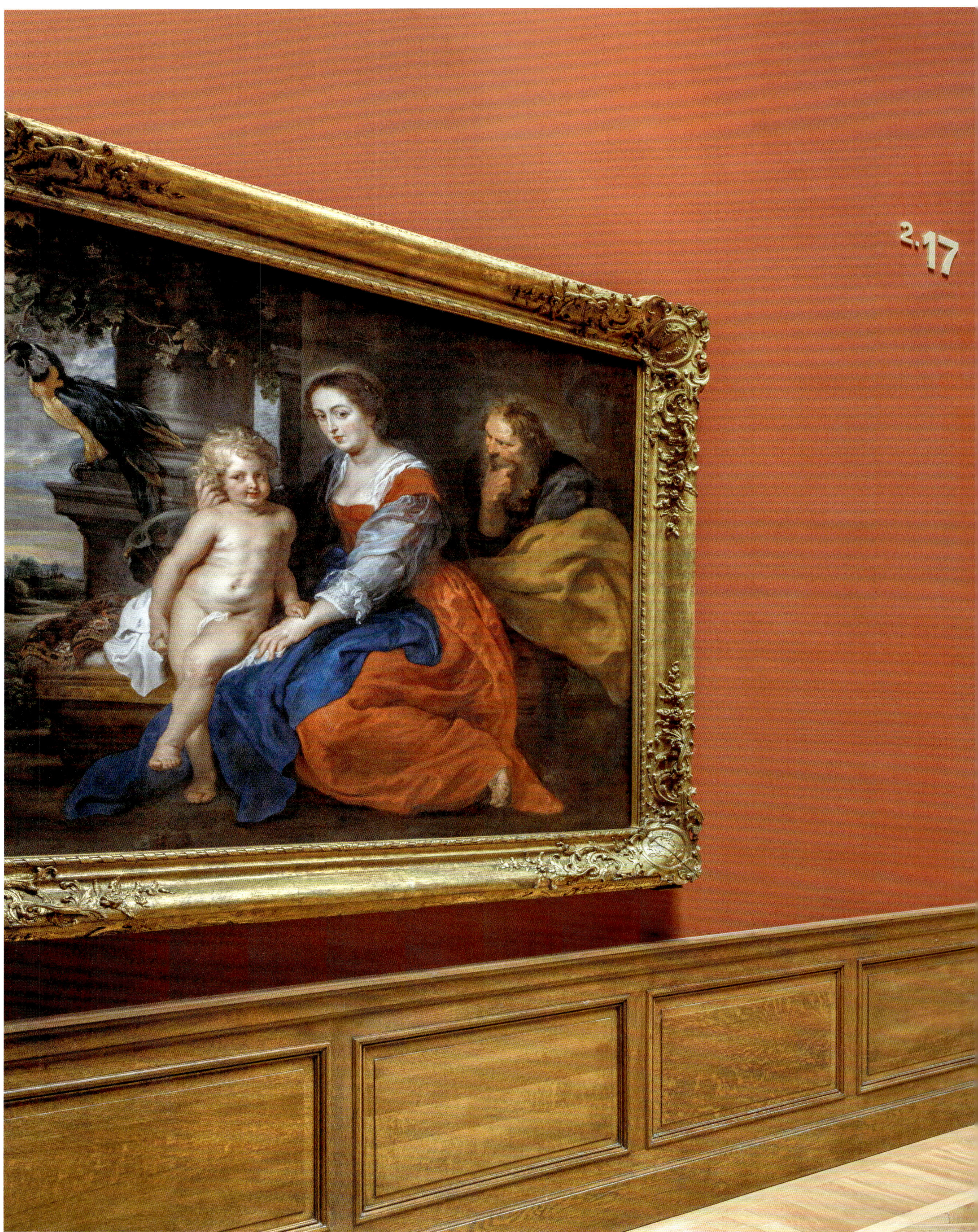
2.17

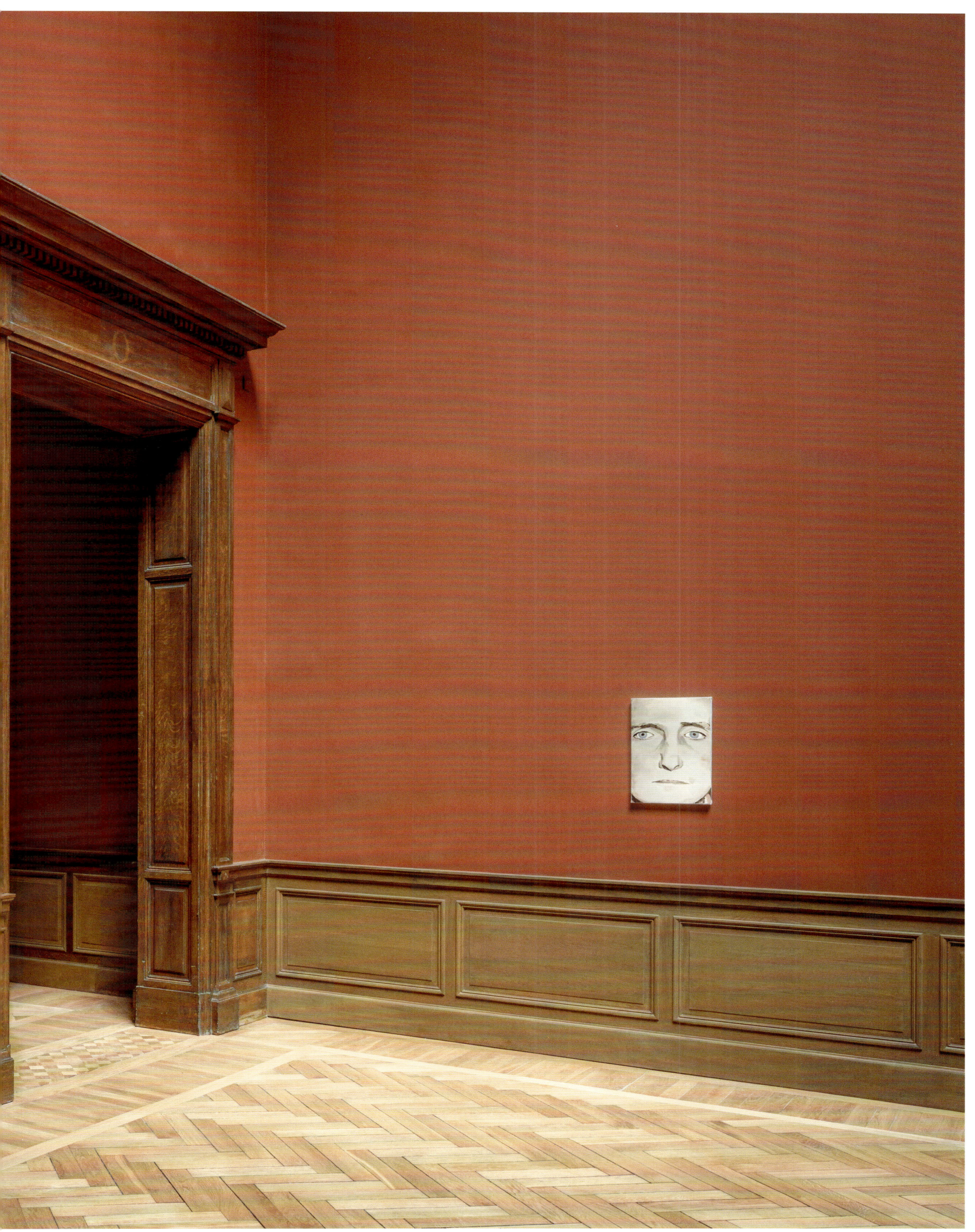

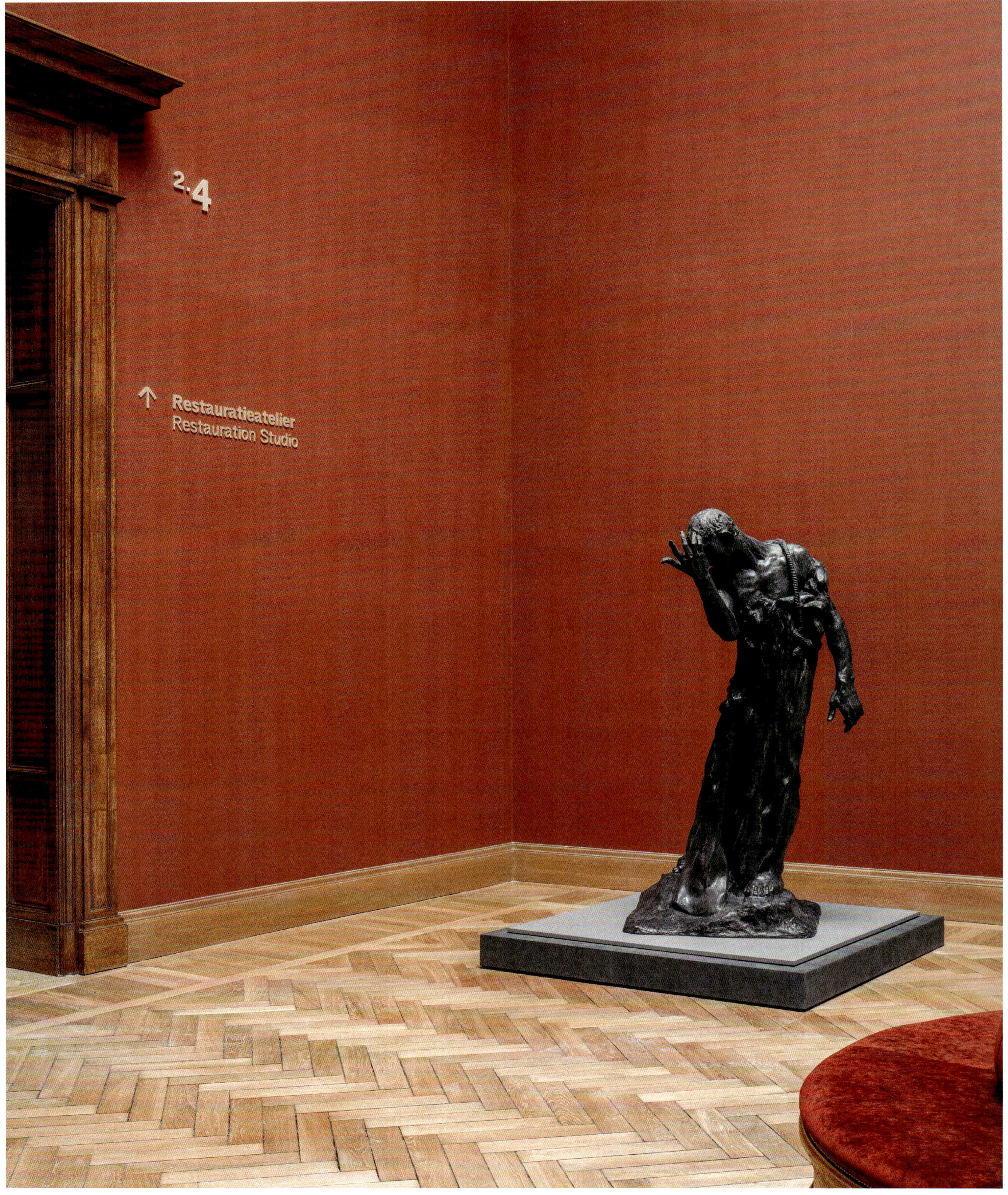
2.4
Restauratieatelier
Restauration Studio

4. INTENSIVE CARE: THE CONSERVATION STUDIO

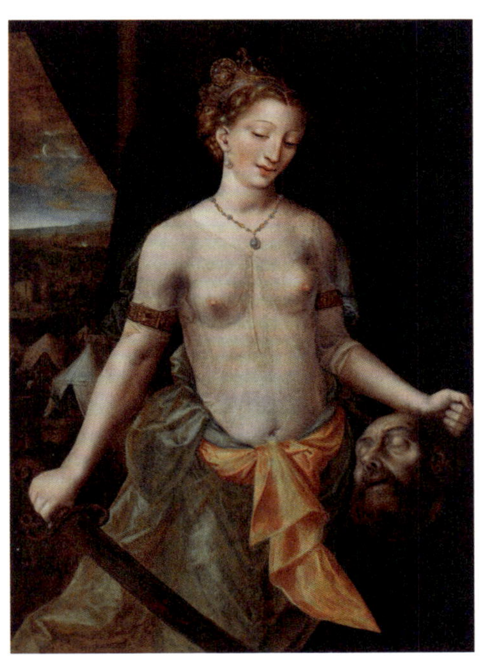

Jan Massys, *Judith*, c. 1554, oil on panel, 116 × 82.5 cm, inv. 5076. Restored with the support of Fonds Baillet Latour, 2015.

One of the prime responsibilities of cultural heritage institutions such as the KMSKA is to preserve the treasures in the best possible condition for future generations. This mission fits in seamlessly with another aim of the museum: to give contemporary audiences the best quality access to the artworks. That is why all the works on show in the new KMSKA have been recently treated. A great advantage of the long period of closure was that it gave us the time needed for ambitious and long-term projects. The work carried out in the studio ranges from extensive restorations, which attempt to return a work to the original intention of the artist, to conservation treatments, which are intended to prevent deterioration. The work is done by both in-house restorers and external parties, with the help of many partners.

Top condition

Let's step back in time to 1999, long before the museum closed in 2011. That is the year when the KMSKA established its own conservation studio, at the behest of its director at the time, Dr Paul Huvenne. From then until this year (2022), almost 200 restorations have been completed. Hundreds of works are inspected every year – in-house and on-site – or receive minor treatment. Frames are treated or replaced, framing is improved, weak wooden panels are reinforced. Works that go out on loan must be in top condition. The studio also ensures that they can be transported safely. Initially, the KMSKA studio treated only paintings, but now it also preserves sculptures, works on paper and, last but not least, picture frames.

A number of KMSKA works were restored by conservators from other museums during the closure. In today's museum world, this is often part of a barter deal; the KMSKA loans a work on the condition that it will be restored by the museum borrowing it before it is exhibited there. For example, this happened recently with Rubens' painting *Venus Frigida* and his portrait of the Antwerp city jurisconsult Jan Gaspard Gevartius. Those two works (among others) were treated by the J. Paul Getty Museum in the US.

Gwen Borms is Head of the conservation studio and Dr Nico Van Hout is Head of Collection Research. Both are also conservators. Gwen Borms: "Everything starts with good conservation – that's how you prevent restorations. It is an evolution that I also see in the newest generation of conservators: they find active and preventive conservation very important, and that includes maintaining an optimal climate in your storage depot. To do the job of a conservator, it's important that you have a passion for art, of course, but also for research and how it's evolving. As a conservator, you have to be able to apply that research to art. This is very different from the past, when restorers were often painters themselves, and would adapt parts that they felt were not perfect." Nico Van Hout: "The restoration world has indeed undergone a major professionalisation in recent decades. It has evolved from being a craft to a profession with many scientific elements."

Chain of knowledge

Gwen Borms: "Multidisciplinary collaboration between art historians, conservators and universities is a key factor in this evolution. Conservation is also a collaborative effort, contrary to the image you often see of the conservator working in solitude. Working together minimises the margin for error. Archival and provenance research are also important. In this way you can find out the reasons why a work is in a certain condition. *Judith* by Jan Massys – which I restored – was resold and subjected to quick repairs many, many times. That work was a textbook example of what can go wrong during the life of a painting. *Judith* was covered in drips of a very aggressive product that corroded the paint.

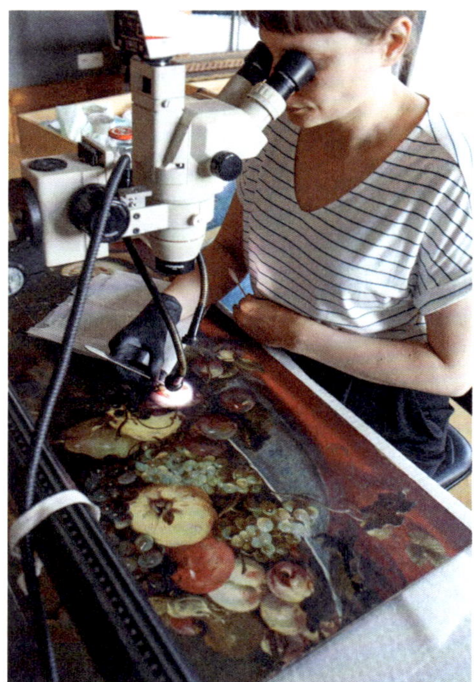

Restorer at work. Frans Snijders, *Still Life*, oil on wood, 58.5 × 83 cm, inv. 907. Restoration thanks to the support of players of the National Lottery, 2022.

In addition, the artist himself used unstable and often relatively cheap pigments that have lost their colour over time. Large parts were painted over to conceal the degradation and damage. In addition, the painting was hung in a 19th-century frame that clashed with the work, so we replaced it with a historically correct frame."

Nico Van Hout: "Thanks to the presence of in-house art historians and conservators here at KMSKA, we have a great deal of knowledge about the collection, in terms of content as well as regarding material-technical aspects. Moreover, we also have people here who translate the research to a wide audience across all possible communication channels. Every employee is part of the knowledge chain. That's a very powerful instrument. The outcome of restorations is shared in exhibitions, publications, lectures, the website, the *ZAAL Z* magazine. We make the collection accessible to visitors, internet surfers and readers."

The whole world in Antwerp

Antwerp, Brussels, Paris, Seville, Palermo, Cologne, Hildesheim, Berlin, Dresden, Tallinn, Krakow, Cuzco, Mumbai: it sounds like a list of cities that you might visit if you were going on a world trip. These are actually the names of places with universities that have sent students to the KMSKA conservation studio in recent years. These future conservators are attracted by the collection or by the reputation of the studio. They restore or conserve art objects or examine the deeper layers of paintings; each project can be completed during an internship period. While in the studio, the students also gain in-depth insight into the latest trends, such as reversible techniques, for example. Gwen Borms: "This involves using materials that can be easily removed, so that the difference with the original remains clear. For example, we don't fill cracks with oil paint, even if it's an oil painting. It will discolour and become so hard that it's difficult to remove such a layer again."

"These young people also bring with them the experience and knowledge of their own teachers. This intensive exchange ensures a global cross-fertilisation of knowledge. People from all over the world have come here to study restoration, especially if we include the trainees too: from France, Spain, Italy and Bolivia, from Estonia, Japan and India. This way you get an exchange between the knowledge that we've built up over more than 20 years of restoration and all of the education programmes our students come from." Nico Van Hout: "Actually, the conservation studio is a kind of mini-university, a knowledge centre. We are proud to be working together so well with all these top restorers. And also with the University of Antwerp, to get specific scans that we can't do ourselves."

Shiny and new

Which recent KMSKA restorations would the restorers themselves like to put in the spotlight? It's a difficult choice to make for people who see 'their' paintings as 'their children'. Gwen Borms: "A memorable restoration for me was *The Pink Bows* by Paul Delvaux. That was an artwork that did not appeal to me at all. After the restoration, which was made possible thanks to the Friends of the KMSKA, it became much more mysterious. All the research on the use of varnish by Delvaux also made it more interesting for me. It offers a fascinating insight into the creative process."

Nico Van Hout: "With James Ensor's *The Oyster Eater*, the difference before and after restoration was phenomenal. It wasn't possible to understand the full meaning of this work until after restoration. Before, the work seemed a bit dingy and very 19th century. Now, it's considered a beacon of modernity. Jules Schmalzigaug's work also demonstrates a very significant difference before and after restoration. The freshness of image needed to interpret his art is clouded by the patina of varnish, which the work really can't tolerate."

Gwen Borms: "Because of layers of dirt and thick varnish, the painting *The Laundress* by Henry Van de Velde was a vague study in brown. Restoration revealed a work rich in contrasts and material experimentation. The play of light, in particular, was revived and you can now clearly see the various shapes again, like the sunflowers. It ended up on our list of key works in the collection: The Finest Hundred."

"With every restoration, you secretly hope to reveal something hitherto unknown. And on the anonymous *The Members of the Guild of the Old Crossbow of Mechelen*, we actually did: a crippled beggar tucked into the cloak of a bishop! A predecessor had painted over it during a previous restoration. Presumably to cover up the man, because his presence in the picture didn't fit the sensibilities of the time."

Nico Van Hout: "All our Rubens paintings were covered with a layer of dark brown varnish. You couldn't really figure out which colours he'd used, because the yellowing varnish always made the work appear much redder. With unrestored paintings, you tend to think that Rubens should have used a little more blue to balance out the picture. But that's the illusion created by the varnish. Each and every one of the restorations is a small miracle. Rubens' colour palette has an unparalleled vibrancy that was not visible in our collection before. Now, you can make even-handed comparisons between the already restored works here and paintings elsewhere."

The KMSKA has undergone a metamorphosis. And so has what is, after all, the ultimate purpose of a museum: the art. Thanks to all the intensive work being done behind the scenes. In the new museum, some of it will also be done in full view of the public: visitors will have the opportunity to watch the conservators as they work.

Paul Delvaux, *The Pink Bows*, 1937, oil on panel, 120.9 × 158.8 cm, inv. 2850, before and after restoration. With the support of the Friends of the KMSKA vzw, 2021.

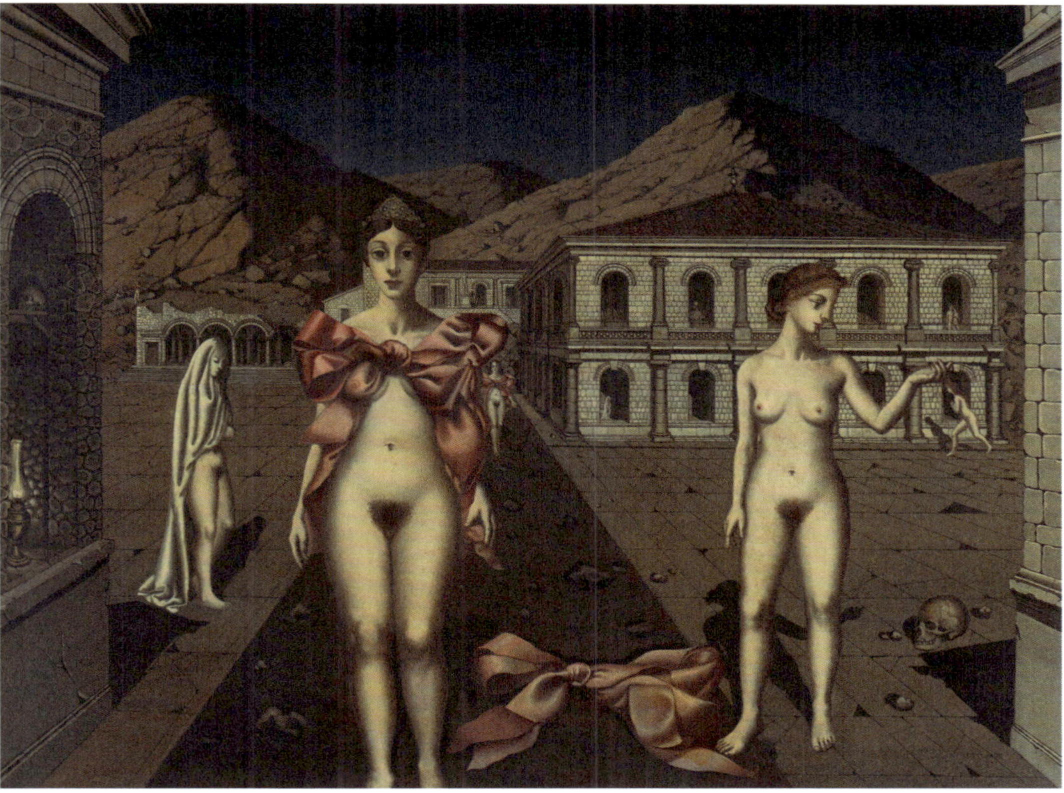

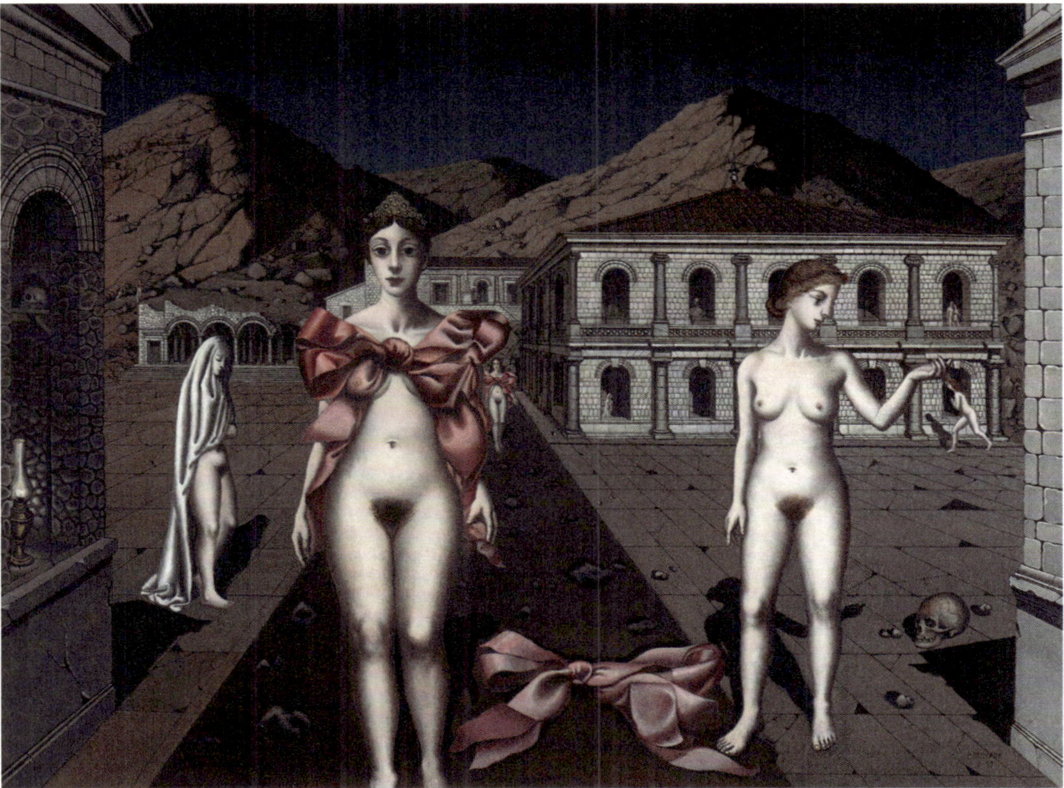

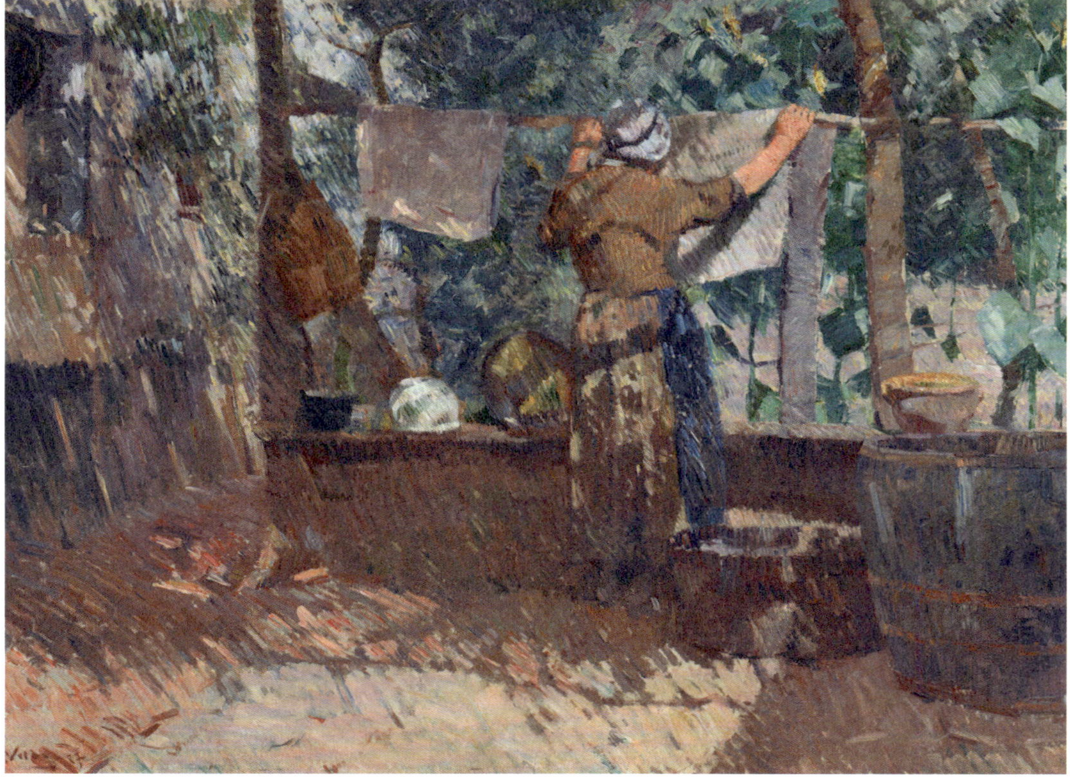

Henry Van de Velde, *The Laundress*, 1887, oil on canvas, 115.7 × 151 cm, inv. 2594, before and after restoration. With the support of Thomas Rabe, 2020.

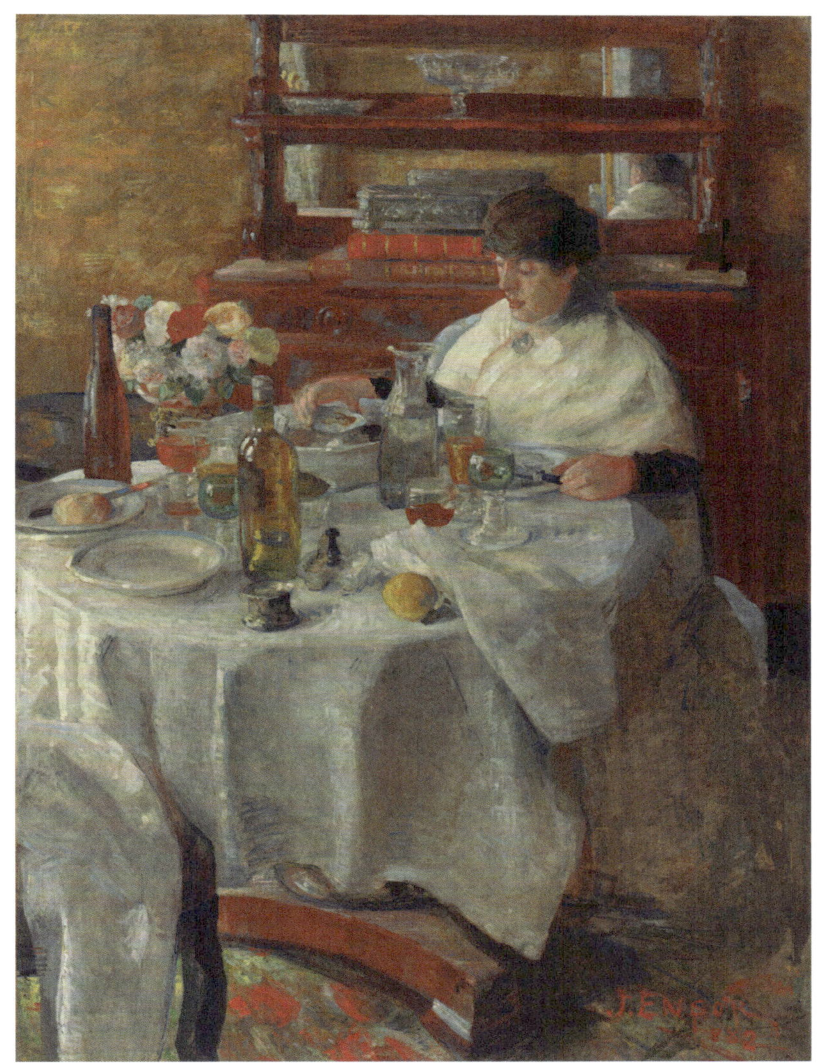

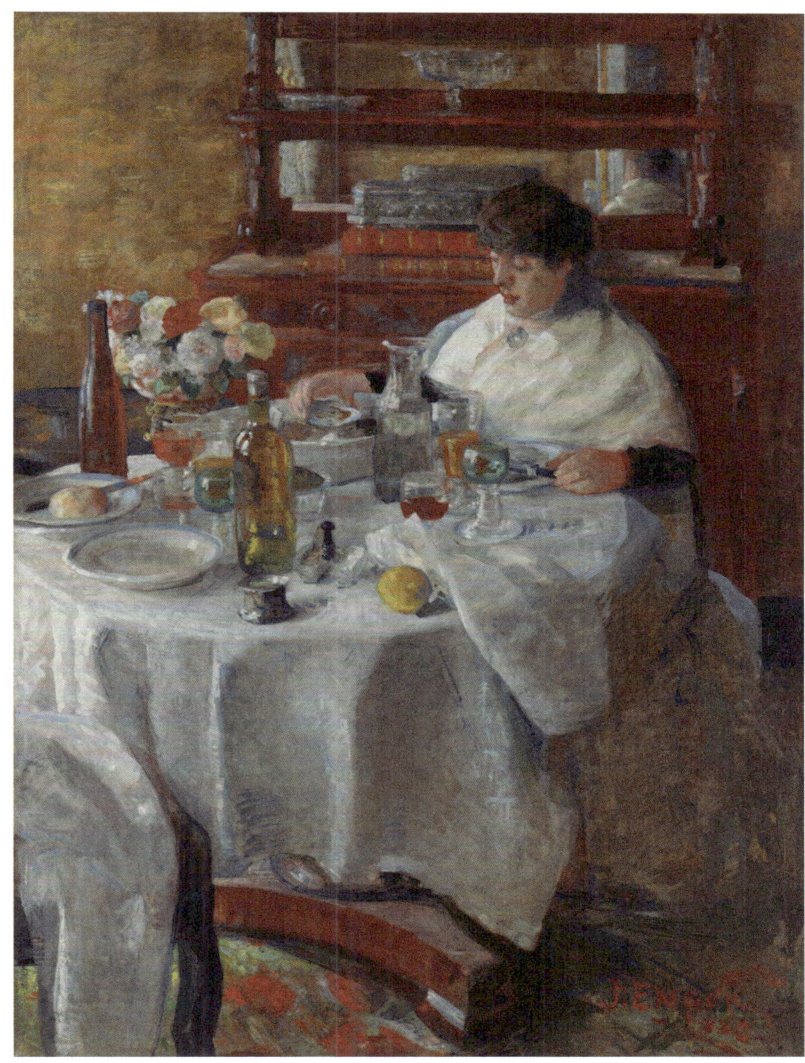

James Ensor, *The Oyster Eater*, 1882, oil on canvas, 153 × 208.2 cm, inv. 2073, before and after restoration. With the support of Fonds Baillet Latour, 2020.

The conservation studio collaborates with and receives support from numerous partners, including: Fonds Baillet Latour, the Belgian National Lottery, Léon Courtin-Marcelle Bouché Fund and Fonds Jacques Bollens (both managed by the King Baudouin Foundation). The Friends of the KMSKA and various private sponsors have also made funds available for restoration projects.

People visit museums to see the art. They tend to overlook the frames, which are a key component of that art where paintings are concerned. It's part of the museum's job to provide pictures with beautiful, suitable and, when necessary, appropriately restored frames.

Theo Van Rysselberghe,
Maria Sèthe, the Future Mrs Henry Van de Velde, 1891, oil on canvas,
118.5 × 86 cm (including frame),
inv. 2690

Mariane Van Obbergen, restorer:
"A picture frame may have various functions. The frame protects the painting and is also an aesthetic extension of the work. Ideally, the colour and shape match the artwork. Traditionally, the frames are chosen by collectors, art dealers or curators, but artists have also been known to design them themselves. In that case, the frame takes on a prominent role and becomes part of the overall concept. *Maria Sèthe* by Theo Van Rysselberghe is a good example. The artist continues the pointillist painting technique in the inner frame, using dots in a complementary colour. The portrait is framed in a modest, gilded outer frame with a grey inner border. The guidelines for the framer can still be seen: "*Prière de faire mettre ce ton ci = un peu plus sombre serait préférable*." ('Please use this tone here = a little darker would be preferable.') In this way, Van Rysselberghe has created an inseparable link between the work and the frame. During the restoration of the frame, missing pieces in the gilded outer frame were replaced and colour-matched. The frame has also been cleaned as evenly as possible, so that the whole achieves a harmony again."

Nicaise De Keyser,
Baroness Adelaïde Vanden Hecke-Baut de Rasmon, 1863,
oil on canvas lined on panel,
173 × 110 cm (including frame),
inv. 1043

This elegant portrait of a woman was placed in a very striking oval frame, elaborately worked and full of references to the important legacy of the model, Baroness

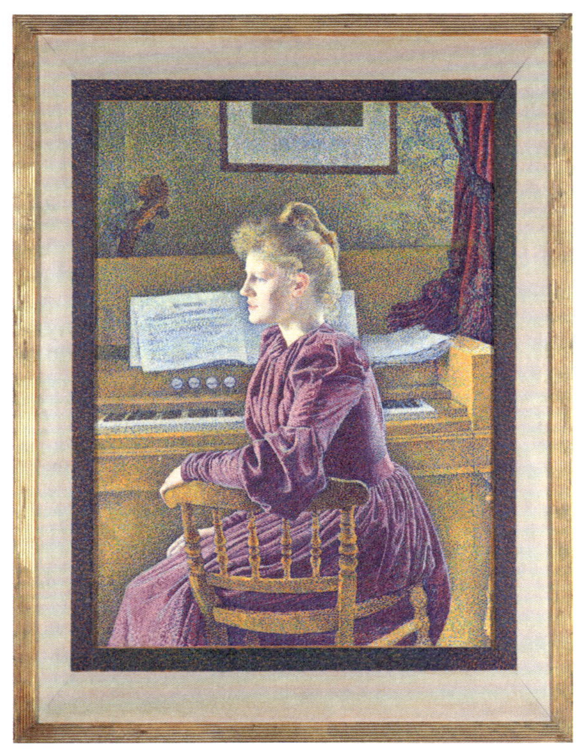

Theo Van Rysselberghe, *Maria Sèthe, the Future Mrs Henry Van de Velde*, with pointillist painting technique continued on to the frame.

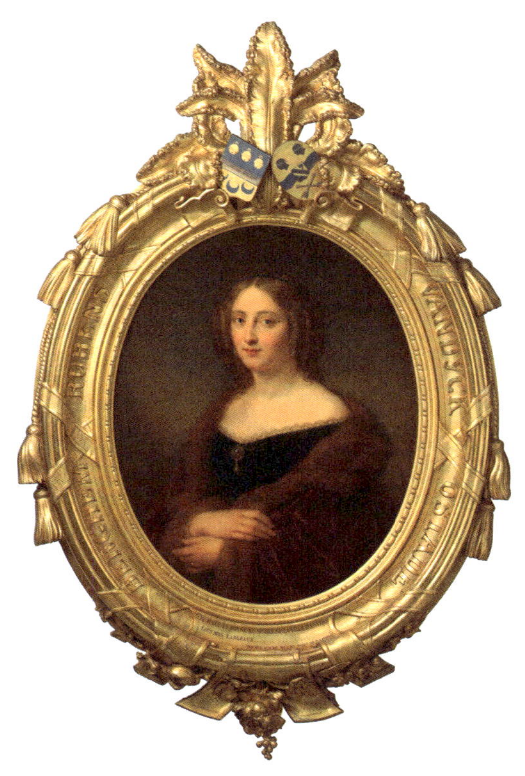

Nicaise De Keyser, *Barones Adelaïde Vanden Hecke-Baut de Rasmon.* Missing pieces in the ornamentation were recreated using an epoxy paste.

Adelaïde Vanden Hecke-Baut de Rasmon. At the top are the family arms and at the bottom a quote from the will. Mariane Van Obbergen: "Restoring this 19th-century frame with its many curlicues was a real challenge. Missing pieces in the ornamentation were recreated using an epoxy paste that is easy to work with after it hardens. The new pieces were gilded, to integrate them harmoniously with the whole. Loose ornaments were stabilised, and the entire surface was cleaned. The Baroness is ready to shine again."

Lucas Cranach the Elder,
Caritas, (1540), oil on wood,
64.1 × 48.2 cm (including frame),
inv. 43

Lies Vanbiervliet, restorer: "This masterpiece was restored in 2020. It no longer has its original frame. In the past, works of art in museums were often all set in one particular kind of frame, to suit the fashion of the time. In the case of the KMSKA, these are the so-called Paalman frames. The Brussels frame maker Paalman provided many works with a frame consisting of a gilded inner and outer frame, separated by a decorated flat frieze. The Paalman frame of this *Caritas* was deemed unsuitable, which is why the museum went in search of a more historically justified frame. Recycling was the option we chose – the gilded and decorated flat frieze has been given a new, dark finish. The result is a simple wooden frame. It's not only in very good taste, it also suits a painting from the 16th century much better."

Joachim Beuckelaer,
Vegetable Market, 1567,
oil on wood, 169 × 237 cm
(within frame),
inv. 5045

Eva van Zuien, conservator: "Before the recent restoration, Beuckelaer's vegetable market had a non-original, gilded frame. It was in poor condition and also didn't match the painting aesthetically. Frame maker Bart Welten has made a new frame that better reflects the time period of the original: dark with gilded edges. That has contributed significantly to the total metamorphosis of the painting."

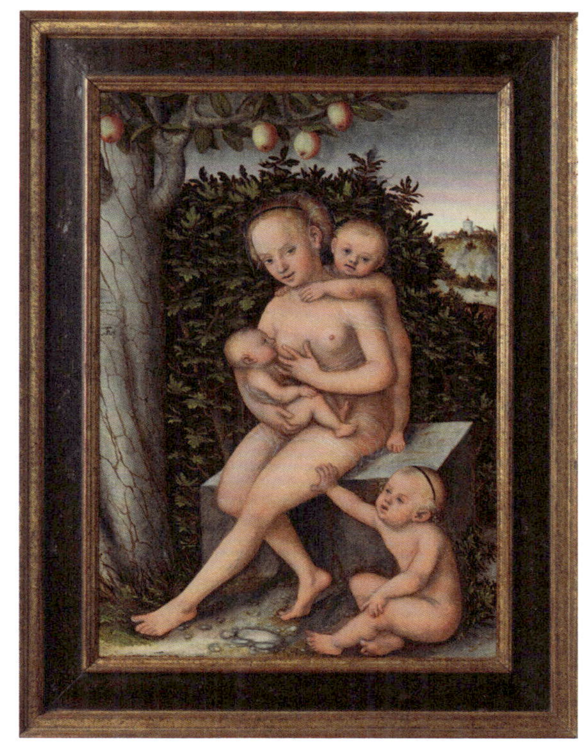

Lucas Cranach I, *Caritas*,
with a recycled 'Paalman frame'.

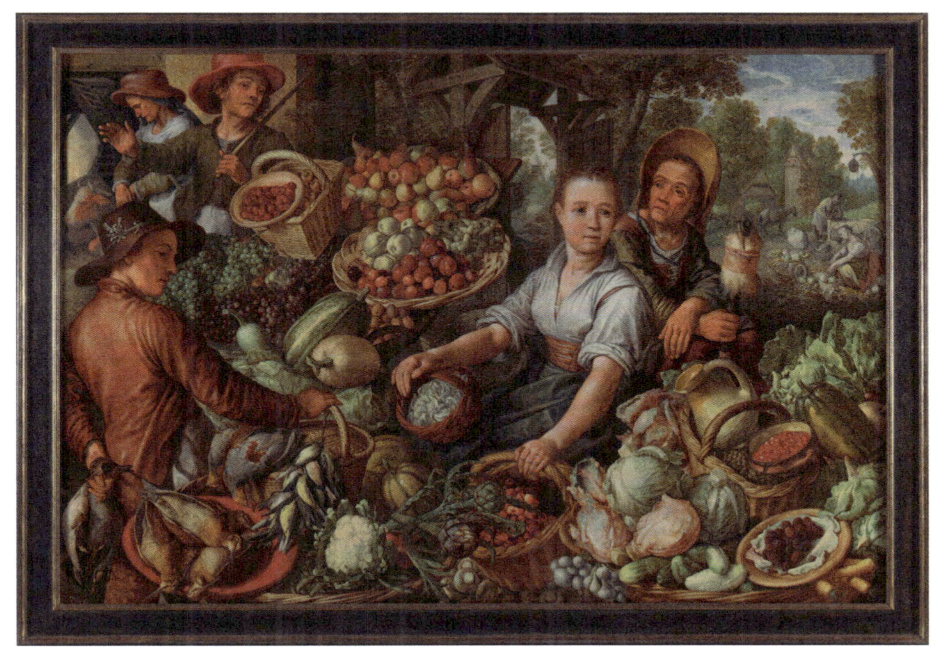

A new frame for Joachim Beuckelaer, *Vegetable Market.*

5. THE INVISIBLE BASELINE: THE LIGHT AND CLIMATE OF THE MUSEUM

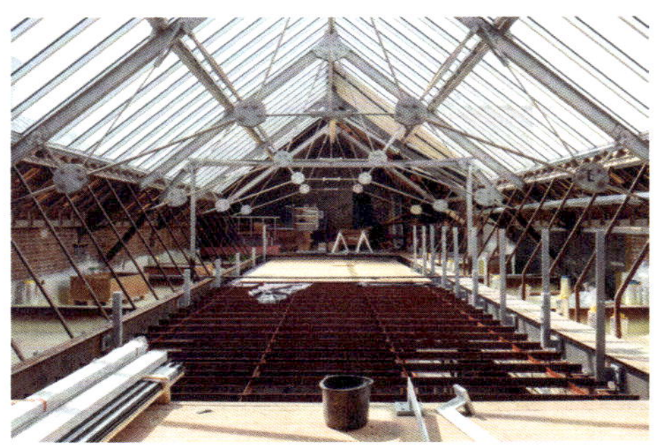

The 19th-century museum is a daylight museum. Two blinds above the glass ceiling regulate the amount of light that enters the building.

1977: The KMSKA is – finally – going to have a climate control system worthy of the name and also (in 1976) electric lighting for the first time. By no coincidence, 1977 is the great Rubens anniversary year.

2019: The new masterplan includes a new climate control system and an improved 'light show'. Visitors will not be aware of it: the system will be hidden from view. The interior climate and, of course, lighting are crucial for a museum, for its collection and for the visitor experience.

The light of day

Walter Hoogerwerf, Project Leader at KAAN Architecten and designer of the climate and lighting plan for the KMSKA, about the light in the historic museum: "The late 19th-century building is being restored as a monument, which also includes the way daylight is allowed to enter the building. We went back to the initial design as our starting point. We are particularly pleased that we were able to retain this aspect, it really is intrinsic to the building: the dimensions and proportions of the museum spaces and the skylights were fashioned entirely around the daylight coming in. The new volume is also a daylight museum, and there too the way in which we bring light into the room is proportional. But there we worked with light measurements and computer simulations to create a similar light quality in a more modern way."

It is a familiar discussion in the world of museums: how should daylight and artificial light interact? As ideas about the conservation of objects and exhibition scenography develop, artificial light is starting to gain precedence over daylight, sometimes. Sustainability thinkers, however, tend to see the construction of spaces with daylight as an investment in the future. Alex Ockhuysen, an engineer at Royal HaskoningDHV, made the technical translation of the design. "In the case of the KMSKA, there was a lot of coordination with the architect about this issue. Naturally, we started at an early stage to look at how we could ensure the daylight experience would also match the conditions required to protect the collection. We incorporated studies on climate and light sensitivity of artworks in our light calculations. With the knowledge of these requirements and the orientation of the building, we were able to calculate how to bring in as much light as possible. Then we came up with a lighting design system in consultation with the architect."

Skylights

Daylight – a word that comes in many colours, literally. There are sunny days and cloudy days, days with bright winter light and days with fuzzy autumnal light, colourful days and grey days. Walter Hoogerwerf: "In the 19th-century museum, we can regulate the amount of light that comes in with two screens that slide open and closed above the glass ceiling. We can use these to temper the surplus of daylight on the sunniest days. This optimises the visitor experience and the conservation of the artworks. When you walk through the museum, you still feel the effect of the outdoor light. In many contemporary museums, this is not the case and you find yourself in a box where the light is completely under control; each room is practically identical. Here, there is a great diversity of lighting situations. As architects, that was very important to us. You experience a building not only through its dimensions, but also through the lighting and acoustics."

The 198 skylights provide a divers array of light experiences.

The word *daylight* had been used up to this point. It would be more accurate to say *northern light*. Because that is the light that enters the new museum through the 198 skylights on its roof. As is well known, this is also the light that artists prefer to have in their studios. Walter Hoogerwerf: "We wanted a maximum of northern light, as it is the best light by which to view works of art. The skylights are positioned as 'light grabbers' facing exactly north. By angling the slope of the glass just so, we succeed in avoiding direct sunlight and only capturing indirect light. We have shaped the light grabbers in such a way that they guide the light downwards while diffusing it. It is abundantly present on the top floor, but thanks to the four, 23-metre, floor-to-ceiling open spaces created in the former patios, the indoor gardens of the museum, daylight also reaches the lowest floor of the new wing. Owing to the distance it travels from the top to the bottom, it becomes very soft and diffuse. Using their scientific knowledge, Alex and his colleagues have ensured that our skylights, aesthetic objects in their own right, not only look beautiful but also produce the right amount of light and light incline. The reflection of the white floors on the upper level of the new museum also contributes to a beautiful and even distribution of light on the walls."

A breath of fresh air for the artworks

And then there's climate control: regulating temperature and humidity to meet specified standards. These systems need equipment that can be real eyesores in museum spaces. Navigating that aspect also required rather intense collaboration during the construction and restoration of the KMSKA. Walter Hoogerwerf: "Climate control systems take up a lot of space in a museum. As an architect, I find it very important that this aspect is part of the thinking process regarding the structure of a building from the very beginning. We have constructed a new volume in the six patios of the historic museum, which also contains the installations that 'creates' the climate. We connected them to the entire museum through the two front patios, as well as from a separate floor solely occupied by technical equipment. I see the new museum as a kind of iron lung… it ensures that the climate in the entire building, including the old part, are in order. Alex and I spent many, many hours together integrating all of the elements."

Alex Ockhuysen: "Ventilation in particular receives far more attention today than in the past. We designed the ventilation system in the 19th-century museum in such a way that we target only the walls on which the artworks hang, with precisely guided fresh air. In other words: we only climatise the air around the artworks, not the entire space. By using this alternative approach, we have reduced the capacity to about half that of a traditional museum ventilation system. By controlling the climate with such precision, you also end up needing fewer large conduits and inlet openings. As a result, we were able to install the ducts and grids almost invisibly."

Colossal

When it comes to climate control, the renovation of the historic museum building could be seen as a kind of transplant: a new organ has been inserted into the old body. What was the biggest challenge in the conceptualisation and implementation? Alex Ockhuysen: "The combination of unknown factors that you have to deal with. You have a building that's been used for several generations, and to which things have been added over the years that are obstructing the process. One major thing was the removal of the asbestos."

Walter Hoogerwerf: "The diversity in this building is so enormous; it is also truly colossal, and the rooms are all very different. It was never going to be possible to apply one and the same principle to all the spaces. The next hall always turned out to be just that little bit different, and of course the blueprint you're looking for can never be found when you need it. Drawing on a huge reservoir of patience and by just continuing with the work, all the galleries do have the same appearance in the end, but there are big differences in what's behind the walls. We were able to maintain the basic principle of integrating the installation as invisibly as possible, but it was a very demanding job. It would have been much easier to run the channels along the top of the cornice. I love that we're now extracting air from the room in the same place that they did in 1890: the perforated brass plates connected to the pitched roof are still there."

Unique in a person's career

And the last item: the climate control system in the new museum. Was it 'permission to do as you like' there? Alex Ockhuysen: "We chose to install a system in which two air flows – with different temperatures and humidity levels – mix in each room in such a way that the right conditions are achieved. This choice was made to minimise the risk of water leakage from the technical equipment to the museum rooms. You run that risk if you humidify or dehumidify locally. We housed all active parts of the climate control system in one central technical room, which minimises that risk as much as possible."

Walter Hoogerwerf: "In the historic museum, the air is blown in from above and descends along the wall, after which it is distributed throughout the entire room. The heat in the room causes the air to rise back up, and at the top it is recovered via grids surrounding the ceiling glass. For the new museum, Alex developed a system that introduces the air slowly through openings at the bottom of the wall and recovers it again in certain areas of the voids. Because those openings are visible, we planned them with an architect's critical eye. As a result, they have become almost invisible. The integration of technology and architecture at the KMSKA incorporates every last detail."

The proof of the pudding is in the eating: how do you know that your system works properly without exposing works of art to the test? Alex Ockhuysen: "You do that by experimenting. A sufficiently long testing period is very important. The climate requirements for proper conservation of the artworks mean, for example, that you have to turn on heat in the winter, and dehumidify and cool in the summer. The exterior conditions influence the installation, so you first have to monitor the circumstances across all seasons before you hang any artworks in the galleries." Walter Hoogerwerf: "And you adjust the system over the different seasons, until it has gathered so much data that it knows how to respond optimally to fluctuations."

Does working so intensively on a building for so many years mean you develop some sort of relationship with it? Alex Ockhuysen: "The museum in Antwerp really is my building now, yes, and I believe the same is true for Walter. We have kind of become interwoven with it. We will never experience a project of this magnitude or with this level of involvement again. It is unique in a person's career."

The climate control system directs controlled air into the galleries through rectangular recesses in the walls.

pp. 124–125: The skylights are positioned to face north, as 'light grabbers'. The angle of the glass directs the light downwards and creates a diffuse distribution of light.

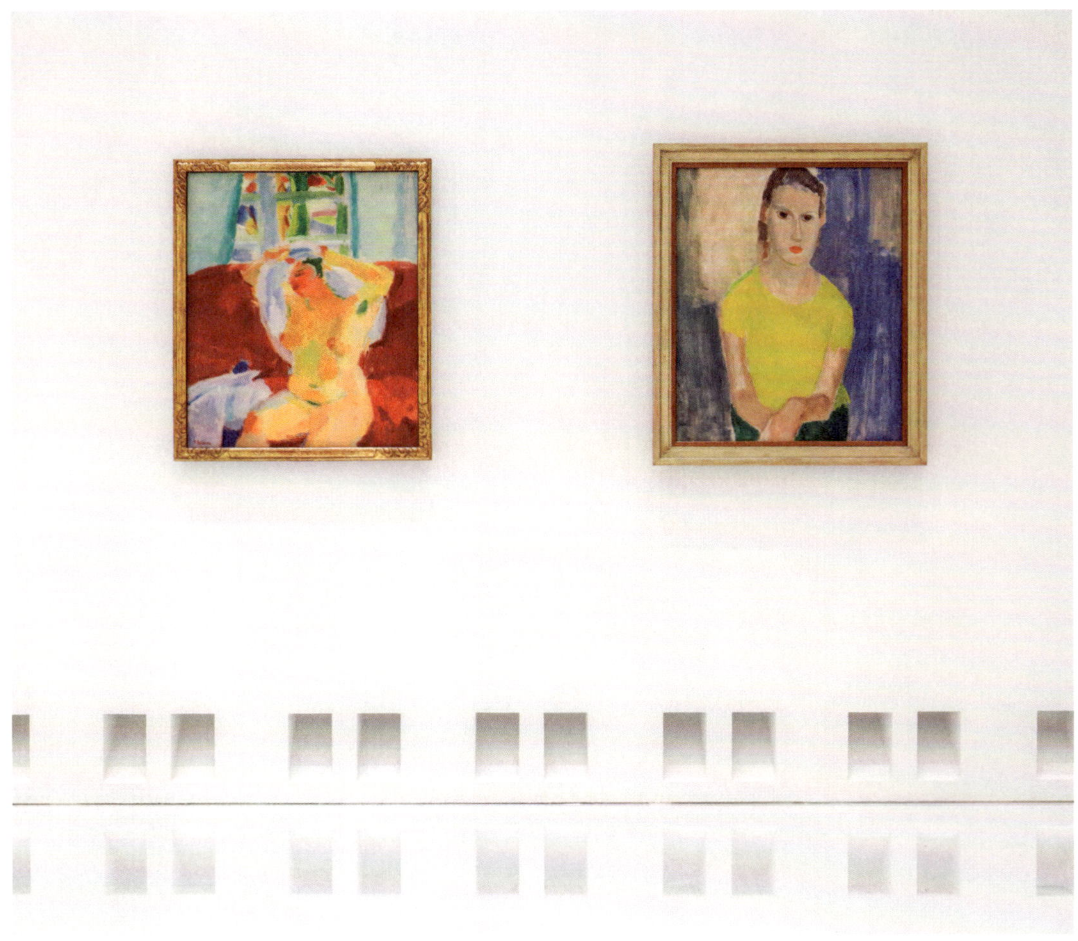

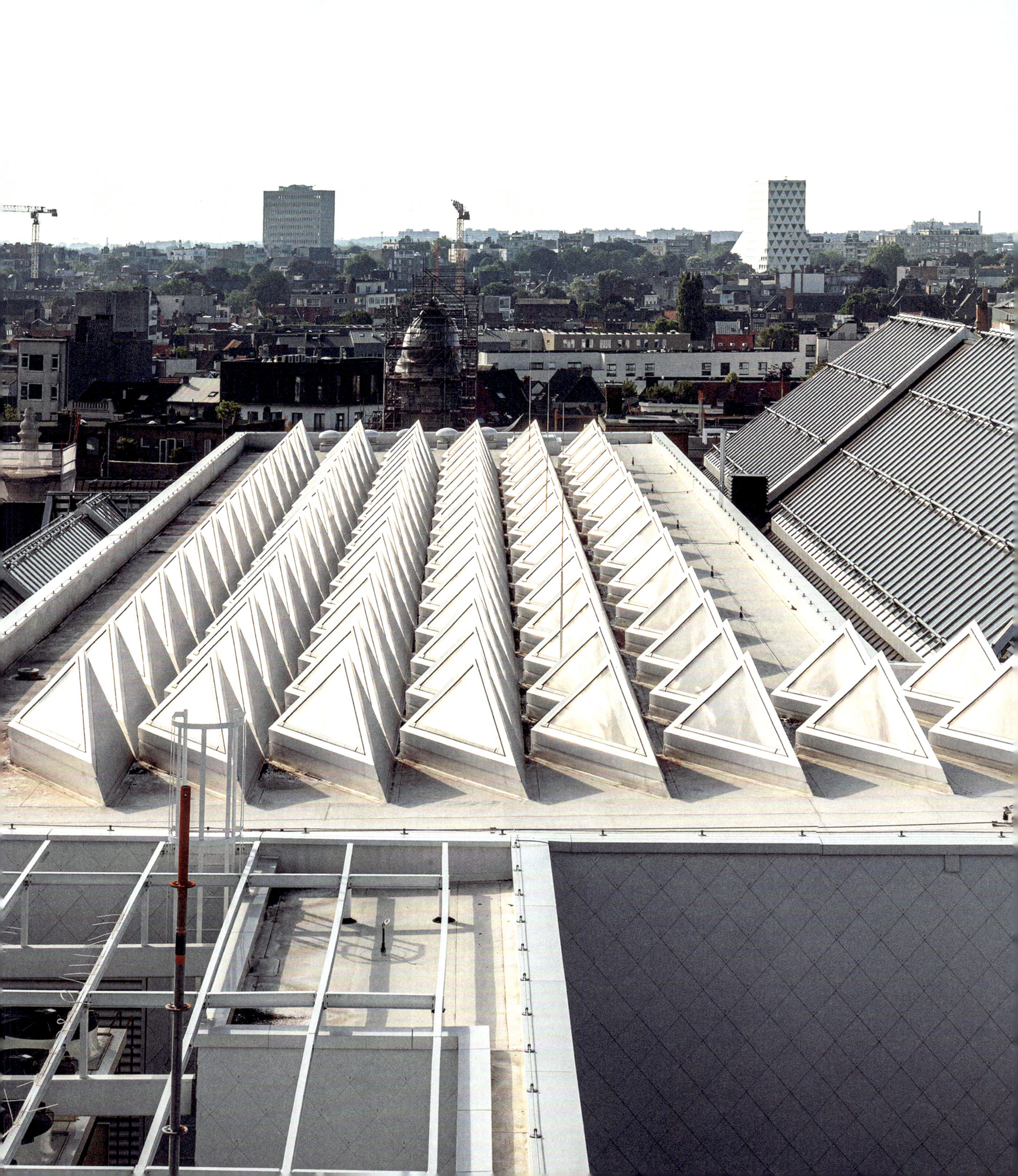

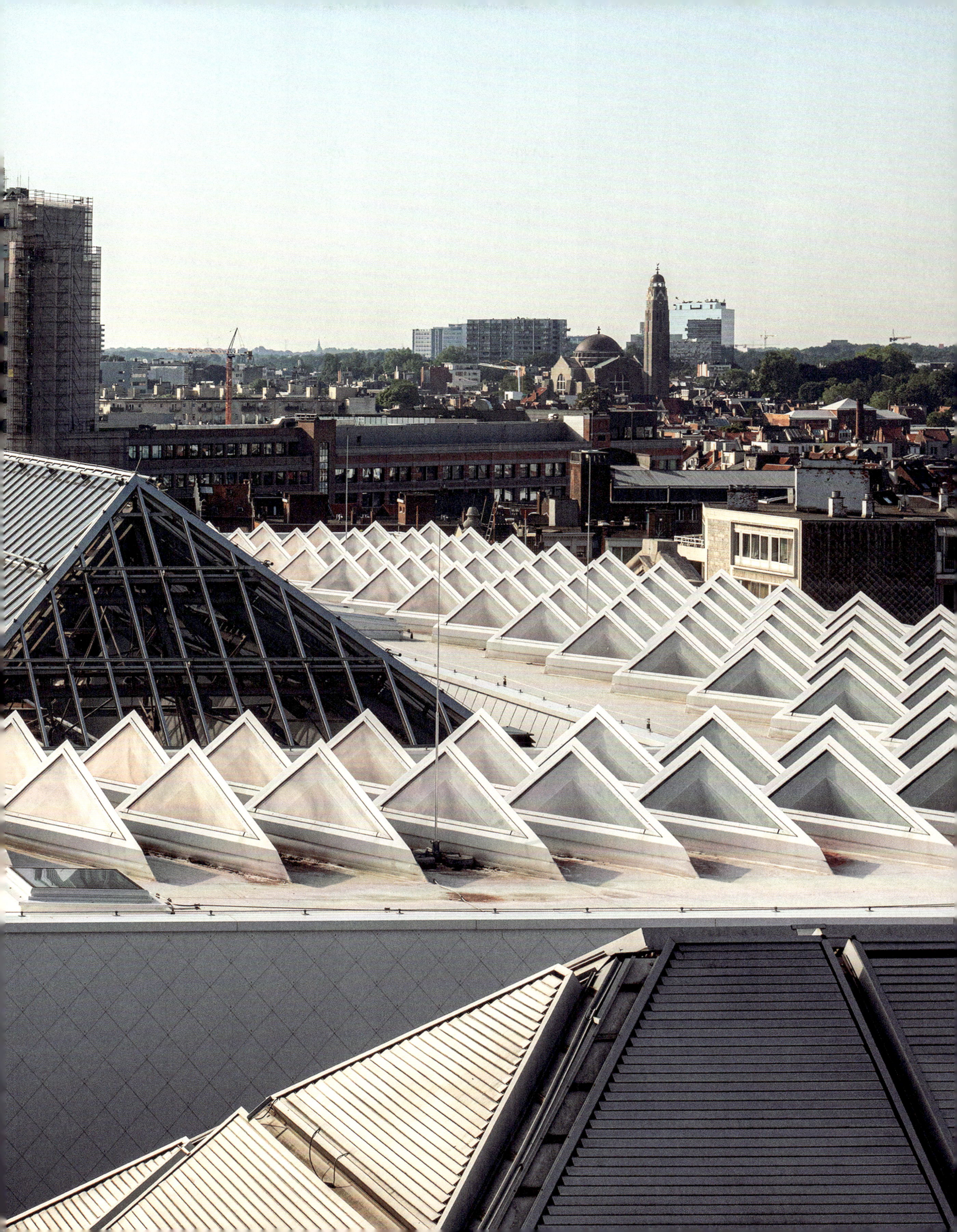

In addition to diligently controlling the climate and light conditions within its walls, an art museum will also take great care when moving and transporting its artworks. Take a 17th-century panel that measures, say, 4.5 by 3.4 metres and weighs more than 600 kilogrammes. Let's suppose that the work has been travelling and now has to be returned to its home in the museum. Or another scenario: a colossal work is coming to the KMSKA on loan from another museum. How do you go about that?

A fine art shipping specialist drives their climate-controlled and shock-resistant truck up to the loading dock of the KMSKA. This is situated at the back along the left façade on the Schildersstraat. The new loading dock measures 6.8 by 2.5 metres, can manage weights of up to 10,000 kilos, and was custom-built for the museum. It can reach a height of 2.5 metres and can also safely 'carry' art handlers. They can roll the artworks over the platform into the museum through a historic entrance.

They then arrive in a room that is part of the exhibition route. How can you prevent temperature fluctuations and flying insects (to name just a couple of concerns) in your other galleries? Architect Dikkie Scipio devised what you could call a 'spinning wall', which pivots on its own vertical axis. If you rotate the wall so that it crosses the room, one part of the gallery is immediately sealed off from the rest of the museum circuit.

In the gallery where artworks enter the museum is an elevator, which transports them inside the museum. It is 3.6 metres high, 4 metres wide and 5.4 metres deep. The elevator accesses all floors, in both the old and the new museum. It is so shock- and vibration-absorbent that you can't even feel it going up and down.

And there is still more ingenuity to come: because some doorways in the museum are too short for the monumental works to move through, slots have been built into the walls. That's how the artworks are moved from gallery to gallery – like posting an envelope through a letterbox. And to move works in and out of the storage depot, slim hatches have been installed in the parquet floors of the Rubens Gallery and its neighbour. When you open the hatch, you can hoist a painting up or down via a pulley mechanism – all thanks to the historic museum's original architects, Winders and Van Dijk.

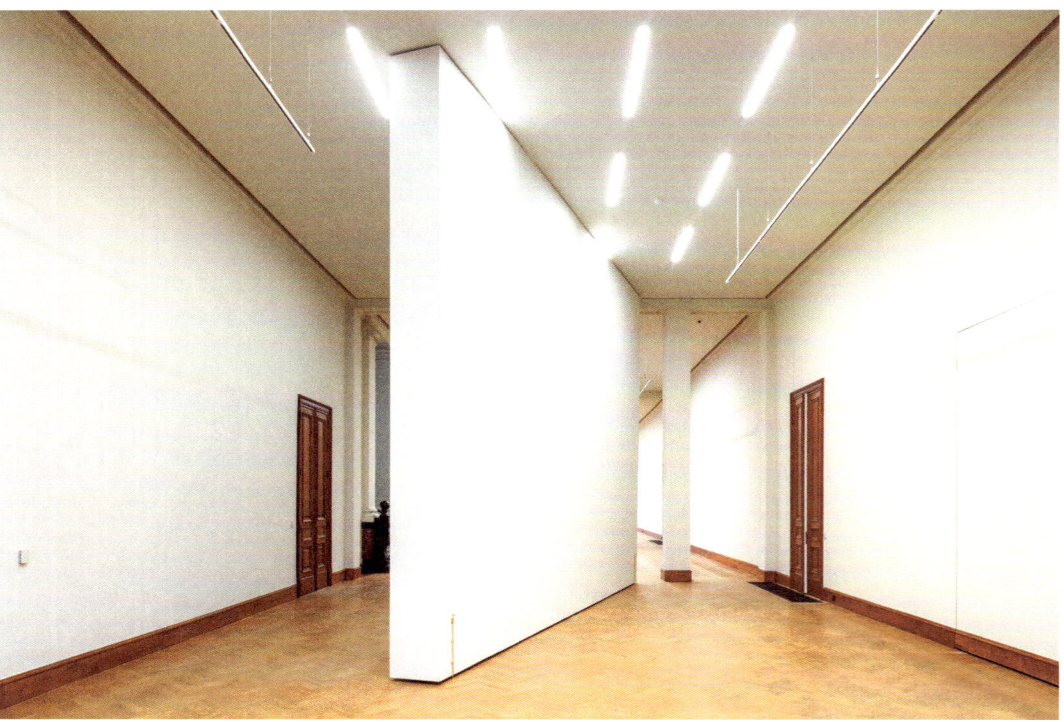

A wall that pivots on its own vertical axis can close off part of the gallery from the rest of the museum circuit.

The architects of the 19th-century museum constructed hatches in the floor of the Rubens Gallery. A hoisting contraption was used to raise or lower paintings through the gullies. This is how monumental paintings were brought to safety in 1939, before the start of World War II.

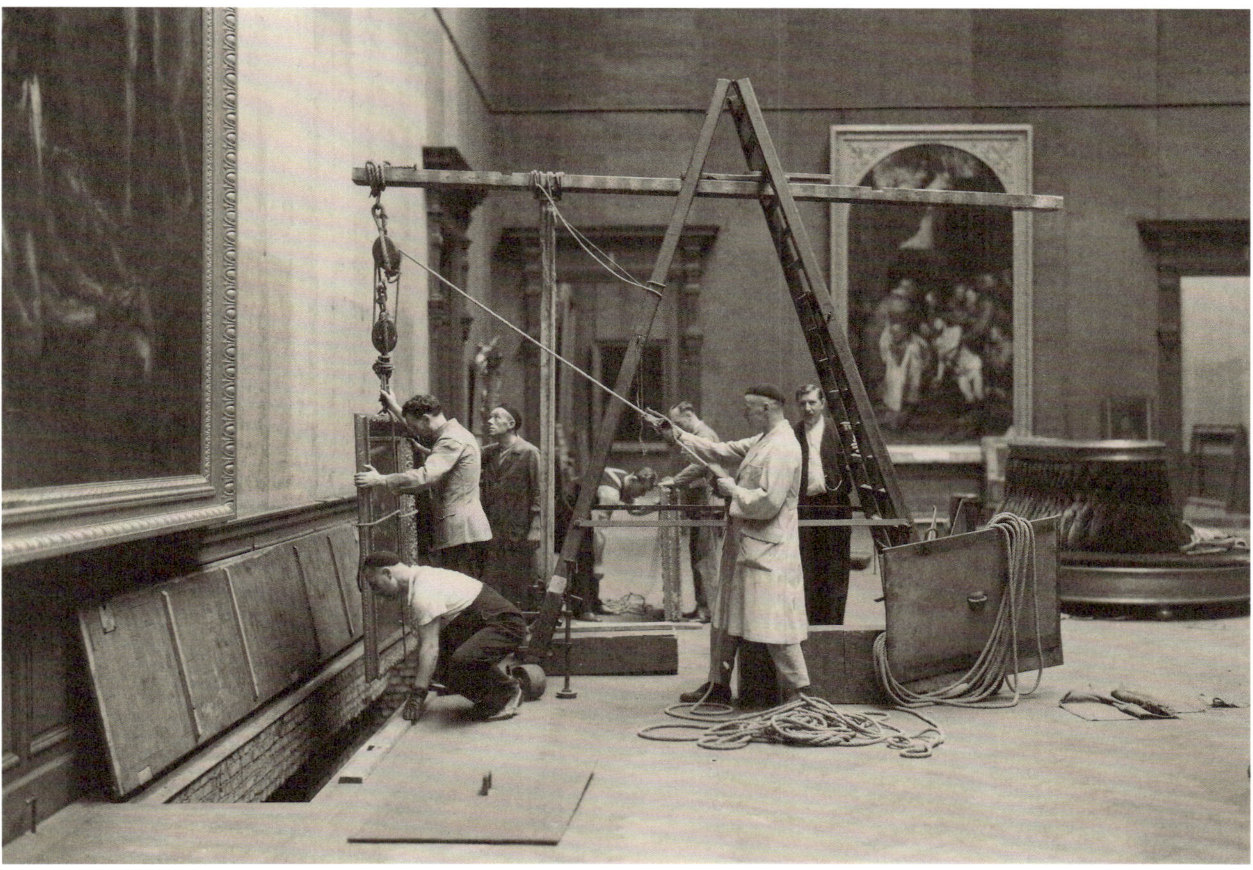

The same hatches are still in use today.

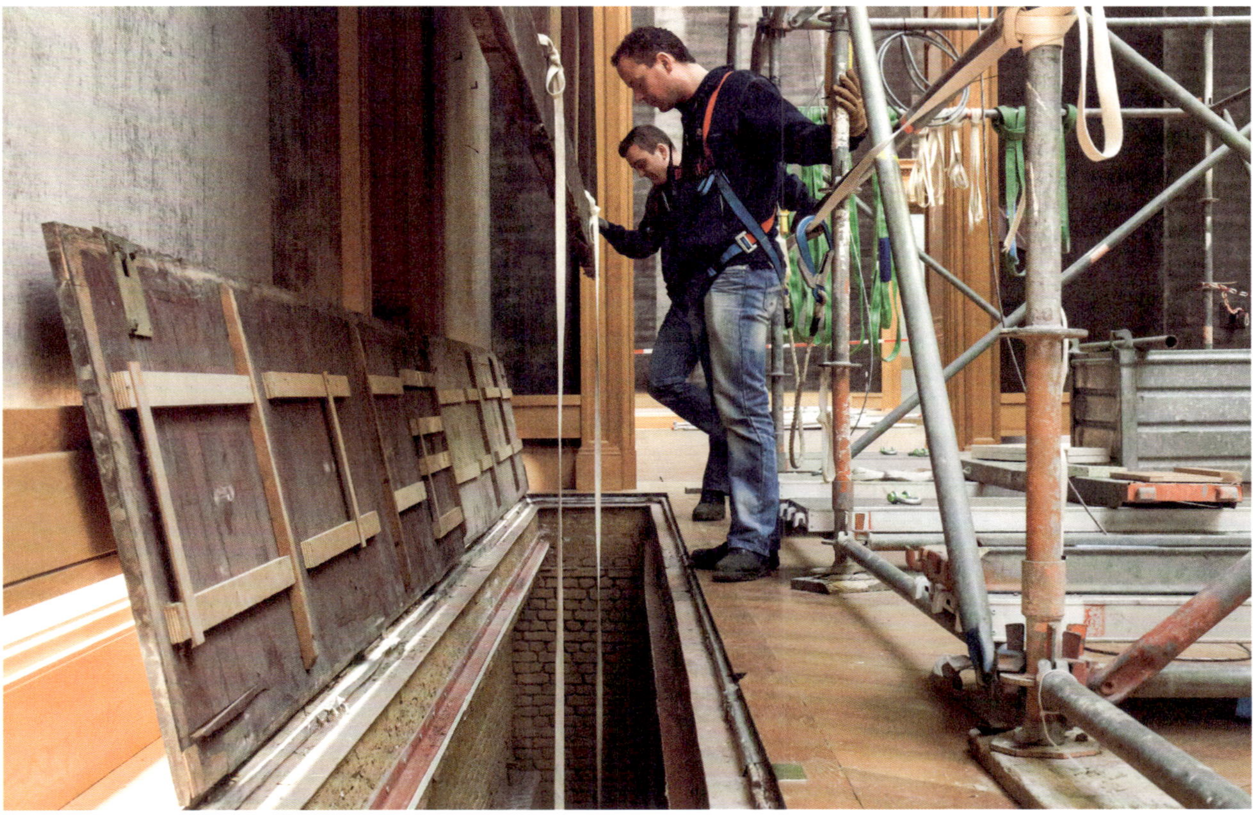

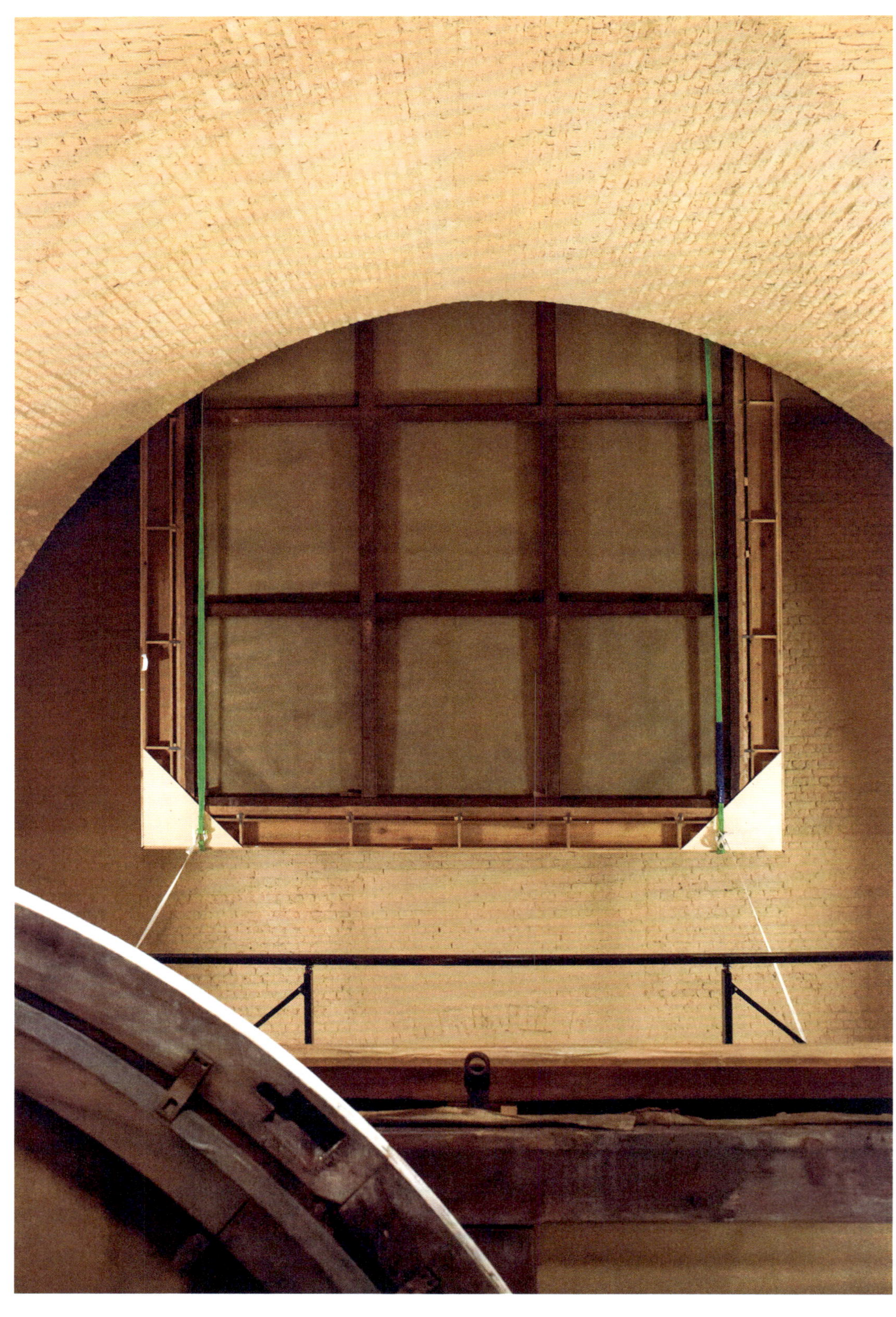

An altarpiece makes its way down through the gully to the storage depot, which is below the Rubens Gallery.

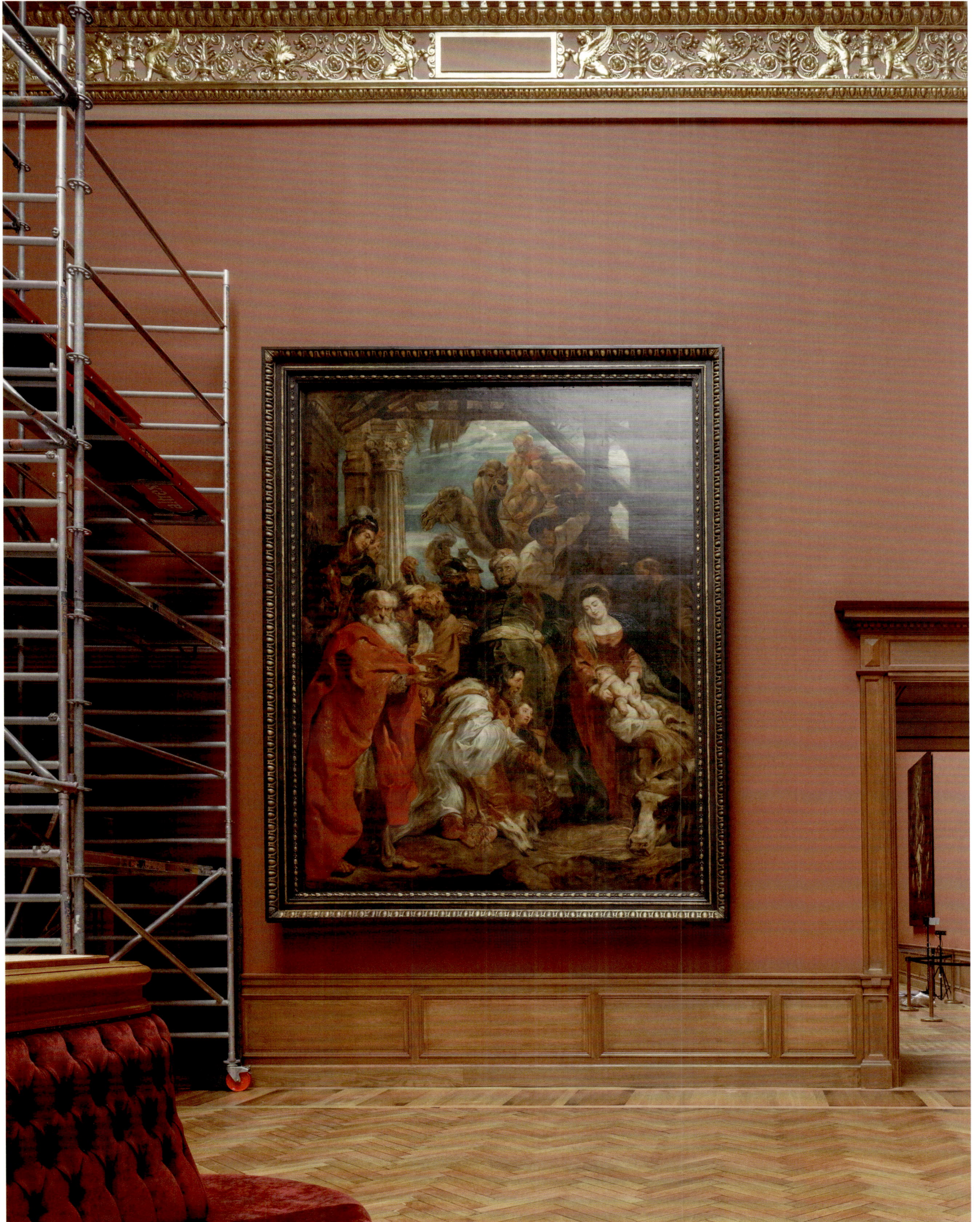

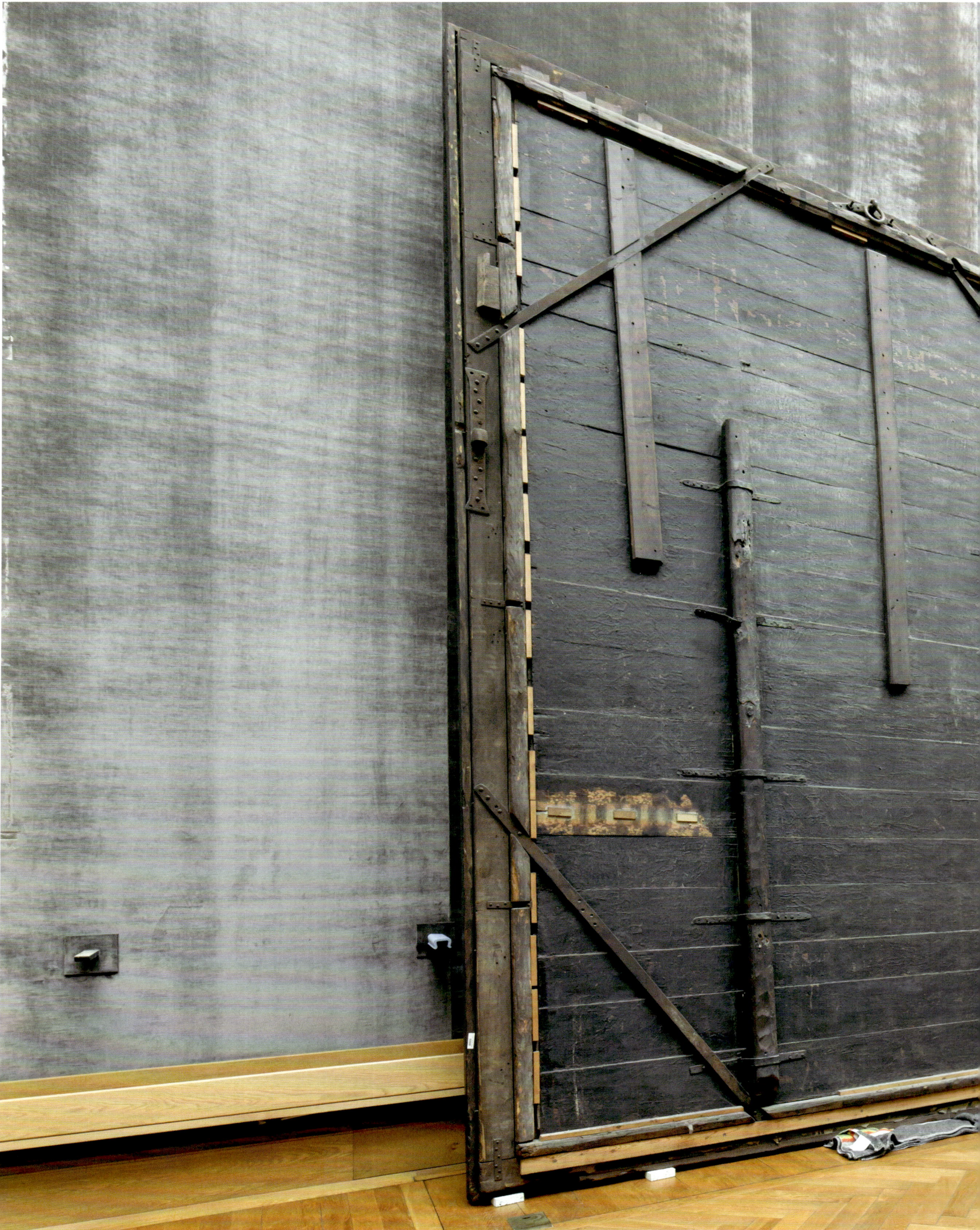

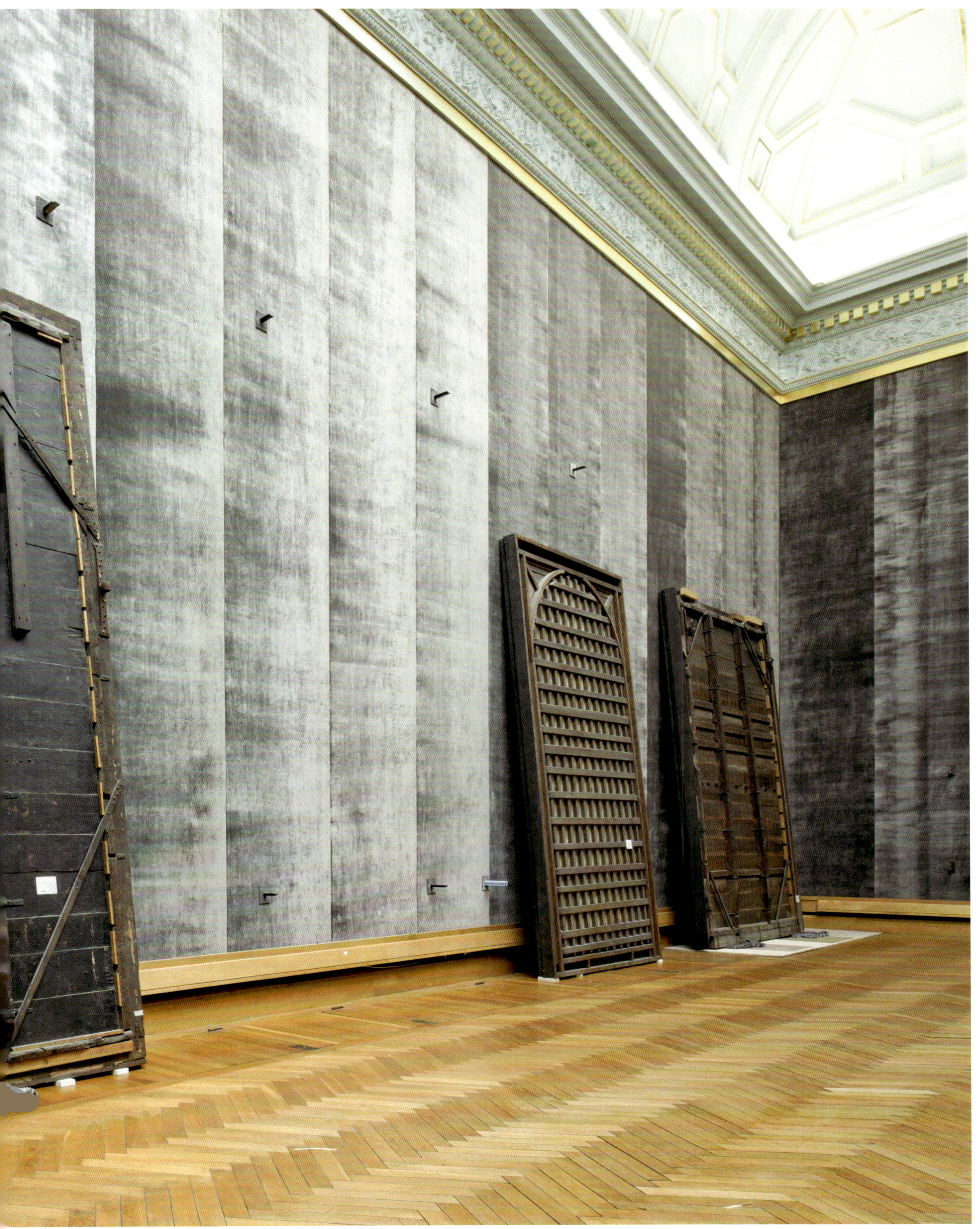

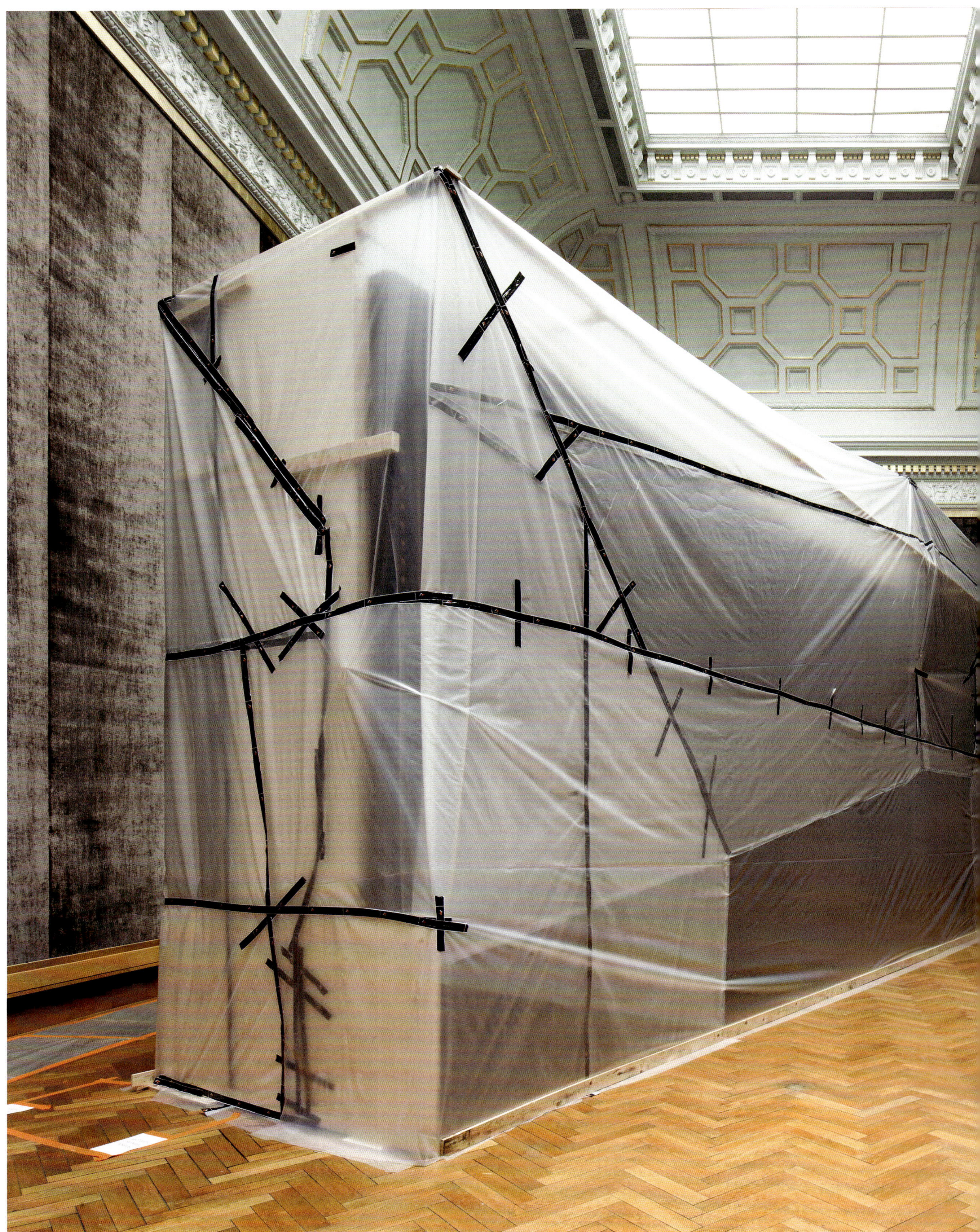

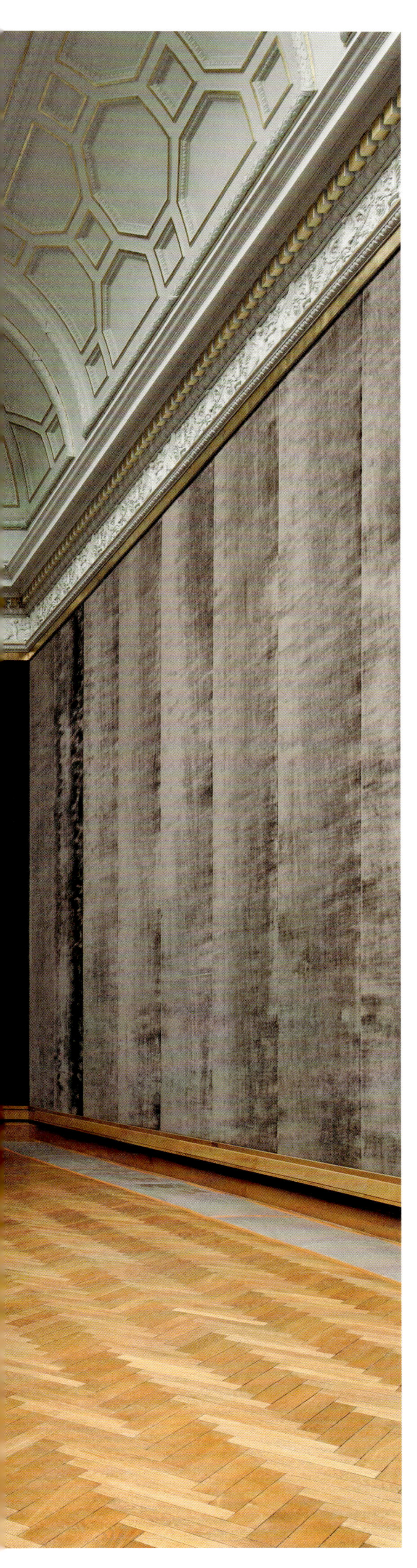

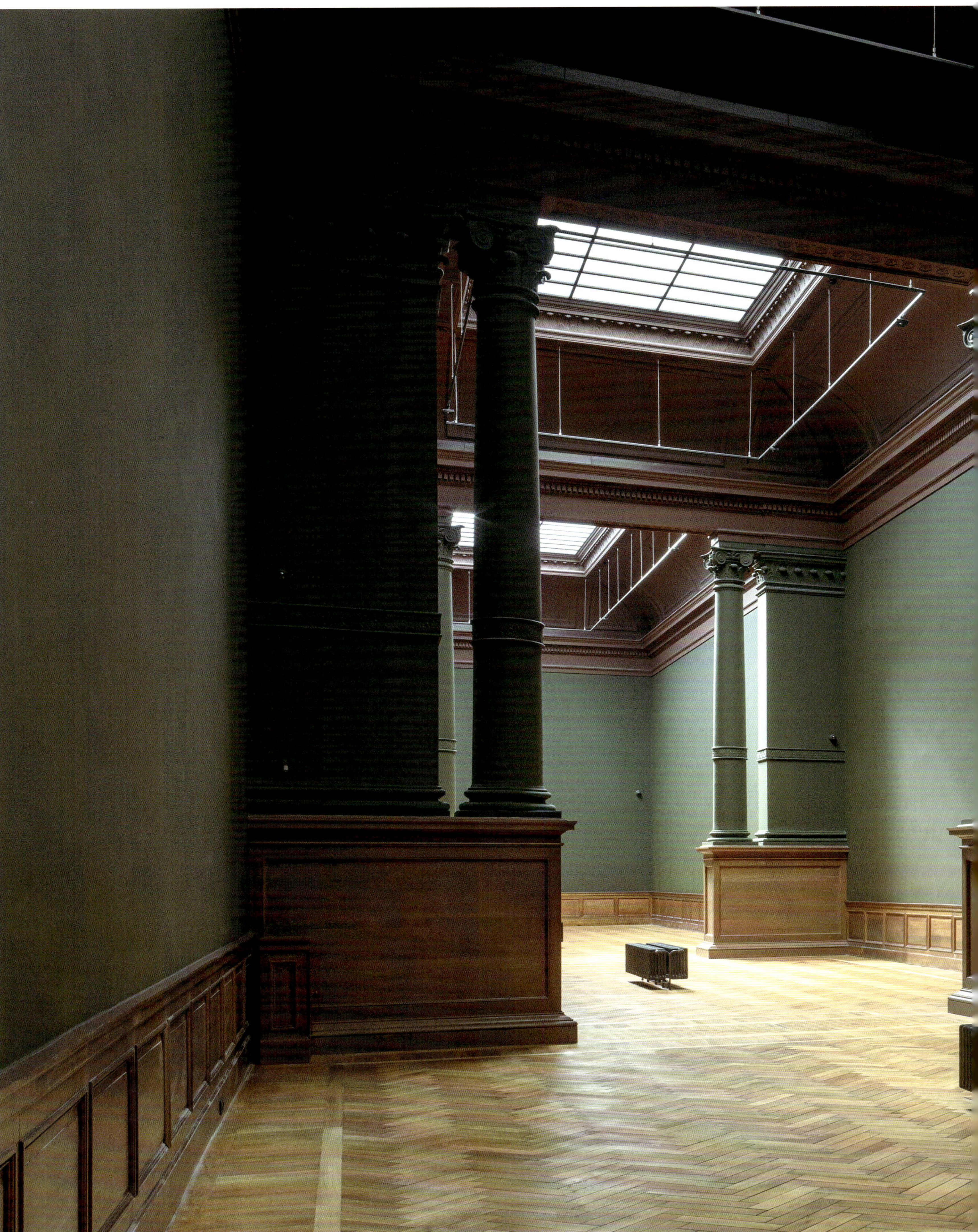

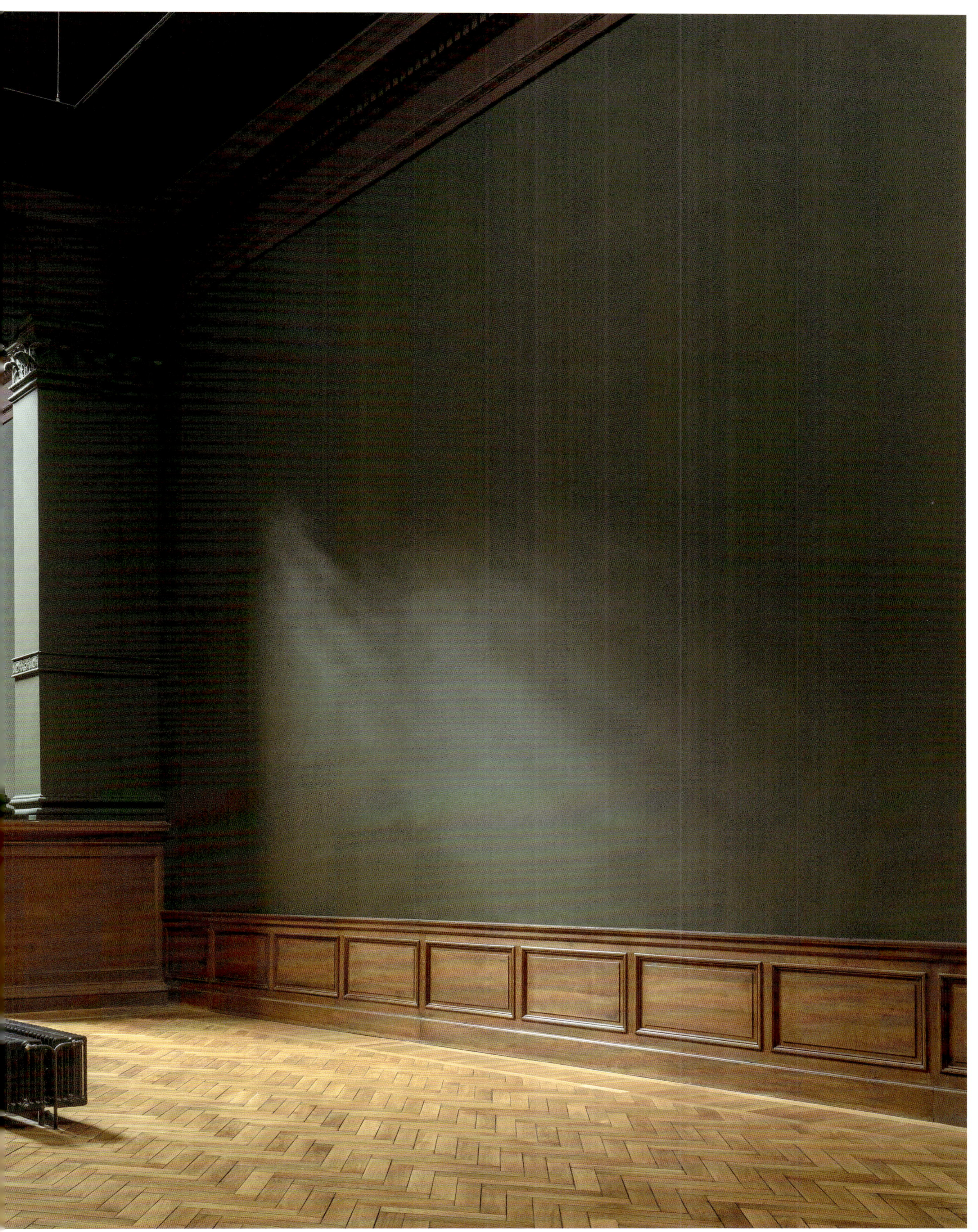

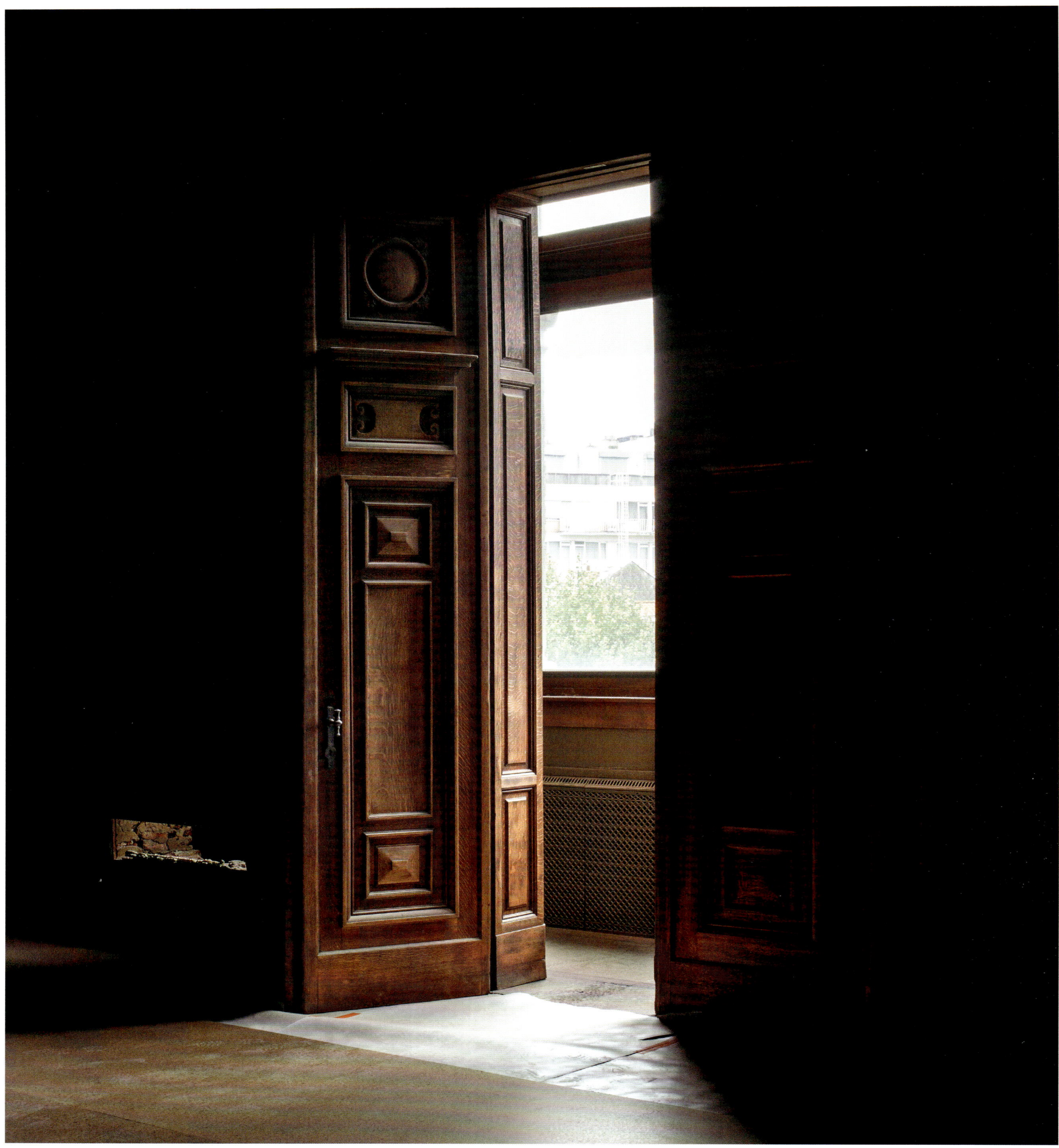

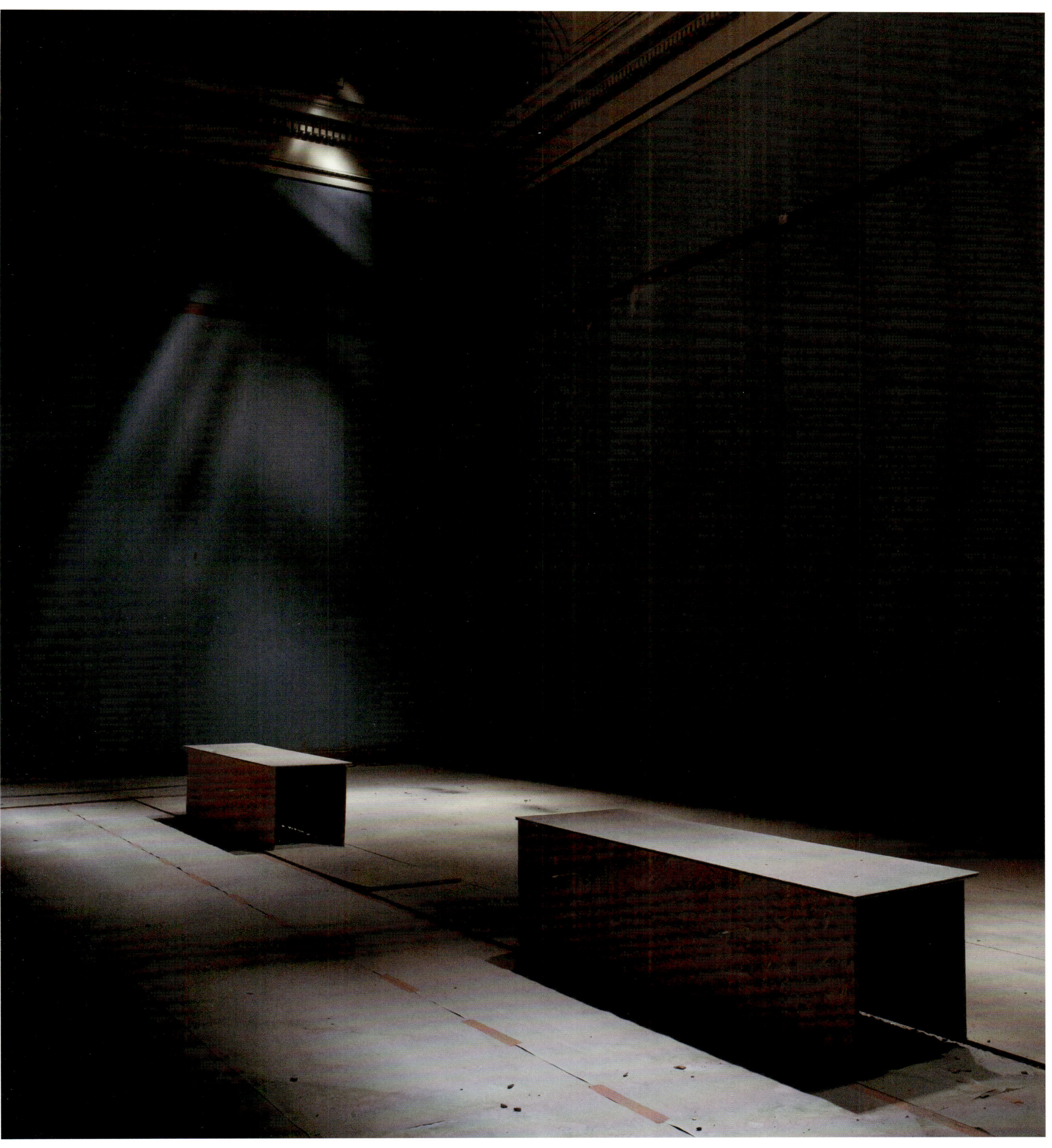

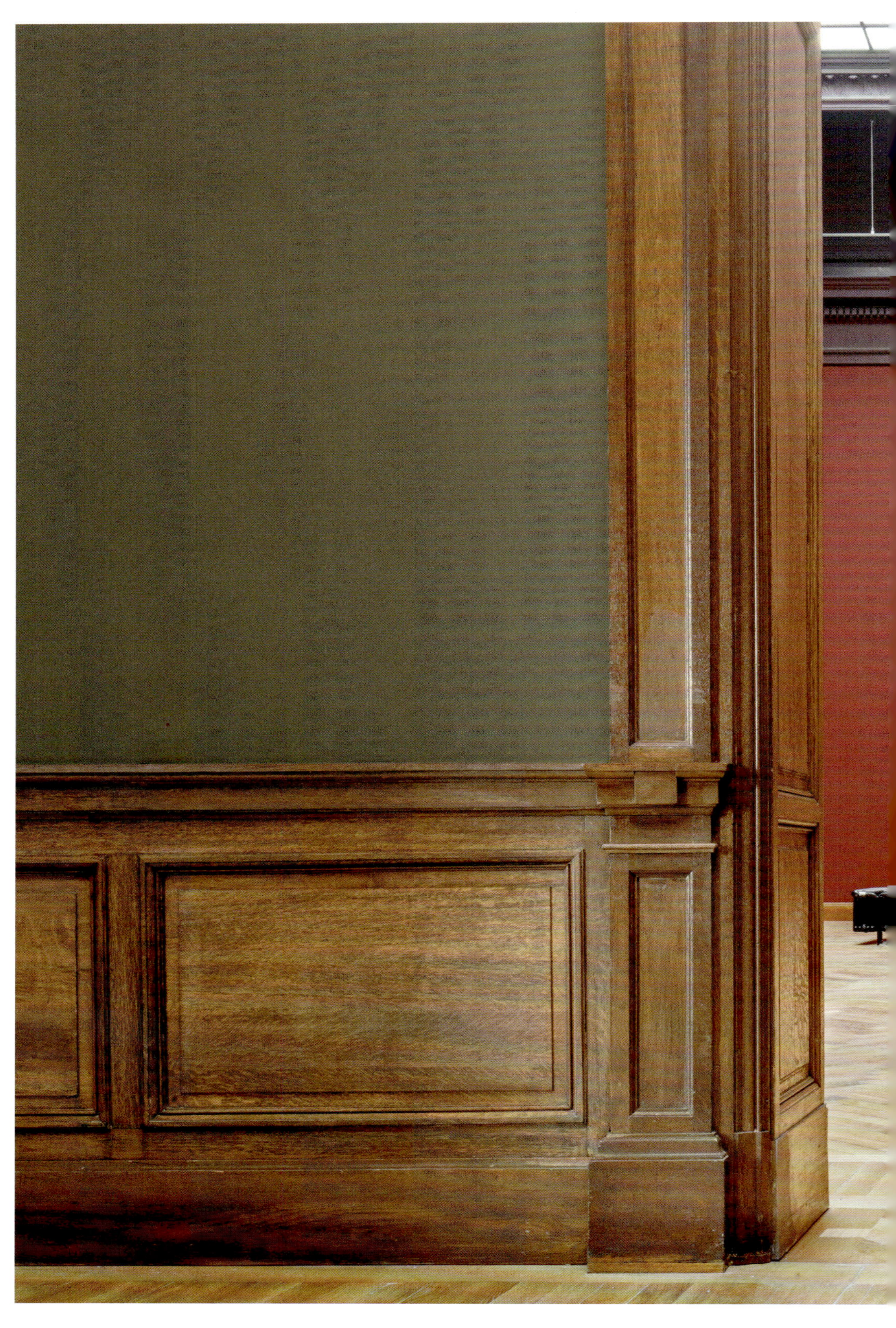

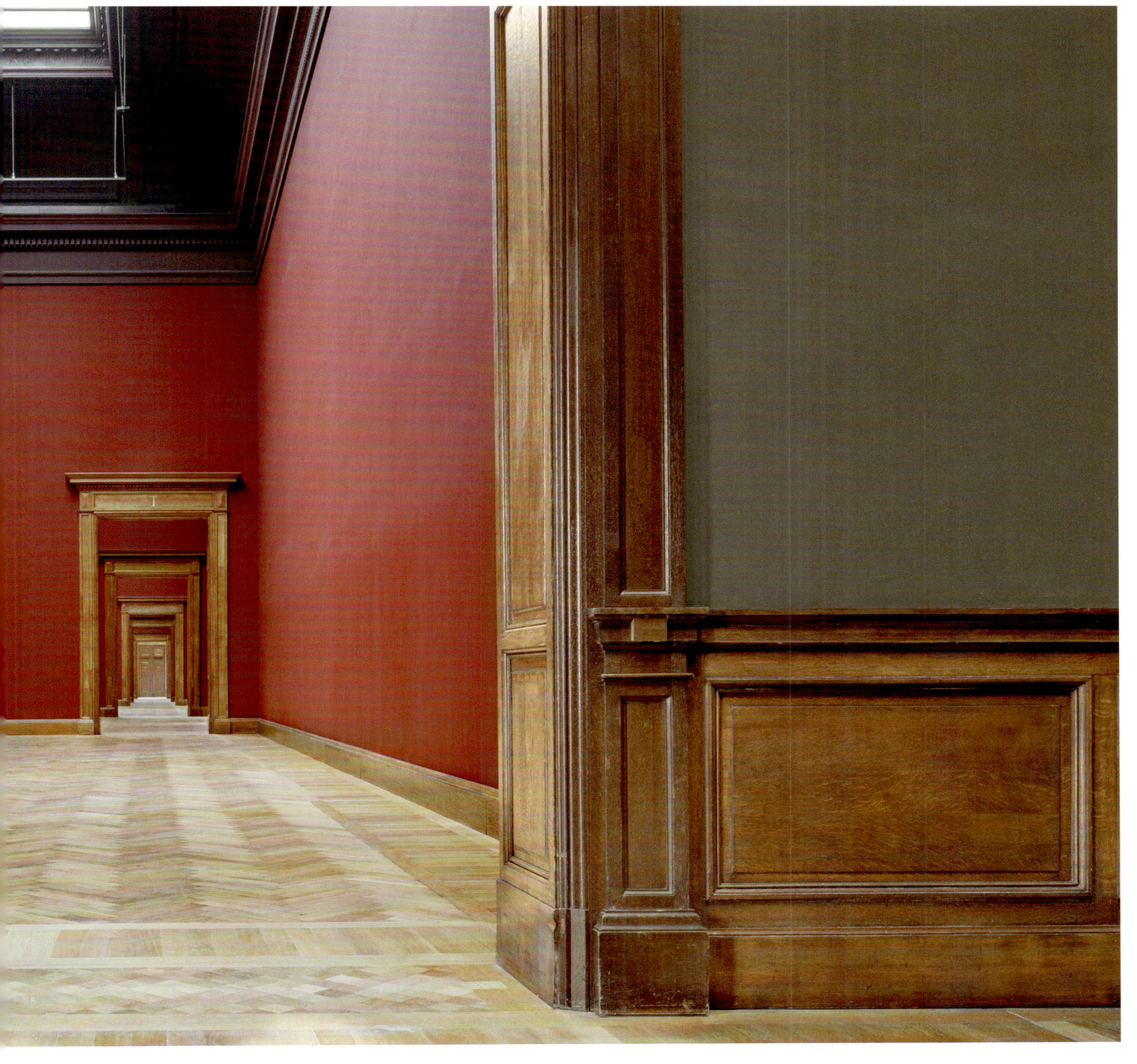

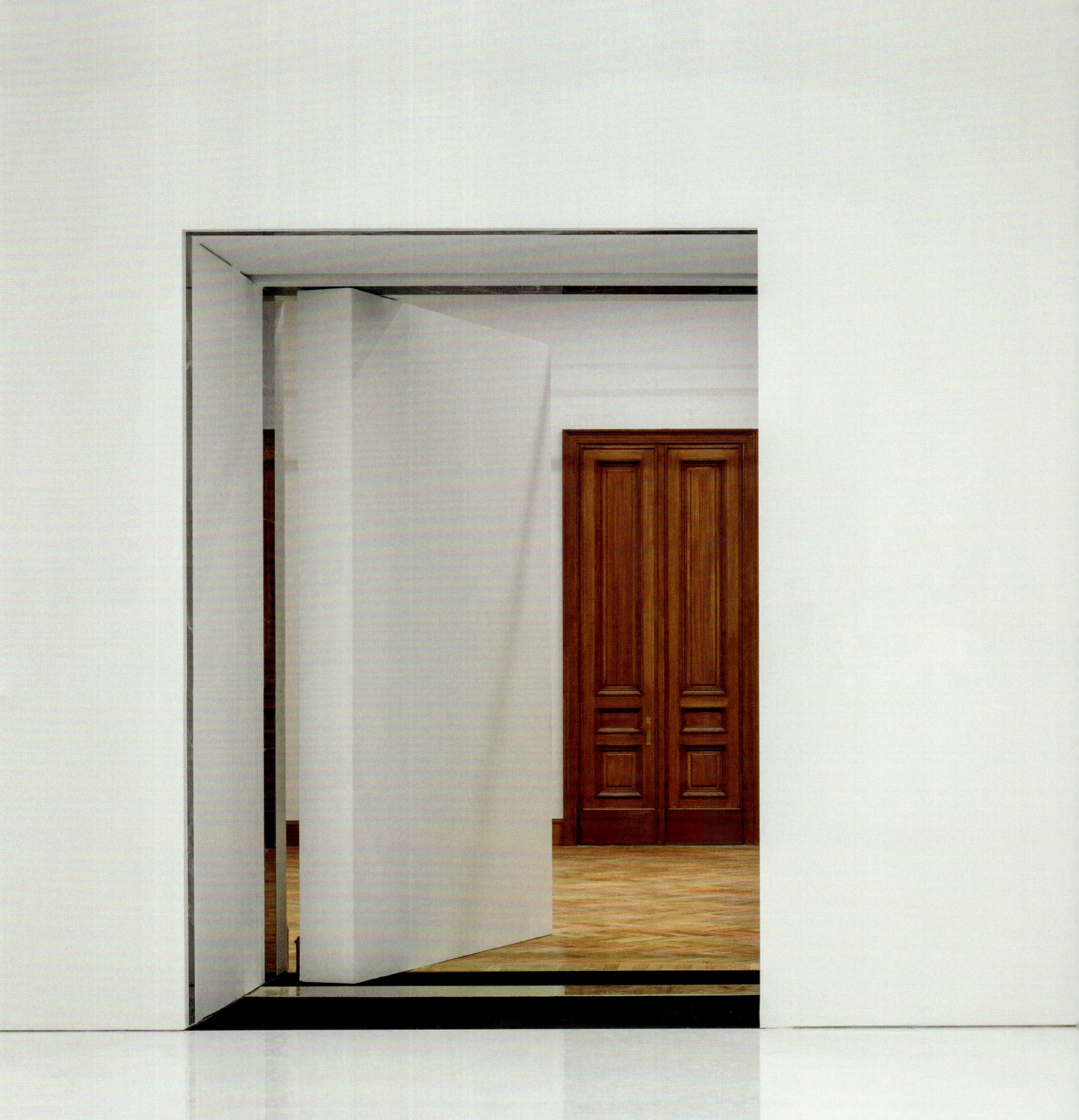

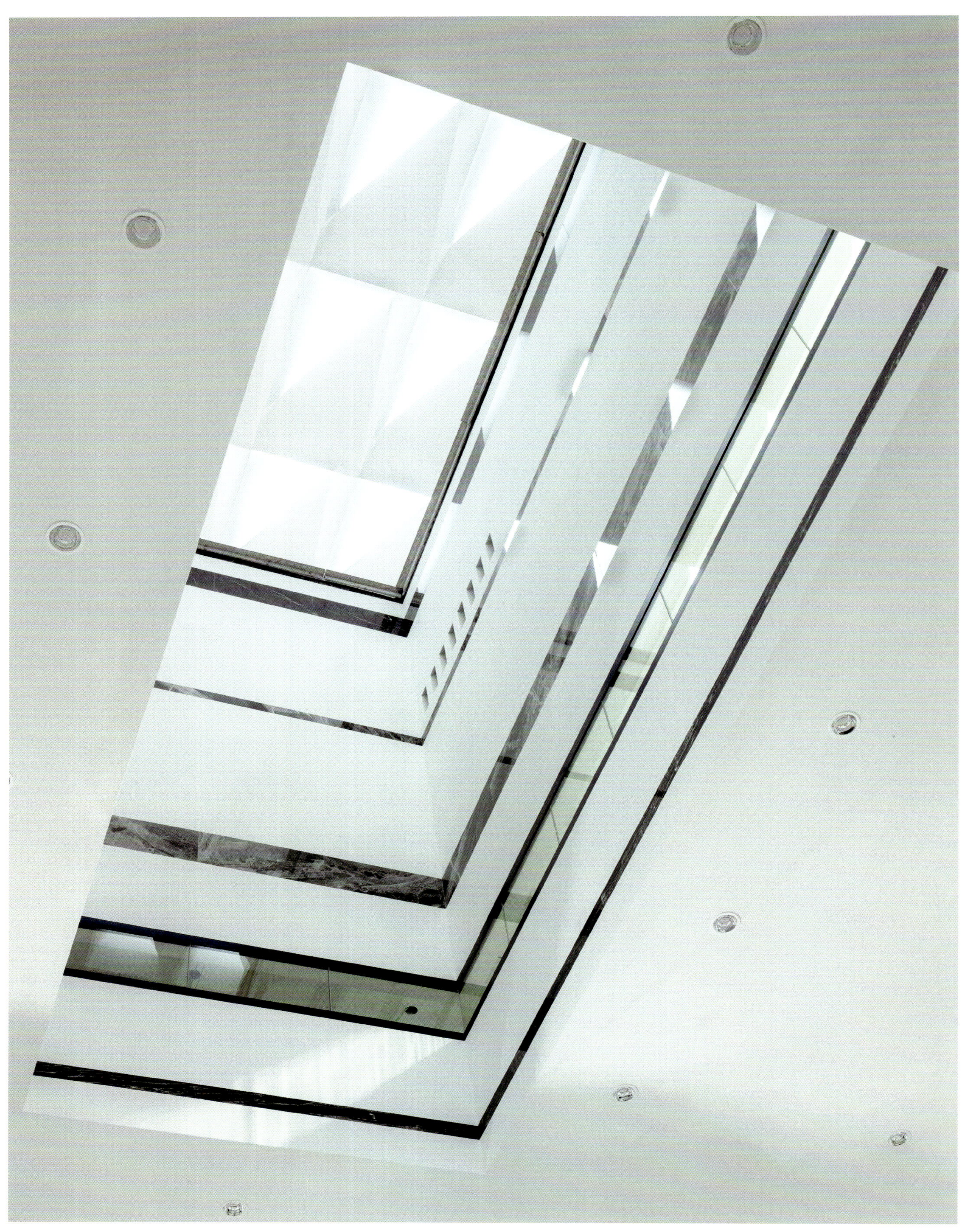

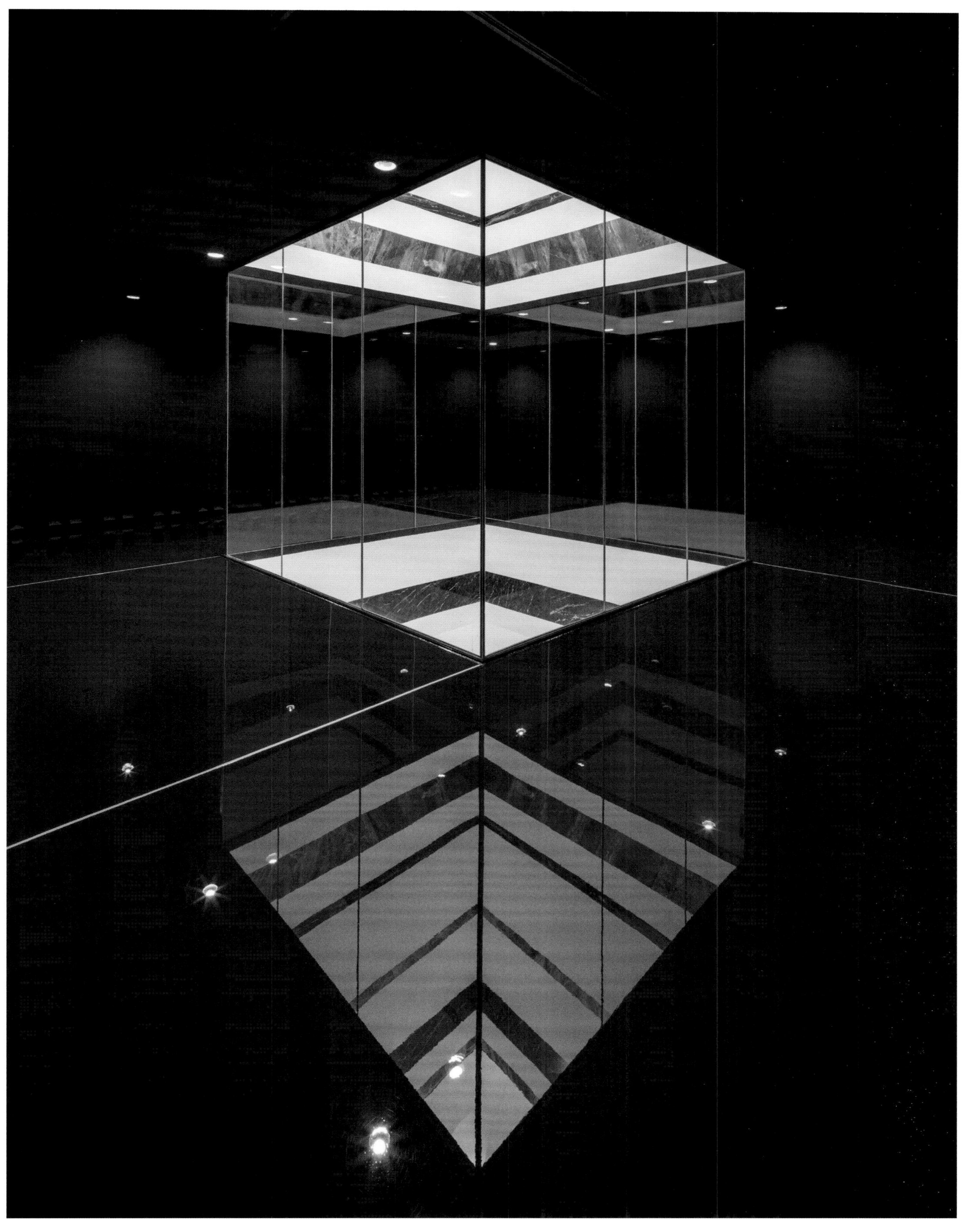

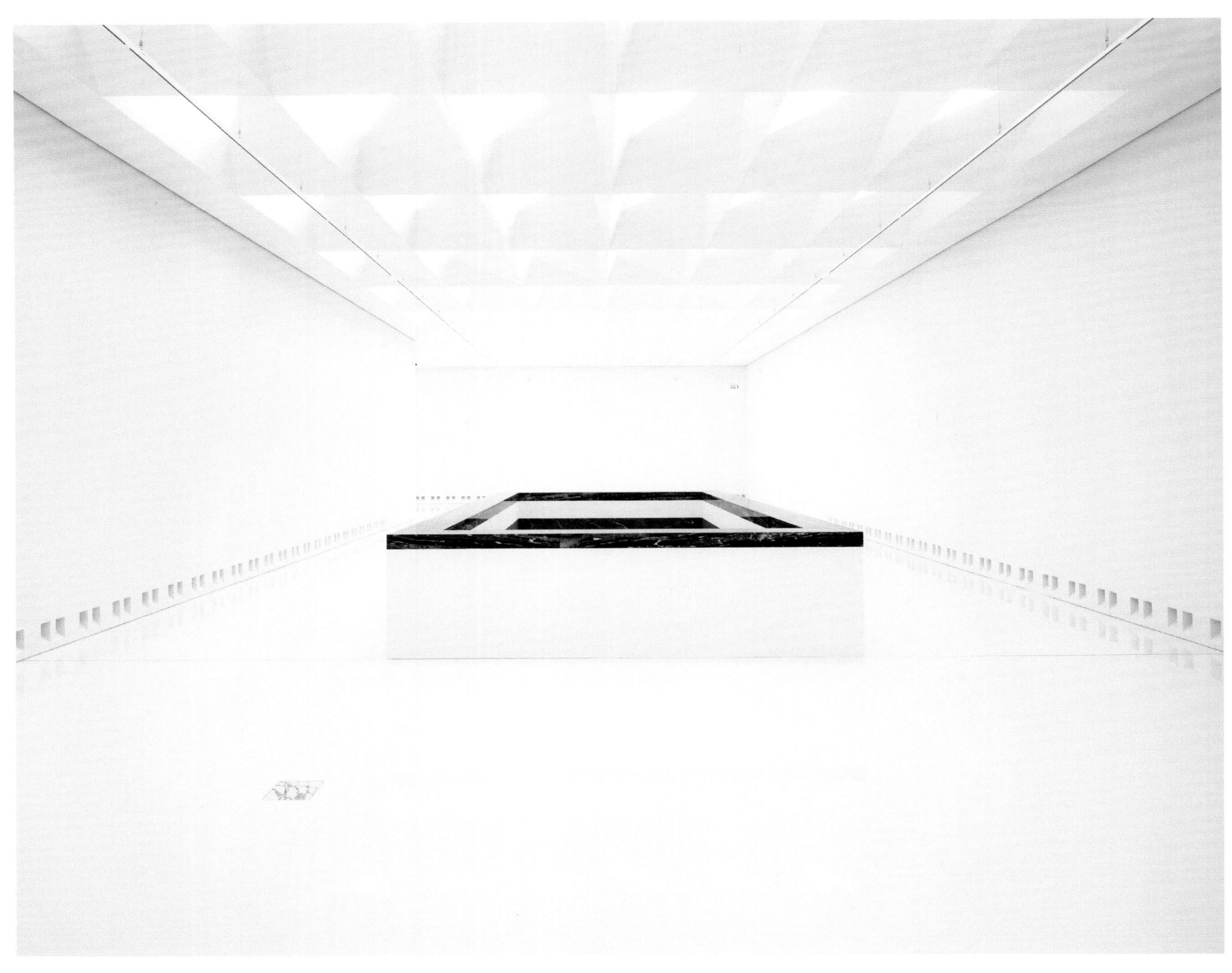

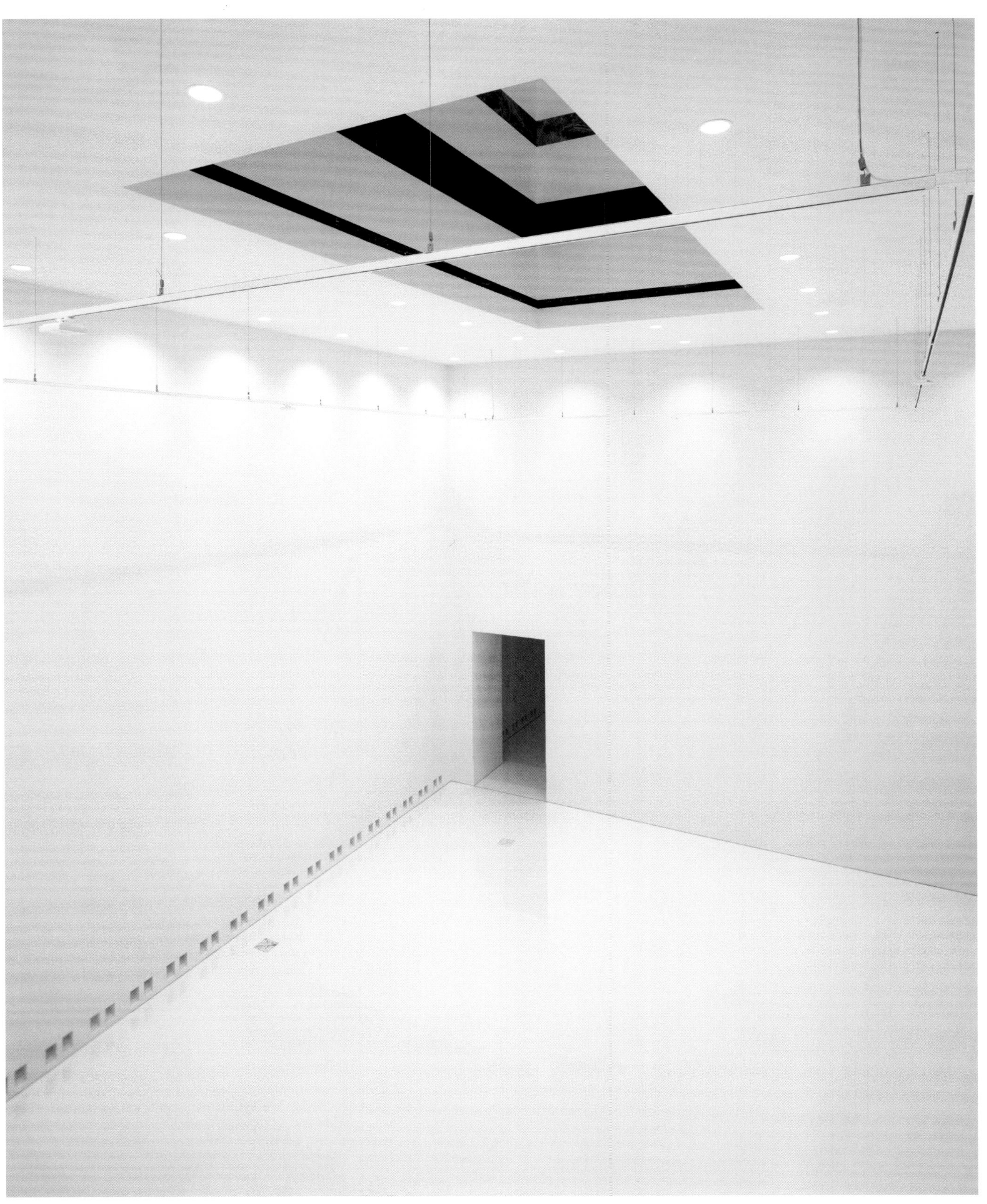

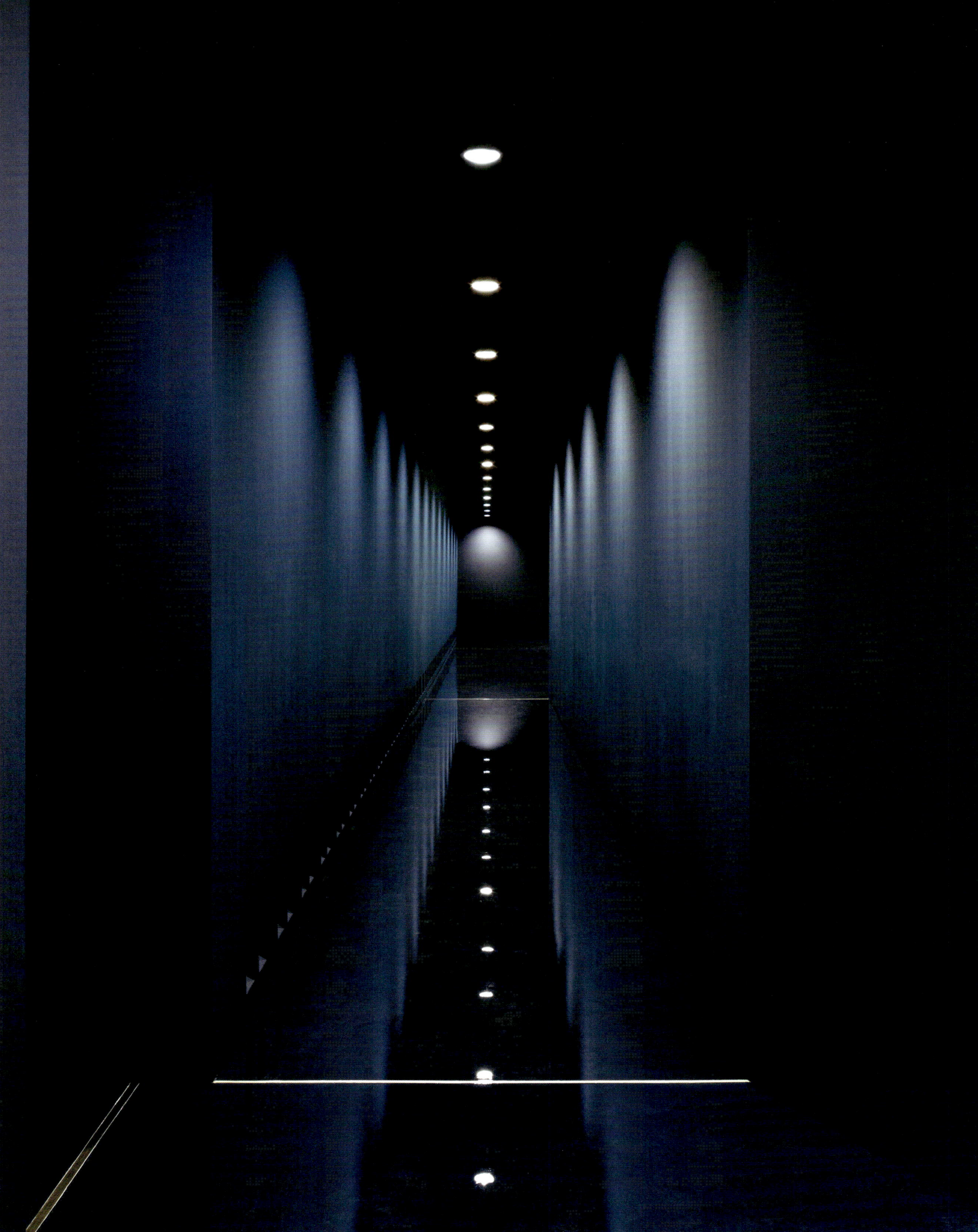

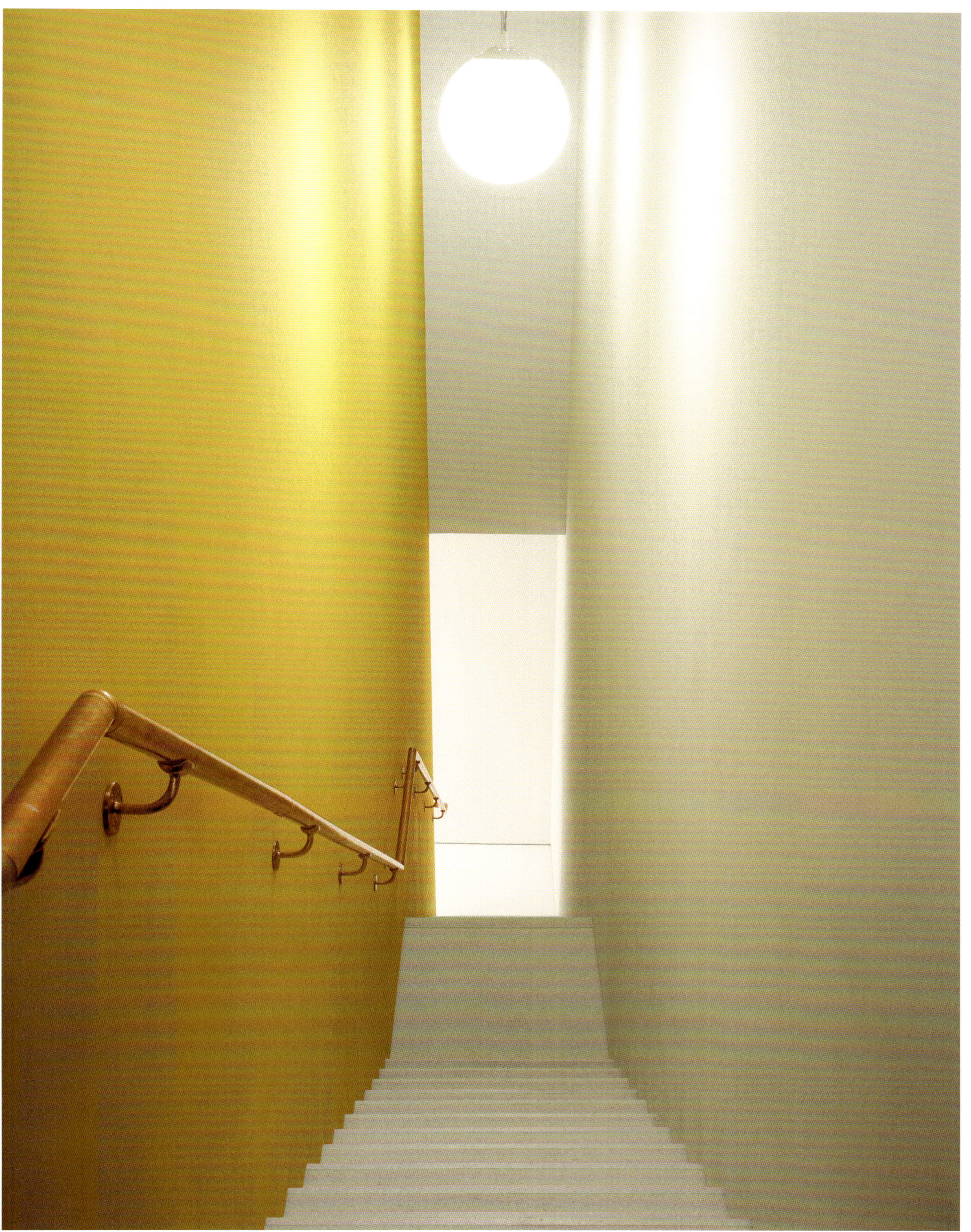

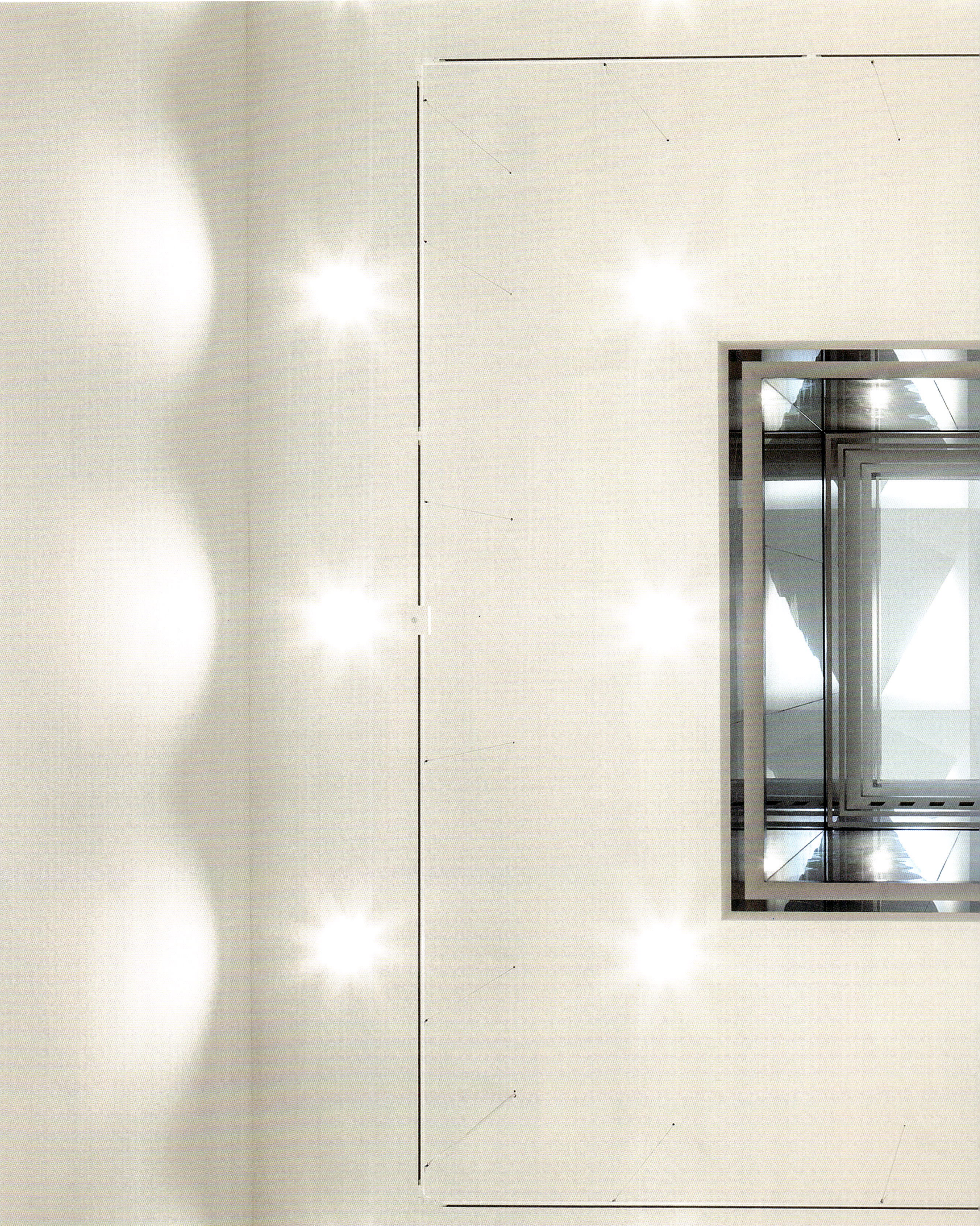

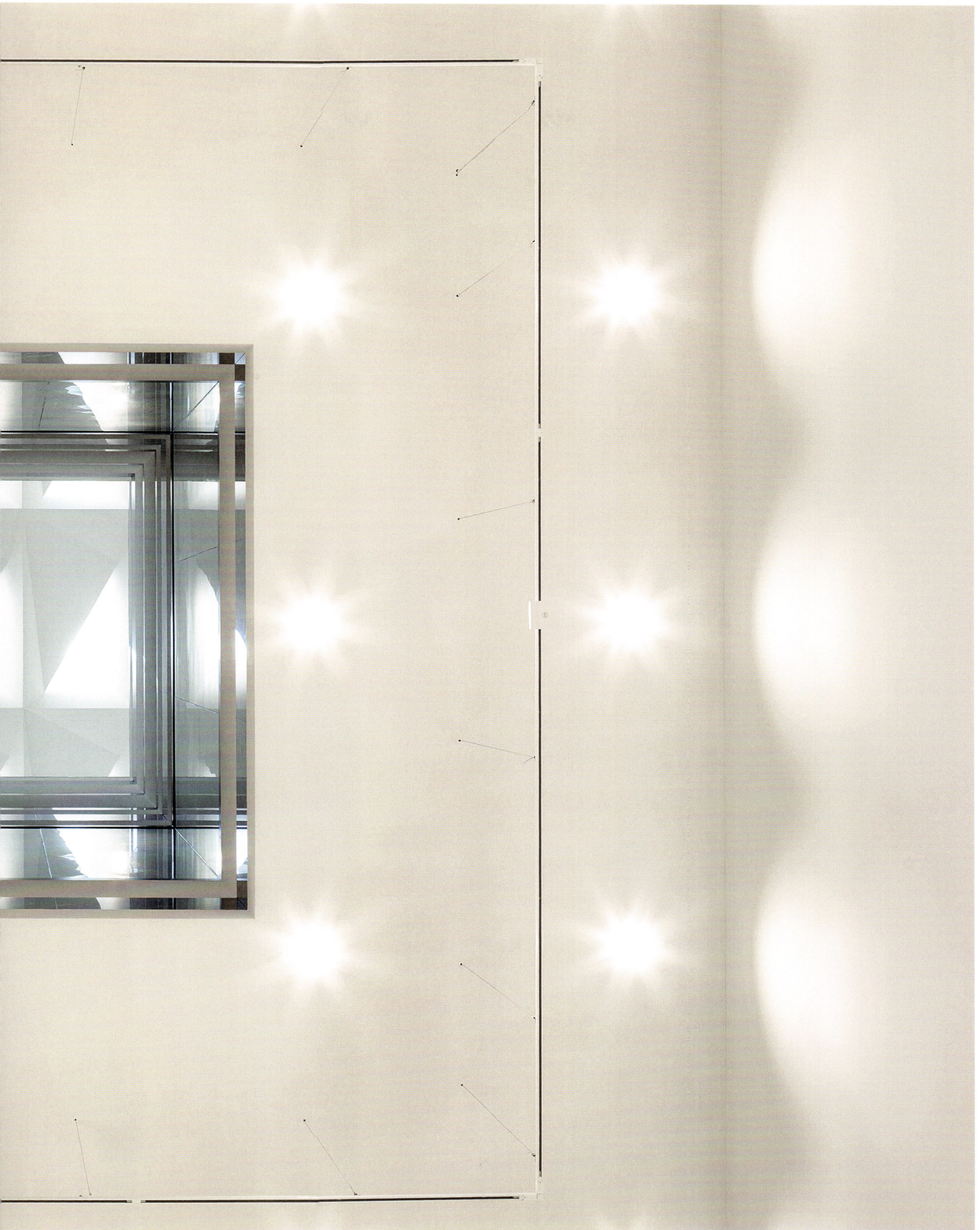

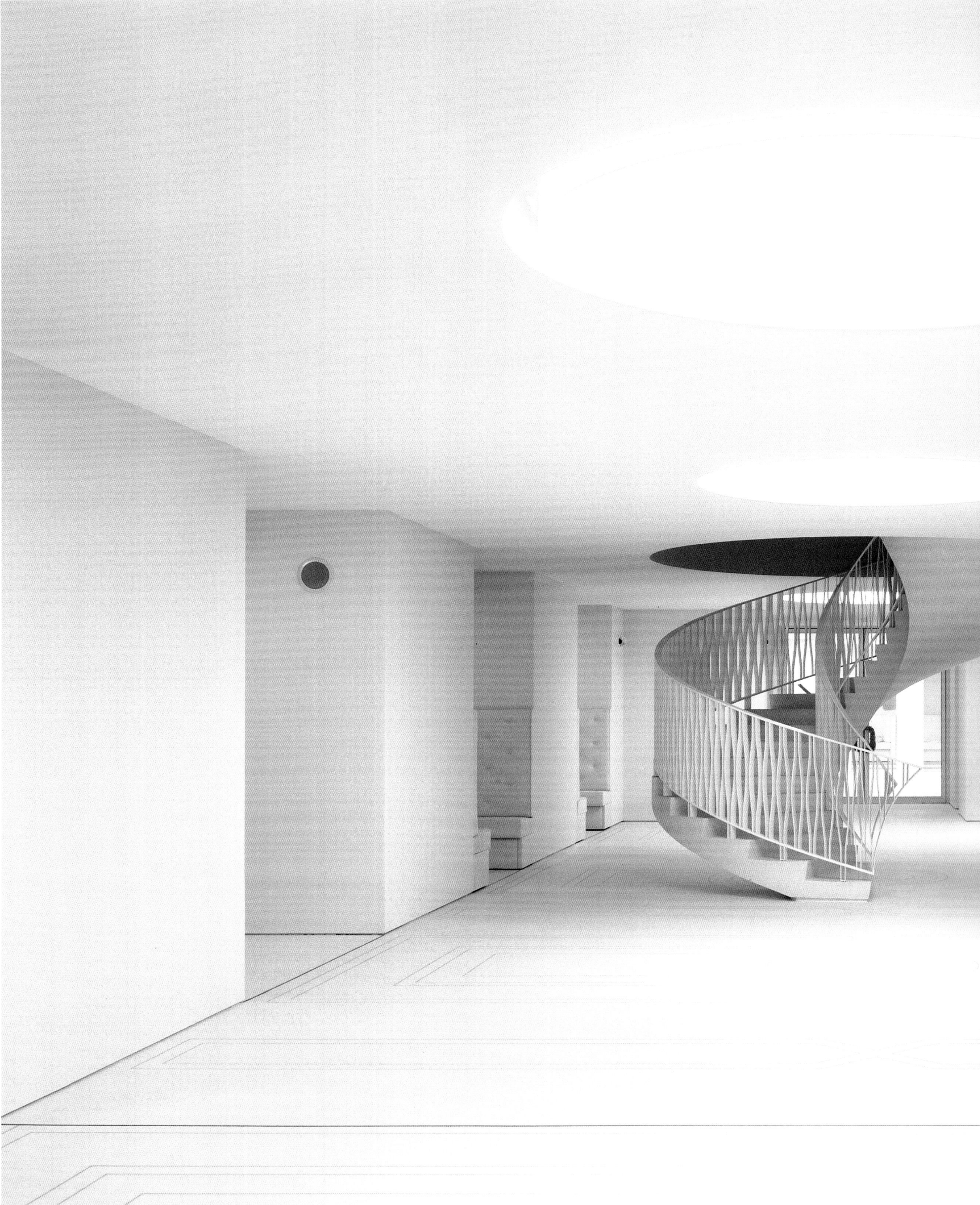

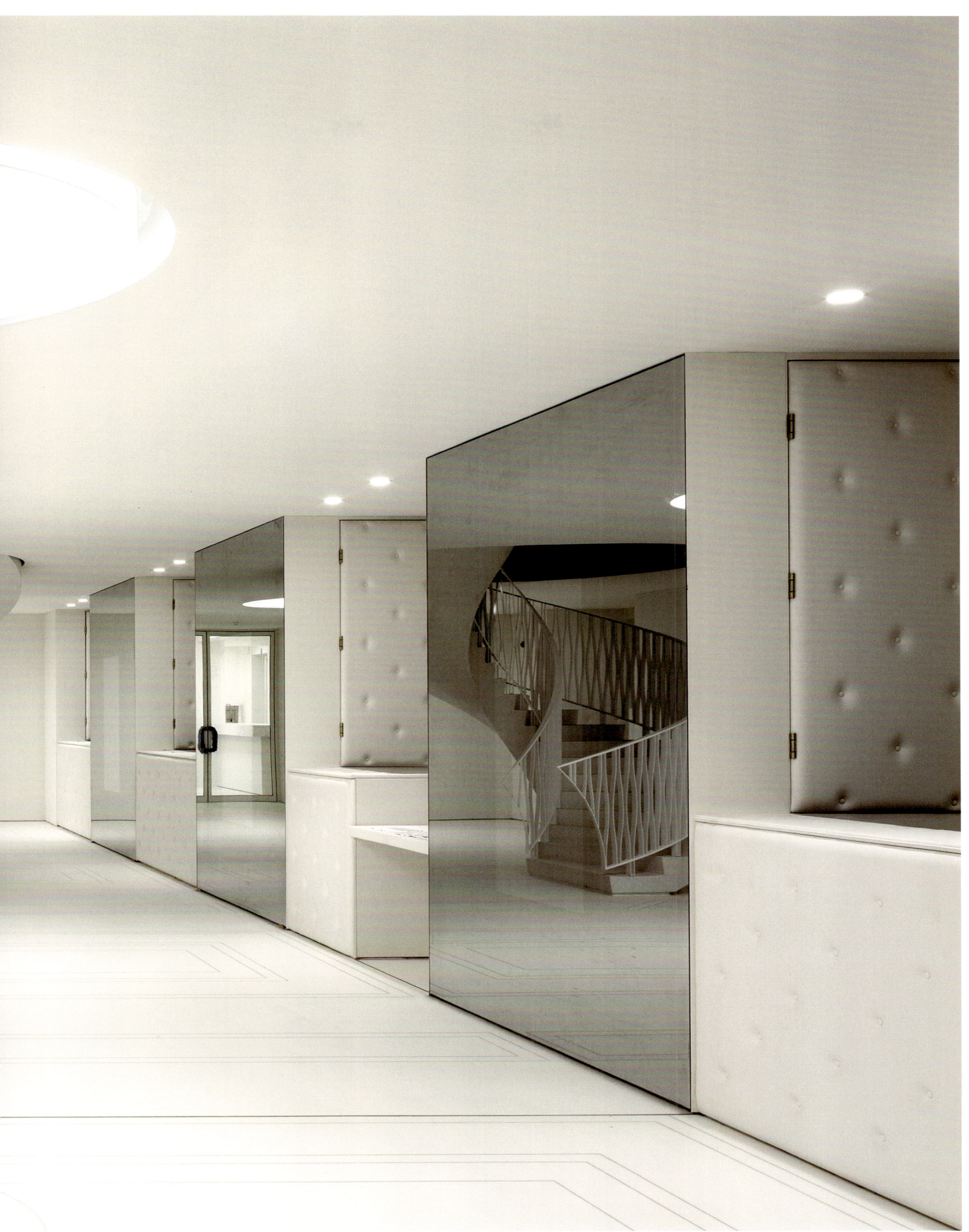

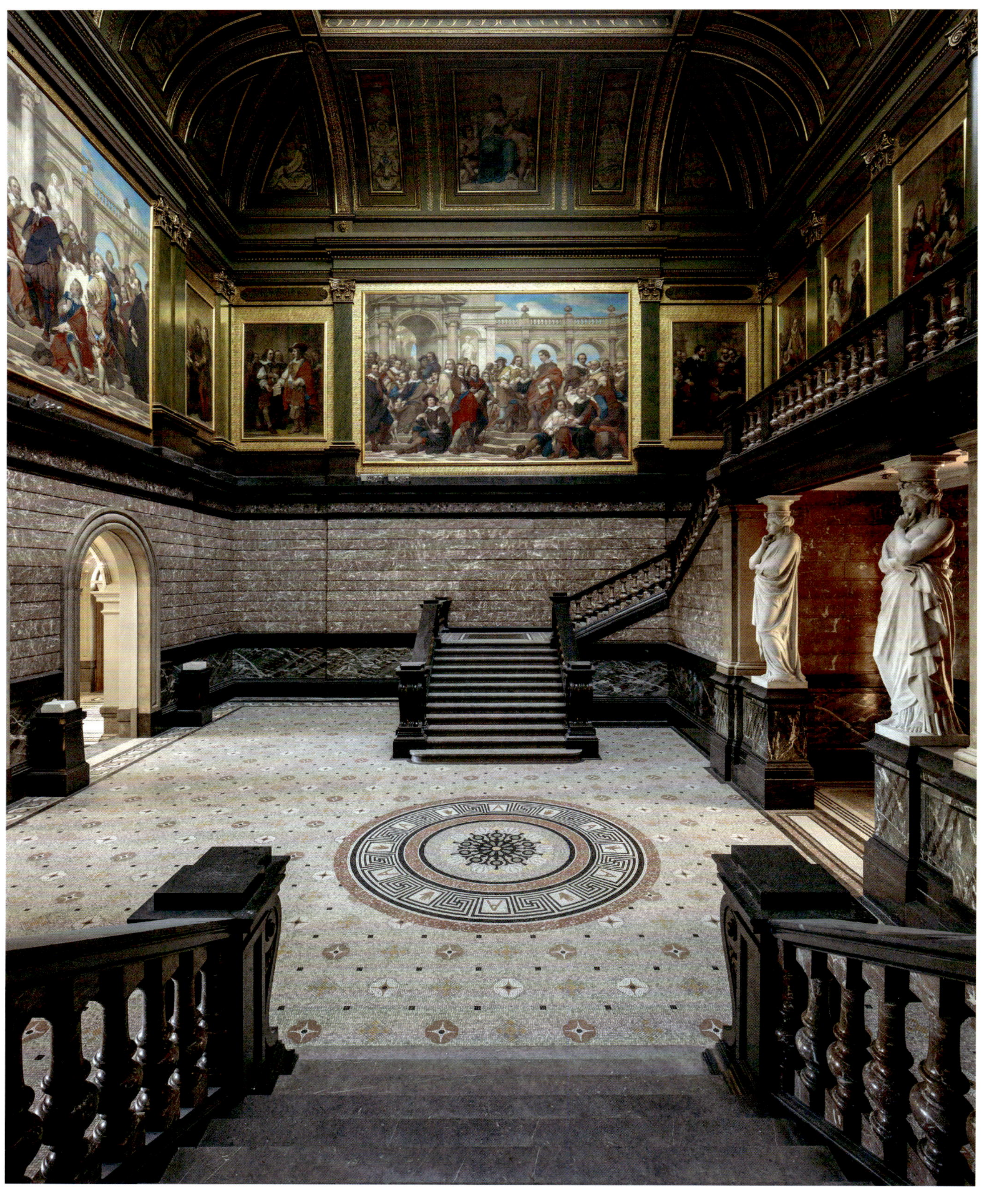

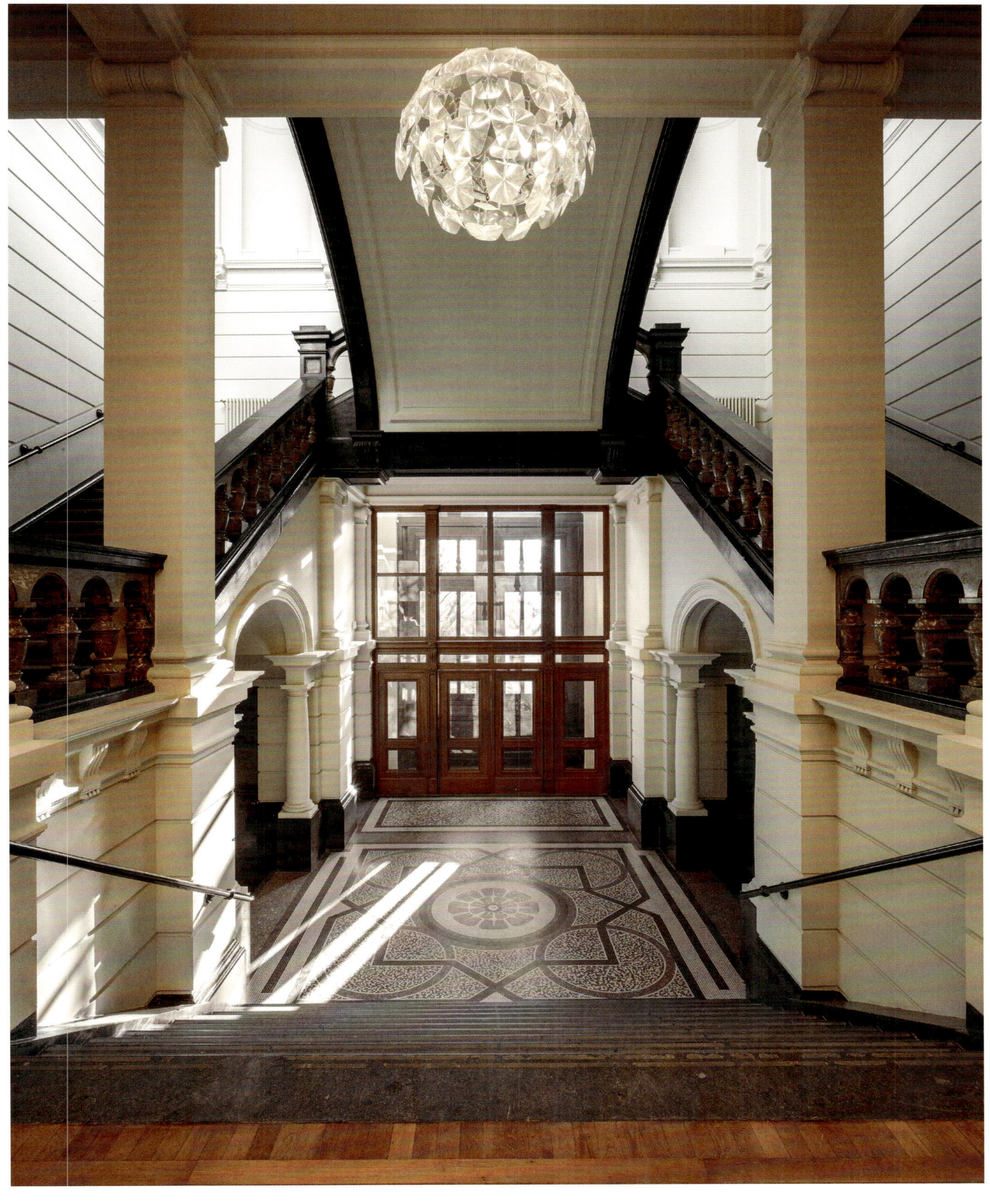

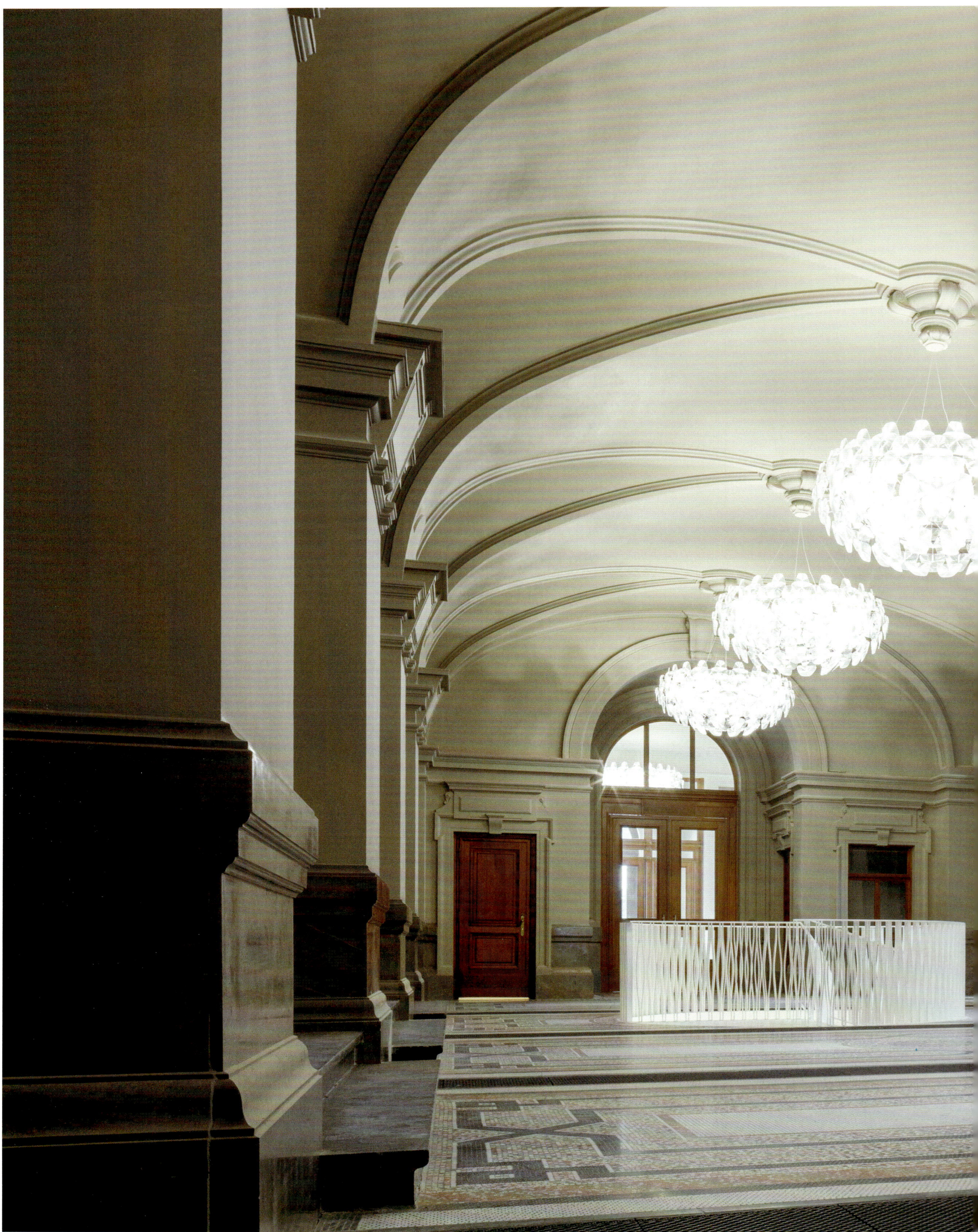

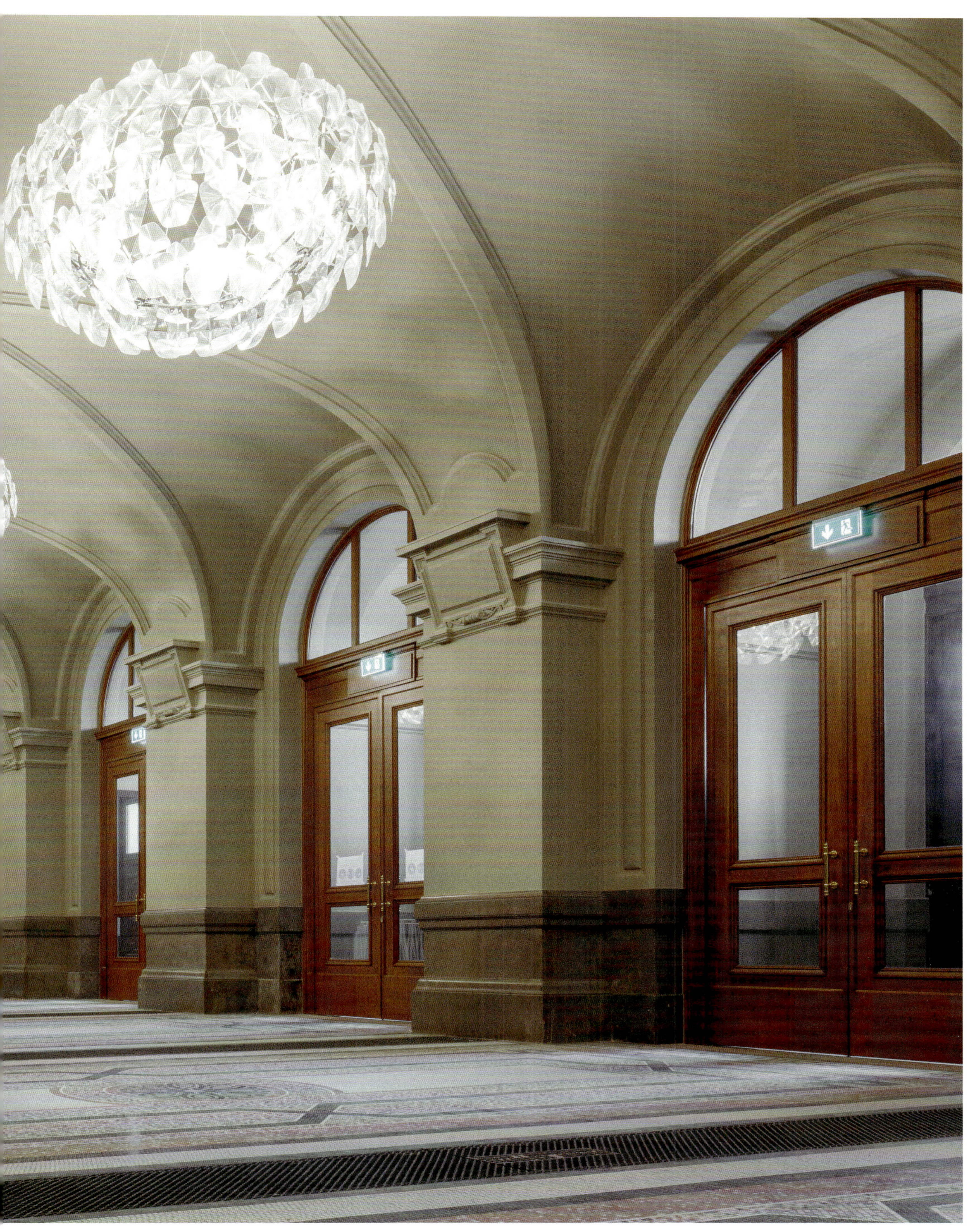

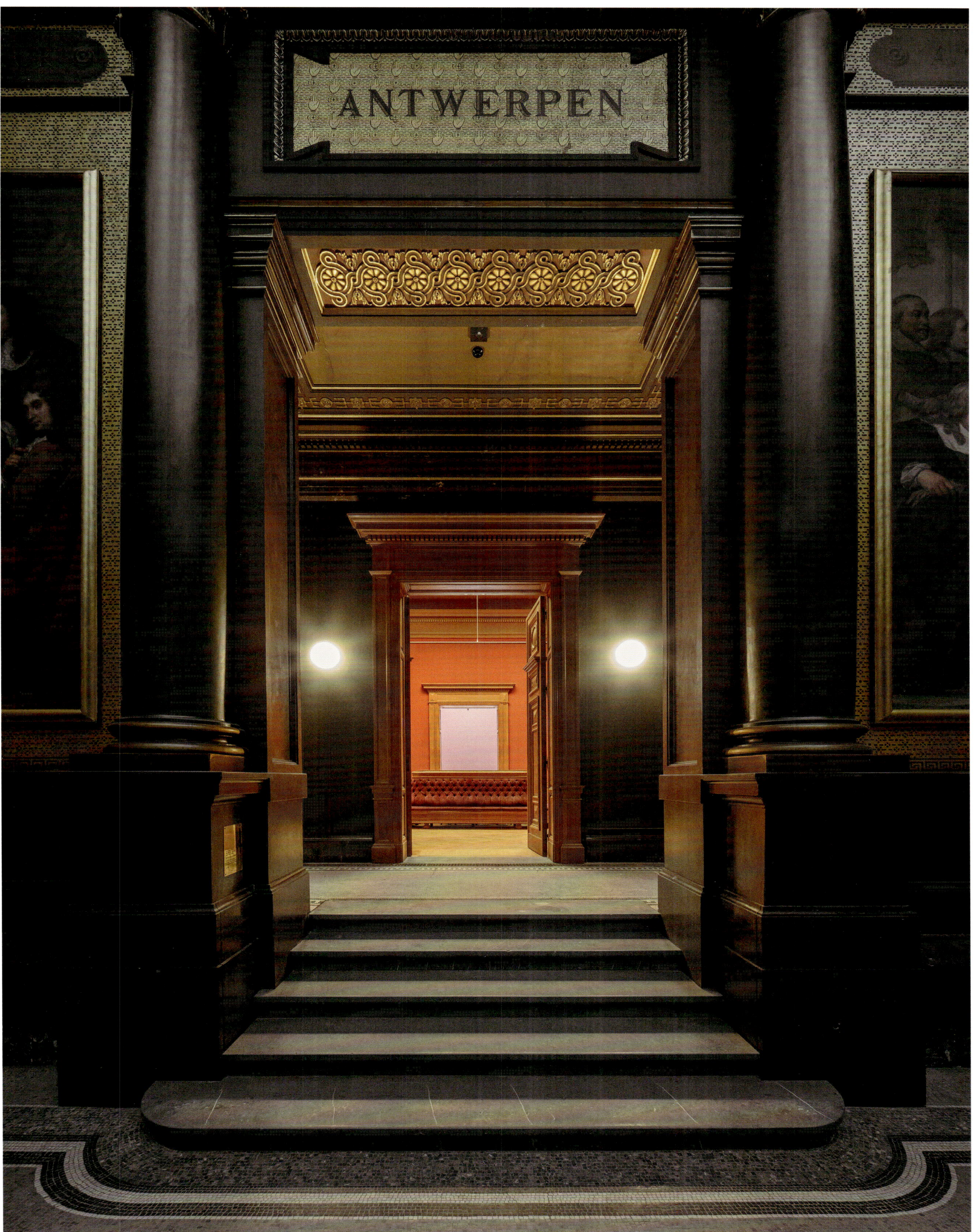
ANTWERPEN

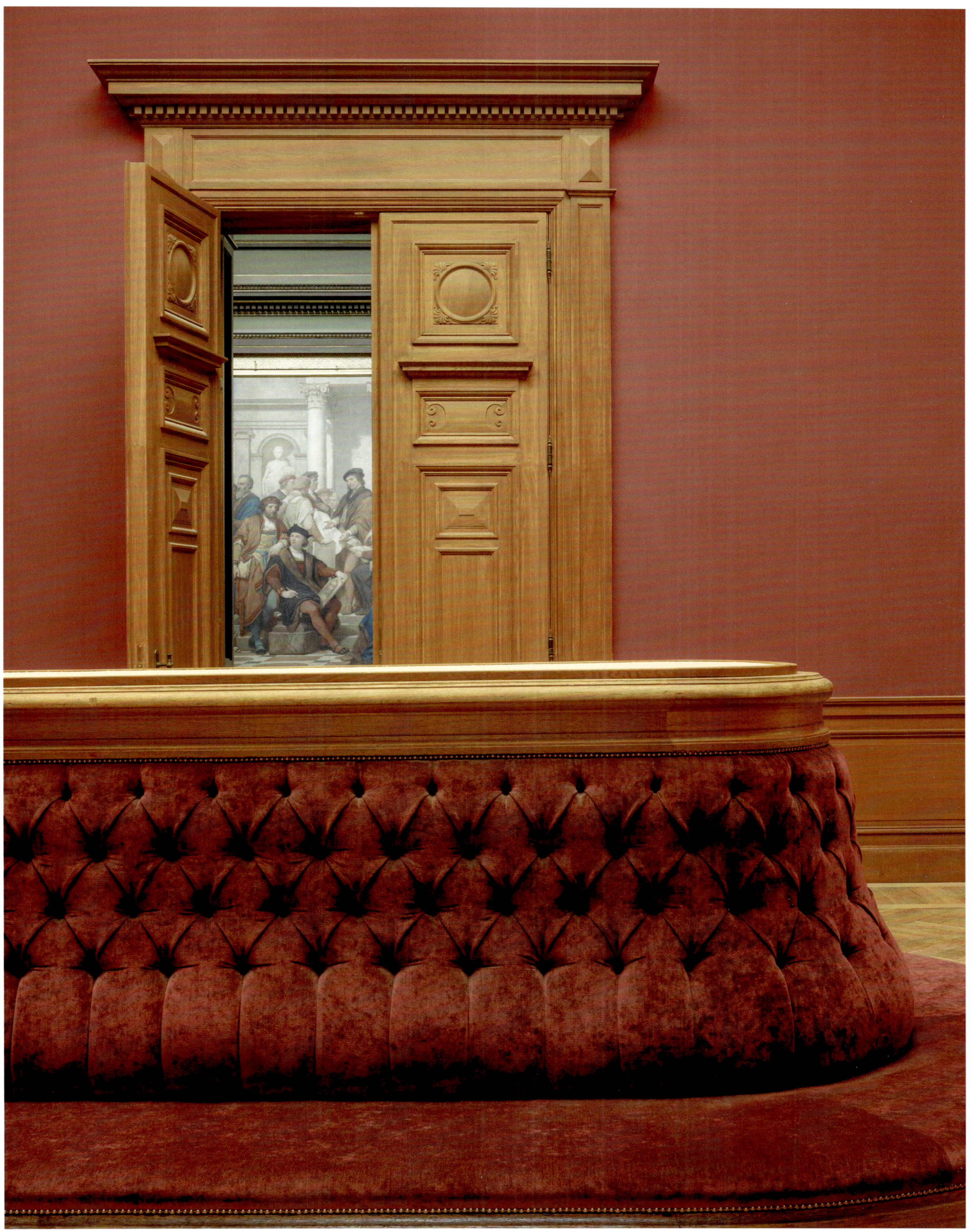

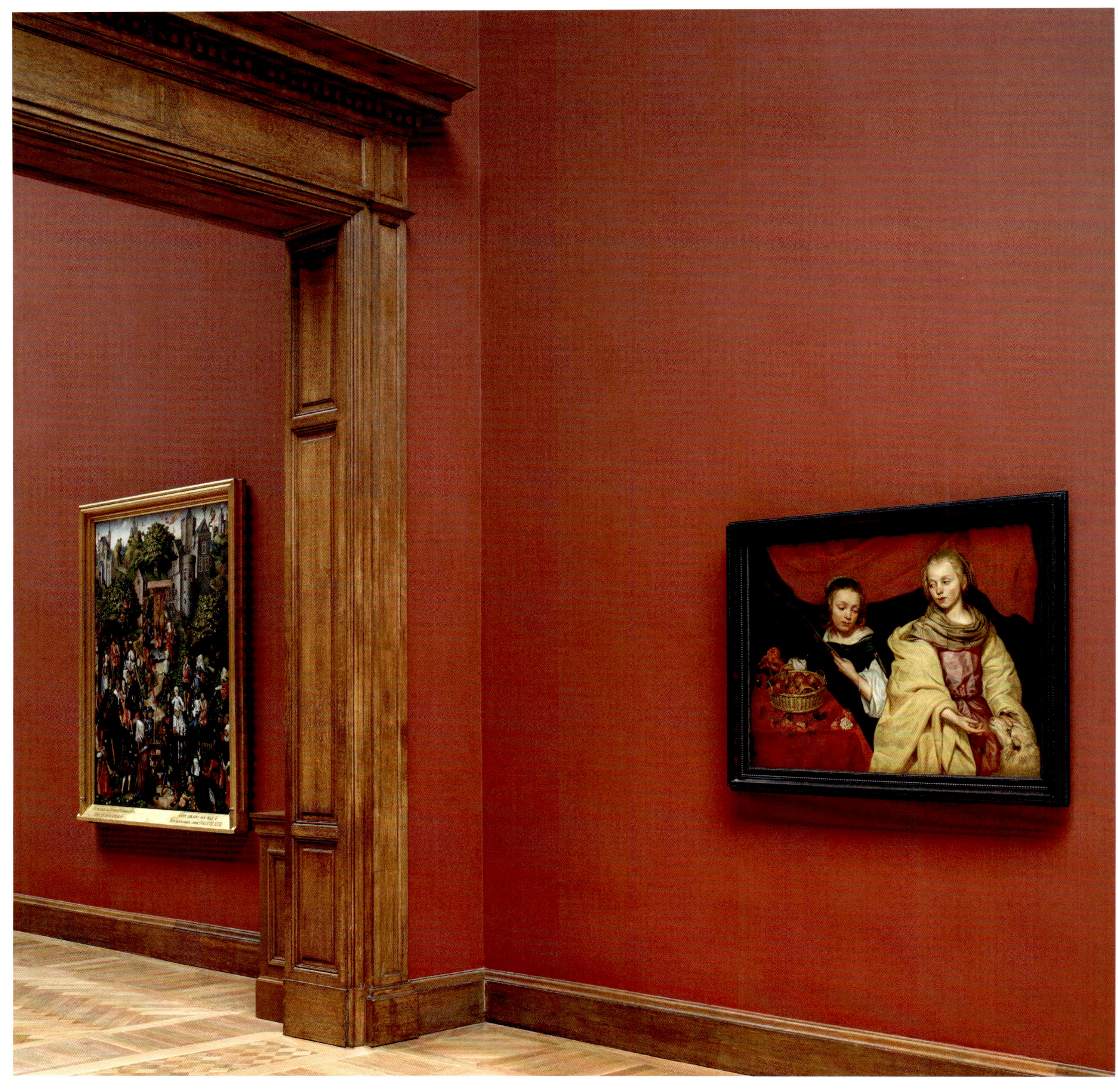

6.

WHAT DO YOU SHOW, AND HOW? PRESENTATION AND SCENOGRAPHY

Dynamic and diverse: the collection on display

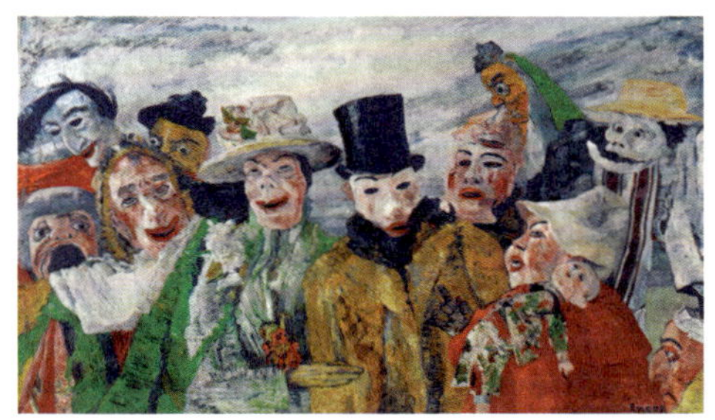

James Ensor, *The Intrigue*, 1890, oil on canvas, 91.6 × 150 cm, inv. 1856

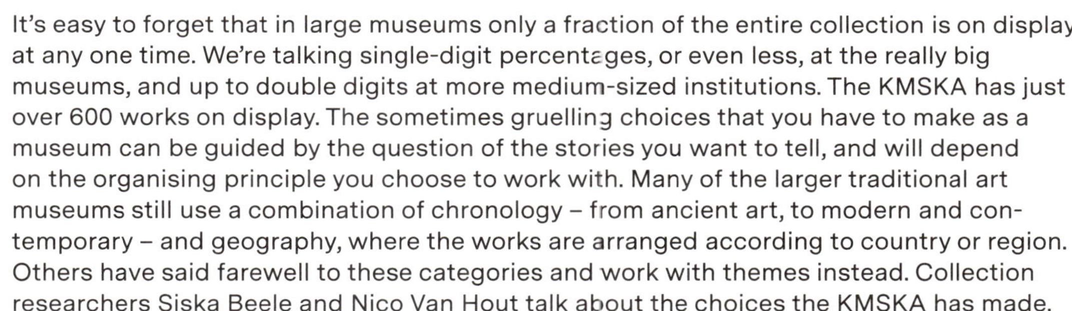

It's easy to forget that in large museums only a fraction of the entire collection is on display at any one time. We're talking single-digit percentages, or even less, at the really big museums, and up to double digits at more medium-sized institutions. The KMSKA has just over 600 works on display. The sometimes gruelling choices that you have to make as a museum can be guided by the question of the stories you want to tell, and will depend on the organising principle you choose to work with. Many of the larger traditional art museums still use a combination of chronology – from ancient art, to modern and contemporary – and geography, where the works are arranged according to country or region. Others have said farewell to these categories and work with themes instead. Collection researchers Siska Beele and Nico Van Hout talk about the choices the KMSKA has made.

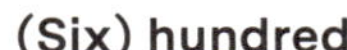

(Six) hundred

Nico Van Hout: "We quite quickly reached the decision to display the collection thematically rather than chronologically. This way, we can show a wonderful ensemble of a very high quality, with a few masterpieces in each room. We anticipated that our visitors will be expecting a new way of presenting the work. Experience has shown that people's historical knowledge is becoming less comprehensive and they can't easily place key figures such as, say, Charles V or Napoleon, in time. The same applies to knowledge of art styles, such as Gothic, Renaissance and Baroque. Also, our collection has strengths and weaknesses: we are very strong in the 15th- to 17th-century period, and with our large Ensor collection we make a nice transition to the modern. But we have no more than a handful of good works from the 18th century."

Siska Beele: "We are exhibiting more than 600 works, 100 of which we have designated our 'key works'. They are evenly distributed throughout the museum. If you have seen those 100 pieces, you've gained a good impression of our collection. Three works also symbolise the three pillars of our collection: Jean Fouquet's *Madonna*, James Ensor's *The Intrigue* and Pierre Alechinsky's *The Last Day*. They represent the old masters up to 1880, the transition to the modern, and the modern period, respectively. The collection on display may be arranged thematically, but art-historical chronology has not been completely abandoned."

"We're not in a position to tell an encyclopaedic story with our entire collection. The best option for us is to assemble the works on display in the appropriate context. This also gives us the perfect toolbox to respond to the fact that narrative – storytelling – is becoming increasingly important, in education and the media, and for our visitors too. This is a way to involve the public more in the display, to challenge visitors and let them discover more about your artworks."

Nico Van Hout: "The new presentation has also become more dynamic. The 100 key works will always be on display, not necessarily in the same locations, but they will form the backbone of our presentation. We're constantly thinking about what to put on display, and it's our aim to respond to new themes and current events. We can also make use of

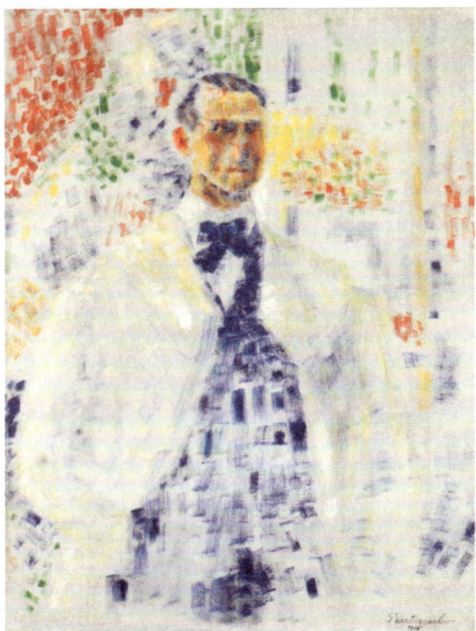

Georges Vantongerloo, *Self-portrait*, 1916, oil on canvas, 100 × 75 cm, collection Mu.ZEE, inv. MZ000070. Gaps in the display are filled through loans or by moving the collection around.

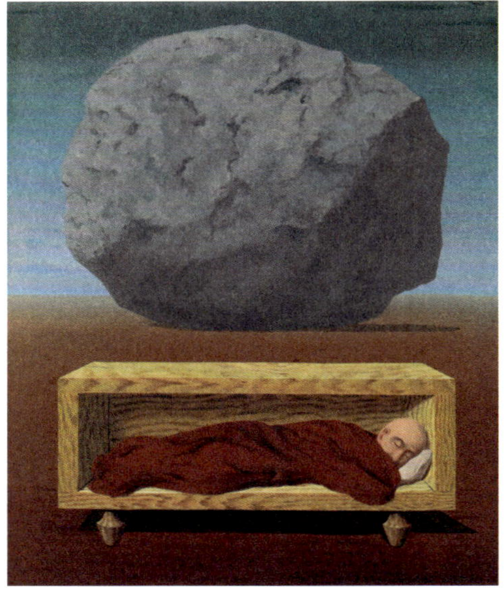

René Magritte, *Le cap des tempêtes*, 1964, oil on canvas, 100.3 × 81.2 cm, inv. 3155. This work interacts with the old landscape paintings.

loans from other museums and private collections to do so. Thanks to this flexibility, we can fill in any gaps: for example, we're going to exchange one of our pieces by Rik Wouters for a Georges Vantongerloo from Mu.ZEE."

Rhythm, diversity and variety

When the museum in the southern district 't Zuid opened in 1890, the walls of a number of galleries were chock-a-block, so to speak, with paintings hanging in closed ranks, from floor to ceiling, with hardly any organising principle. There was only one division: old and (at the time) modern masters were hung separately. This is still the case in the new KMSKA. Also, Rubens still has a gallery all to himself. Nico Van Hout: "In the old museum building, we mainly show figurative art, featuring religion, morality and civil life. Art intended for churches and palaces, informed by the classical concept of beauty and dealing with themes such as power and impotence, evil and suffering, heaven, worldviews, entertainment and abundance. In the new building, we show art that has moved on from those themes and from figuration itself. Art in which light, form and colour have become the principal elements. Here, it's not so much about what's to see, but how it fills the painting."

Siska Beele: "There's also an Honour Gallery at the front of the building in which we go back in time: a room filled with salon art – a kind of time capsule. It's a re-creation of the 19th-century salon with its rows of paintings, one above the other. After all, the Honour Gallery was originally intended for that type of academic art exhibition. There are self-portraits by artists such as Ingres and Fantin-Latour, history paintings by Ferdinand De Braekeleer, Cabanel and Bouguereau, and realistic oil canvases featuring peasants, labourers and beggars by Meunier, Evenepoel, Claus and also Van Gogh. Salon art was brushed aside by the modernists as a *quantité négligeable* (unimportant, basically), but since the arrival and success of the Musée d'Orsay in Paris, it is being appreciated again. Often it concerns works that we have not previously put on display. Another noteworthy change is that there are many more sculptures in the galleries than before the closure. That too is a sign of a revival of appreciation."

Nico Van Hout: "We are also prompting meaningful dialogue across the centuries, in both directions: modern works can hang among the old masters, and vice versa. Fra Angelico from 1435, for example, hangs in the new building, because his painting already contains seeds of Cubism and of thinking in volumes. A work by Magritte from 1964, *Le cap des tempêtes* – which is dominated by a floating rock – fits in comfortably among the old landscapes. Those confrontations are refreshing. But rest assured, we have winnowed the collection quite diligently. 'Kill your darlings' is a very difficult mandate for an art historian, but we didn't want to stuff the halls to the gills. Now, the circuit has rhythm, diversity and variety, with diverse scenography too, and here and there an almost empty hall giving you space to look at only one, or just a few, masterpieces."

Cherchez les femmes

The KMSKA has also taken a critical look at itself. At certain gaps in its collection, for instance. Nico Van Hout: "Our 20th-century collection needs to expand its female and international presence. We already have taken some initial steps. I'm thinking of Marthe Donas, who can be brought into dialogue with Archipenko. Or Jules Schmalzigaug, who has close ties to the Italian Futurists."

Siska Beele: "Nicaise De Keyser's *The Fame of the Antwerp School of Art*, the series of paintings that for many visitors is the first thing they see upon entering, features only men, excepting the allegorical figures. This imbalance is also visible in our collection: among the old masters we have only a few works by women, namely Catharina van Hemessen, Clara Peeters and Michaelina Wautier. In the 19th-century salon, we're now showing work by three women: Virginie Demont-Breton, Henriëtte Ronner-Knip and Adèle Kindt."

Nico Van Hout: "This is actually a statement we're making in the museum square. *Deep Fountain* is by Cristina Iglesias, the circular bench is by Ann Demeulemeester, our new mosaic at the top of the stairs is by Marie Zolamian and, since the reopening, a work by Lili Dujourie has found its place on the high plinth on the left."

Marthe Donas, *Still Life*, 1917, oil on canvas, 34.5 × 53 cm (within frame), inv. 2948

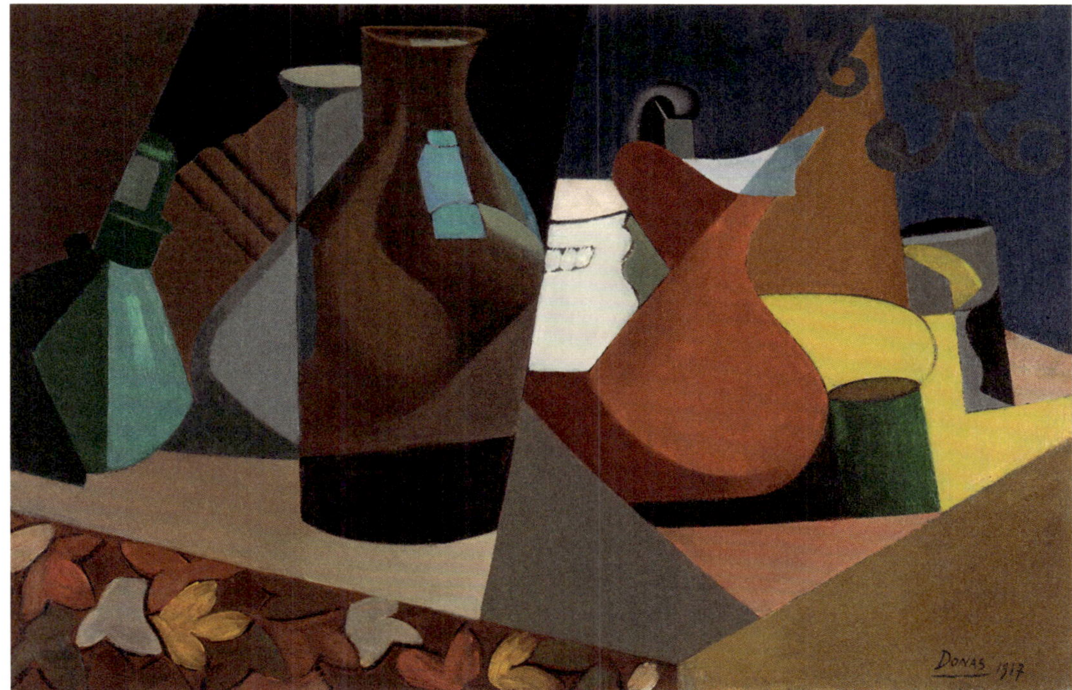

More female artists: the new mosaic by Marie Zolamian (under construction).

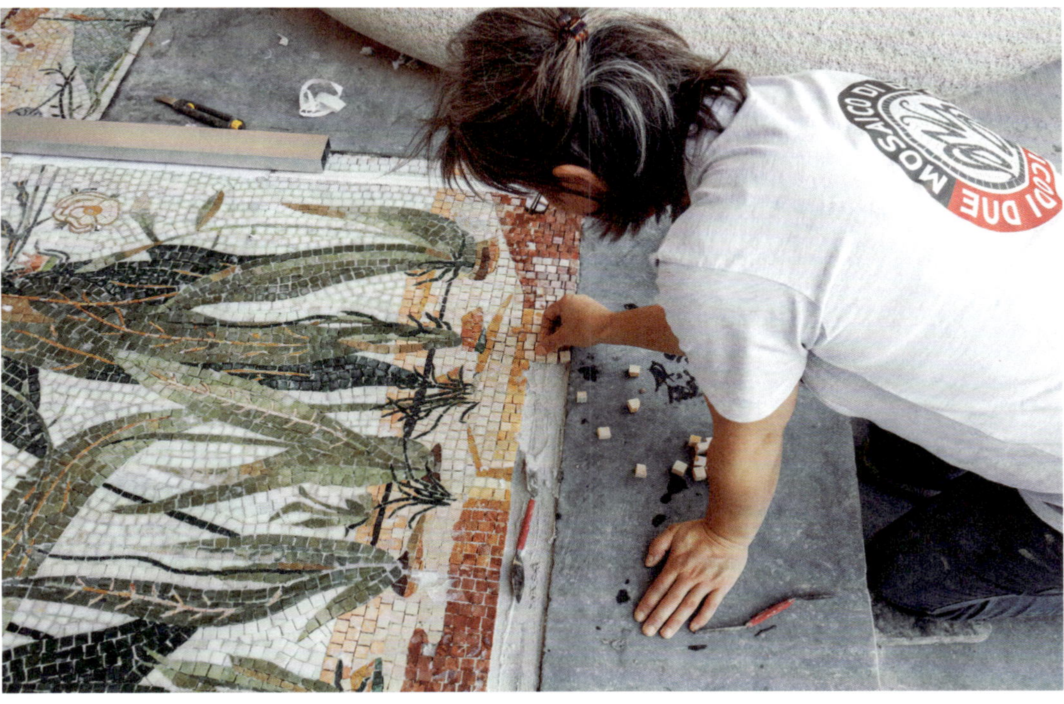

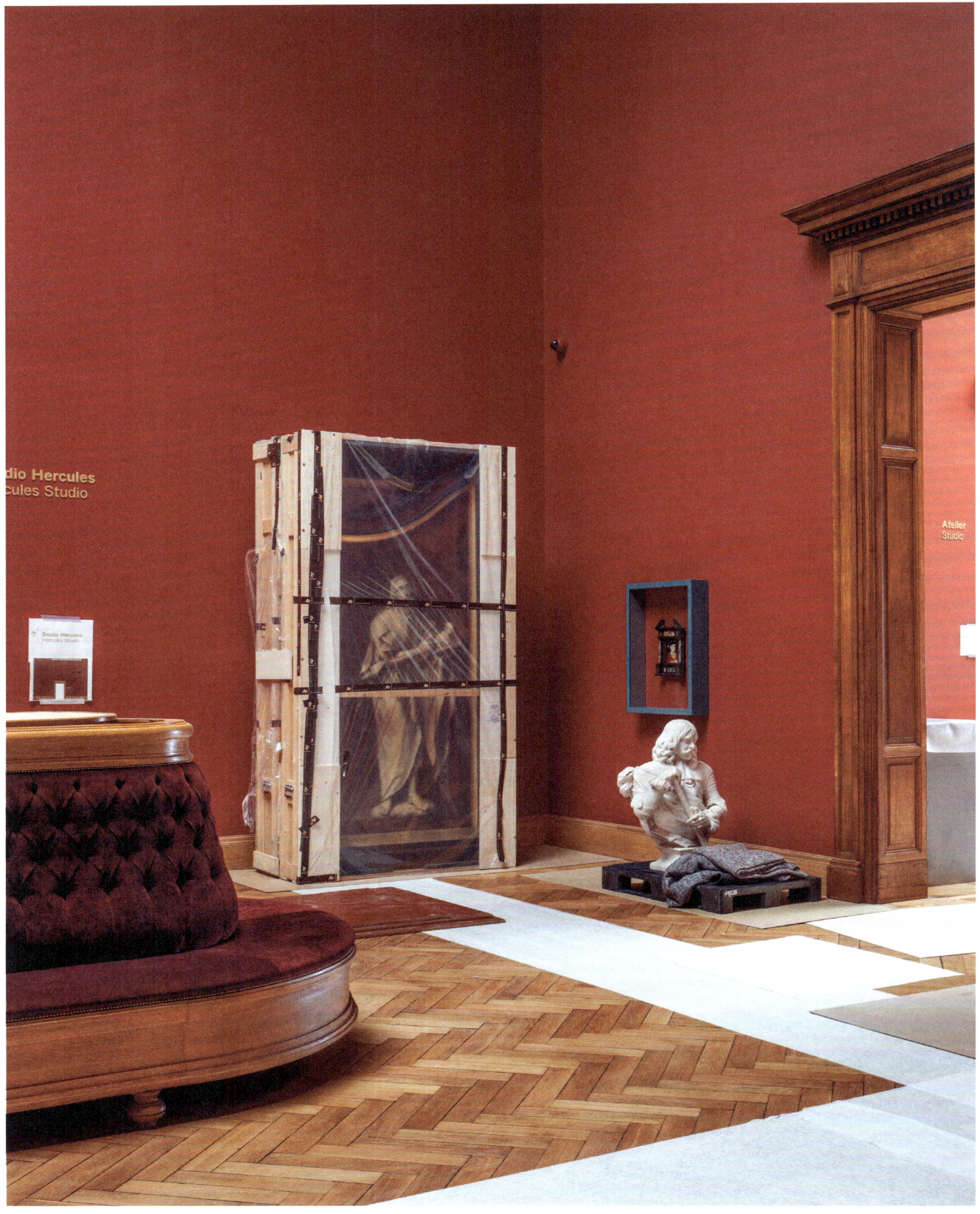
dio Hercules
cules Studio
Atelier
Studio

Putting the artworks on display, summer 2022.

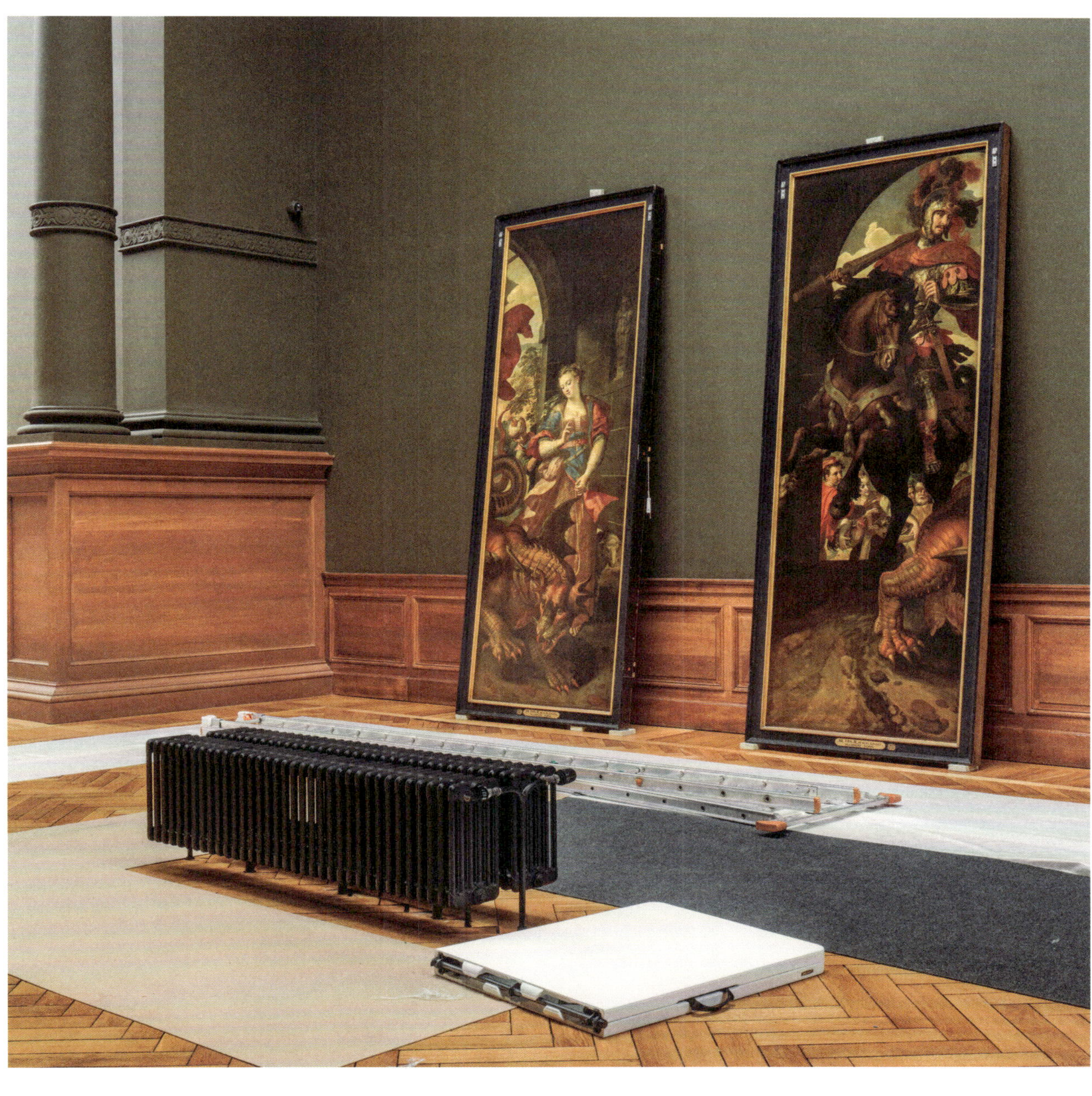

One big family: the scenography

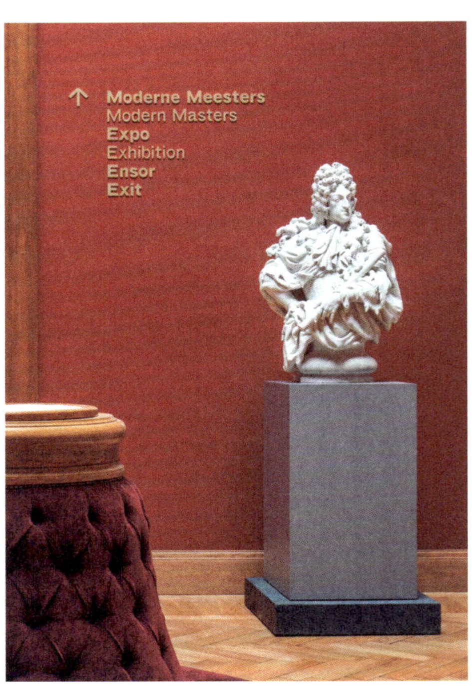

The shade of grey chosen for the pedestal depends on the sculpture.

According to the Cambridge dictionary, scenography is "the art or job of designing and creating scenery for a show or event". A rather narrow definition of a facet of the museum world that is highly important. In museums and exhibitions, scenographers are helping develop the entire design, and therefore also how visitors view the exhibited works and experience their visit. How are the works (safely) installed and mounted? What kind of display cases do you use, and which suspension systems? What is the atmosphere – or rather, the atmospheres – of the various galleries? And what does the route look like that visitors are to follow? What needs to be communicated, and what font do you use?

Aslı Çiçek developed the scenography together with Robbrecht en Daem Architecten. Lies De Rauw is Project Manager at Meyvaert, a firm that specialises in designing museum display cases. They describe the basic premises the KMSKA followed in the scenography.

Coherent

How do you create a connection between two very different museum atmospheres? The classical atmosphere of a 19th-century museum and the contemporary atmosphere of a 21st-century museum? Linking these two together was the main ambition throughout the process of designing the pedestals, display cases and other elements of the KMSKA furniture. Each element has its own character, but, above all, they form a recognisable 'family' for visitors as they make their way through the museum, regardless of which part they're in. These recognisable and, over time, familiar features have another advantage: they're interchangeable. In this way, as a museum, you can deal flexibly and sustainably with the furniture of your art presentation. In these times, we'd expect no less.

The objective of creating a visible link between classical and contemporary in the old and new spaces of the museum also determined the choice of trimming materials – brass and bronze – used with the various components of the scenography. Their warm presence and colour give a classical touch, while their modern finish provides a contemporary look. They are used for the room numbers, the lettering in the signage, the pictograms that help point the way, the text label holders and so forth.

The core idea behind the interior design of the KMSKA is simple: to ensure uniformity, repetition, cohesion and coherence. All for visitor comfort. Everything is connected with everything else: from the size of the decorative perforations in the furniture to the details of the finishing touches in wood, bronze and brass. The brass signage was designed especially for the KMSKA, as were the holders of (among other things) the gallery texts and object labels. These required separate production: the label holders are pleated with a special v-cut technique to achieve a nifty detailing at the corners. That is a precise and artisanal piece of work.

Five greys

You will also find craftsmanship in the museum in places where you wouldn't immediately expect it. Take the plinths of the pedestals, with their light relief. They are cast in bronze as separate pieces, using a sand casting technique, and then welded together invisibly. Invisibly, because the bronze is hammered and patinated after casting. You could also call that a form of colouring. Again, this process involves a lot of craftsmanship. To give you an idea: the making of one pedestal requires 16 working hours. The bronze is heated with an open flame, and chemical products are added to provoke a reaction. Then colour is added with a brush and a dabbing technique, and finally there comes a protective layer of wax. Each stage, each element and each material makes its own contribution to the final appearance of the plinth.

The pedestals have wooden elements that are varnished in five different shades of grey, from almost white to almost black. The choice of shade for each pedestal is tailored to the sculpture standing, sitting or lying on it. The greenish plinths are a link to Cristina Iglesias's *Deep Fountain* on the square in front of the museum. The same grey and green trim can be found in other 'family members' throughout the interior of the museum: the display cases, altar pedestals, stools and lamps in the reading room of the library, among others.

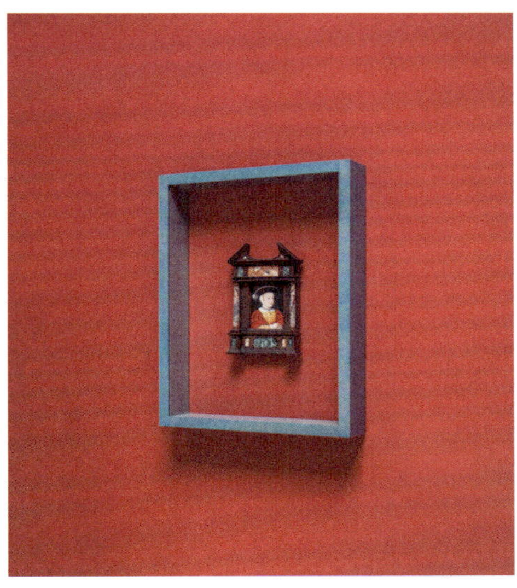

The wall display cases are minimalist in design, keeping hinges and lighting out of sight.

Minimalistic

The KMSKA uses wall-mounted display cases as well as freestanding ones. Their design is minimalistic, with shallow dimensions and a finely built frame. The design brief included the need to "make the hinges and lighting disappear" – a complex undertaking with hinges that sometimes have to hold a glass pane measuring 160 x 190 centimetres. Such shallow display cases do pose a challenge with regards to stability; when you open them, the centre of gravity lurches forward. To counteract this, they must be very firmly attached to the wall, and brackets have been used to fortify the wall's load-bearing capacity. This is how to achieve minimalist, yet stable wall-mounted display cases.

Once again, the challenge in the detailing of the display cases and pedestals was to ensure visual consistency throughout the museum. This was a separate issue from the system for opening the display cases. Which in turn is related to the size of the object inside the case and therefore to the size of the door-opening, the placement of the display case (against the wall or freestanding?), the speed required to evacuate works of art... Also, note the unusual profile at the bottom of the glass cloches. This is a distinctive and bespoke design for the KMSKA.

The unique scenography to be found in the KMSKA since its reopening was realised by pooling our insights, setting clear objectives, choosing creative ideas and sourcing sophisticated craftsmanship. All with one goal in mind: to offer visitors an intense experience.

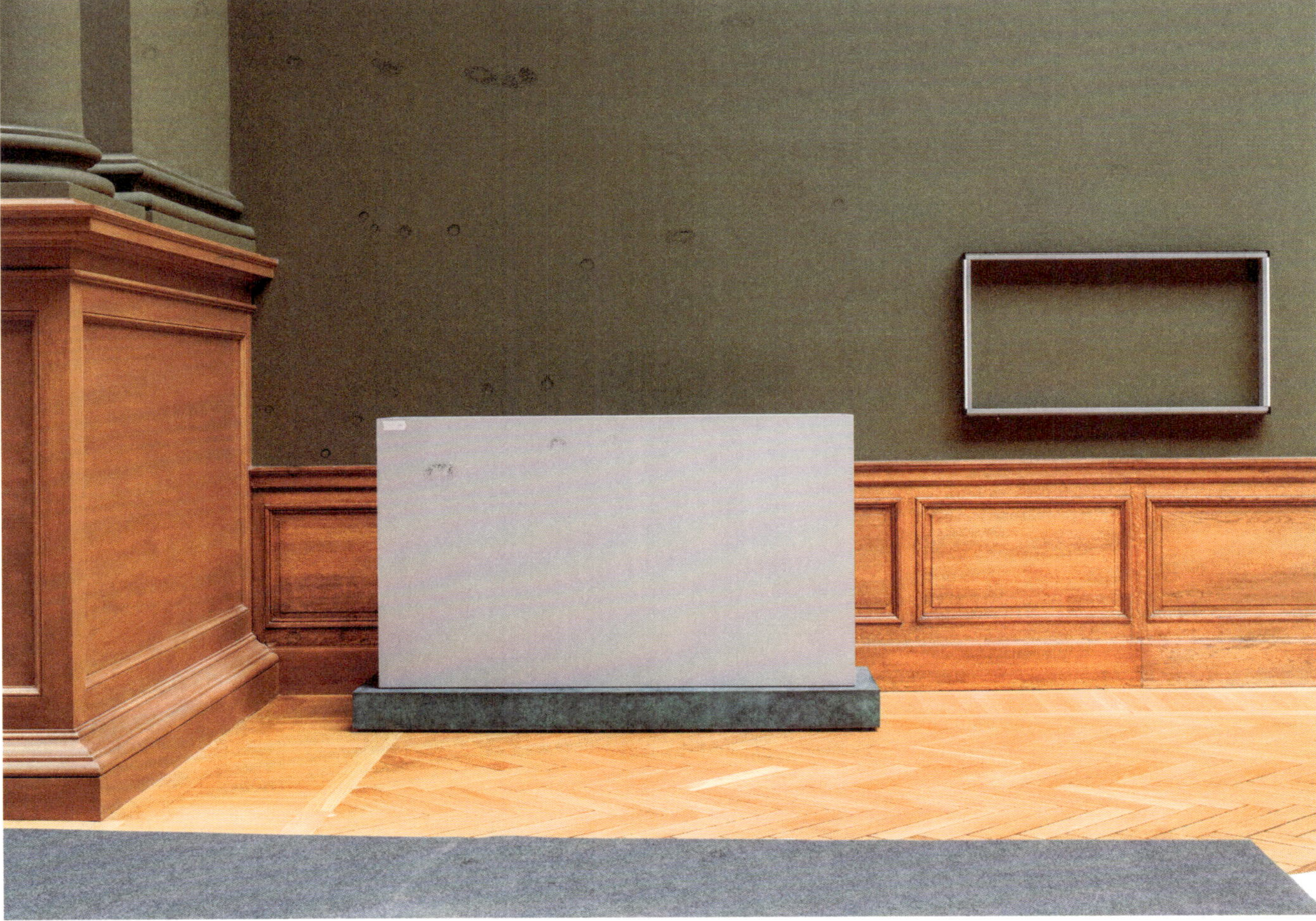

The pedestals, display cases and other elements of furniture provide visual links between classical and contemporary, between the old and the new museum.

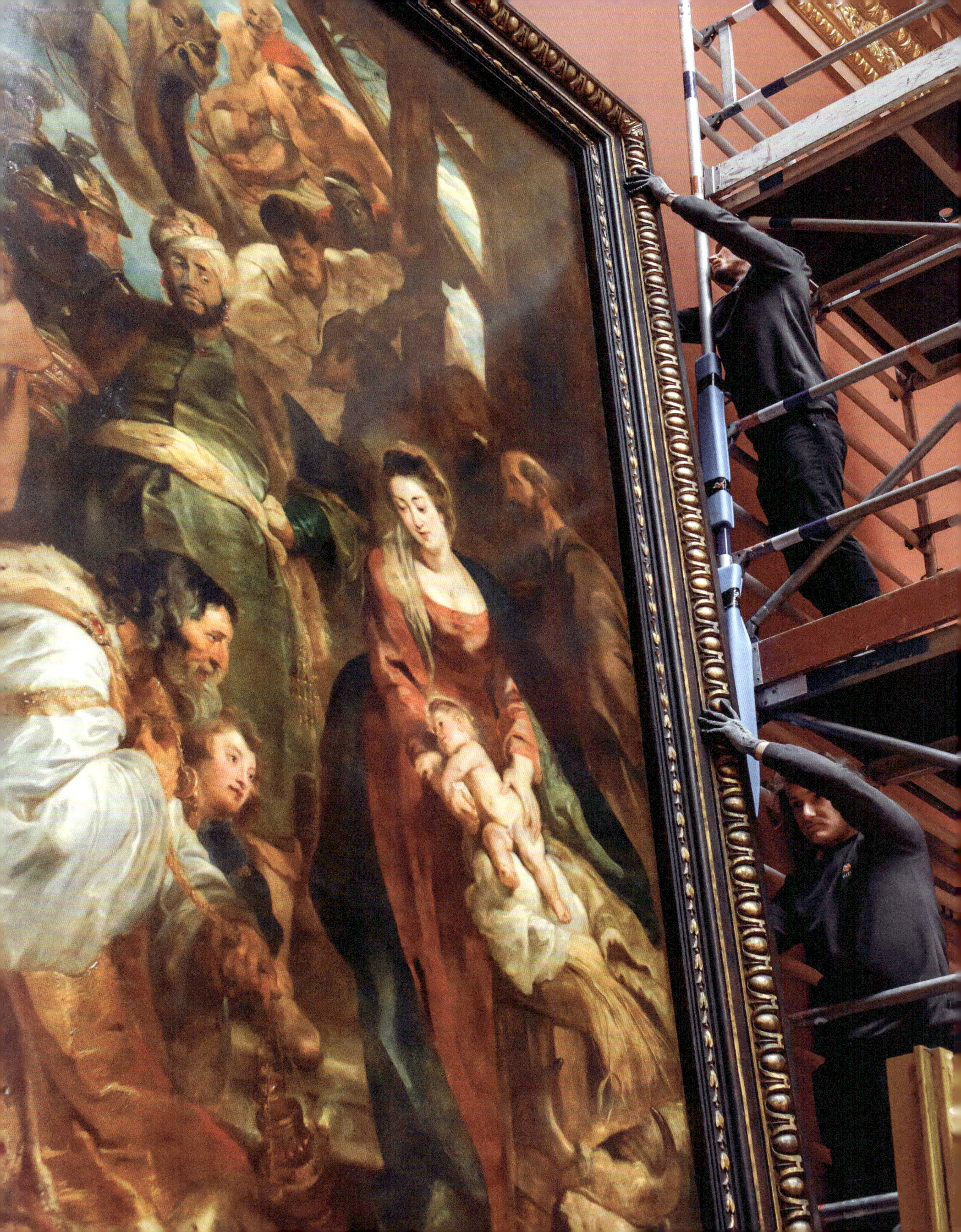

A monumental Rubens such as *The Adoration of the Magi* weighs more than 600 kilogrammes. The panel supports weigh 36 kilogrammes on their own.

When you see art on display in a museum it seems so simple: there is a painting, large or small, and there is a sculpture, large and small. So what? It's like what you do at home, but on a larger scale and with many more artworks.

Giant Rubens

It is, of course, not quite that simple. Take an enormous Rubens such as *The Adoration of the Magi*, for example, which weighs more than 600 kilos. The panel has been mounted in the Rubens Gallery again, no doubt for years to come. How can that be done safely, aesthetically and elegantly? And how can you successfully balance good conservation and maintenance with the enjoyment of the visitor? How do you discreetly but unmistakeably show that some works are protected? What do you do if it turns out that the wall on which your Rubens is planned to be mounted contains air shafts, which is not exactly ideal considering its weight?

At the KMSKA, the specialists of Etoile Mécanique solved many such problems, each one presenting a unique challenge. They have experience working with the notoriously strict British Museum, among others. Known as 'mounting and pinning' in English, our museums call the specialism by its French word, *soclage*. Etoile Mécanique carried out their work in close consultation with the registrars and conservators – who know better than anyone where the weak spots are in works of art and where support is most needed – as well as stability engineers and art handlers.

The solution? Chemical anchoring behind the air shafts with *tiges* (threaded rods) that are firmly attached (aided by filming the wall's innards with a camera), and with tubes around the rods that distribute the point load over the wall's stones. At the bottom of the artwork, the supports must have sufficient, well, supporting capacity. In the case of the enormous Rubens panel, the supports themselves weigh 36 kilos. The suspension system at the top of the work offers great adjustability, to accommodate old paintings that may be crooked or warped. Thanks to the flexibility of the system, the art handlers can hang heavy panels flush with the wall. All paintings weighing more than 150 kilos use this specialised support system.

There is another type of painting that is exhibited away from the wall: the triptych. These are mounted on a freestanding pedestal. This too must be done securely.

Vulnerable sculptures

It's not only the giants that are vulnerable. Small sculptures are too – imagine if a visitor accidentally bumped into one... Consequently, they are also protected and stabilised. The stabilising element is usually inside or at the back of the object. This requires a special preparation process, for which the rough shape of the pedestal is made in the museum itself. First, the workshop technicians sit together with the scenographers and curators, who explain their story. Using sketches, together they decide what the stand will look like. Often, several small objects and paintings end up in one display case, in a carefully considered arrangement. Once the positions have been determined, the sensitivities of objects have been discussed, and the feasibility of the suspension has been investigated, the sawing, bending, fitting and adjusting begins – on site, in a mobile workshop. The various parts are then numbered and sent to the workshop for finishing. Pedestals are preferably made of non-ferrous metal and given a low-solvent coating, with additional protective layers around it. Purpose: to avoid corrosion so as not to leave any contact marks, not even after years of loyal support.

All things considered, *soclage* is the search for a balance between function, security, substance and aesthetics. It is – as will be clear by now – an art in itself.

pp. 170-171: Hanging Rubens' *The Baptism of Christ*, more than four metres high and almost seven metres wide, on the wall of the gallery was no easy task for even the most experienced of art handlers.

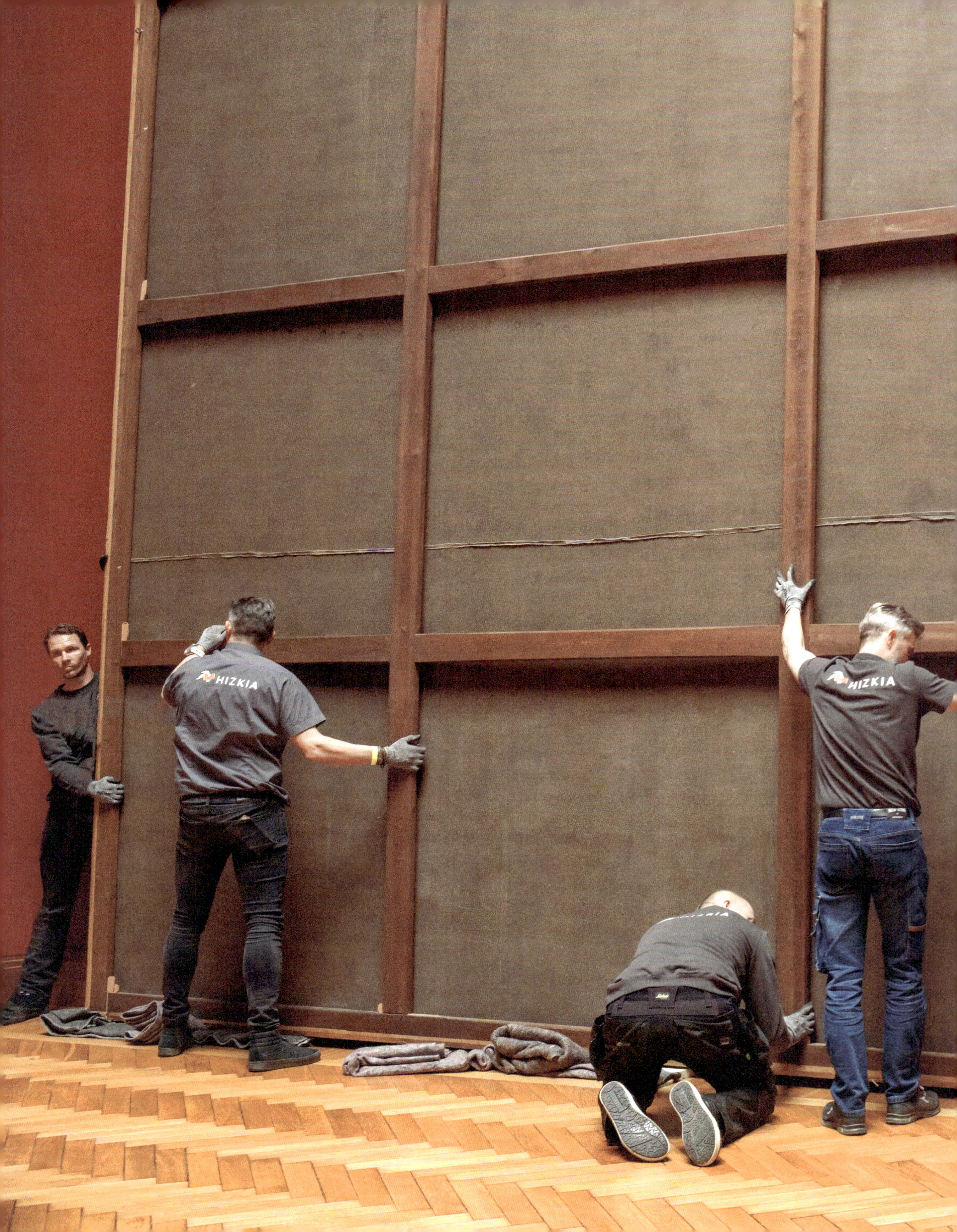
HIZKIA
HIZKIA

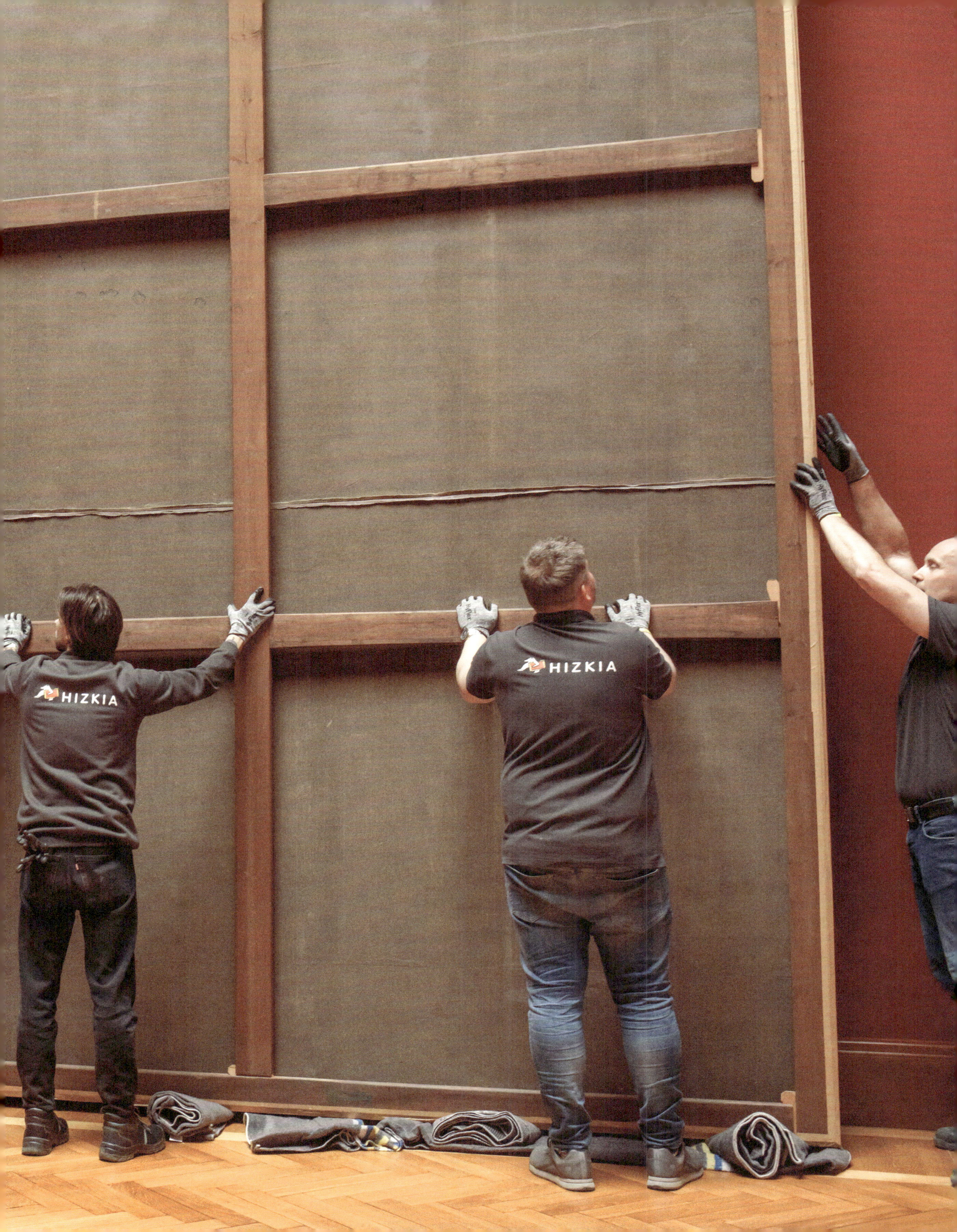
HIZKIA
HIZKIA

7. A RENOVATED OPERATION

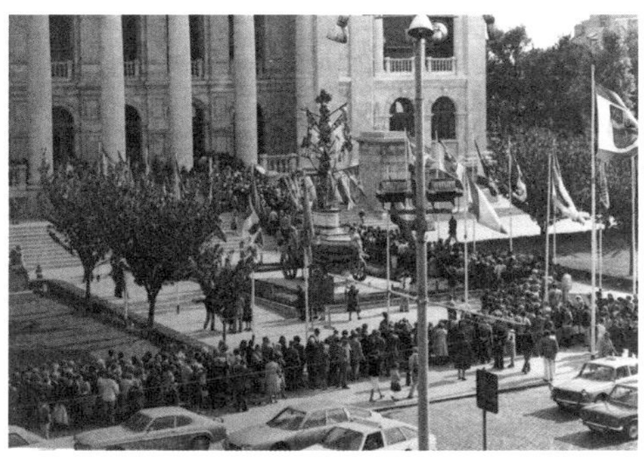

The Rubens exhibition in 1977 drew 625,000 visitors. In those days, people stood in line patiently.

"I think it's a striking image, and it's wonderful to reach so many people who would otherwise never visit a museum, but…" Birgit Pluvier, Head of Marketing at the KMSKA since 2018, is looking at an iconic image from 1977 of a long queue of people waiting in front of the museum. It was the famous year when lines of people queued patiently on the Leopold de Waelplaats to see the KMSKA's mega-exhibition of work by Peter Paul Rubens, in his 400th birthday year. The queue included many people who wouldn't normally visit a museum. The final tally numbered about 625,000 visitors.

The visitor's journey

Birgit Pluvier explains where the "but" comes from: "Standing in a queue is a pet peeve for most museum visitors. Even worse is when it's so busy that you can barely see the artworks you've come for, as is sometimes the case in large museums. We do everything we can to avoid that. We really aim to offer a first-rate visit, even though as a museum you can't have everything under control. But you can apply the art of crowd control. That means, for example, that at very busy times you can go up to roughly 1,500 visitors being present in the museum at the same time."

There's a new concept gaining ground in museums: the visitor's journey. Also called the customer's journey. Companies, airports and hospitals have been working with this idea for some time. Birgit Pluvier: "How do you make your visitors feel welcome – from the first moment of contact (these days, this usually takes place digitally), but especially, of course, during their visit and also after their visit? How do you create a feeling that makes your visitor form a bond with the museum, and want to return? What do people with families expect from their visit? And what does an art aficionado expect? Or someone short on time? At what moments is their experience enhanced, or vice versa – what in your museum might be blocking their experience? This involves literally everything: the facilities, the garden, the reception, the bathrooms and of course the route that people take in your museum and the collection that they get to see. But it's also about the visit to the website, your social media, your posters, your PR… If you identify and map out those moments, you can do something with them as a museum. Do they enhance the experience, or do they spoil it? These are all tools you can use to adjust the visitor experience. Research has shown, for example, that if you offer 'something nice' at the end of a visit, you positively reinforce the general feeling that visitors take home with them."

Museum puzzles

"I strongly believe in the power of the experience that people get from their museum visit. That is why, for example, the friendliness of your reception staff is so essential. And why it's important that, if you aim for a diverse audience, that ambition should also be visible in the museum team. The KMSKA has made a purposeful choice to make vacancies as accessible as possible and to fine-tune communication channels to reach our target audience. This way, we manage to get other groups of people to apply for vacancies. That is a learning process for many museums, including us. We've come a long way."

"You should also not forget that coming to a museum is not a given for many people, that it's not something they find easy to do. Other people want to plan their visit down to the very last detail, on the website: what can you do in which spaces, where is it going to be busy, where can you expect what…? All of that is going to be possible. New technologies are very helpful. They can identify quiet or very busy moments, for example, so that we can react accordingly. We've been working with a test audience and focus groups in

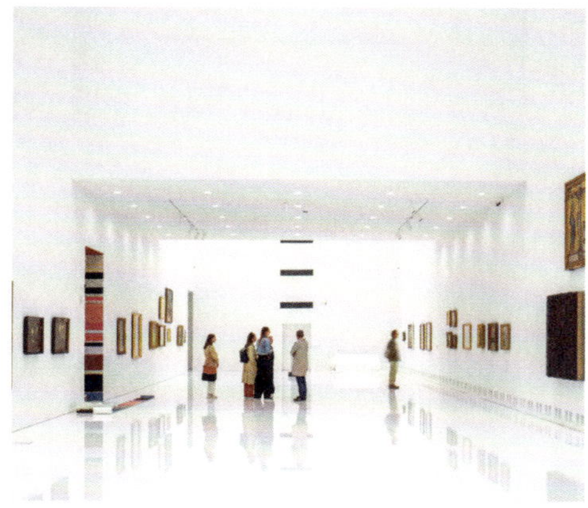

The Light gallery on the first floor in the new museum volume.

the run-up to the reopening. This yielded a great many ideas and wishes. We've tried to accommodate as many of these as we could in our way of doing things and in our route through the museum. Lots of little puzzles to be solved. I'll give just a few examples: people experiencing poverty, people in wheelchairs, people with a visual impairment…"

Framework

Everyone is welcome. A beautiful and noble goal. But who is everyone? The general public, young and old, both the seasoned art connoisseur and the newly interested? Birgit Pluvier: "It's impossible to reach everyone. We started by broadly defining target groups – or *personae* – each with their own profile and interests. These people have a certain level of knowledge when it comes to art; these choose certain leisure-time activities; these may or may not experience certain difficulties during a museum visit; these have their own motives for coming to the museum… We then tested these personae with audience research in order to get rid of certain assumptions. Our own blind spots, so to speak. Then we announced the personae throughout the organisation. That's how they came to life. It has helped us to provide a new framework to everyone who is working with the public. And to develop a reflex to think from the perspective of the visitor."

"What I also think to be of importance: it has led us to offer layered information on different formats. For all the Highlights, for example, we use both short and longer texts, and texts that go into more detail about what you're seeing. That way, people can choose how much information they want to absorb. That is the reason why we are working and writing for a specific audience: to know who you are doing this for. I know that such an approach has sometimes been viewed with scepticism in the museum world, but in the end everyone can see that it makes sense."

"If I compare the museum world from around 2000 with that of 2022, an awful lot has happened. Back then, museums certainly weren't so intensely engaged with their audiences. On the contrary. There was almost no layering, many texts in museums were quite specialised, audio guides were sometimes simply a recorded catalogue. Museums didn't make it easy for their visitors. So I'm happy that the KMSKA has experienced such a long renovation and restoration period. It has given us the opportunity to review and renovate our operations too. As the cliché goes, museum curators/conservators and marketing people sometimes have different wishes. As a museum, you have to find a middle ground. I'm convinced that in recent years we've moved mountains at the KMSKA, and that we've grown closer to our goal: on the one hand, recognising that you're working and writing for a specific audience and, on the other, realising that by working in layers you can go in-depth and remain relevant at the same time."

Thinking from the visitor's point of view

The competition within the museum world is not getting any smaller and people's expectations are getting bigger. How do you deal with that? Birgit Pluvier: "By offering a range that is polyvalent and diverse. For the KMSKA, there is, of course, the building and the collection, but also the beautiful garden, the lovely café, the feeling that you're welcome, the varied offering that focuses strongly on experience. With that whole package you can entice people to come and visit. But yes, the competition is fierce, especially when you're talking about families. You have to be able to guarantee that people will have a good time, that they'll get value for money and that they'll feel 'comfortable'. It's therefore a real trump card for a museum to be tailored to family visits. In any case, we have worked extremely hard on the hospitality, which the KMSKA wants to extend to everyone."

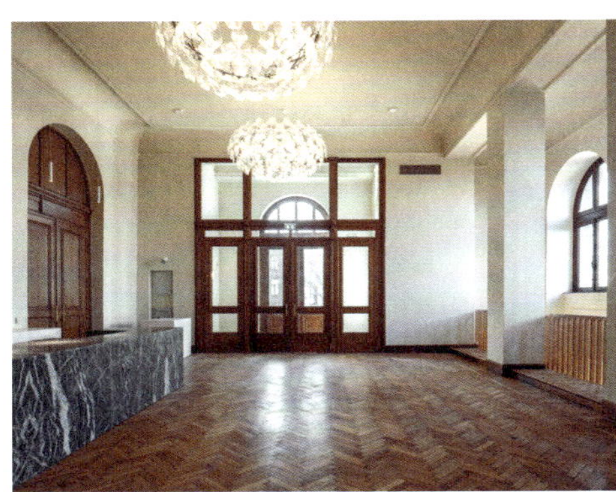

The museum café and restaurant, before decorating.

Museums such as the KMSKA are also gathering places. And where people gather, it doesn't take long before their minds turn towards food and drink. Museum cafés and restaurants have therefore become an important part of the contemporary museum world. They're a contributing factor to the ambience of the museum, expressing core values such as hospitality and sustainability at all levels. 'Madonna' is the name of the KMSKA's new café-restaurant. It is managed by Jan Jacobs, also manager of Fiera in the Antwerp Handelsbeurs. Lorenz Lievens, who helped shape the concept of the café, is in charge of marketing. He is also a neighbour of the museum in the South district, 't Zuid. He fell for its charms in 2021, during a catering event: "We were blown away by this new incarnation of the museum and by the atmosphere of the crew. It was almost magical."

Lievens: "Obviously, by using the name 'Madonna', we're referencing Fouquet's iconic artwork, but we're also taking a broader view. There's a very strong link between Antwerp and Mary, the patron saint of our city. There are 150 Madonna statues scattered throughout the city. These used to be illuminated sites, where people gathered – similar to our function now, in the museum. And to top it off, we discovered that there are more than 70 Madonnas in the KMSKA collection."

"This is first and foremost a place for everyone to feel comfortable. We want to enhance the museum experience with catering and hospitality suitable for every moment of the day, seven days a week. Giving people space and time to talk about what they've seen in the museum. But we're also here for people from the neighbourhood who'd like to have a drink, and for a younger crowd who could well first discover the building and then, perhaps, the museum by way of our cocktail bar on the ground floor. Or for those who are after a fine dining experience in an internationally alluring city such as Antwerp. We're located in what is, after all, one of the jewels in the Antwerp crown, and in the high-quality restaurant district of 't Zuid."

"We thoroughly enjoyed browsing the museum's collection, including items that will not be on display. This has also inspired our menus – for example, the names of dishes. It would be a missed opportunity if we didn't do anything with oysters and a glass of champagne, or with flowers and vegetables, in a museum where you can see *The Oyster Eater* and *Flowers and Vegetables* by Ensor. Tavern scenes from genre paintings put regional beers with a snack on the menu. In this way, we hope to also remind our guests of works they may not have seen. This can be done by making links with the online collection and by incorporating paintings in prints."

"KAAN Architecten did a fantastic job for the museum, with the delightful contrast between old and new, and the two very different atmospheres they conjure up. It was a challenge for us to connect the two worlds, but I think we succeeded, both in our menu and in the decoration and furnishing of the interior. The interior designers, VERBRAEKEN x BISET, made sure of that. Striving for a total experience for our guests was our first priority: by using high-quality materials, by working with plants to bring a little bit of the garden inside, by offering comfortable seating in the various zones, by the tableware, the employee uniforms, the right lighting for the time of day, good acoustics… All this combined is what hospitality means to us. We are well aware that we are part of the face of the KMSKA, and that we help to create goodwill for the museum, among visitors and also among partners."

THE SHOP: AN EXPERIENCE TAILORED TO THE MUSEUM

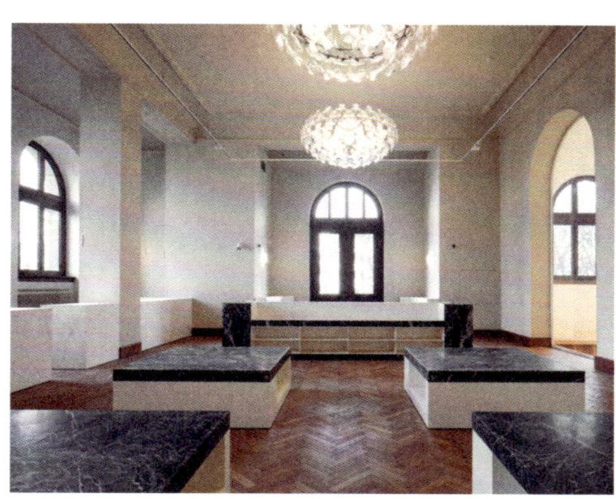

The museum shop, before decorating.

BAI, the operator of the museum shop at the KMSKA, has a great track record in the sector. In 2011, BAI opened the shop at the MAS in Antwerp, and since 2018 it's has been the concession holder of the AfricaShop at the Royal Museum for Central Africa in Tervuren. The company, which also publishes artbooks and designs cultural merchandising, runs temporary pop-up shops for Europalia, BOZAR and the Royal Greenhouses of Laeken, among others.

"Our relationship with the KMSKA has a long history," says Manager Kathleen Borms. "In 1988, we published our first museum catalogue for them, for the Henri De Braekeleer exhibition. Later on, we created the catalogues for the Van Dyck exhibition (1999) and for *Fatal Women*, a collaboration between the KMSKA and the Groninger Museum (2003). Many doors opened for us after that: it led to a collaboration for the merchandising for Lille 2004, European Capital of Culture, among other things. The circle is now complete with the concession for the museum shop at the KMSKA."

"In the finest museum of the country, we present the finest shop," says Borms with a smile. In fact, her statement captures the entire philosophy behind the BAI museum shop. "In the shop, we're offering an experience that is an extension of the museum itself. The bar is set high, and we want to deliver on quality and class. We work with designer and artist Christophe Coppens, for example. He has made accessories – exclusively for our shop – inspired by the ten interventions he created in the museum galleries. For each one, he chose a detail from a painting, which he enlarged and is exhibiting in the gallery as a sculpture. Coppens hasn't made any accessories for ten years, so that's a scoop for the KMSKA shop. We've also teamed up with Essentiel: they design, among other things, kimonos inspired by paintings by Fouquet, Ensor and Wouters."

In addition to this rather exclusive merchandising, more standard items such as postcards, magnets and pins are also on offer, plus books and catalogues that accompany the KMSKA collection and temporary exhibitions. "Obviously we don't want to offer only the more expensive range. Everyone should be able to find something to suit them. But we don't sell ties or scarves with motifs from the paintings. We want to be very selective with the limited space we have."

There's also room in the museum shop for a so-called 'coffee corner'. "There too the emphasis is on the experience, with high-quality Antwerp, and by extension Belgian, treats: coffee from the Antwerp roastery Cross Roast and an excellent barista, with chocolates from Jitsk, Antwerpse Handjes (local biscuits), and products from the De Koninck brewery. The plates are designed by Ann Demeulemeester, the cups and tables are by Vincent Van Duysen and the chairs are by Muller Van Severen."

The museum shop and coffee corner can be visited without a museum ticket.

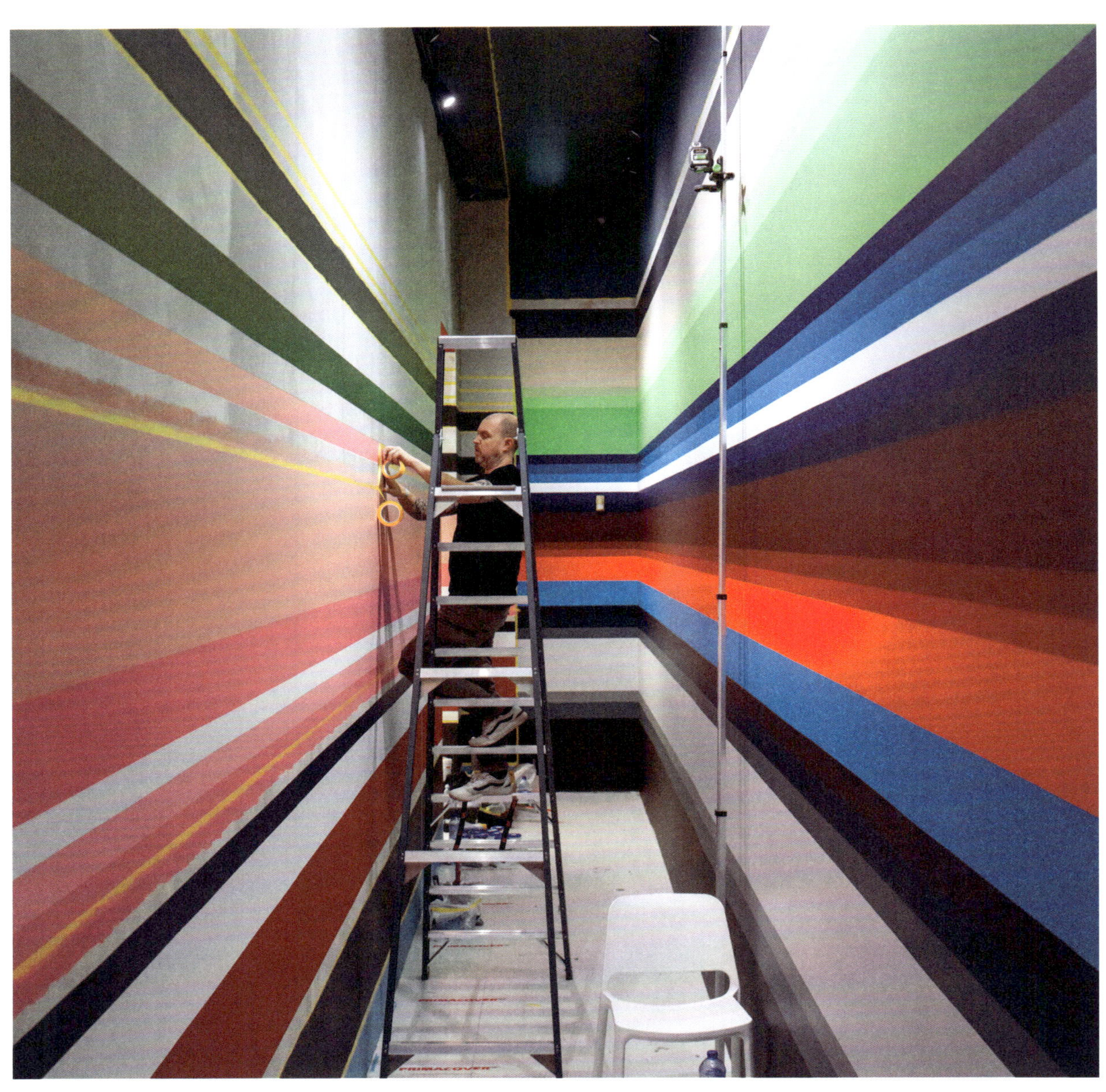

Cartouche 2022. Conflict Painting by Boy & Erik Stappaerts while it's being made, July 2022.
The space displaying this artwork is connected to the Light gallery.

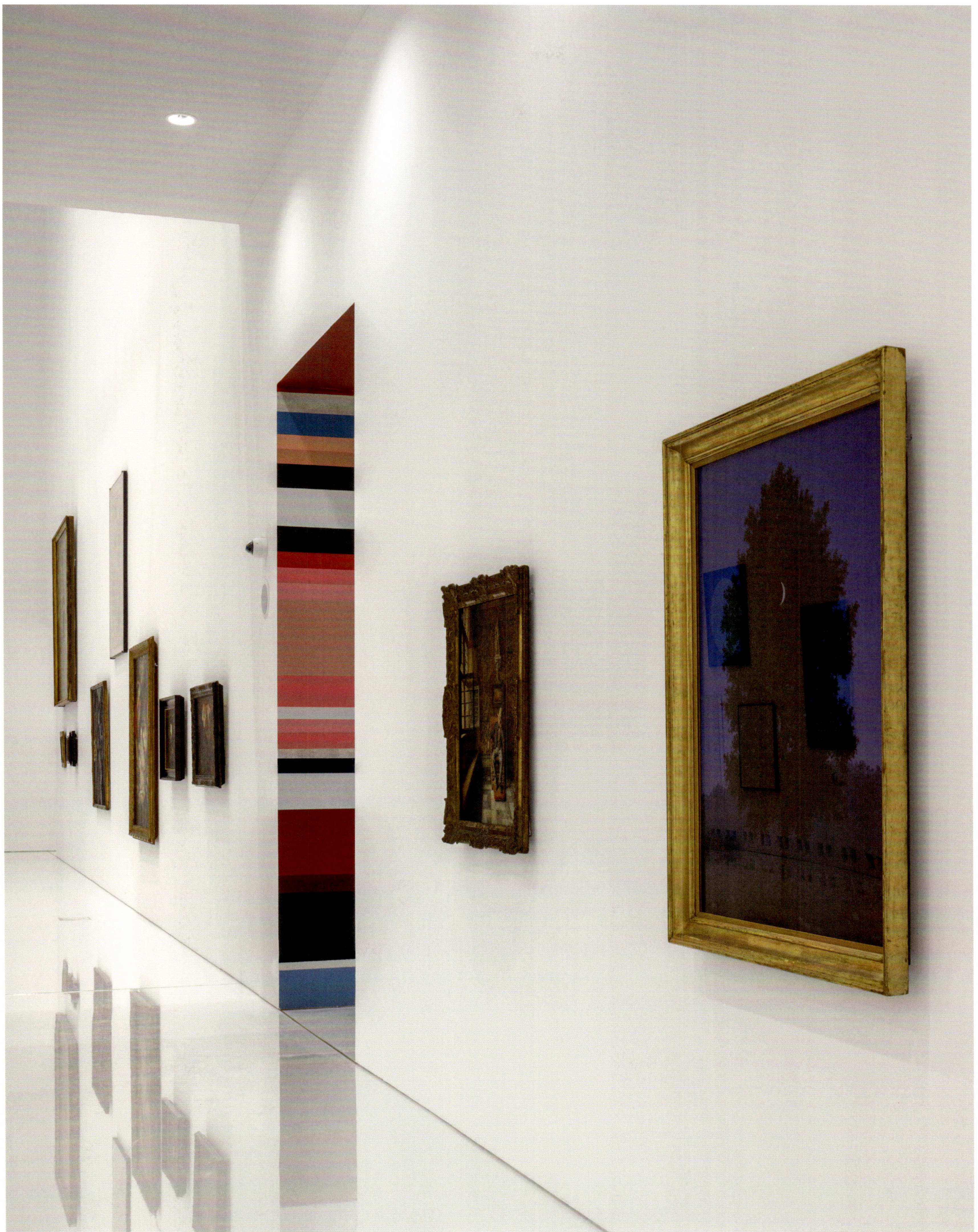

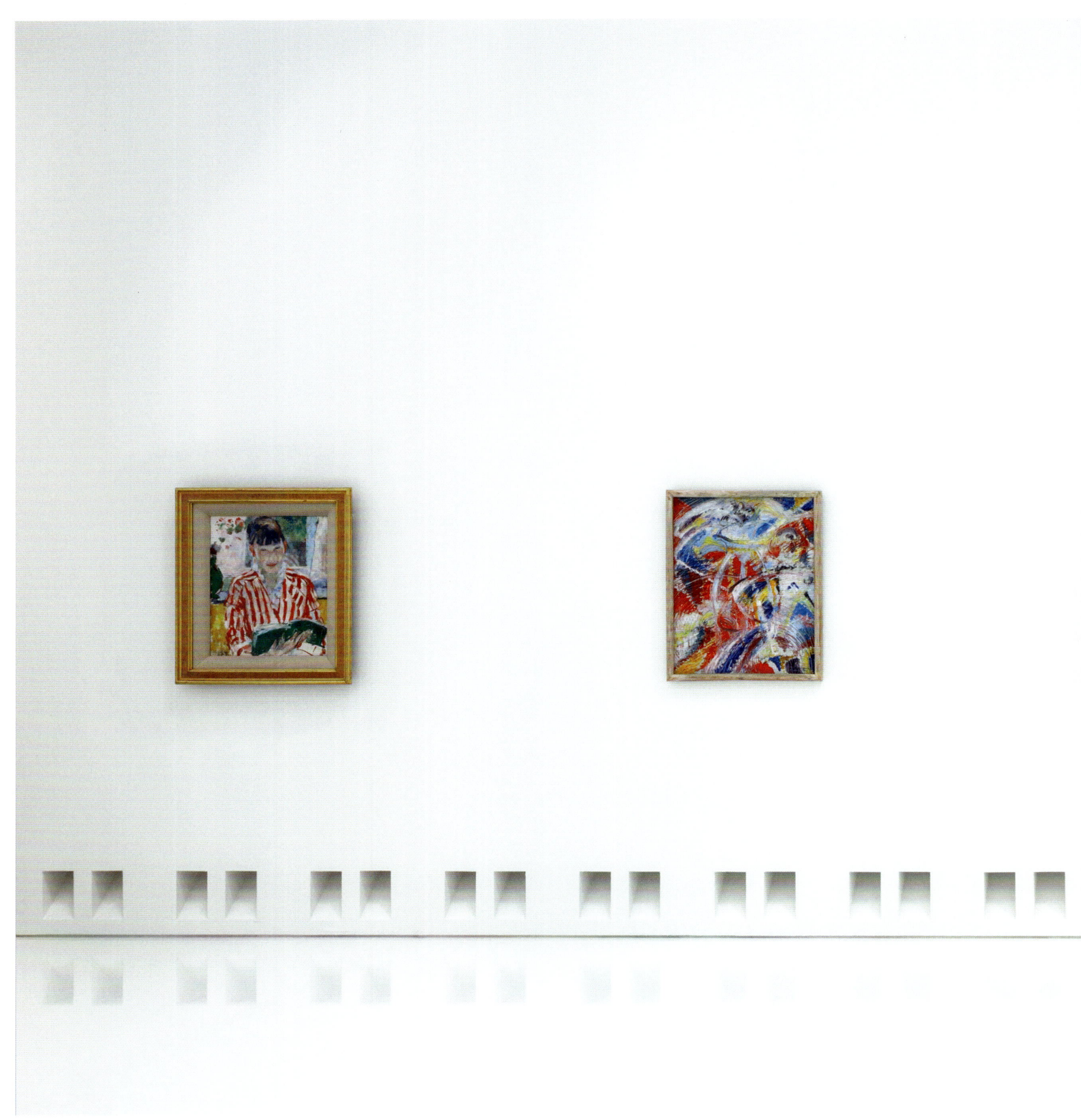

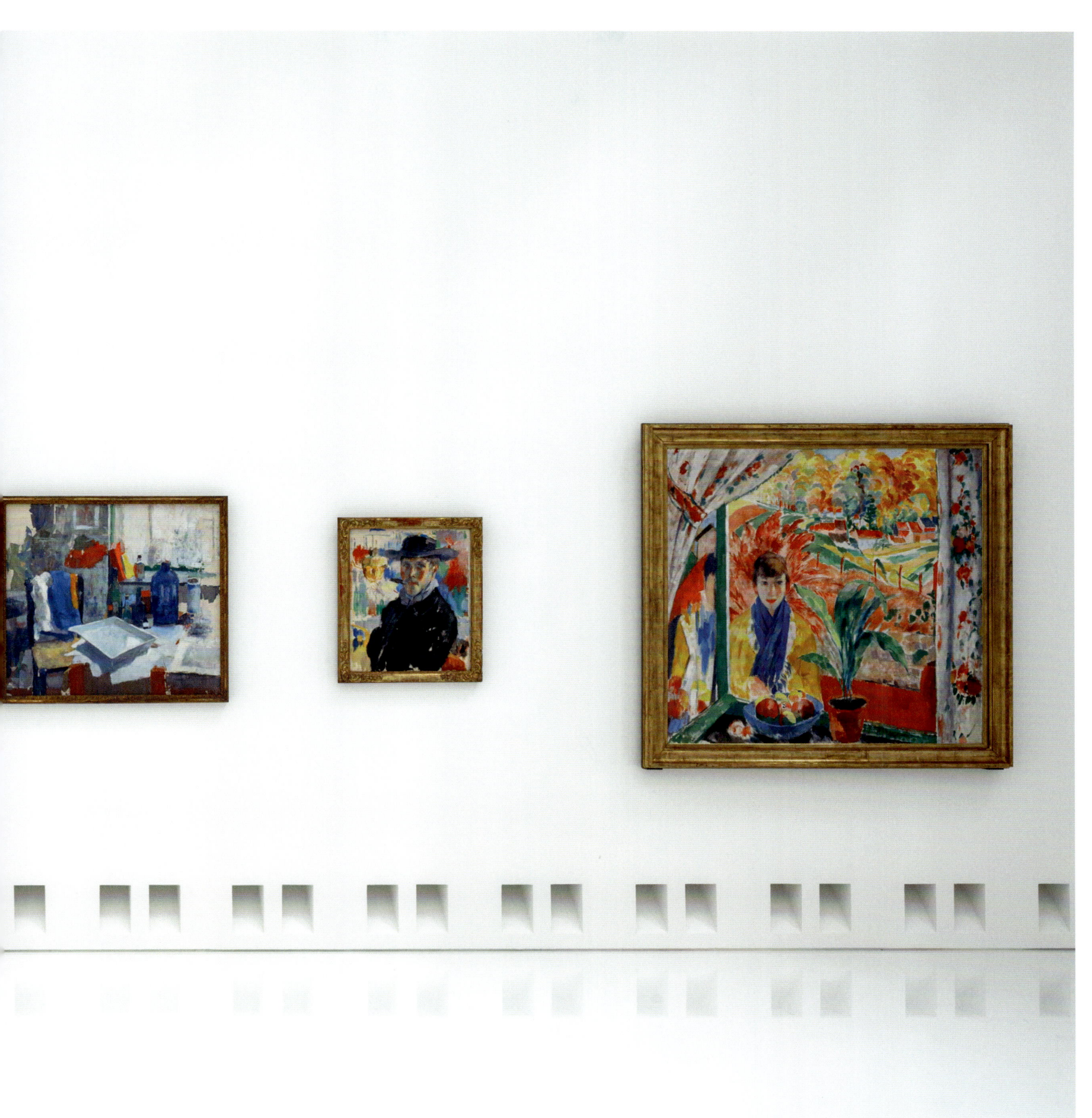

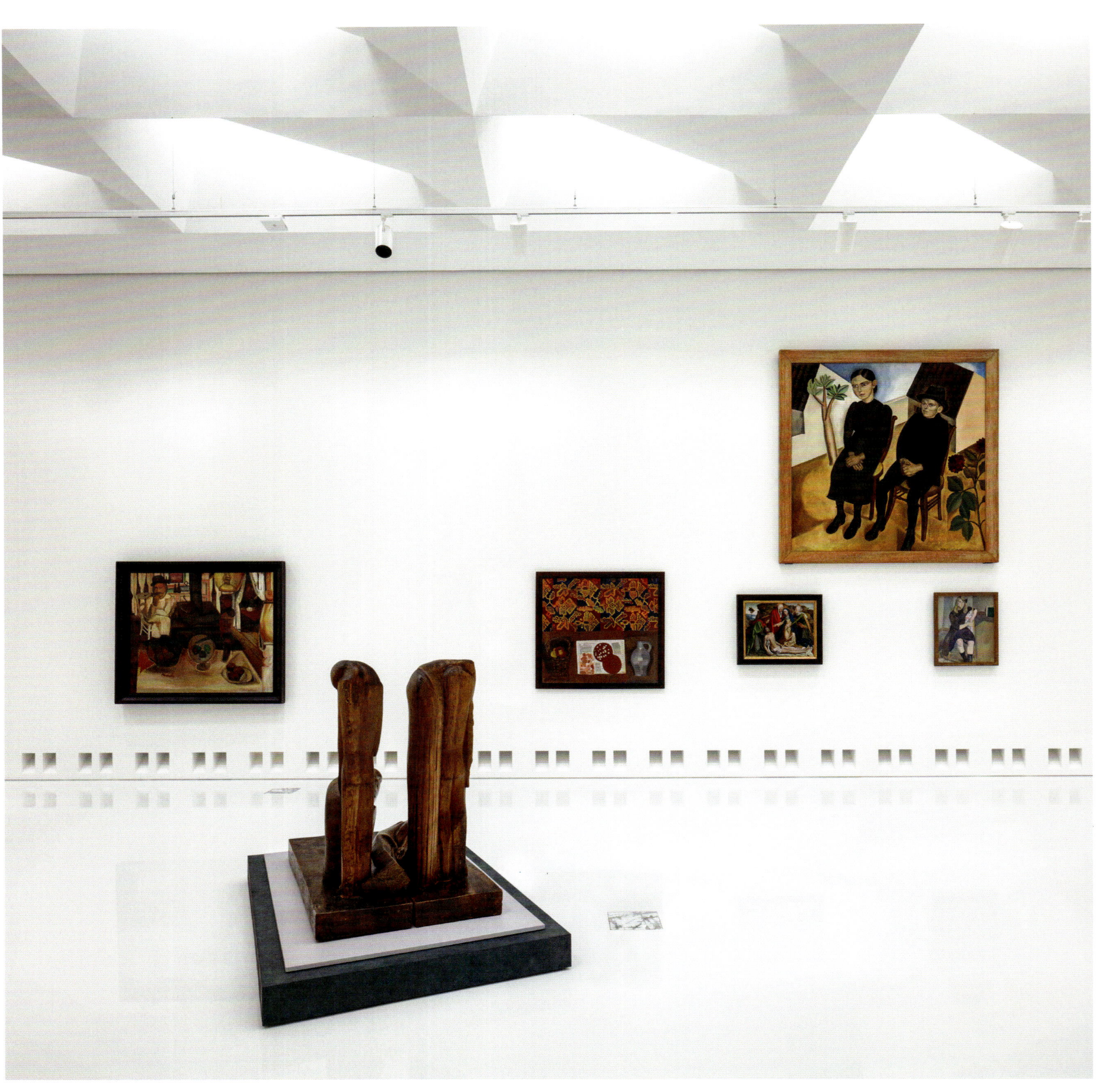

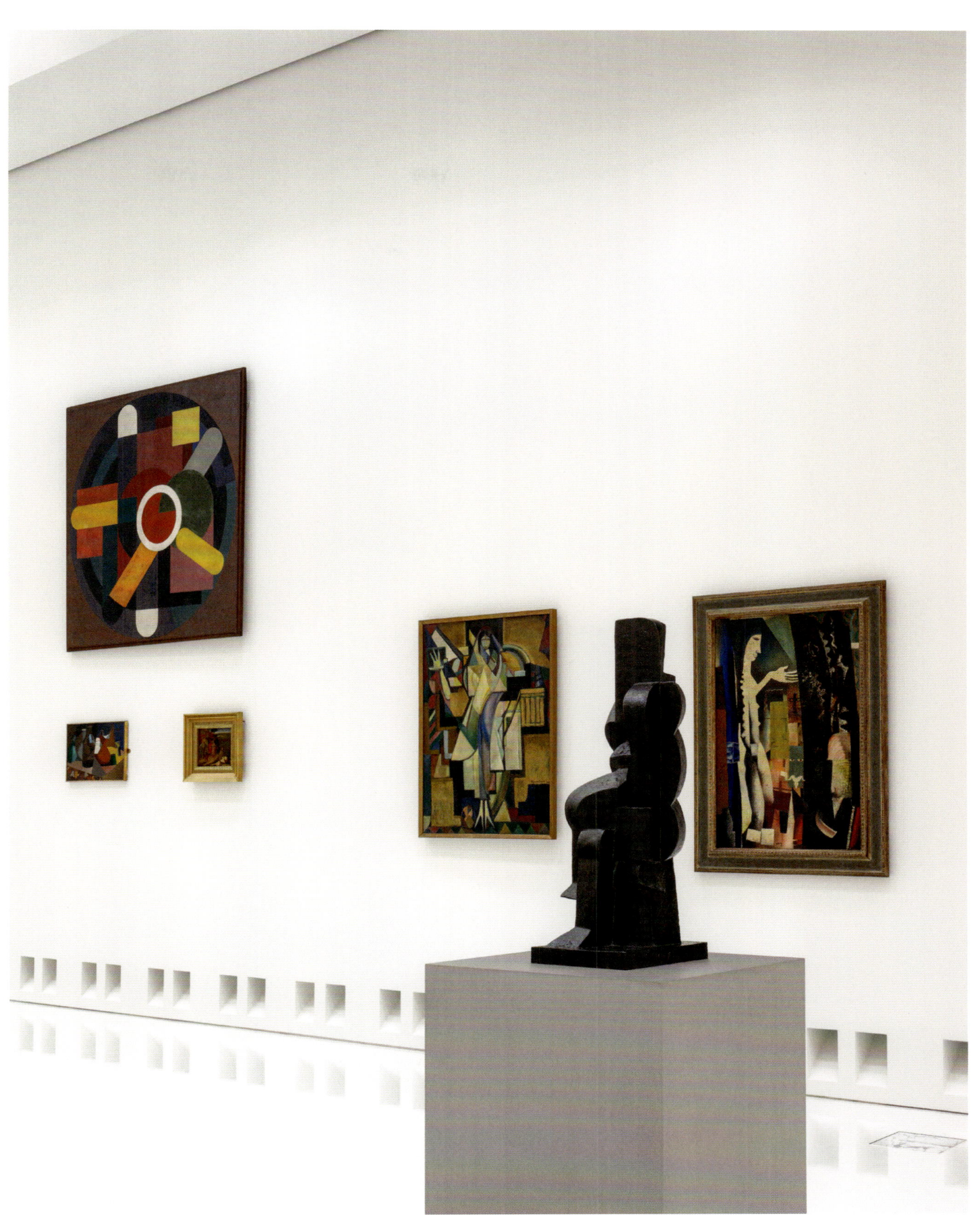

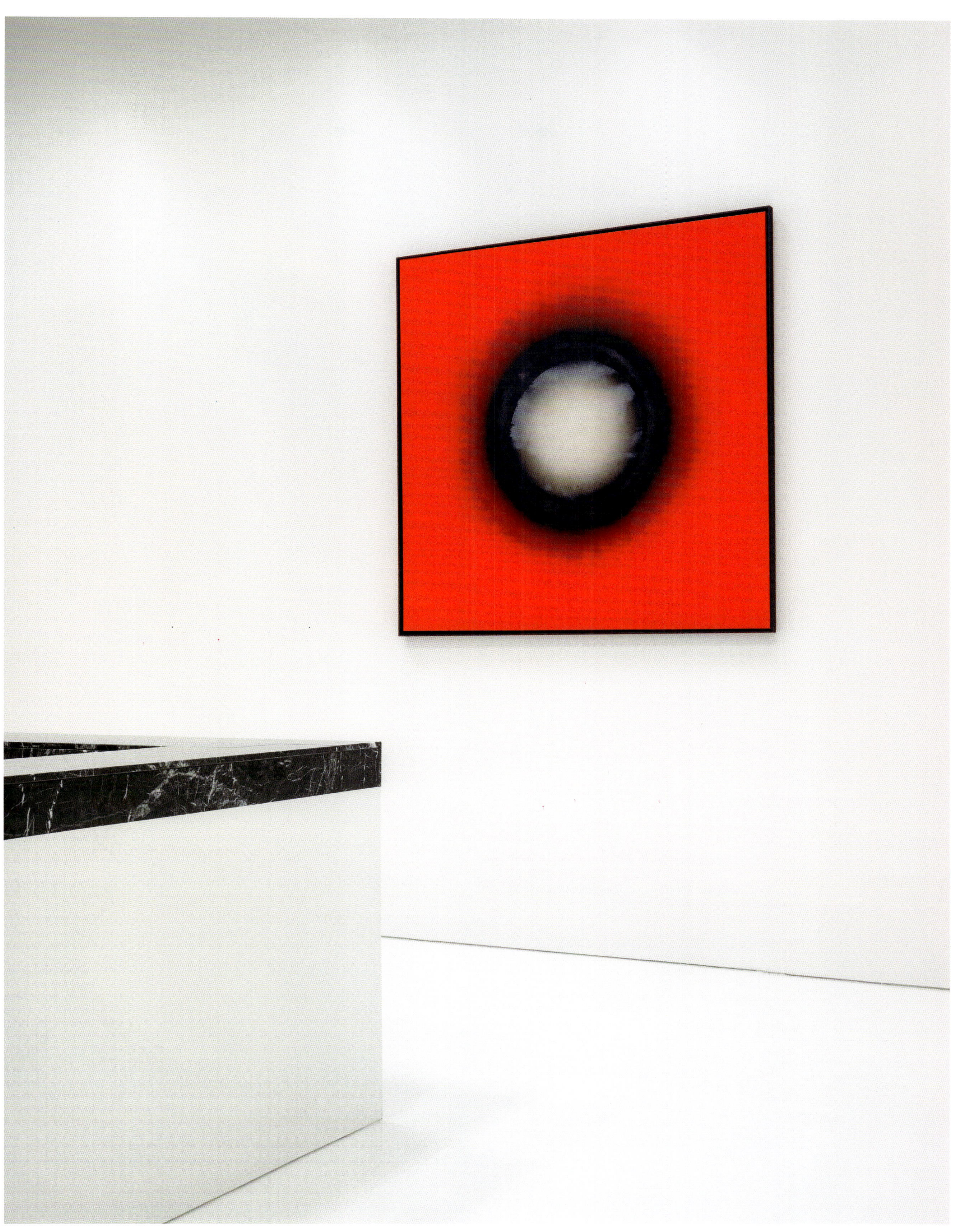

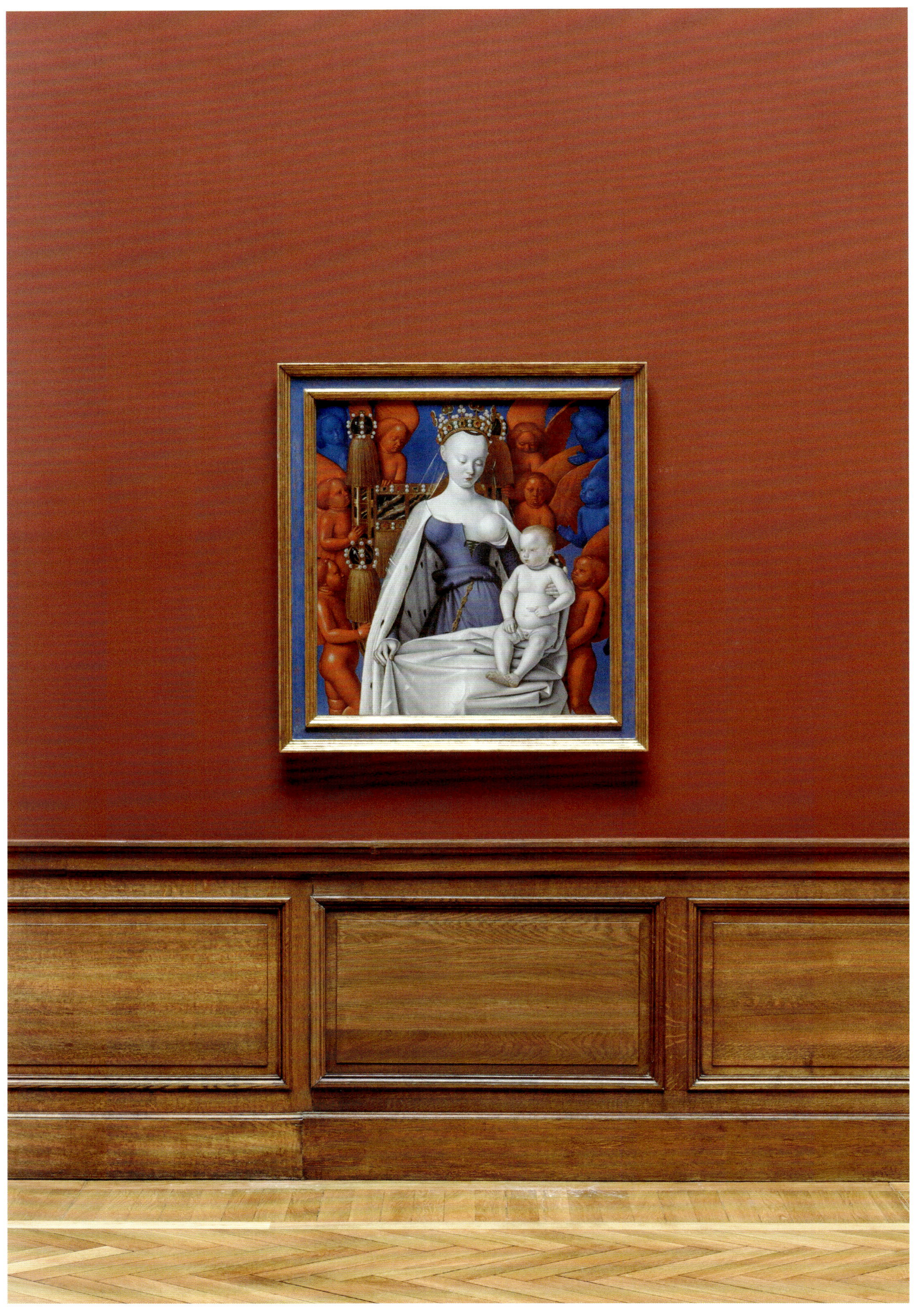

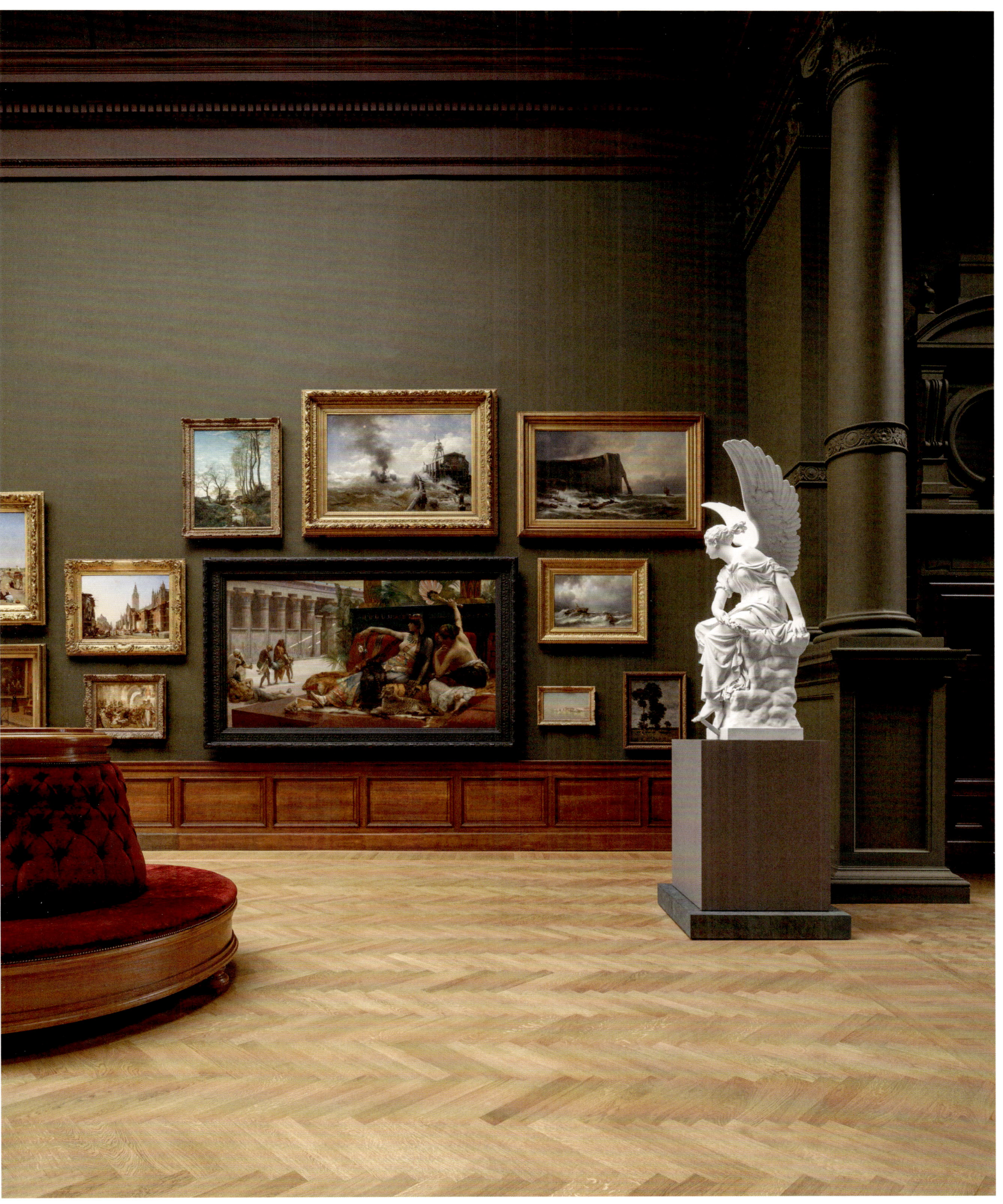

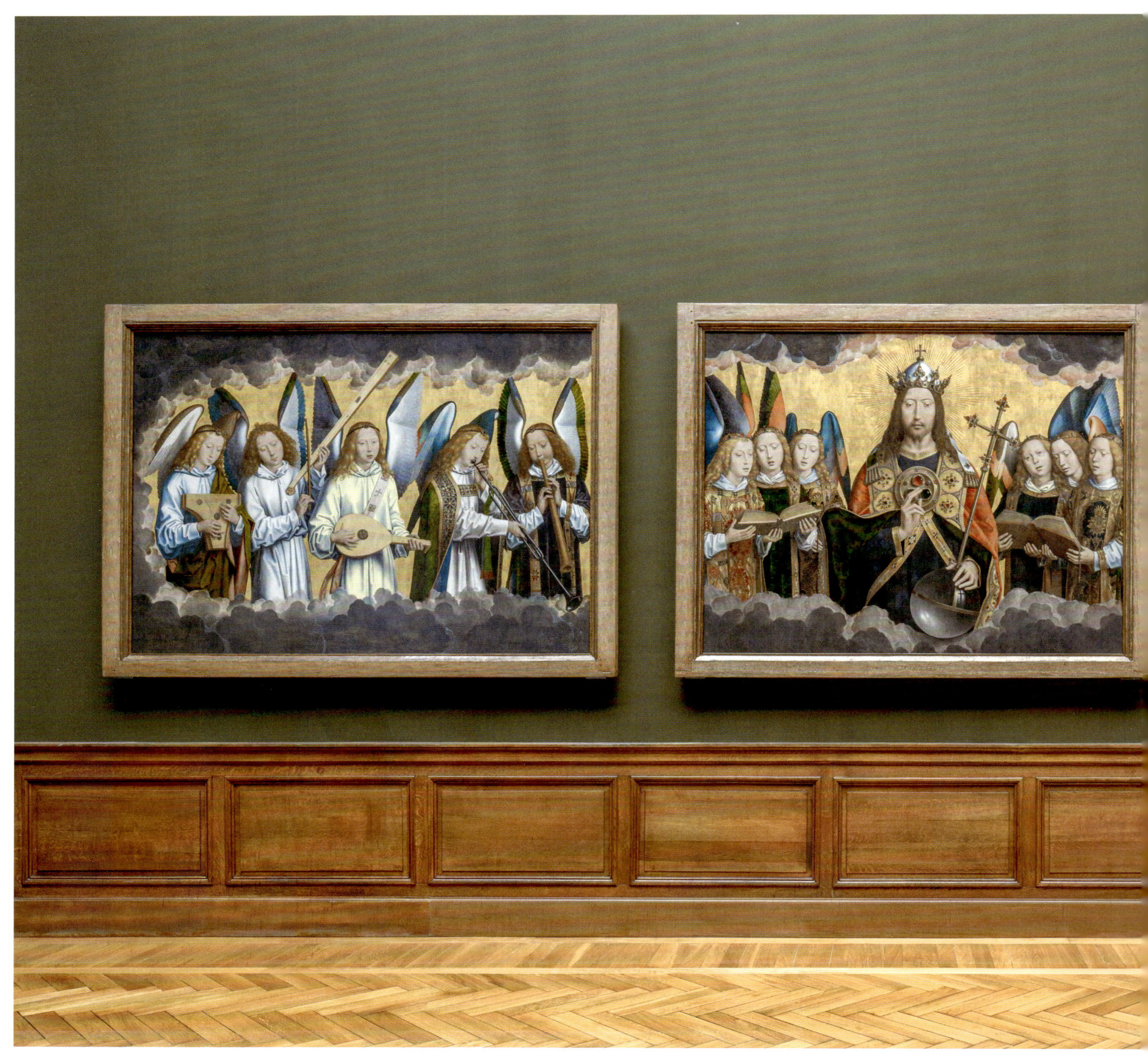

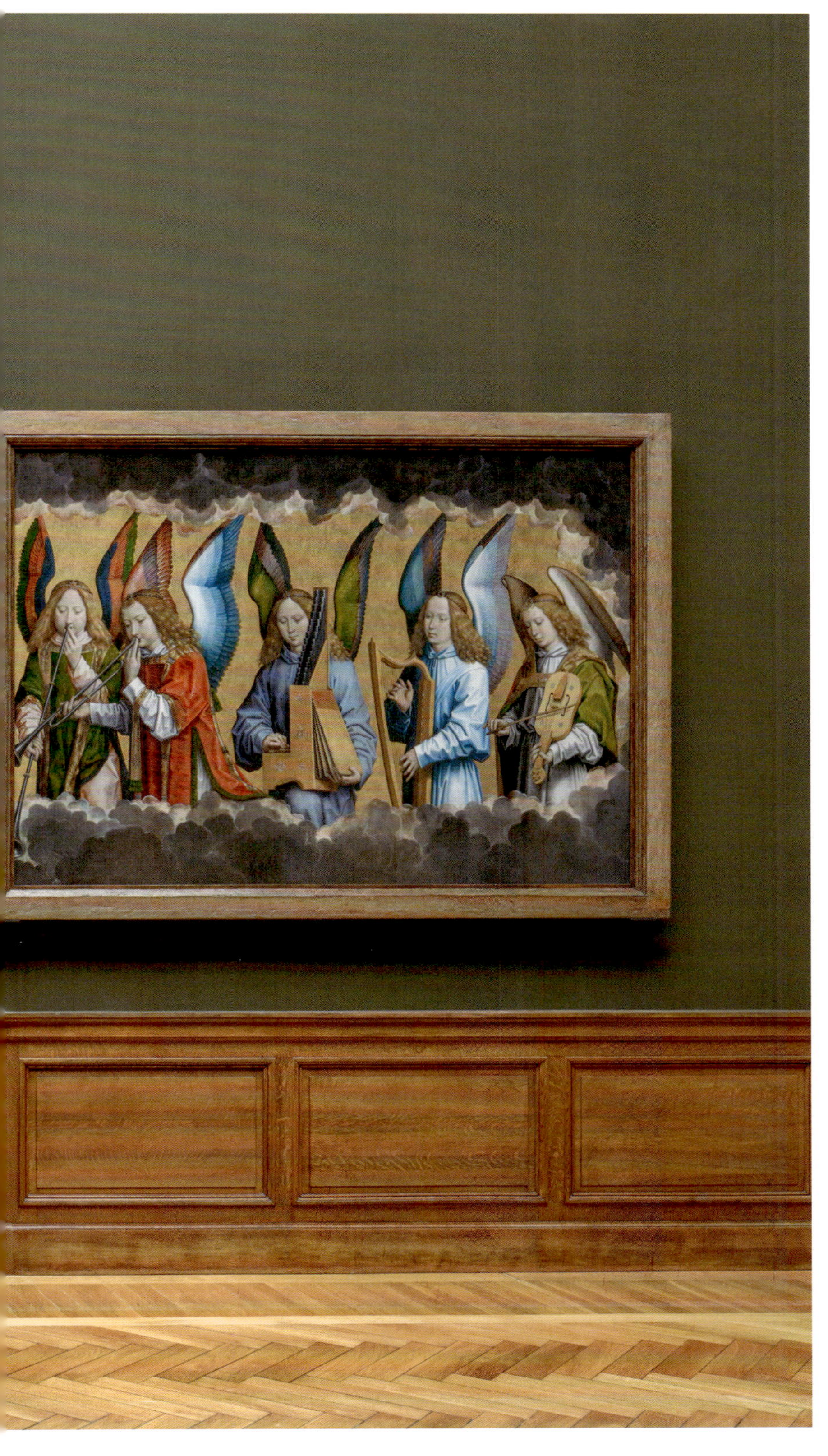

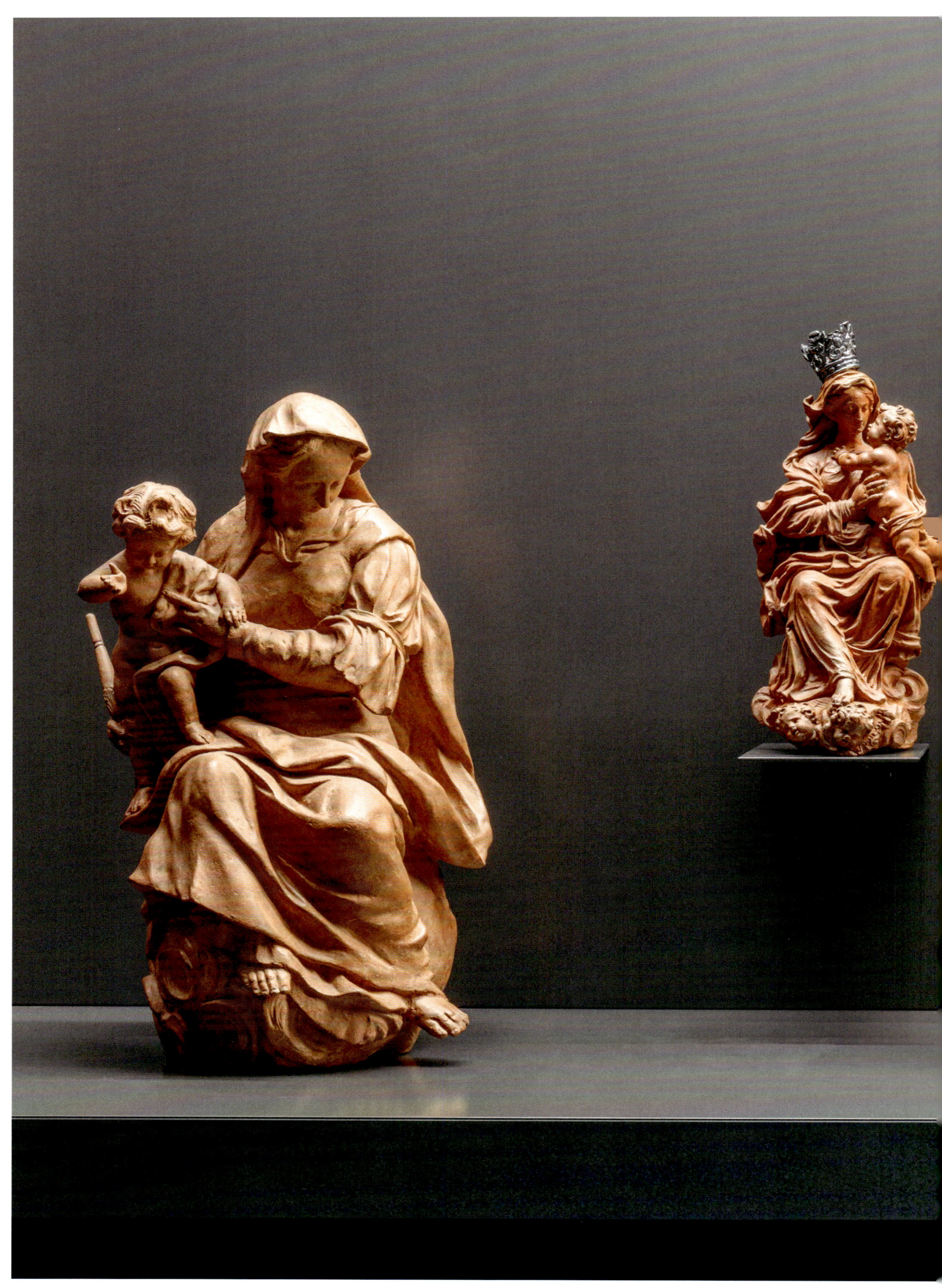

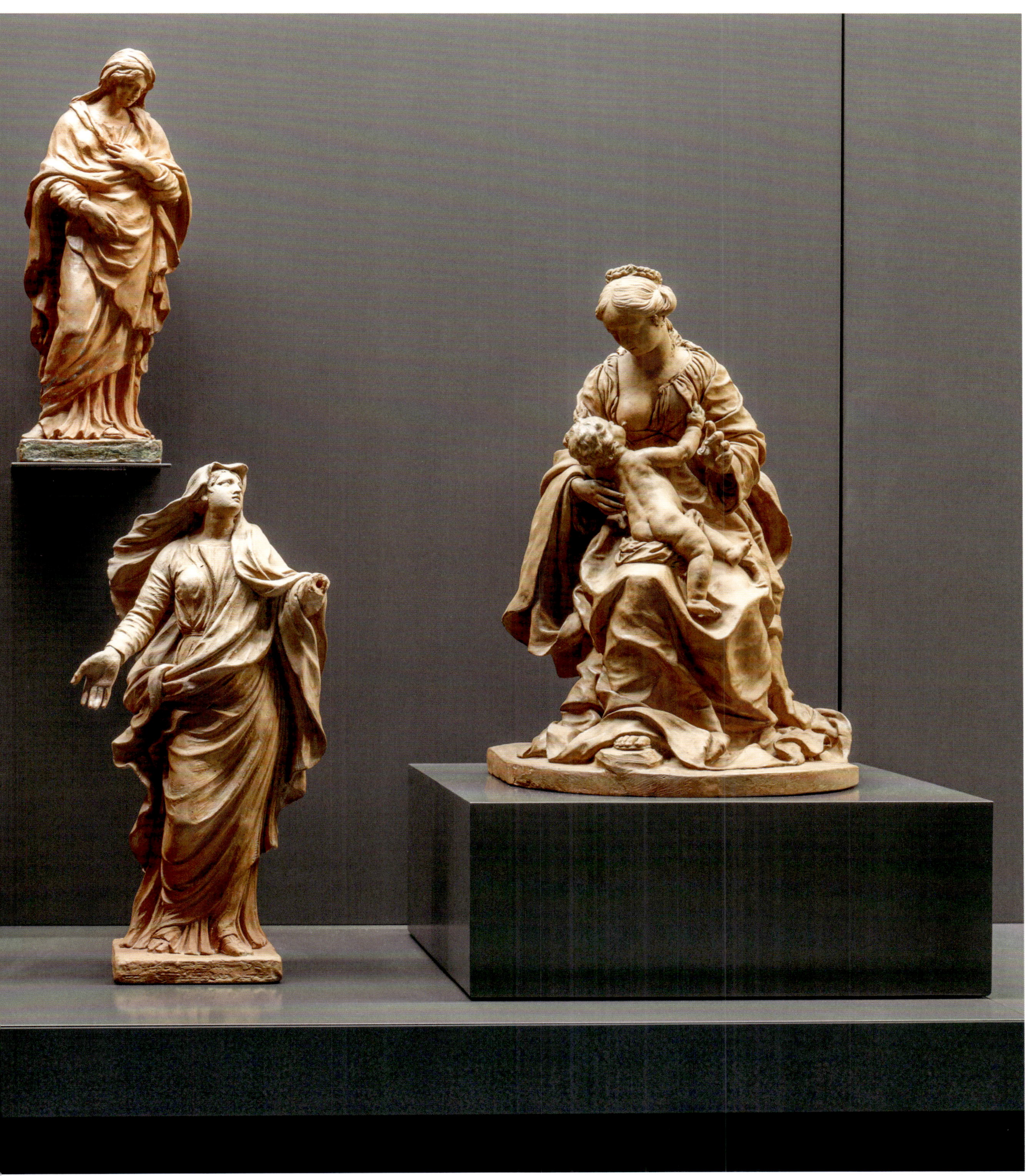

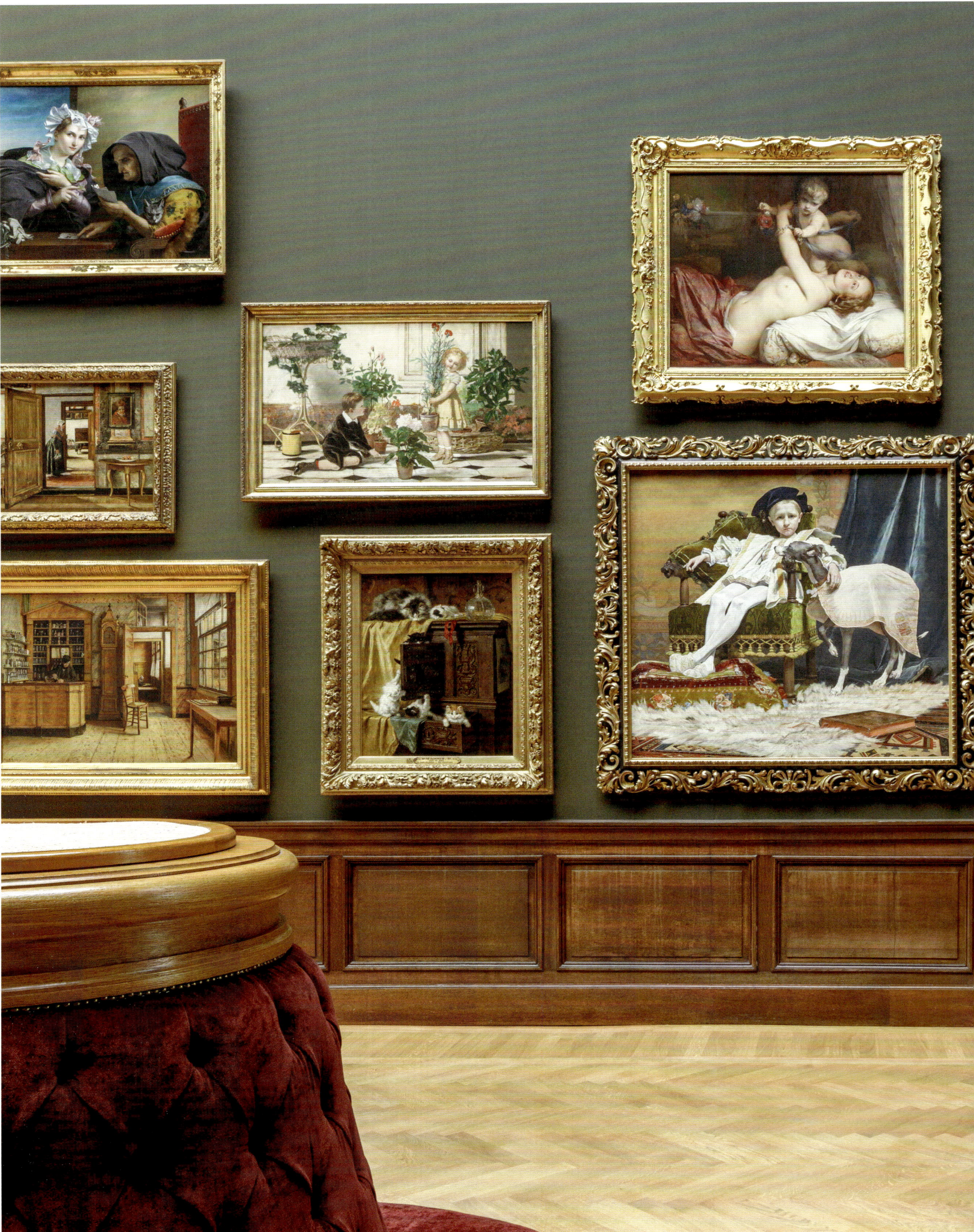

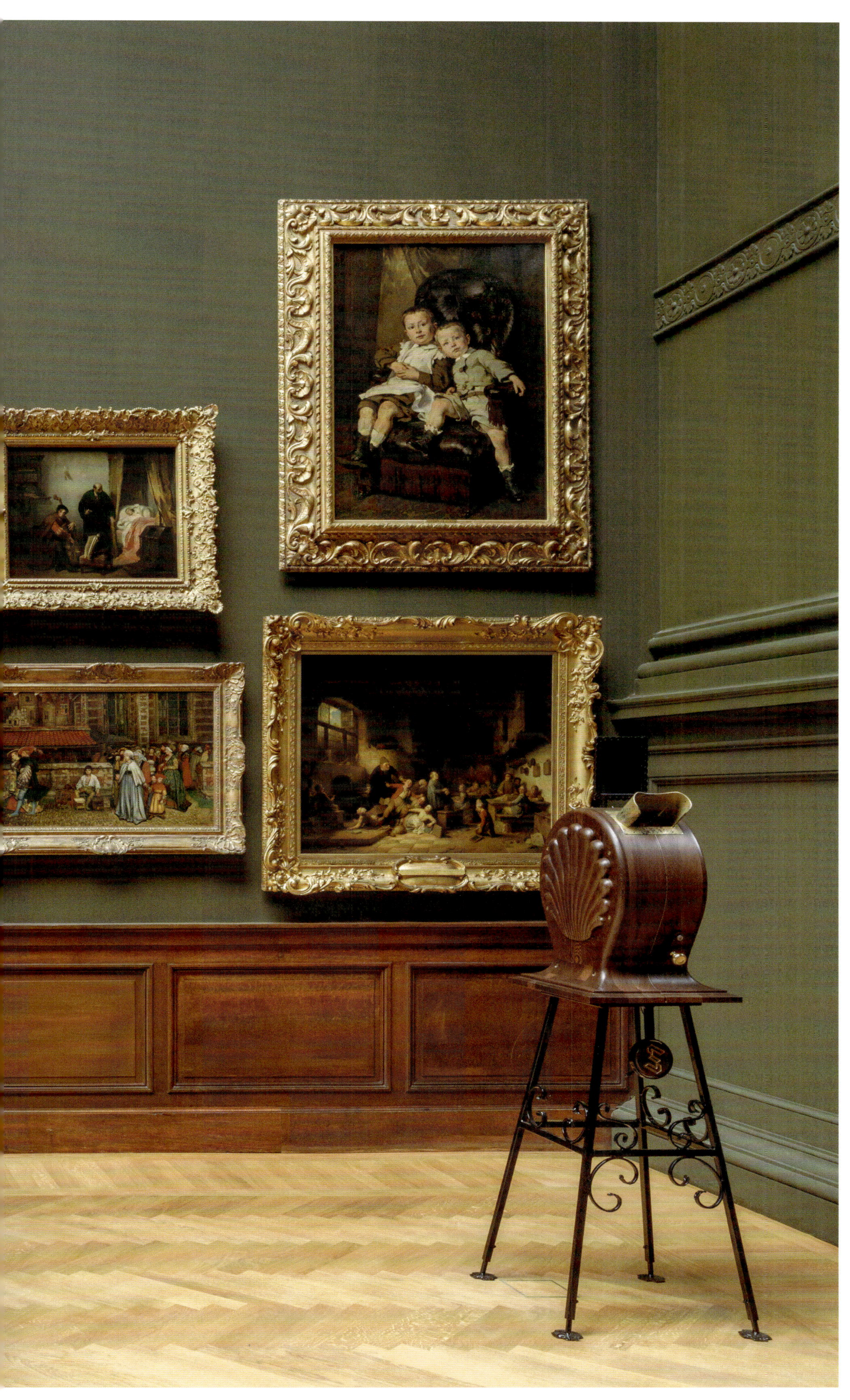

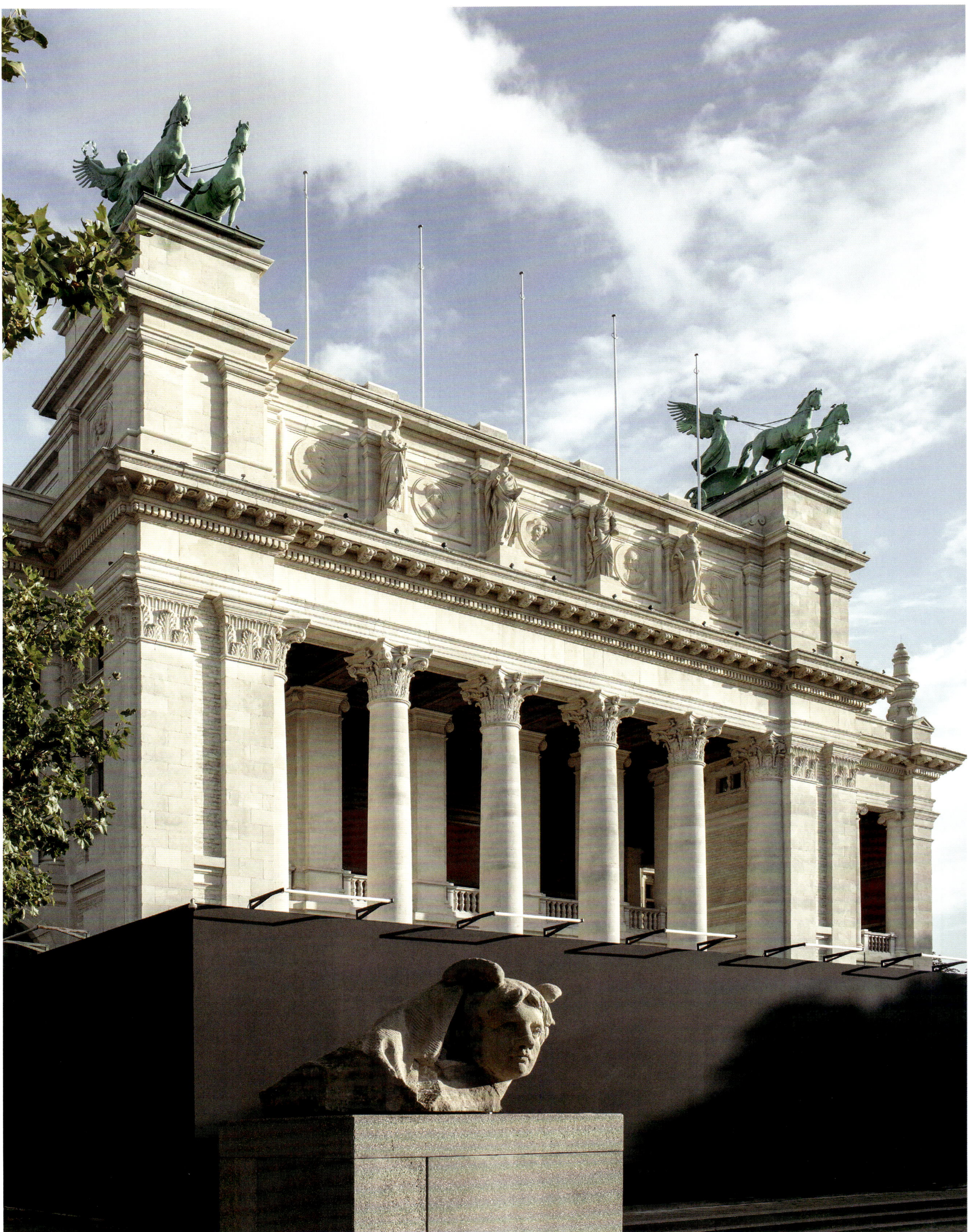

8. REMOVING ALL BARRIERS: THE KMSKA OPENS UP

Like all heritage institutions, museums have to adapt to the ongoing transformation of society. What does today's zeitgeist mean to us? Societies are becoming increasingly diverse. Everyone has the (human) right to participate and should be given that opportunity. We appreciate and embrace the constructive input of people from all walks of life. It also means that institutions such as museums have to be accessible to everyone, in the largest sense of the word. Diversity, inclusion, participation and accessibility: these are the core concepts of the contemporary heritage and museum world. You can embody them in nine letters: turn the museum into an 'open house'. How do you open up, coming from the white and male bourgeois past in which, and thanks to which, you flourished? How do you remove the thresholds to the temple that the museum also is?

Looking

Veerle De Meester, Head of the Audience Engagement team at the KMSKA: "I remember a museum director once saying at the start of a presentation: 'We are not the visitor.' That really hits the nail on the head. As a museum employee, you can't just assume that you know all about what your visitors want. So you should engage in conversation with a wide range of groups and people, and look at what their needs are. We at the KMSKA have done just that during the closure. If you want to be an open house for everyone, then you need to consider everything from a great many angles: how to welcome visitors, how to help them find their way around the museum, the gallery texts, the audio guide, the variation in the depth and the width of the information that you offer, the various atmospheres in your galleries, the composition of your staff... There is a risk of becoming excessively ambitious and envisioning projects that are too grand. Our approach is to embed openness as an attitude and as a policy throughout our whole organisation, in everything we do. Let it grow, step by step, pay unwavering attention to it and be creative. It is a daily practice and, to be fair, never enough. It's also important to dare to be vulnerable: conscious of the fact that we are going to make mistakes."

In a museum of fine arts, you can apply the core concepts to the universal starting point: looking. "At the KMSKA, we want to deliver the message that there are many different ways of looking at art and that they are all valuable. You are there as a museum for all: art enthusiasts, young people and families, schools, budding museum visitors, newcomers... There is no 'one correct' way of looking. Everyone can think and feel about it in any way that suits her, him or them, and that's okay. The collection is rich enough for that. You can provide the tools to achieve that goal, and that's what we do. We are fortunate that there are quite a few bridges between the collection researchers and audience engagement team."

Countless stories

An Sijsmans and Sophie Verbeke from the Audience Engagement team are helping to throw the doors of the house wide open. Sophie Verbeke: "As Veerle says, we first and foremost want to invite people to look at our collection with their own eyes. What personal points of reference do they find to connect with? Of course, as a museum you're also sharing knowledge, but we want to enable diverse perspectives and encourage visitors to enter into a dialogue with each other. Maybe then, because of the different ways in which it is possible to view artworks, they will look at the world differently. That is the heart of our message. There is no single truth in art, truths can co-exist."

"It is true that as far as the art makers is concerned, the collection is rather one-sided: male, white and bourgeois. But it is possible to draw many different stories from it. We also do this in our programmes for schools, where you meet a really very diverse audience: our whole society in miniature. That's why we explore links with other art disciplines, beyond the visual, and with artistic traditions from all over the world. Sometimes we discuss the influence of African masks on the form experiments of some of the modern masters; sometimes we place the abstract signs and patterns you can find in the museum next to Arabic art. Or we talk about the expensive pigment lapis lazuli, which travelled a long way to get here from Afghanistan centuries ago, making it possible for the Virgin Mary to be draped in such a piercing blue mantle. We also don't avoid the more difficult questions: why are there so many scantily clad women? Why is it that there are hardly any women artists or artists of colour in the collection? It's really interesting to discuss these things and to invite young people to think about them with us."

Comfort included

Museums can contribute to people's well-being, and we are seeing a rising trend in this approach. An Sijsmans: "Slowing down, coming into contact with other people and their gaze, these are good examples of things that achieve well-being in a museum. A big question today, also for museums, is: what gives people energy and satisfaction? Helping others, playing sports, reading a book? In our case, the next question is: can you turn it into a museum activity? The trend of 'slow art', among other things, is part of this evolution. The KMSKA was a pioneer, as the first Belgian participant in the Slow Art Day. This day invites people to look at a single work with a group of fellow visitors for one hour and to share their observations with each other. The guide becomes more of a facilitator than an explainer. We got amazing feedback. People told us: 'It has recharged me', 'it gave me a peaceful feeling', 'I will always remember this work'."

How can you ensure that all those visitors with all their different wishes, talents and limitations feel welcome in your open house? By trying to make that visit comfortable for everyone, it's as simple as that. An Sijsmans: "A good example is how we have developed our audio tours. Experts said you shouldn't make a separate tour for the blind and partially sighted, because that's how they are always made to feel like an exception. This is now outdated. The move now is to make your regular, classic audio tour inclusive, by adding visual descriptions and context. This makes your tour accessible to everyone and, if you're visually impaired, you can chat with fellow visitors about the works. It's not an easy task, I admit, but that's how we're going about it. We tested it especially with those concerned. Or take people who are deaf or hard of hearing. There had never been a specific programme in the museum for them. We asked the deaf community for their thoughts and developed a Visio tour: videos of the highlights with sign language. They can view this whenever they want in the museum app. The insights continue to develop and the technology is also lending a hand. People are becoming more self-reliant. Of course, we also asked people with physical disabilities for advice on how they experience accessibility."

"There is also a Tourism for Autism project, which enables people with autism to prepare for the particulars of their visit on a website, with the use of step-by-step plans and lots of details. That starts with the moment of getting off the tram, walking to the museum, making use of the cloakroom, and so on. Such a step-by-step plan is also useful for other groups that experience barriers, such as people in poverty. It's wrong to assume a museum visit is evident for everyone."

Sophie Verbeke: "This is a work in progress, we are well aware of that. And it's not just a project alongside other projects. It is one of the KMSKA's core objectives. If your objective is 'to provide every visitor with a warm and stimulating museum experience', then you must constantly ask yourself: what does that really mean, viewed through the lens of diversity, inclusion and accessibility? We will stumble and get up again. We will make mistakes and we will own them. You have to continue to screen all aspects of your operation – your programme, your staff, your audience, your partners – and you have to continue to diversify. The more perspectives, the better!"

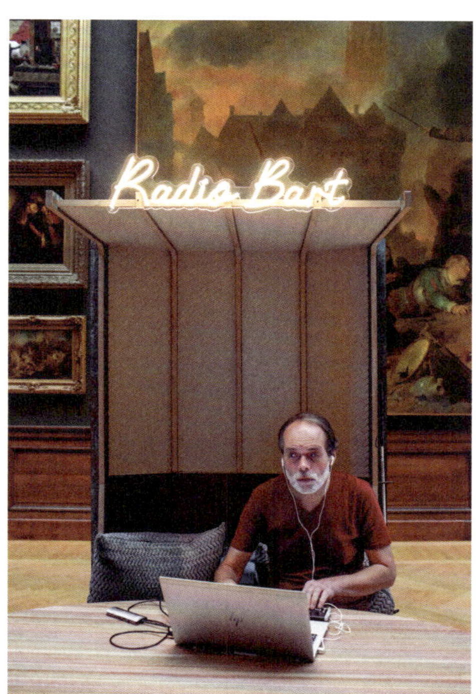

In his mobile broadcasting studio, Bart Van Peer talks to visitors about how they experience the artworks.

Bart Van Peer is one of the KMSKA staff. He makes a radio programme in the museum. Not just any radio programme either: "For the Radio Bart broadcast, I sit in a mobile studio in one of the galleries. Visitors can approach me and start a dialogue about how they experience a work of art. Because I'm blind, I ask people to describe the work to me. I ask them what they see: to describe the shapes, colours, size… But I'm also curious to hear what they think the artist is trying to say. I have a couple of openers, such as: 'Does this work call up any memories for you?' Or: 'If you could get into the work yourself, which part would you want to go to, or who would you like to be?' That makes for some interesting conversations."

"Research shows that on average people only stand in front of a work of art for a few seconds. 'Looking differently and seeing more' means, among other things, that you take the time to really take in a work. When you ask questions, people quickly start to notice things that they didn't see before. And for them, by having a conversation with someone who can't see the work, a different way of looking is unlocked. You look again and are challenged to find the right words: how do you explain an image, brushstroke or colour to someone who can't see? In the meantime, I can let my imagination run wild. This makes the conversation a win-win situation for me and the visitor."

"It's nice that visual impairment or blindness often leads to new conversations. People ask questions like: 'What can you still see?' 'How do you imagine certain colours in your mind?' 'How do you look at art as a blind person?' 'Were you born blind?' People also sometimes feel uncomfortable using the words 'see' and 'look', even though I do, all the time. They assume that blind and partially sighted people can't enjoy fine art, or have no use for it. The opposite is true. That's an eye-opener for many. The conversation therefore not only provides insights about the works of art, but also about being blind. And every conversation is unique."

The mobile studio was designed by the ONBETAALBAAR collective with financial support from the King Baudouin Foundation. Hans Bourlon, entrepreneur and CEO of Studio 100, is the ambassador of Radio Bart.

Ten. That's the number of works that artist Christophe Coppens (b. 1969) chose for his design for a permanent visible route through the museum for the KMSKA's youngest visitors. When he started out, Coppens' work hovered at the intersection of fashion, design and art. Over the past ten years, he's been directing theatre and opera as well as focusing on visual art. And now on the KMSKA collection.

The Ten, as they are now called (with the definite article), is an artistic intervention through which Coppens offers his own innovative look at ten details from the KMSKA collection. Playful, exciting, adventurous, funny. The way children like to look at things.

Coppens: "When we first discussed this project, I was instantly very enthusiastic, but at the same time cautious. Coming up with ten new artworks to be placed among all the masterpieces seemed to me to be a very delicate intervention, an exercise in humility too. I am a fussy museum visitor myself: I don't like the clash you see between the typical type of installation for children and the works of art in a museum gallery. My first thought was that the paintings themselves should be enough to appeal to their imagination; that my input would be superfluous."

"But highlighting a detail, as we have done, can (among other things) light a spark in that child's imagination. It encourages you to look again and discover different things. It turns a museum visit into an exciting adventure. By the way, my own first museum experience as a child was right here at the KMSKA. My grandfather took me with him. I was always deeply impressed, especially by the Rubens Gallery, with its towering walls and red velvet benches."

"For The Ten, I consulted the list of artworks on display with the curators. That's how we came up with a preliminary shortlist. It was not just a question of 'what inspires you?', but also a puzzle full of practical considerations: you have to take into account the limitations of the gallery, the distribution across the museum, safety issues… This assignment is not about me, it's not a solo show! That's the challenge that inspired me: creating strong visual work that also disappears in the space. The Ten is intended for all children, but should not seem childish. I also wanted it to appeal to adults. I saw before me a series of tactile works, with sound or movement, that stimulate the mind and the imagination. They should invite visitors to step into the painting."

Sixty people were involved in the making of The Ten: "The ten works are all made in very different ways. Instead of collaborating with different workshop studios, I chose to make the link with another great Belgian institution: La Monnaie/de Munt opera house in Brussels. My previous experiences with their studios, and the artists and craftsmen who work there, were so positive that I really wanted to involve the team in this. It has become a true interaction. A nice bonus is that we are building a bridge between two beautiful Belgian cities and cultural institutions: Antwerp and Brussels, a museum and an opera house."

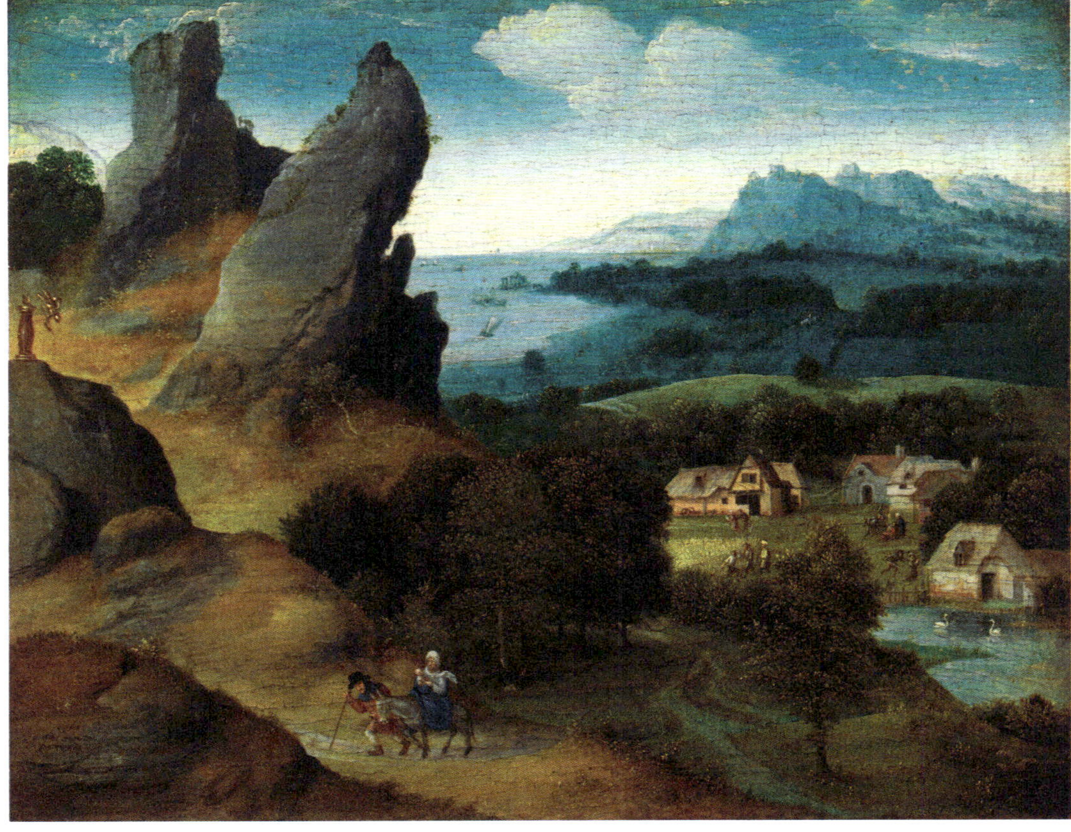

An XL edition of a rock from a work by Patinir, the size of a hand, in the Horizon gallery. Joachim Patinir, *Landscape with the Flight into Egypt*, 1516–1517, oil on panel, 18.2 × 22.2 cm, inv. 64.

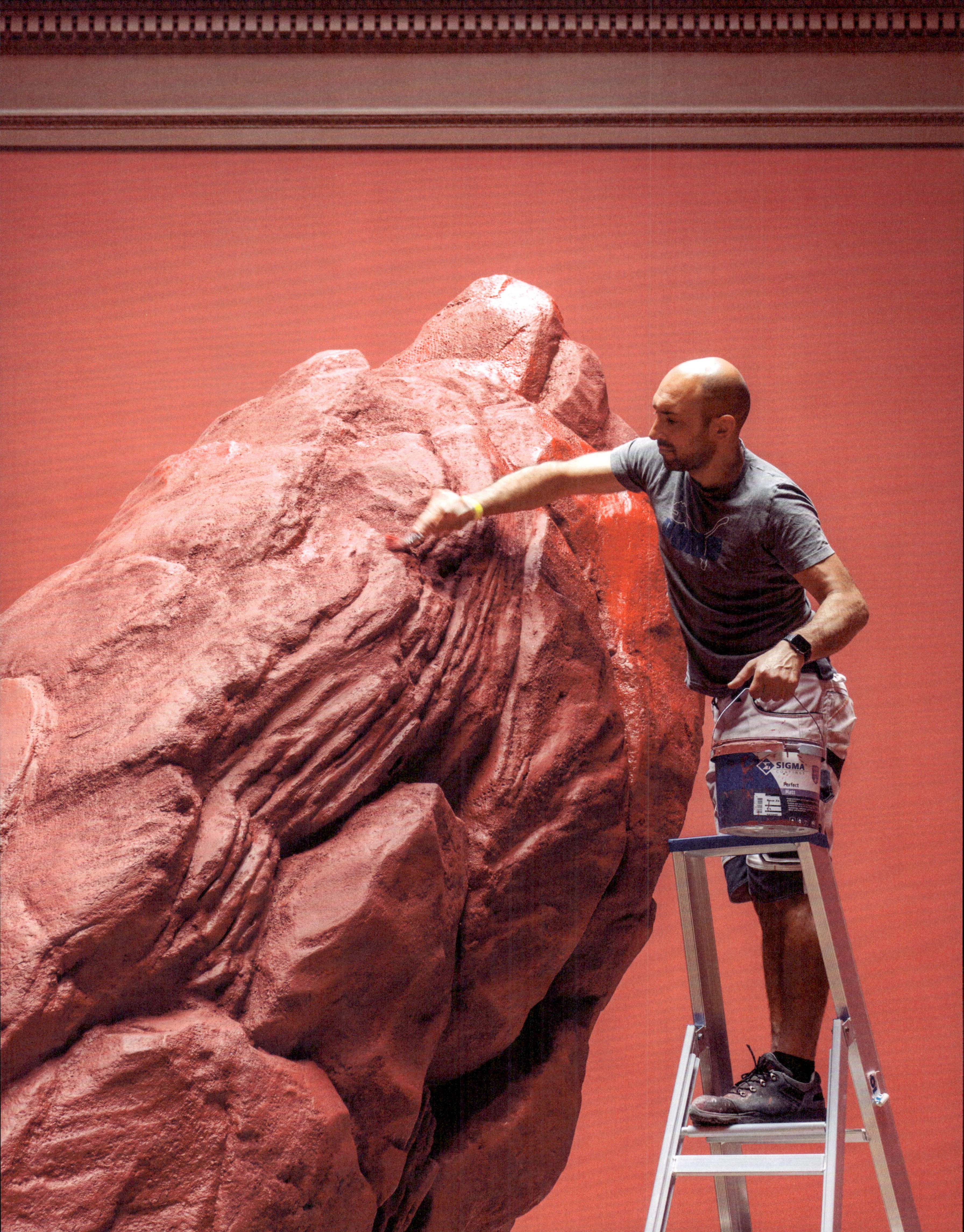
SIGMA
COATINGS
Perfect
Matt

Enamul Haque, 28,
owner of newsagent Het Museum

"Six years ago, I opened a newsagent in the Verschansingstraat, close to the museum. A suitable name was quickly found: Dagbladhandel Het Museum ('Newsagent The Museum'). My sign is illustrated with the museum's façade with the horses, after an original design by my neighbour across the street. As a child, I often went to the museum with my school class… it's where I saw a pointillist painting for the first time. That became my favourite painting style. Now I'll be able to visit with my new wife and show her my favourite works."

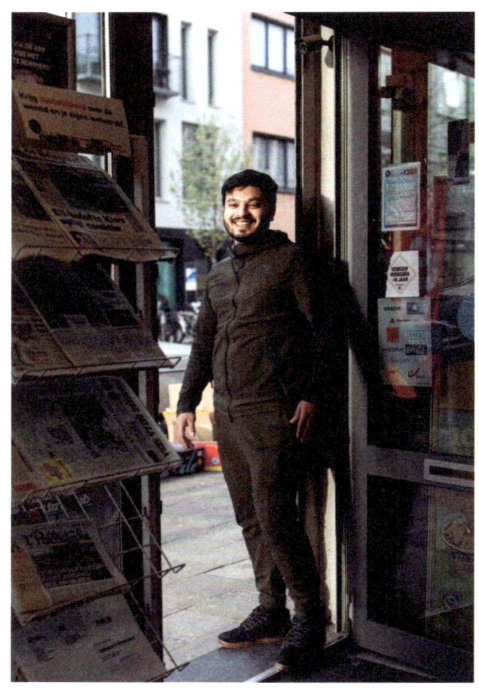

Judith Van Pelt, 33,
florist

"When I was a little girl, my dad often took me on short visits to the museum on our way to the bakery. After we discovered a painting with a beautiful lady who had the same name as me, I often asked to go and look at *Judith*. My dad hasn't made it to the opening of the museum, but I can now see 'my' painting again and think back to the adventures we had in 'our' museum."

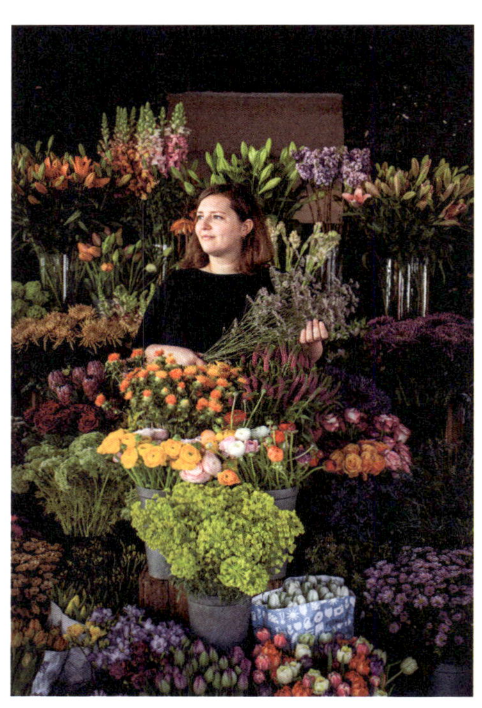

Paul van Rutten, 62,
waiter at Café Hopper

"A few days before 9/11 in 2001, the second edition of the literary festival *ZuiderZinnen* took place, with the KMSKA as its glittering centrepiece. But it was raining cats and dogs, and the entire outdoor programme was rained off. In the years since then, we organised another ten editions of the festival. Always with the steps of the museum as the area for spectators and a platform on the pavement in front of the fountain as a stage. It never rained again during *ZuiderZinnen*… It's wonderful that those steps are now open again and the square can once again truly fulfil its public purpose."

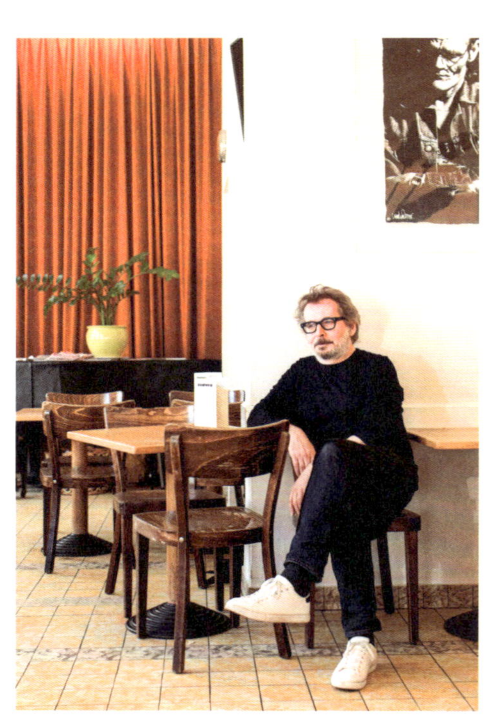

Sarah Vanwelden, 33, owner of Newchild Gallery

"The stately building in the South district of Antwerp always fascinated me. My earliest memories of the museum are the interactive tours, which were followed by a creative workshop. Later, during my years as an art history student, I went there often. Despite my passion for contemporary art, my love for the old masters has never diminished. Now I can rediscover the museum's many treasures, and once again set eyes upon my favourite work by Titian."

Dominique Vilain, 40, kindergarten teacher BSGO Kunst Doet Ontdekken ('Art Leads to Discovery')

"As a child, I climbed the majestic steps of the KMSKA in the company of my mother. A skull on a vanitas painting was my first introduction to iconography. So art was more than techniques or those pointless 'beautiful or ugly' discussions. Ensor's painting *The Intrigue* only fuelled my admiration for art, and later I discovered his socially critical prints. With the reopening, I will be able to introduce my students and daughter to the brightly visible and intriguingly hidden world of the fine arts."

Leo Van Hamme, 71, retired

"Although I was born in the South district, it was mostly by accident that I ended up back there when I was 25. That's how I came to live in this warm and friendly neighbourhood, which has gradually become more vibrant over the years. The reopening of the enlarged museum with its newly landscaped garden is another jewel in the crown. We can walk into our beautiful museum again – it's a fitting symbol of the friendship, harmony and well-being that characterises our neighbourhood."

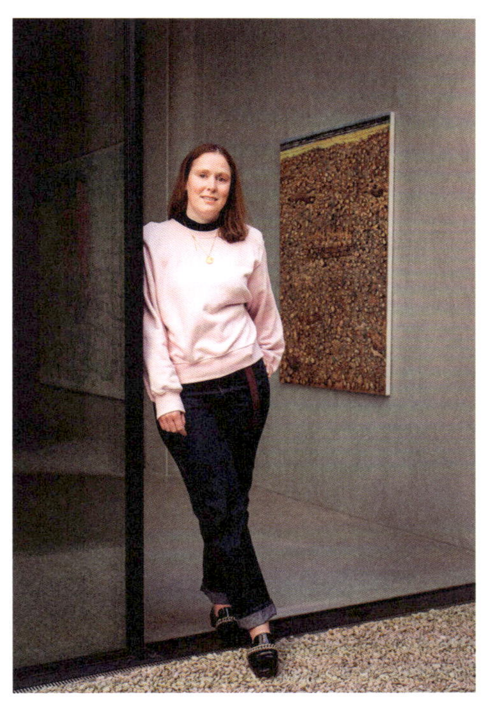

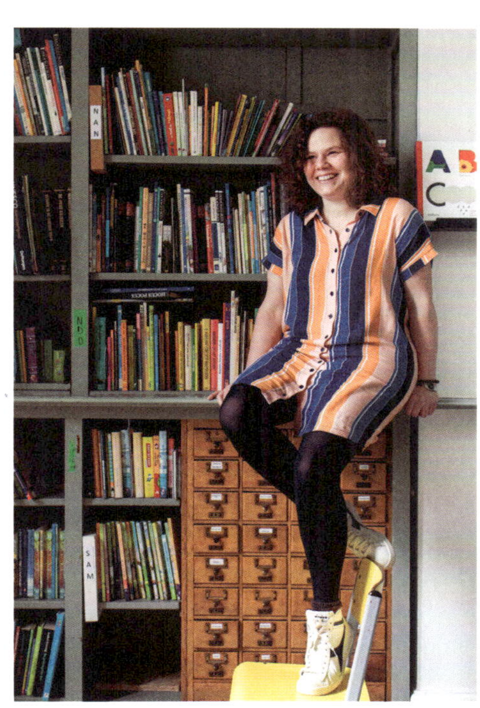

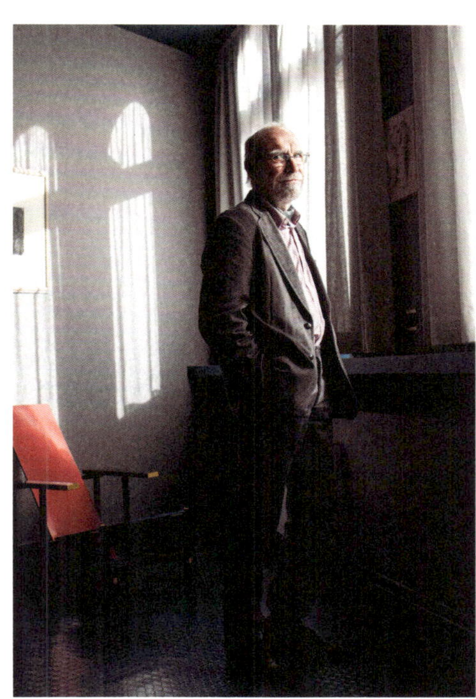

9. THE FINEST FAÇADE: THE EXTERIOR

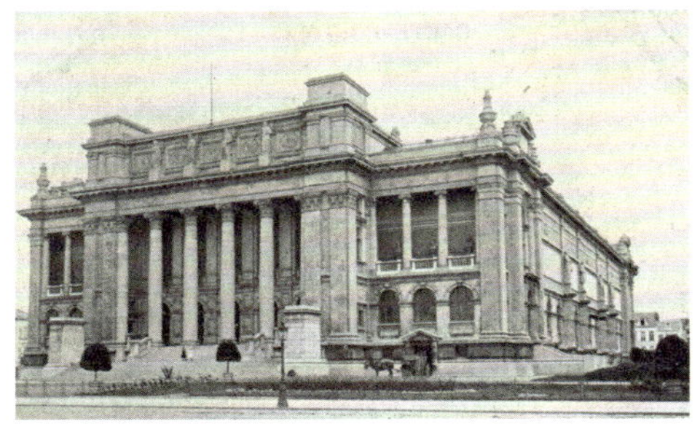

The museum before June 1905. The iconic horses of Vinçotte – symbolising the triumph of the fine arts – were not yet in position on the roof.

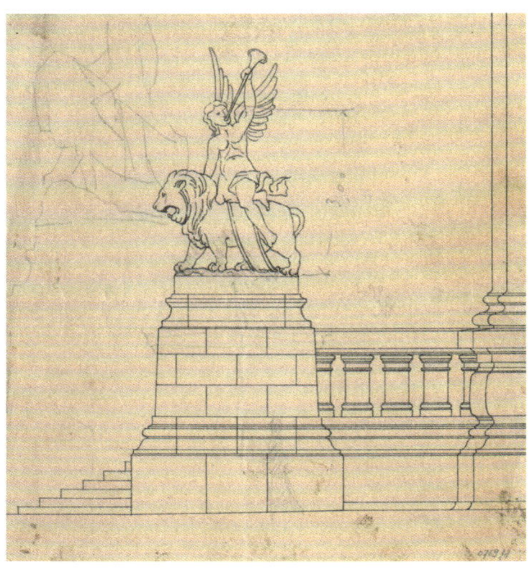

Design by Winders and Van Dijk for the pedestal of the monumental stairs.

"At the moment the façades are lamentably barefaced," wrote a newspaper when the KMSKA opened in August 1890. What was going on? And how does the museum's façade look to visitors and passers-by today?

Tribute to the arts

The monumental steps, the numerous columns and pilasters, the cornices and all the other architectural elements that catch the eye on the exterior – the museum *building* was finished when the summer of 1890 came around, but the many sculptures were not. That work had been ordered too late. We're talking about the friezes, busts, medallions, bas-reliefs and the sculptures in the round.

The entire sculpture programme, consisting of dozens of pieces, had been clearly specified by the architects, Winders and Van Dijk, right down to the dimensions, type of stone and so on. The whole was to become a tribute to the art history of Europe, starting with four monumental freestanding female figures above the cornice. They symbolise the four great art disciplines: architecture, painting, sculpture and printing. They are truly monumental in size: the statues range from six to eight metres in height. The seven medallions alongside them depict the busts of artists from the Low Countries who practiced the four arts. Each one is 1.5 metres high. And in the loggia are another 11 busts, this time of internationally renowned artists, including Michelangelo, Raphael, Velázquez and Rembrandt. The two tall pedestals in front of the anterior façade, on either side of the steps leading to the entrance, were not used, even though two statues were designated for them. The two double-horse chariots on the roof are described at more length elsewhere in these pages.

The art-history lesson continues on the side elevations, where allegorical women stand between the round-arched windows, representing different periods in art history, ranging from Egyptian and Greco-Roman antiquity, to Byzantine and Arabic art, up to the Gothic and even the art of the 19th century. The friezes with their garlands beneath the cornice give the whole building a festive élan.

A total of 22 sculptors – many of them respected masters from Brussels and Antwerp – were involved in the sculpture programme. They first made designs in plaster that were approved, rejected or modified by a jury. After many consultations, they worked with blocks of stone that originated mainly from Lorraine. The entire undertaking received its crowning glory – literally – in 1905, when the two horse-pulled chariots flew up on to the roof.

Bomb damage

On to the masterplan of the early 21st century. Let's zoom out and visualise the entire exterior of the museum. What needed to be done? What problems came to light, including after an inspection by Monumentenwacht? And what does the exterior of the new KMSKA look like now? Project Manager Isolde Verhulst, from PERSPECTIV architects, can tell us all about it. Cleo Cafmeyer, Sculpture Conservator at the KMSKA, followed the process: "We started with a general examination of the building in October 2016. Such preliminary investigations are carried out by various means: cone penetration, tests, recording any damage, on-site examination, research into archives and old specifications, drawing up restoration plans, and so on. For example, we had to check the interventions that had taken place in 1976, such as the replacement of bricks, the cleaning of the façades and a moisture-resistant treatment. The details of this couldn't be found in the archives."

"During those first examinations, we discovered bullet or shrapnel impacts in the north façade – nothing alarming. But we did notice a serious crack in the south façade, in addition to other cracks. We suspect it could have had something to do with the air displacement and suction of the German V2 bomb that fell here on 13 October 1944. It wreaked havoc,

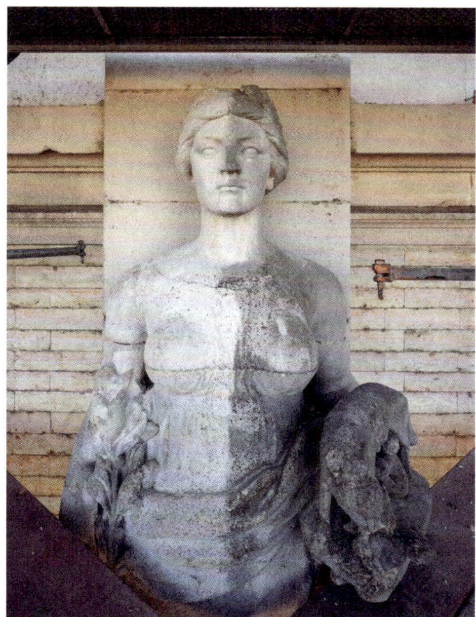

The weathered sculptures on the façades were cleaned and consolidated.

causing 32 casualties and extensive damage to the building. The north façade, where the bomb fell, was actually in better condition than the south façade. Anyway, the museum has a 'stronghold' base on the remains of the demolished citadel of Alva."

Colourful

If you think back to the KMSKA building at the start of the 21st century, you'll probably see in your mind's eye a rather grey and monotonous building. Isolde Verhulst: "The use of many types of stone originally gave the museum a more mottled appearance, although the polychromy of the façades, as the architects themselves had imagined it, had already been greatly reduced during construction, partly due to financial constraints. Most of the colour variations are on the front façade; since the restoration, you can once again see pink, pale yellow, light orange, grey and blue colours there. The conglomerate stone Brèche de Waulsort also stands out, because it gives the large façade of the loggia a speckled appearance. This forms a striking contrast with the Pompeiian red backdrop behind the busts. So the Museum has become more colourful than before the closure, but of course without it becoming colour-blocked."

Back to the beginning of this story: the sculptures that were nowhere to be found in 1890. How was their condition after all this time, and what happened to them during the restoration? "We have been careful with the sculptures. That means: cleaning, consolidating and maintaining their current condition as much as possible. The damage to the friezes at the top of the southern façade is considerable, but because they're so high, it is hardly noticeable from the garden. So we did very little to change that. The statues on the south side are also more affected, but major repairs were not immediately necessary there either."

"In Euville, near Nancy, we selected good-quality, frost-resistant examples of the original stone for the restoration of the sculptures. The stone quality in the original building is of a lesser or – shall we say – secondary quality. The best Euville stone has a compact structure: it's hard and therefore less sensitive to frost. That was a tricky factor in the restoration. Since we were consolidating the images, we had to take into account the coarse grain of the stone used at the time, which makes it prone to faster degradation. Within, say, 50 years, interventions will certainly have to be made again. You can't stop the decay of the original natural stone, but you can decrease it. That's why we also made 3D scans. This allows us to document the current situation, so we can pass it on to future generations. The 3D scans provide very precise information about the restoration sites, the nature of the interventions, the condition of the stones, and so on."

Coda

Isolde Verhulst has two more surprises in store: "We were surprised and delighted to find that all the exterior doors are still original and of very good quality. They just needed a good polish. The glass in the windows has been replaced by burglary-proof glazing, and the woodwork, which was initially varnished, has been given a different, more authentic colour. And we also stumbled upon a fantastic and unprecedented detail. When we were taking heat measurements and scans, we discovered a 'skeleton frame', which we believe could be an old bricked-up grand entrance in the south façade. We didn't do anything with it. Perhaps, it's a not fully completed change that was made during the construction phase?" In other words, how new technology is exposing old secrets.

15 June 1905. Fifteen years after opening its doors, the museum was finally finished. On that day, horses flew through the sky over Antwerp: two pairs of metal horses, each with a winged female charioteer, were lifted on to the roof of the KMSKA. Each driver holds a laurel wreath raised high in her hand, symbolising the victory of the arts. *Triumph of the Fine Arts* is therefore a most appropriate name for this double artwork by sculptor Thomas Vinçotte (1850–1925), a native of Borgerhout. Vinçotte studied in Brussels and Paris before becoming a teacher in Antwerp in 1886. He also created the four-horse chariot on the triumphal arch in Brussels' Cinquantenaire Park. Horse-drawn chariots sitting atop monumental buildings have a long history dating back to the Romans.

Stainless steel skeletons

Rooftop horses catch a lot of wind, and large outstretched wings even more so. Once you know that the KMSKA steeds are made of copper sheets joined with rivets (not of the more expensive bronze, as many people think) and fortified internally by an iron frame, it becomes clear that somebody needs to keep an eye on them. The first restoration took place in 1976–1977 in anticipation of the Rubens 400th anniversary year. Under the direction of sculptor Geo Vindevogel, the artworks were removed from the roof, completely dismantled and restored. The rusting iron frameworks were replaced by stainless steel in most places, and the copper plates were cleaned and joined together again. Then the horses took to the sky once more.

Finely hammered hairs

In 2018, after a thorough assessment of their condition, it was clear that the horses and their drivers needed another round of maintenance. Tiny fissures were appearing in the copper, particularly at points of constant pressure, such as where the wings meet the charioteers' backs. Those joins needed to be repaired. This time, the horses and charioteers could, for the most part, remain on the roof. The KMSKA was covered in scaffolding at the time, so it was easy to access the chariots, but four wings, two hands and one head went on a little outing to the Metafose restoration studio.

Restorer Derek Biront: "Monumental sculptures in hammered copper are rare in Belgium, especially of this high quality. Vinçotte created them to stand on top of the building, to be viewed from ground level. And yet the copper of the horses is chased with thousands of fine hairs. You can't see that from the street, but it does affect how the light reflects off the statues. This is great craftsmanship. The heads of the women have a smoother surface."

"It has been a wonderful challenge to work on these iconic statues, and to make sure they can withstand the test of time again. As I returned the head to its proper place, my heart definitely started to beat faster: this was the culmination of a unique project."

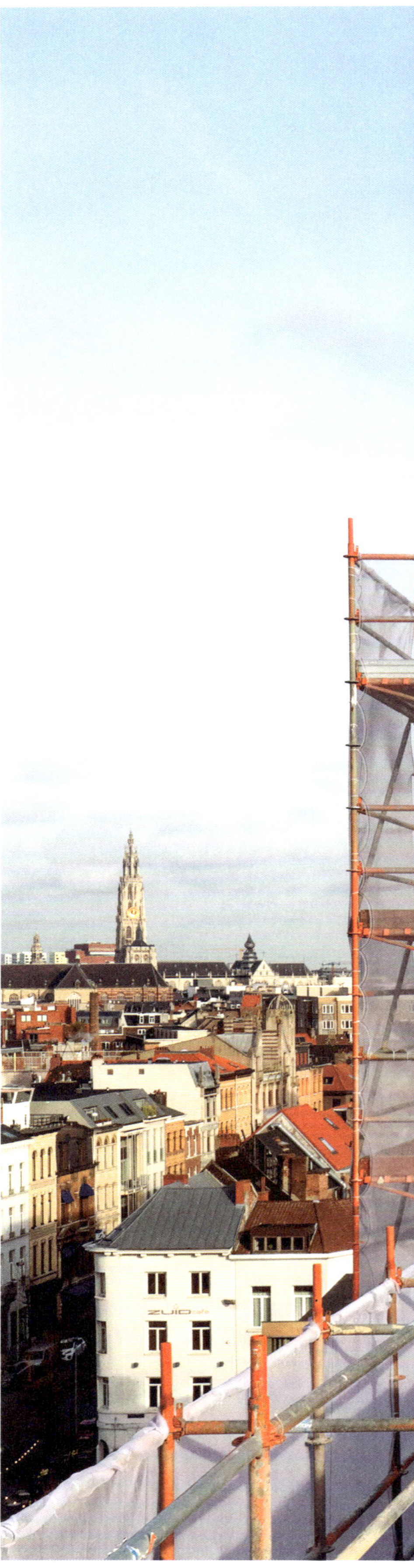

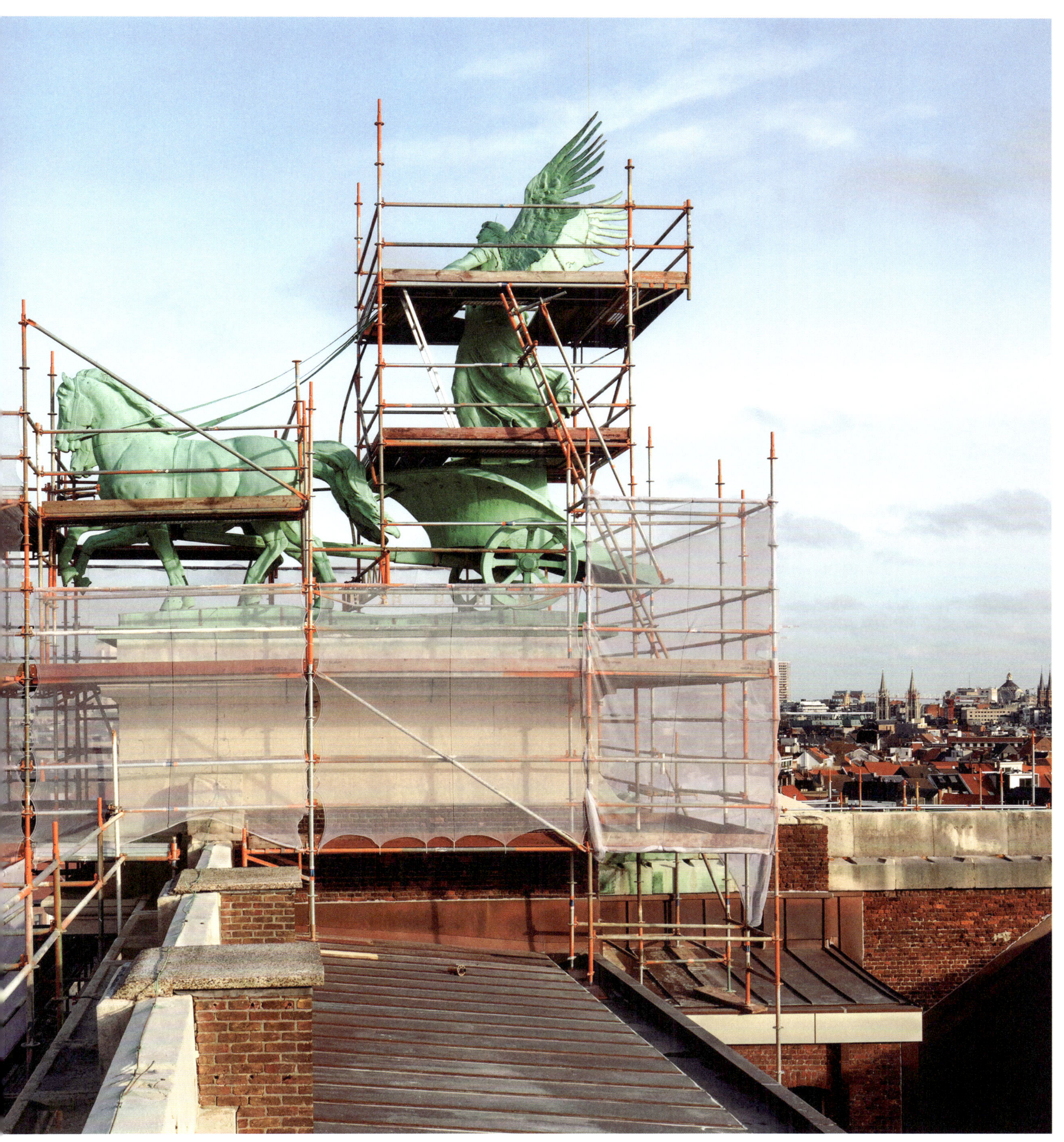

The *Triumph of the Fine Arts* by Thomas Vinçotte is restored in situ, 2018.

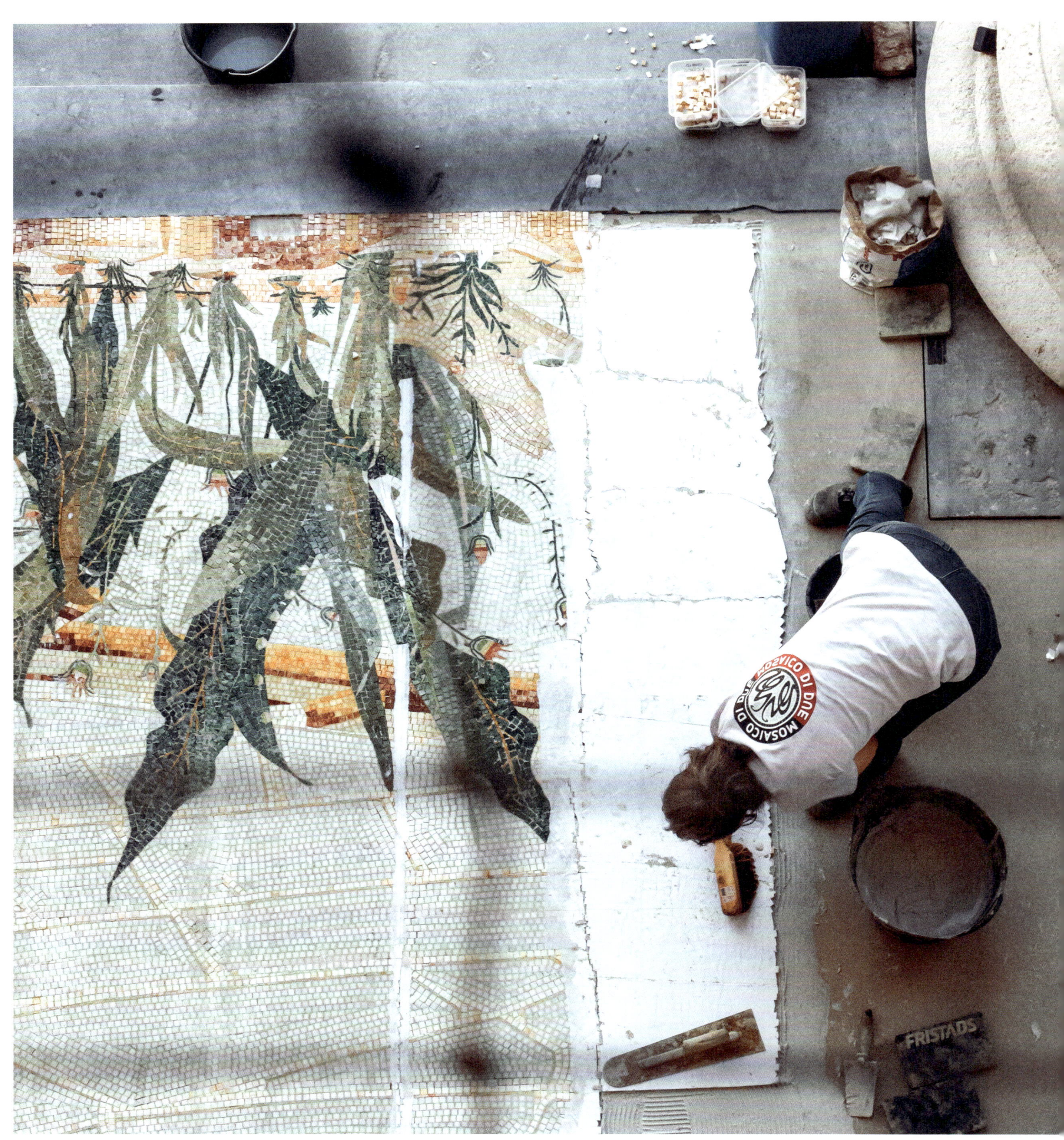

At the top of the steps, a mosaic designed by Marie Zolamian: a welcoming carpet of 480,000 stone pieces.

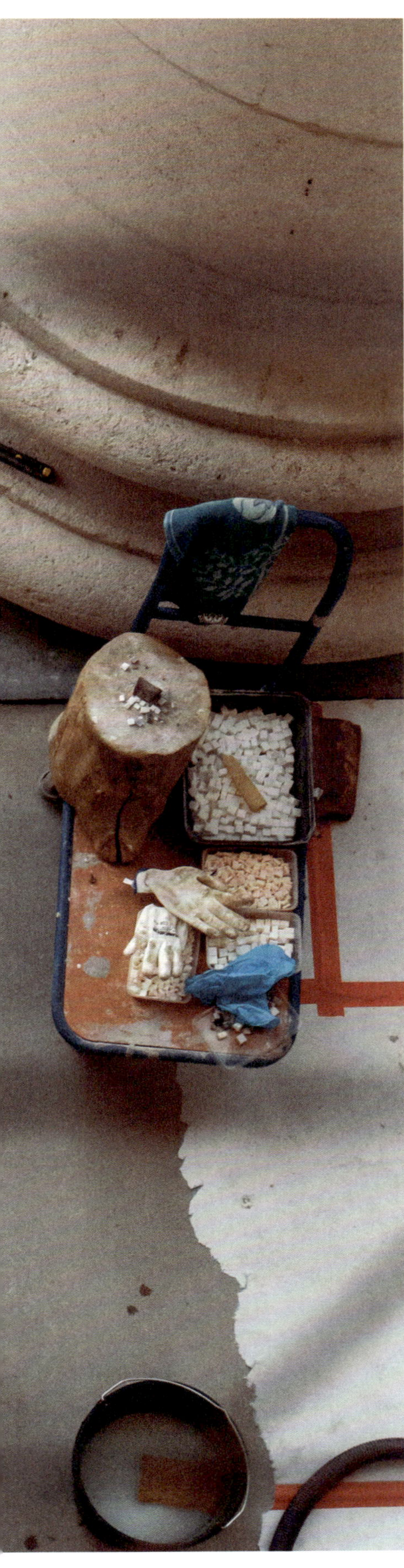

At the KMSKA, you not only stroll past the art but also over it. It welcomes you as you enter: the floors of the reception area and the staircase hall of the historic museum are adorned with mosaic art, as is the front balcony. These mosaic floors were laid in the late 19th century by specialised artisans, the Pellarin brothers from northern Italy.

A new mosaic

At the top of the steps leading to the museum entrance, on the Leopold de Waelplaats, was a 1977 mosaic set in concrete. A copy of the original work, it had been a rush job and it was questionable whether it was worth restoring. So the KMSKA decided to create a brand-new mosaic artwork. Thanks to the generosity of Richard Vander Linden, KMSKA now boasts Europe's largest modern-day art mosaic, composed of 660,000 stones and 60 types of marble sourced from across the world. Creating a mosaic is like painting with stone. As Italian Renaissance artist Domenico Ghirlandaio once put it, the art of mosaic is "painting for eternity".

Paintings caught in mosaic stones

The new mosaic was designed by artist Marie Zolamian, who thoroughly researched the technical aspects of laying mosaics. She studied the history of the museum, its collections and the various art periods they encompass. Zolamian incorporated the city of Antwerp and elements from the city's coat of arms – the hands and towers – in her design. But her main inspiration was the collection itself, taking elements from *Saint Jerome* by Marinus van Reymerswale, the portrait of *The Painter and His Wife* by the Master of Frankfurt, and the hands and crown of Antverpia in the painting by Abraham Janssens. It doesn't stop there: Ensor and the Flemish Primitives also provided inspiration. Even Jan van Eyck's minuscule *St Barbara* is visible in her design, notably the intricate draping of her garment. The designer set herself the challenge of creating one composition out of this rich diversity. Zolamian calls the new mosaic "*un tapis de bienvenue*" ('a welcome carpet').

Puzzle and polish

The design of a new mosaic is only the first step in the path. You need professional mosaic artisans to set the design in stones. At the KMSKA, this work has been done by Sarah Landtmeters, Gino Tondat and his father. Gino and Sarah are the Mosaico di Due team; over the past 30 years, they have restored almost all the mosaics at the KMSKA. They lay mosaics using the traditional Italian method: "After cutting the mosaic stones by hand, you glue them upside down on a sheet of paper. You can then take all those sheets and puzzle them together on location. We use cellulose-rich paper with a rough and a smooth side. We stick the stones using flour-based glue on to the rough side. Once on site, we lay the side covered with the stones in the mortar. The smooth side of the paper is now on top. We wet it so that the glue dissolves and we can remove the paper. Then we fill the seams and give everything a final polish."

Richard Vander Linden

The new mosaic was created thanks to a donation from Richard Vander Linden (1929–2017), a great art lover and Friend of the KMSKA. Bioscience engineer Vander Linden was the creator of Meurisse's ZERO bar, TUC savoury biscuits and Perette chocolate bars. He supervised food production processes all over the world. His legacy supported a number of good causes, including the KMSKA.

10. THE FIRST MUSEUM GALLERY: THE GARDEN

The garden of the KMSKA is what is known as 'living green heritage'. It has historical value. And a social function to fulfil for neighbourhood residents and museum visitors. How do you approach the redevelopment of such a vulnerable green sliver of the city? That was the challenge that Landscape Architect Hannes van Meer and his partner Stijn Thomas – together known as Team van Meer! – faced.

Ensemble

We know from archival sources that the garden had not yet been planted when the museum opened in 1890. What could our modern designers use to base their project on? Hannes van Meer: "Historical photographs show parts of what the garden looked like at the end of the 19th century and the beginning of the 20th. Not in detail, but this provided us with enough to go on. No real garden plan has been preserved, but we are aware of a number of the early proposals. Based on that limited information, it wasn't possible for us to create a reconstruction. You should only attempt that if you have sufficient knowledge to do it correctly. It also wasn't part of the brief that the client, the Flemish government, gave us. Of course, you can sense that the museum, garden and neighbourhood came into existence together, it is a genuine ensemble. The district was adapted entirely around the site of the museum, and the garden design also played a role in this. The old garden proposals all shared the basic principle that the garden supported the grand character of the museum. Except for the row of elms on the street side, it was open-plan. As a result, you were forced to take up position across from the façade everywhere in the garden. We have taken this into account in the new garden design."

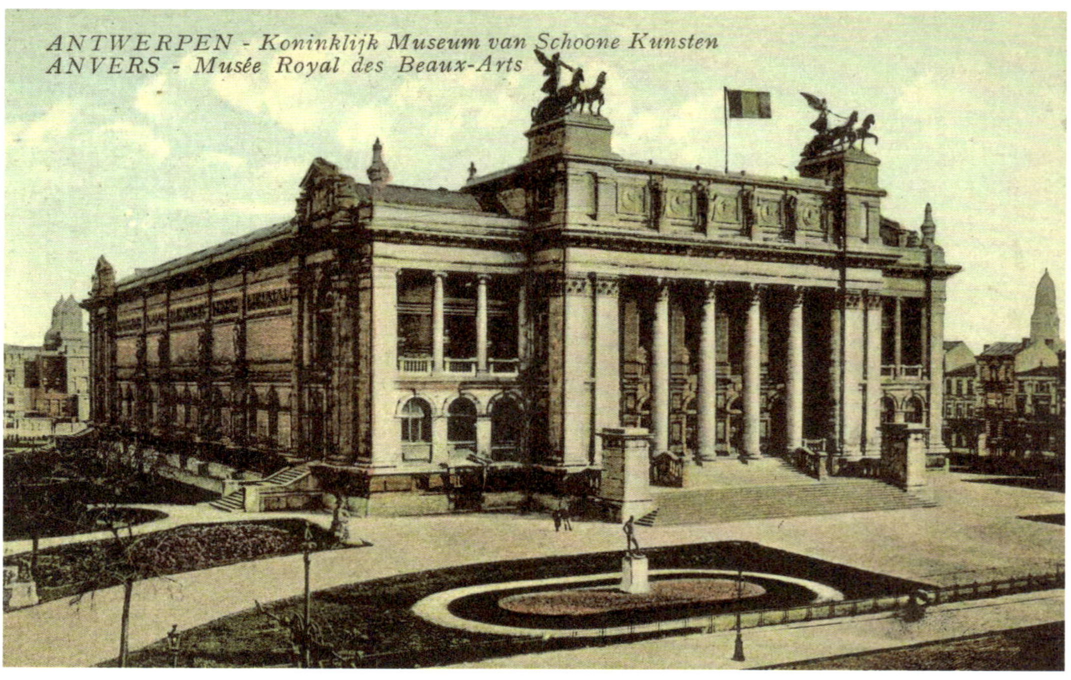

Photographs and postcards show what the garden looked like in the early 20th century. In the foreground, Constantin Meunier's *Dockhand*.

Back in time

A historic garden that has been a construction site for years and that was also extensively damaged in the past is not a clear-cut assignment. Where do you start? " As always, we started with an analysis. We examined all aspects: urban planning, spatial, architectural, historical. It is a major challenge for a designer to reconcile all functions and interests with each other, in a good and, above all, sustainable design that you also feel personally invested in. The garden should be welcoming and accessible to everyone in the neighbourhood. Safety is another important factor. And there are also the artworks, which are an integral part of the garden. It was an exciting challenge to embrace all these elements. The new garden now claims its place back within the museum, garden and neighbourhood ensemble – fulfilling its great potential. We took a look at the principles of the old proposals. The starting point was a green border on all sides, with a strolling promenade. The second principle was the formal axial structure of the paths, based on the street plan of the district. The space in between was filled with attractive greenery, the third principle. We replaced that with active greenery, lawn zones and perennial plants. As a fourth principle, art was placed at the intersections of the axes and sightlines. We also translated that into a new integration of the art. The artworks complete the garden."

Having a picnic

"Of course, as a designer of a historic garden, you ask yourself: what do we need to preserve here? And what is healthy enough to keep? This concerned the row of elm trees and the railings around the museum on the street side. Those are the only elements that are certainly historically correct. We were able to restore the ornamental railings while retaining as much of the existing material as possible. We completed the row of elms with 36 new ones. That is the only bit of pure reconstruction that we did. The *krentenboom* (wild plum) trees are new. We also tried to bring back the concept of the historic route, while changing the contents of the garden. Greenery just to look at no longer fits within a contemporary interpretation of public space. The same applies to the garden as a museum gallery. The art experience today is different; people like to get closer to the works of art. We have designed the entire rear zone in a much more informal way, so that the neighbourhood can use it very casually. In that sense, there are similarities with the approach that KAAN Architecten used in the renovation of the building. Only there is no new building in our case, but a grass meadow for a picnic. That wasn't there before. So you keep the historical aspects, but bring the use of the garden up to date: that's how you can sum it up."

Looking to the future

Designing a garden in a time like ours, by definition also means being attentive to sustainability: "For me, this design is about the smart use of water. The first question was: how do we reuse the rainwater? We don't channel anything to the sewerage system, we allow all the rainfall to penetrate into the soil on our own property. To achieve this, we opted for a permeable pavement that allows water to pass through. We also laid the pavement on a slight incline, so that the water flows to the adjacent green zones. The path is steeper around the various steps. This increases the flow of water, and we collect it in a tube in the ground. Then the water can seep slowly into the subsoil through holes in the tube."

"Sustainability, above all, also looks to the future. A good public space only succeeds if you consider the maintenance that will be required. That too is a sustainability principle. We could easily have designed a very complex garden that requires a lot of maintenance. There is then a real chance that your concept will become completely diluted after two or three years. Maintenance requires a lot of money, after all."

"Upon completion, a building already reflects what the architect had in mind. When you design a garden, it won't be finished until several decades later. In our vision we always try to estimate what the garden will look like when, for example, the trees reach maturity. Or the hedges have become fuller. That's also why it is important to design a garden that needs little maintenance. It's all about achieving that future vision."

Nine sculptures from the KMSKA collection have been planted in the newly designed garden surrounding the museum building. As a result, the garden is the first museum gallery, as it were, where visitors and local residents can appreciate art out in the open air.

The statues in the new museum garden were already in the garden before the KMSKA closed. Nearly all of them were acquired specifically for the garden, at 19th-century salons where important and popular Belgian sculptors would display their latest work (not all these artists are so well known today.) The works exhibited at the salon were models made of plaster; once a sale was agreed, a bronze cast was made, to create a sculpture that could stand up to the weather gods. While the museum was closed, each and every one of them was thoroughly restored and now, once again, have a nice, even patina. The sculptures feature in the new public gardens and along the promenades flanking the museum building. Let's take a look at a selection.

Antwerp sculptures

Dockhand by Constantin Meunier (1831–1905) is an iconic statue for Antwerp, the port city. For decades, it stood in the Middelheim open-air sculpture museum. Incidentally, the city of Antwerp ordered a second copy of this heroic dockworker, which stands next to the town hall, right in the city centre.

A second statue in the museum garden has a special significance for the city on the Scheldt: *Vulture Protecting Its Prey* by Josuë Dupon (1864–1935). The sculpture depicts the drama of two wild animals fighting – an age-old motif in sculpture – in reference to Antwerp Zoo. At the turn of the 20th century, this was the largest zoo in Europe. The Dupon and Meunier statues were both acquired by the museum in 1898 to grace the front garden.

Bucolic vase

Vase with Bas Relief (1879) by Johann Friedrich Drake (1805–1882) is of a completely different genre. This is a decorative garden sculpture, elegant and refined, and typically neoclassical. German sculptor Drake became a member of the academic corps of the Antwerp Academy in 1866, which entailed the obligation for him to create a work of art for the museum of the Academics. The reliefs on the vase symbolise the poetry of rural life. Drake took a rather easy way out for this "mandatory work": he had used the same motif 20 years before, on the pedestal of the statue of King Friedrich Wilhelm III (now in Berlin's Tiergarten).

Modern art

1/24 x 23 x 22 ... x 1 by Bert De Leeuw (1926–2007) is a work from 1974 and therefore not from the same period (late 19th/early 20th century) as most of the garden works. This "totem" consists of six bronze elements that can be mounted in various combinations. The current montage was made at the suggestion of his son, Hendrik De Leeuw, and is in keeping with the title of the work. The project has 24 blocks, which can be stacked and/or presented separately. The blocks can be rotated; they have four different sides. For the more mathematically inclined among us: the title with the 1 above the vinculum refers to the one configuration chosen out of the 24 x 23 x 22 ... x 1 possibilities.

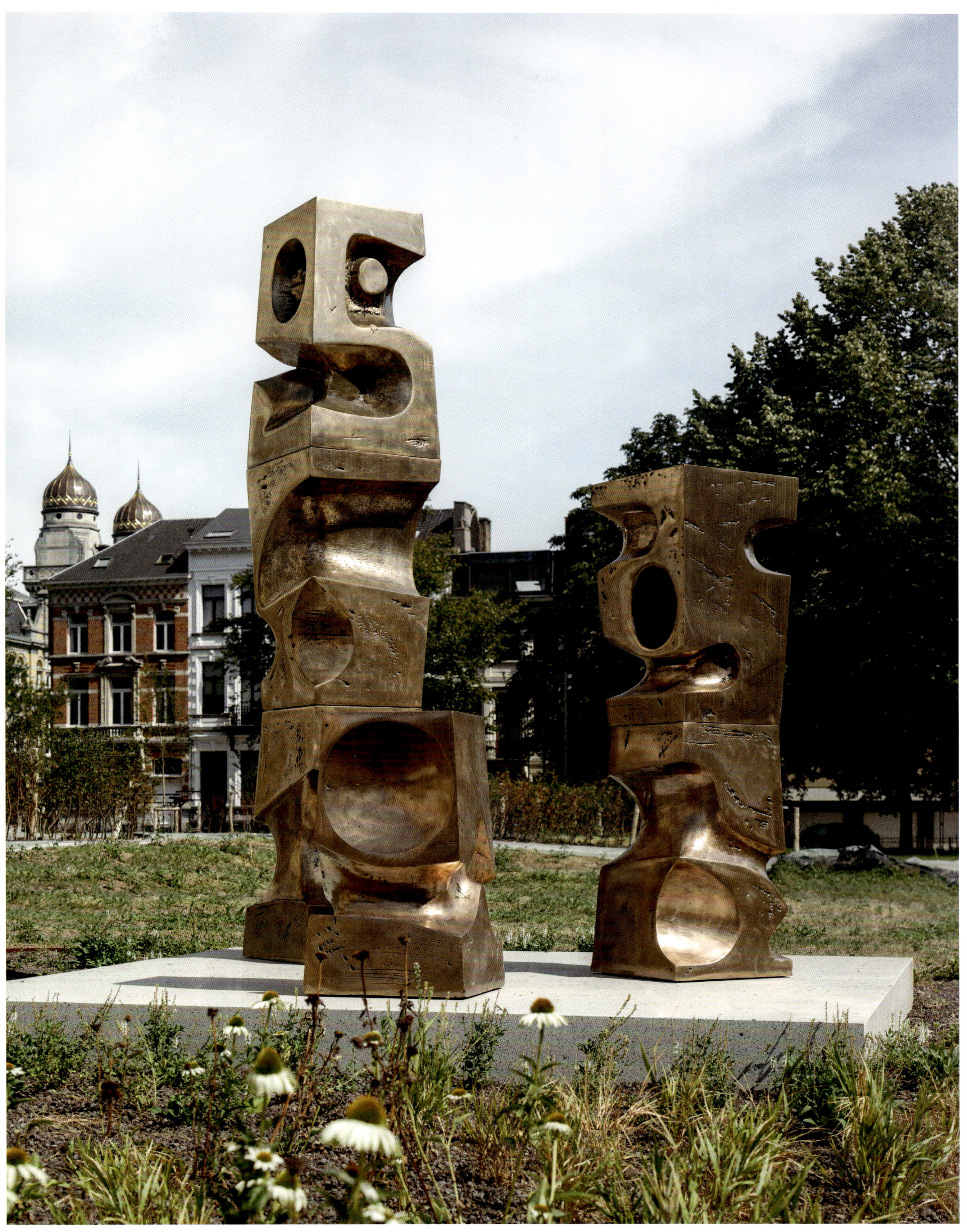

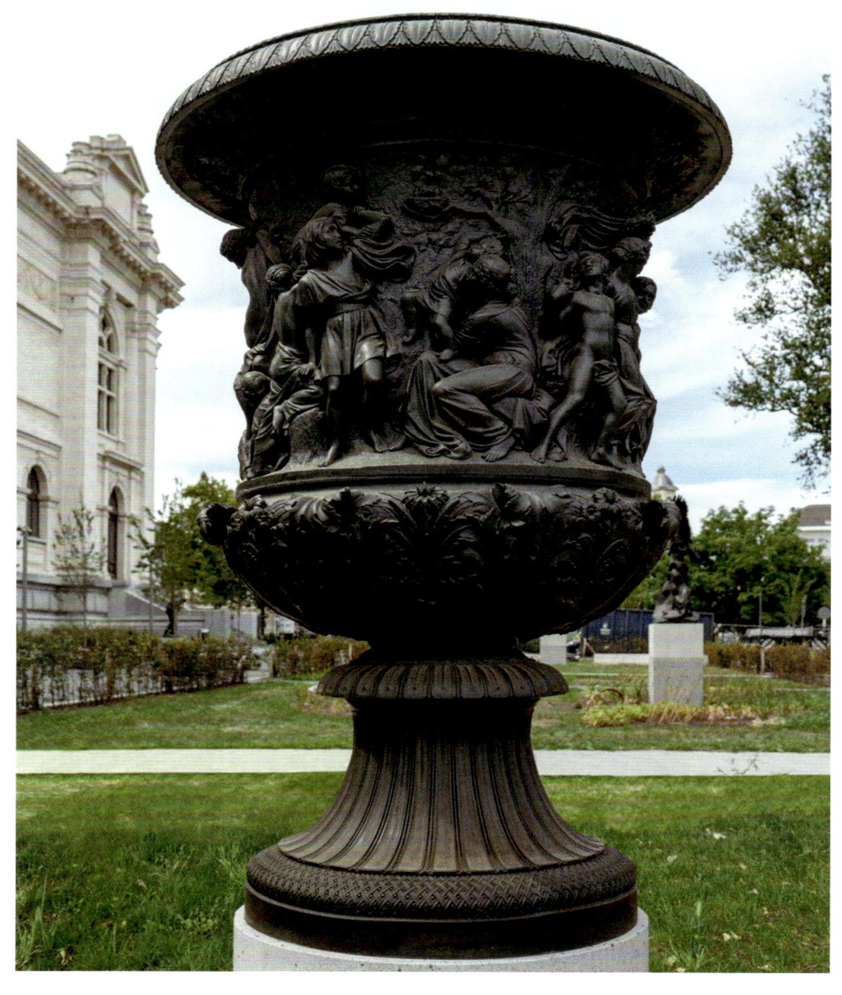

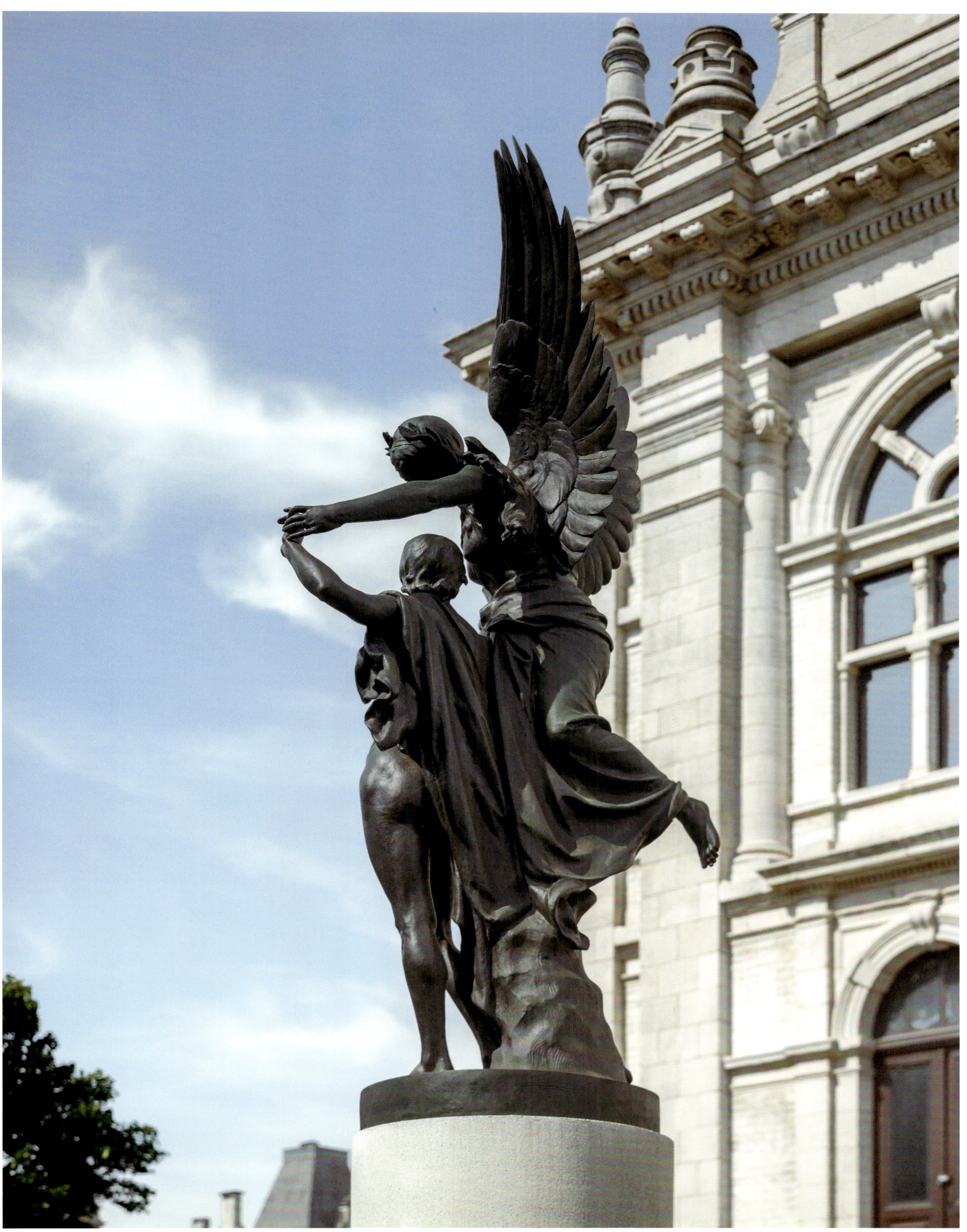

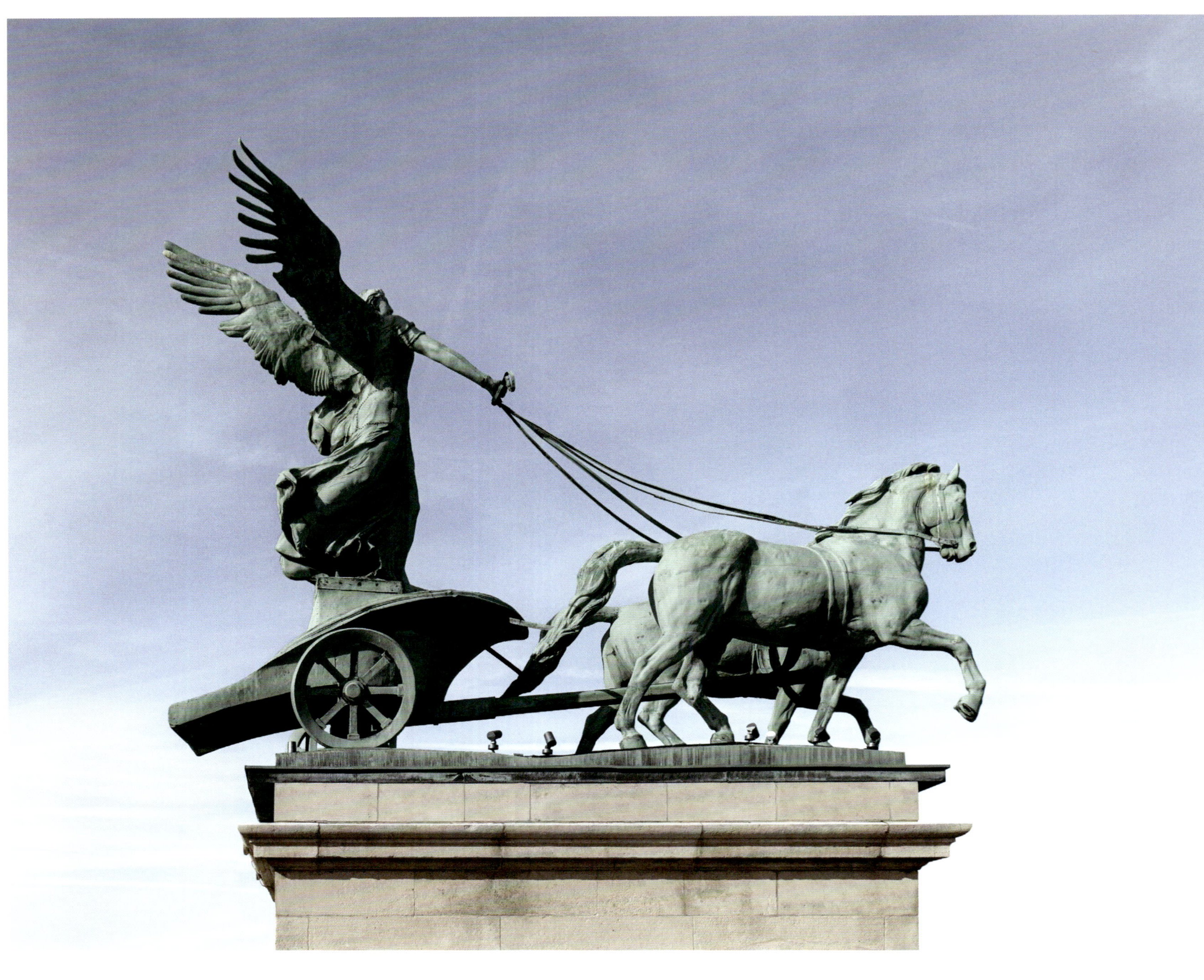

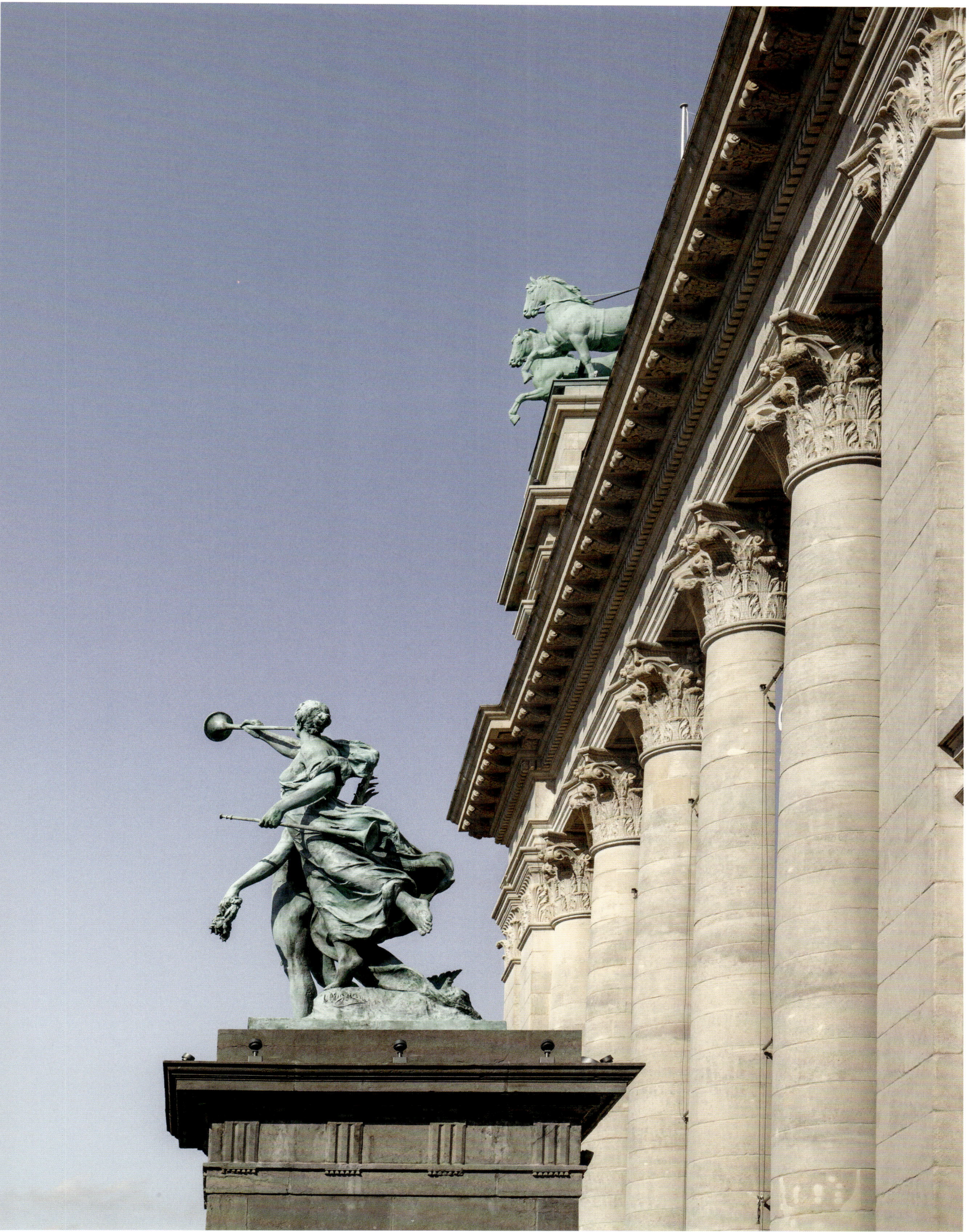

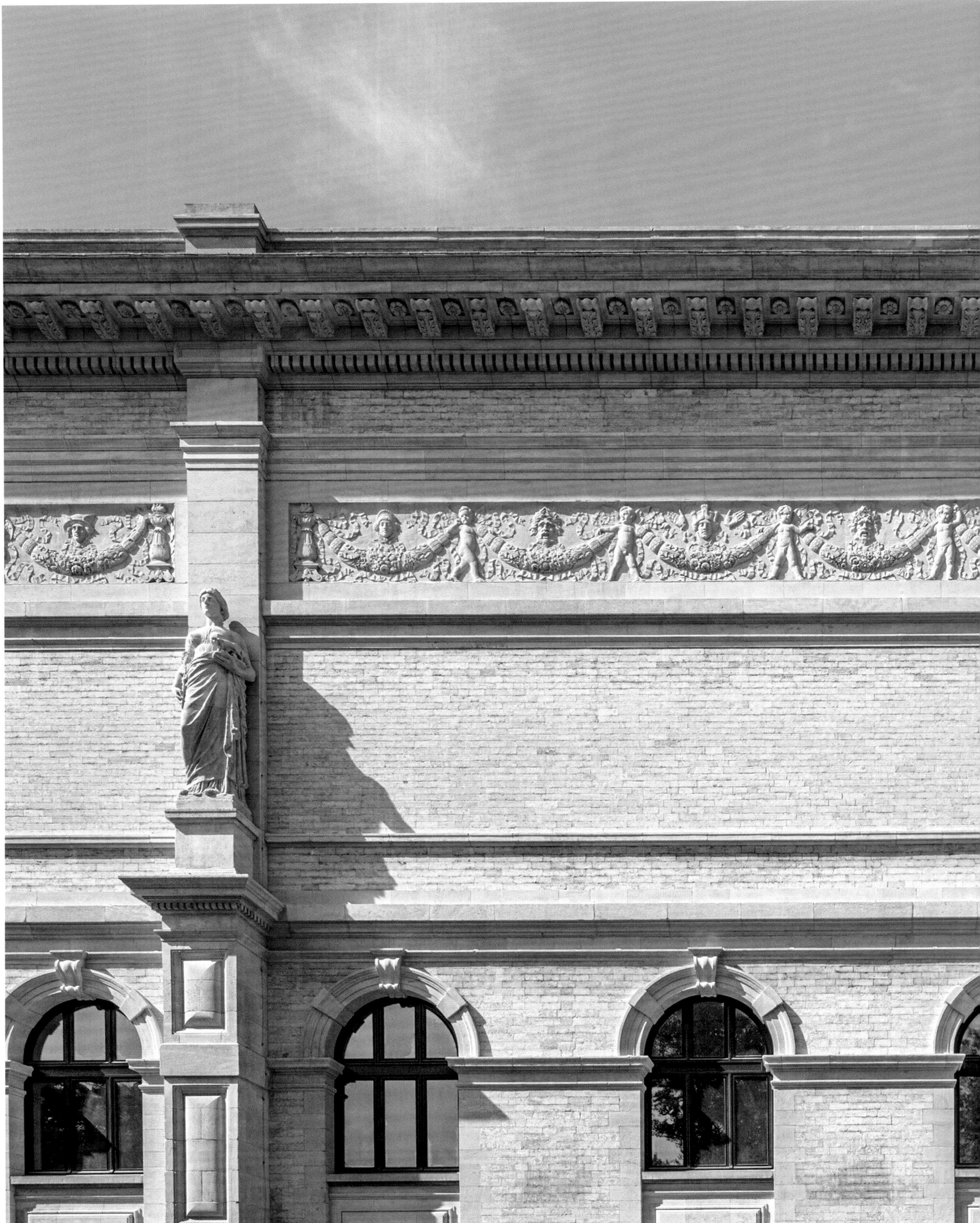

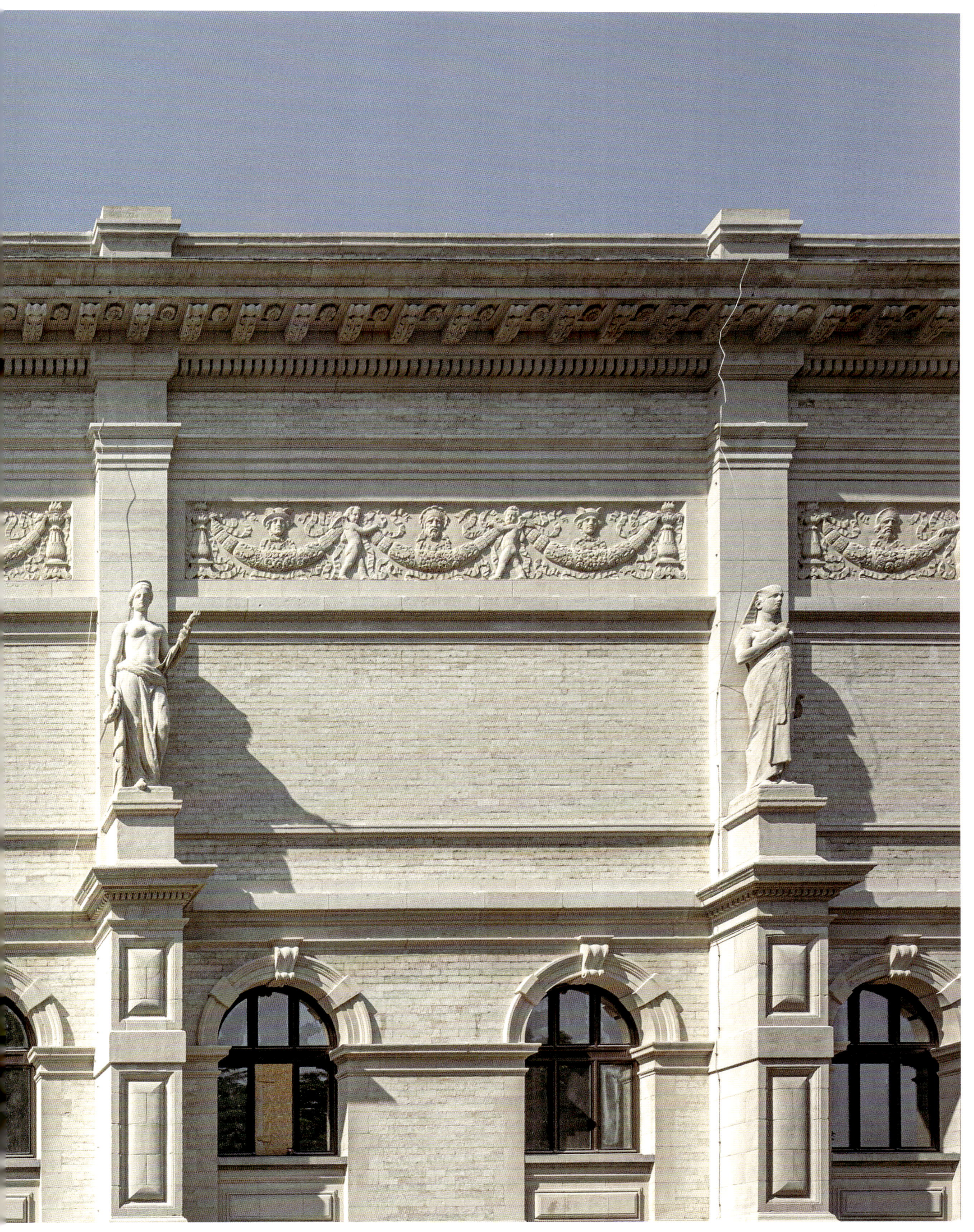

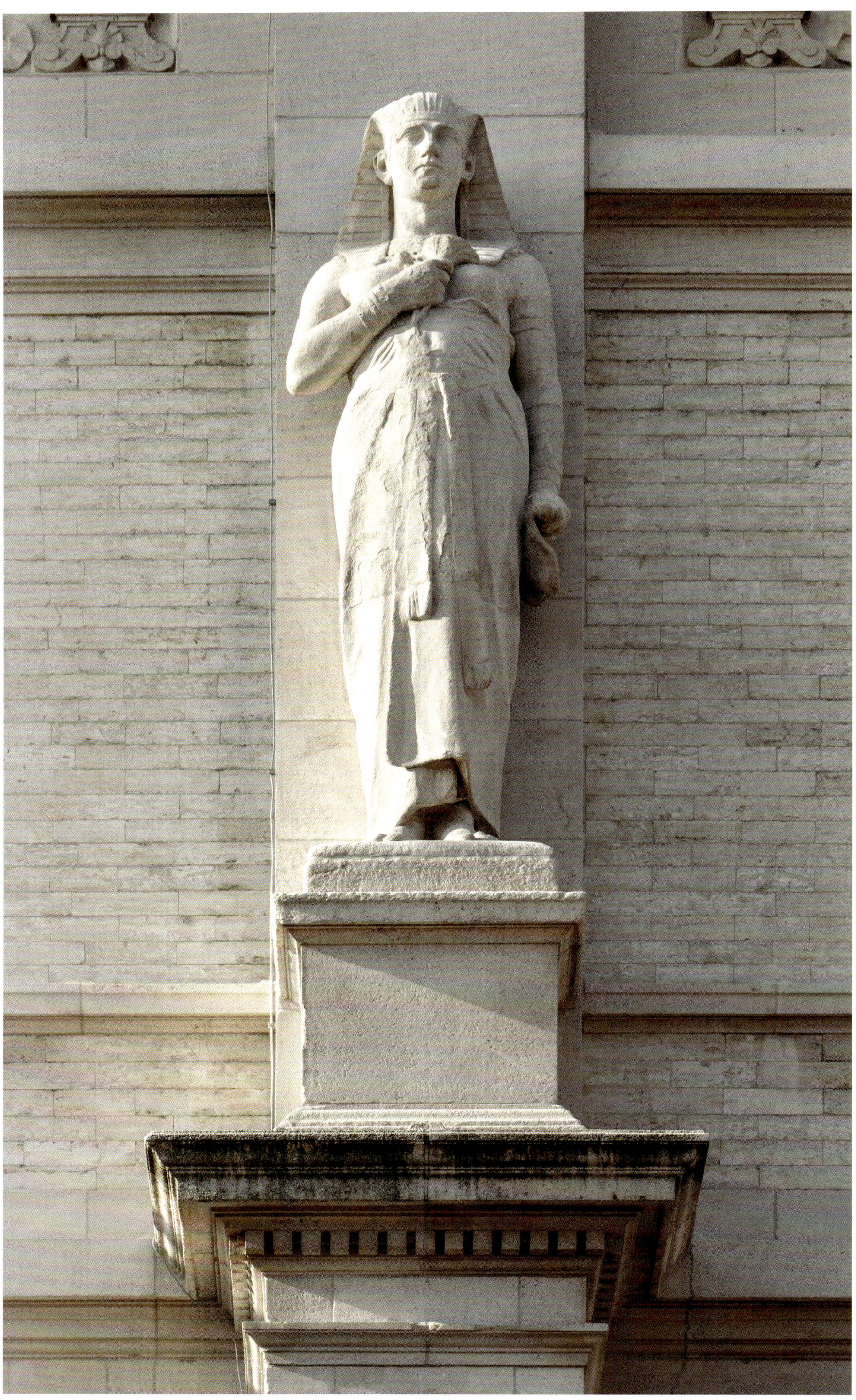

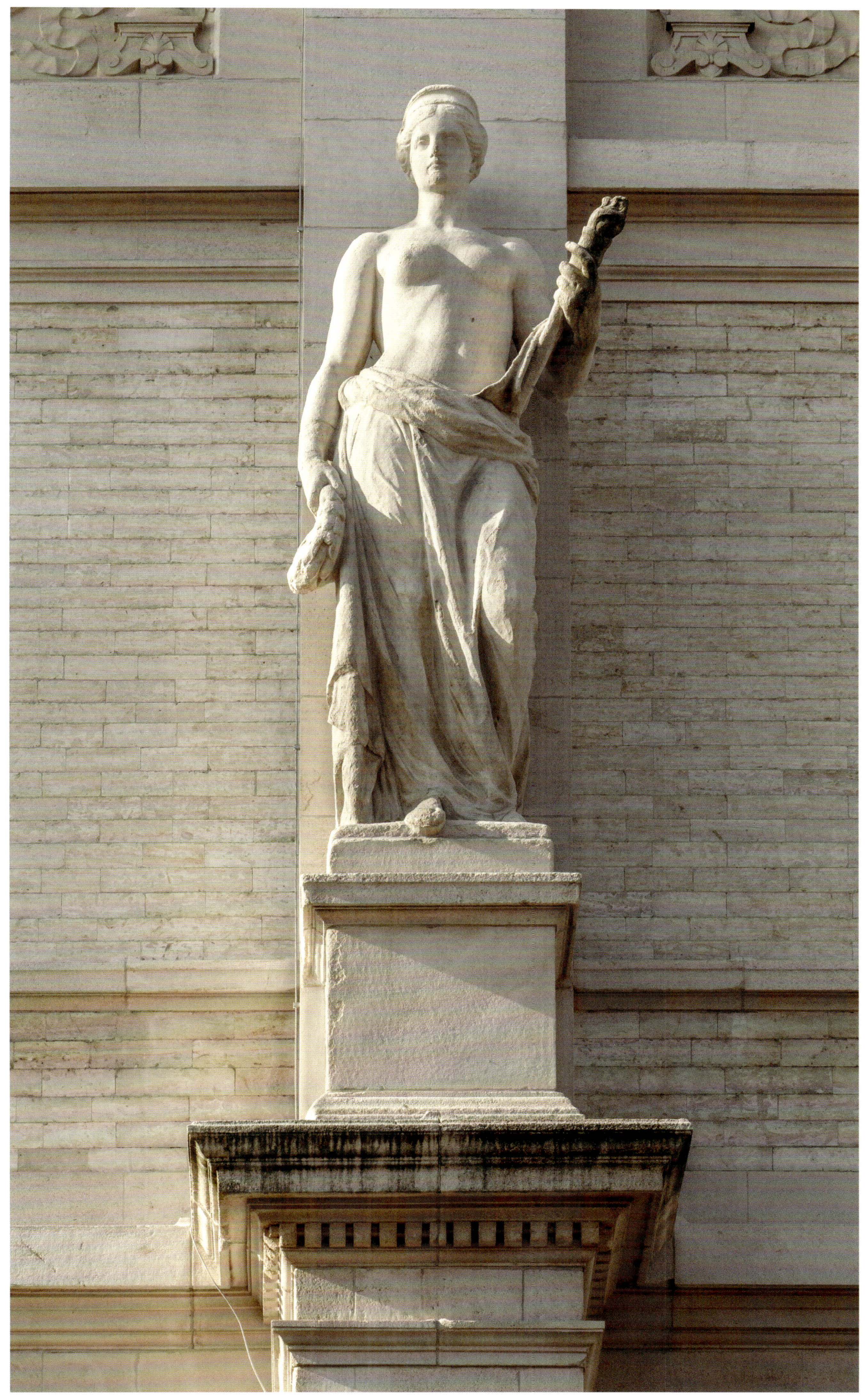

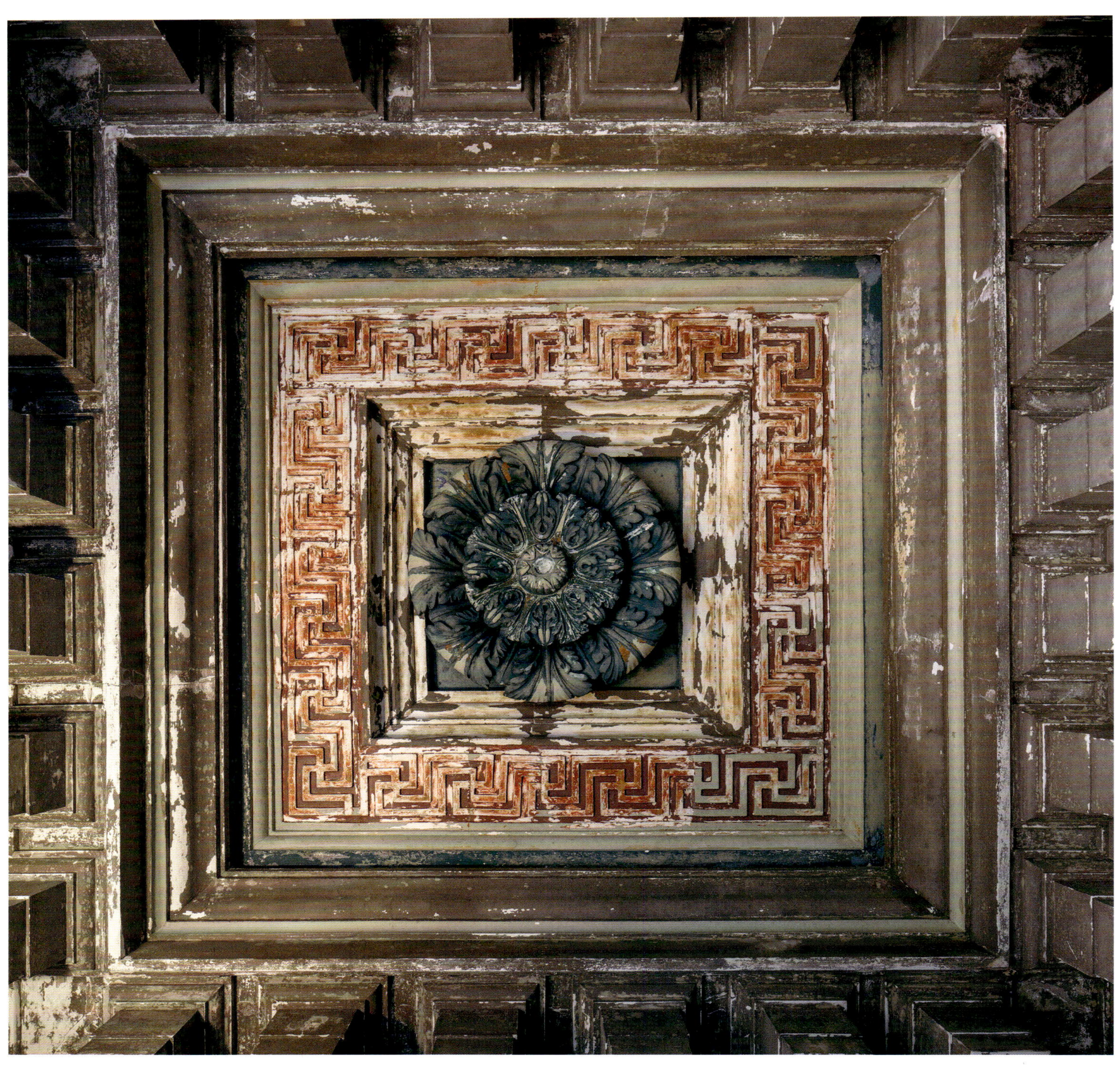

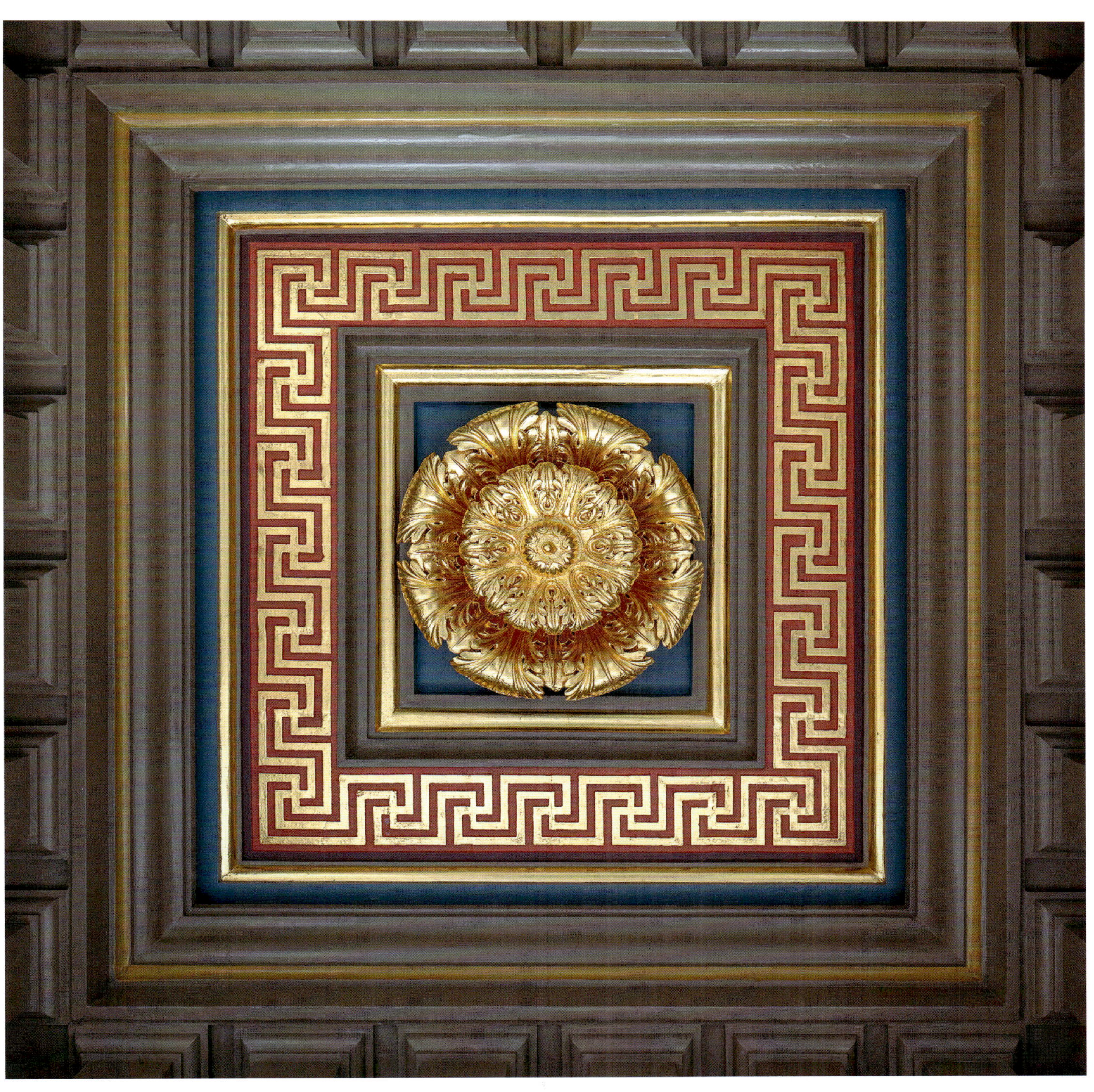

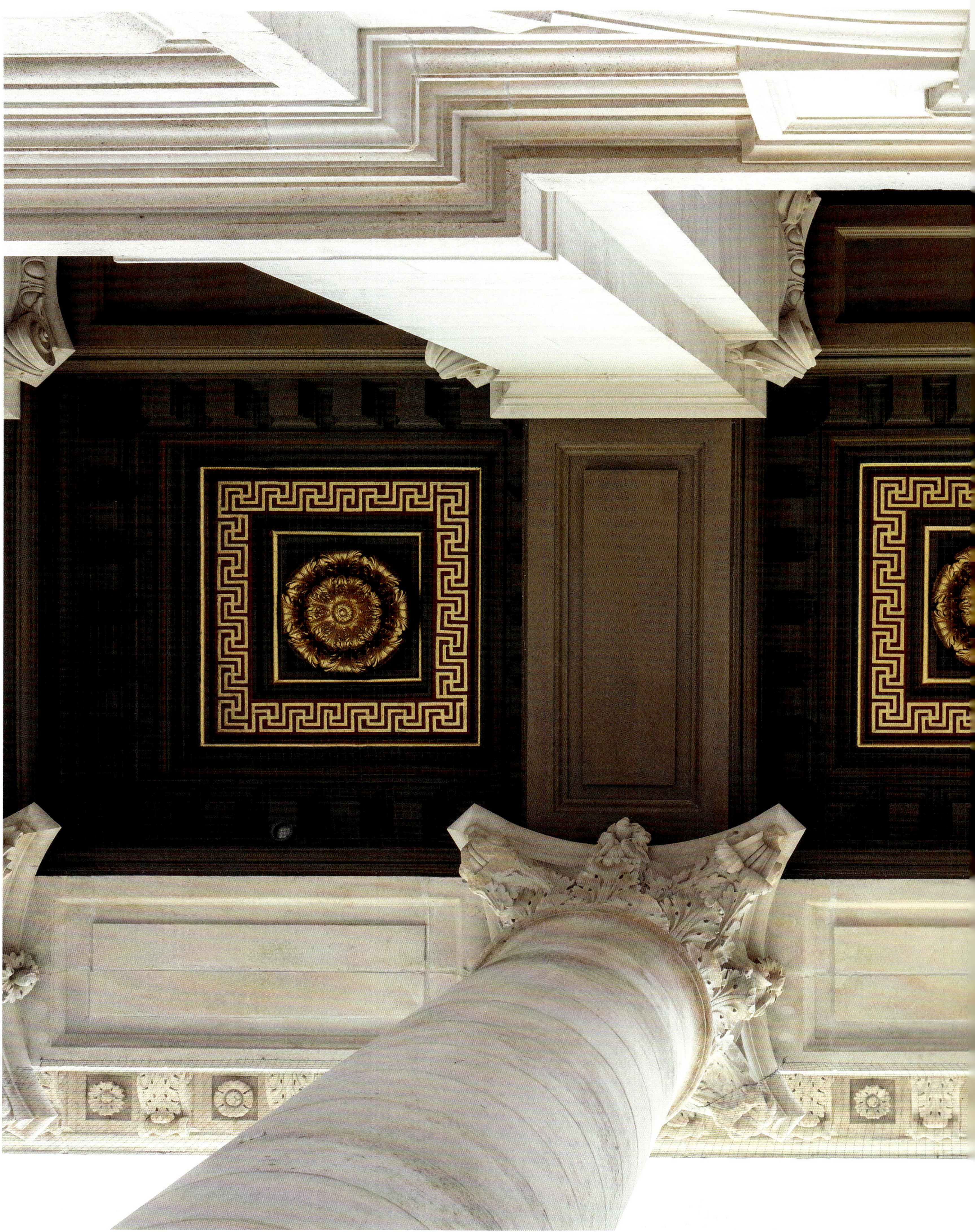

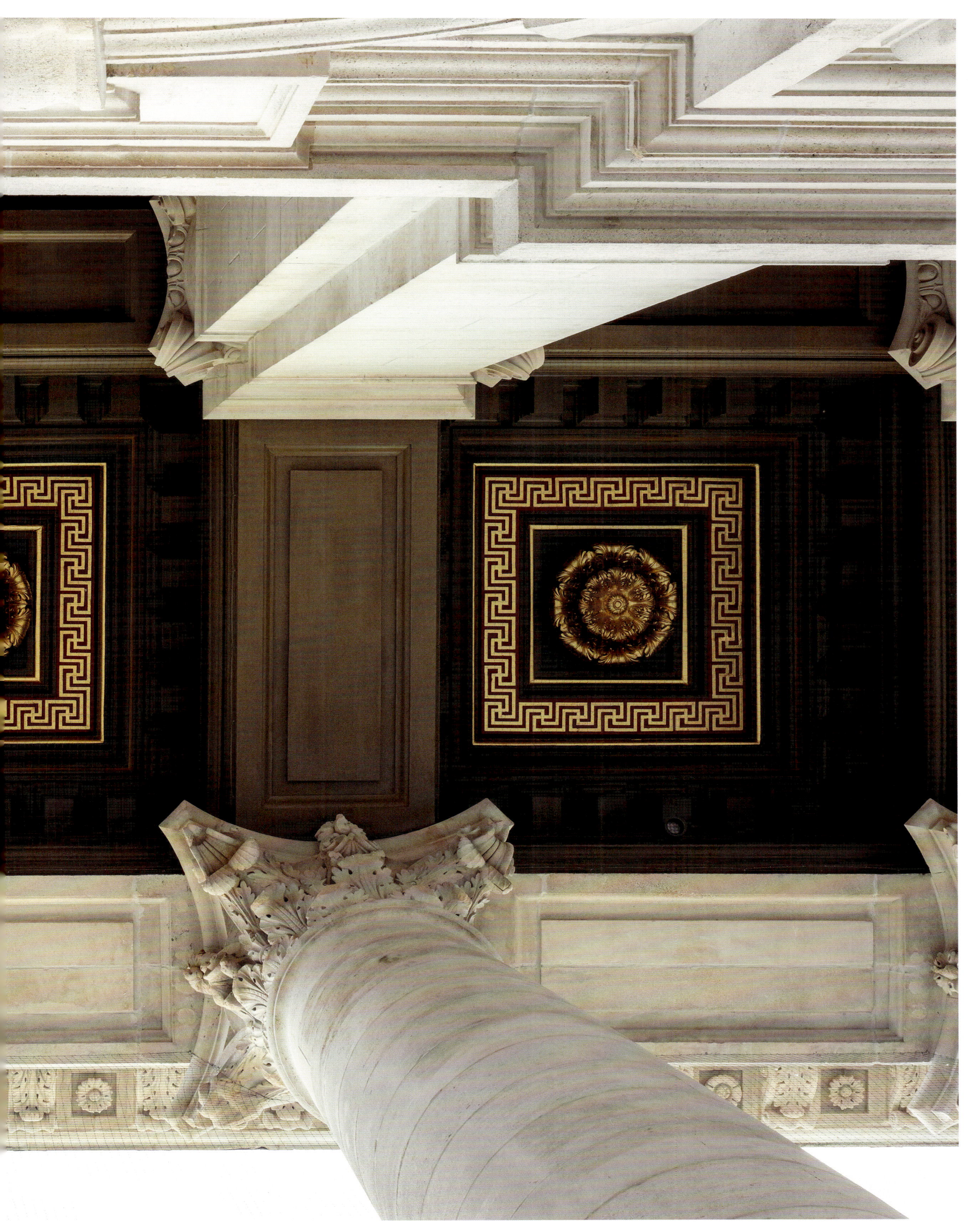

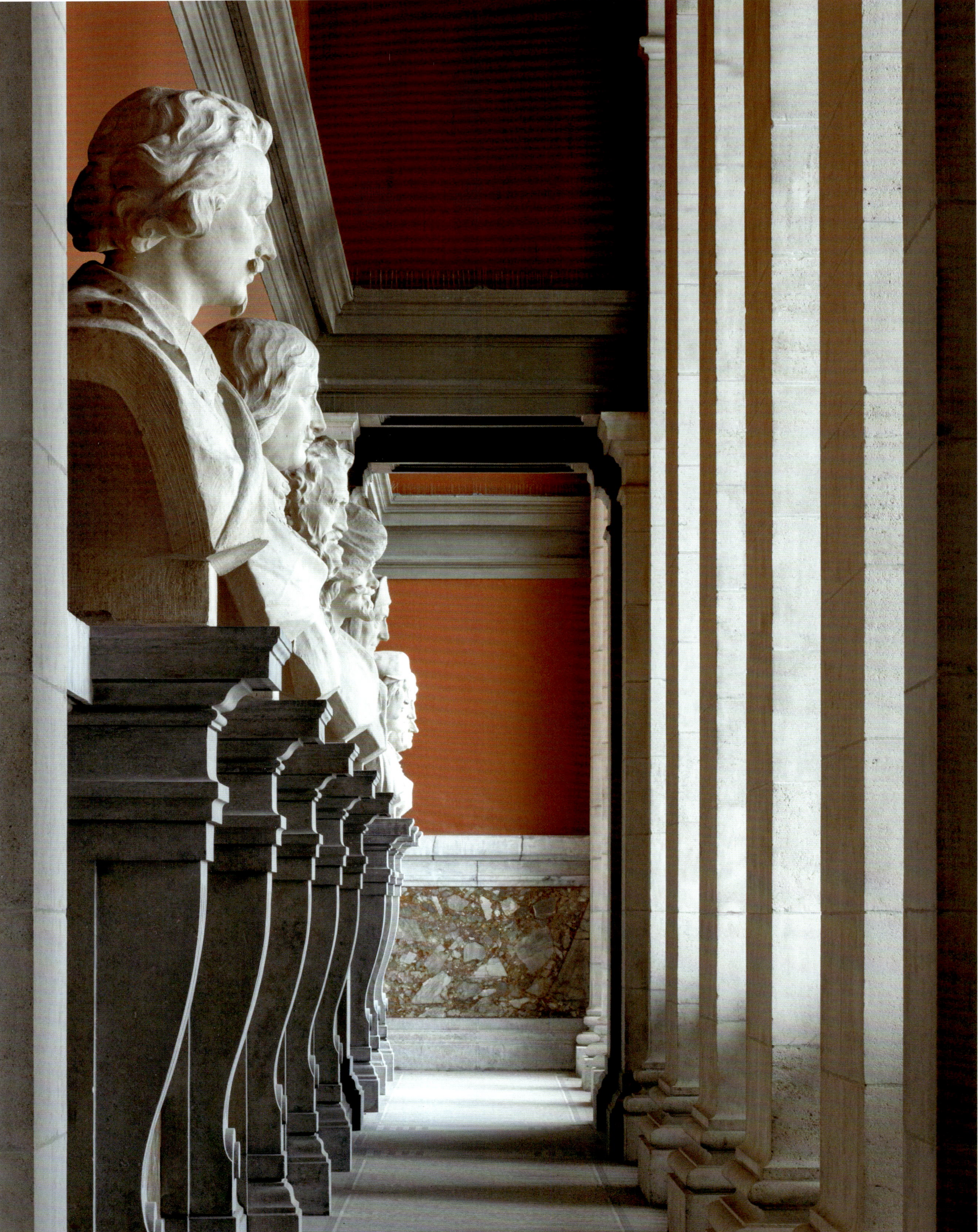

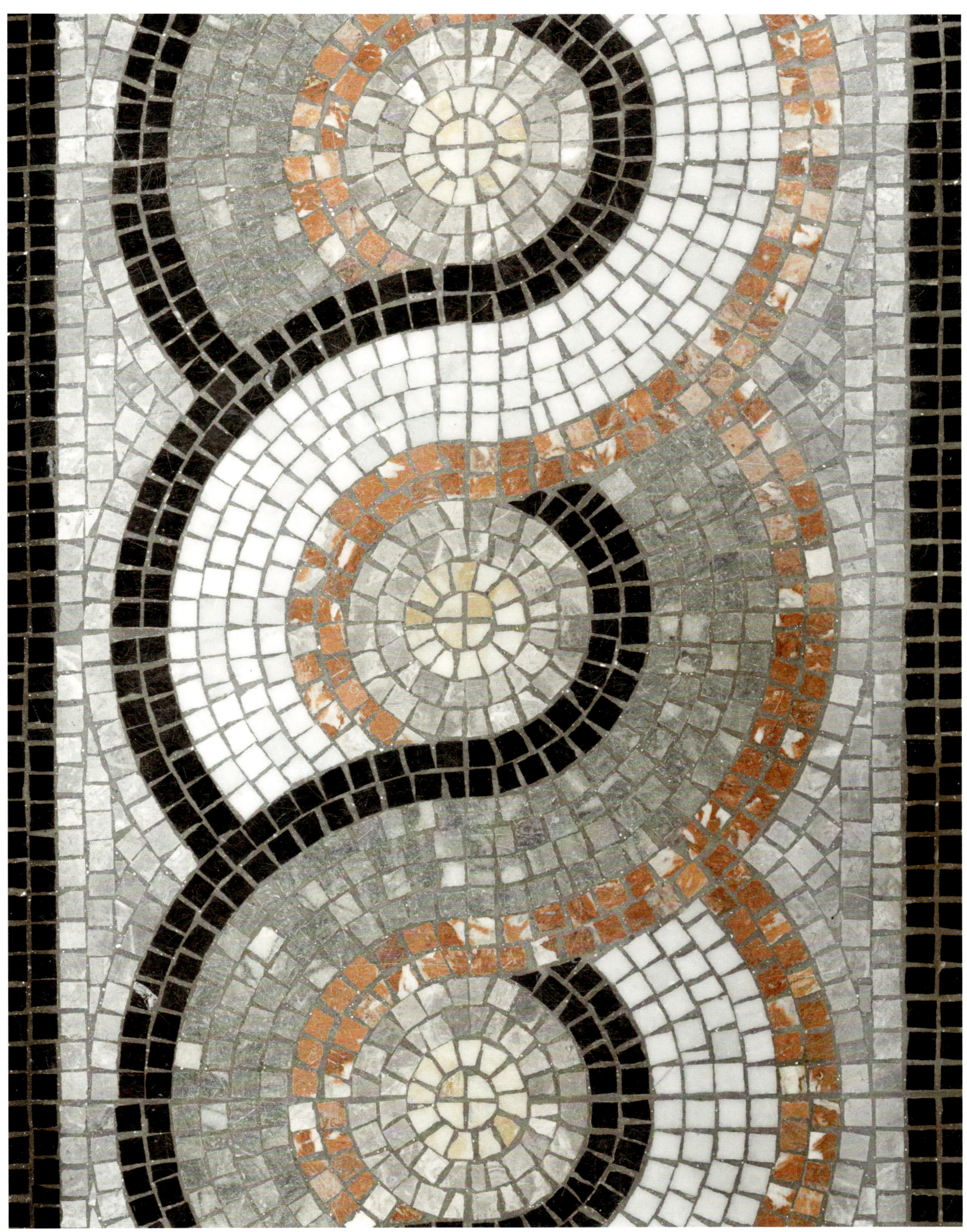

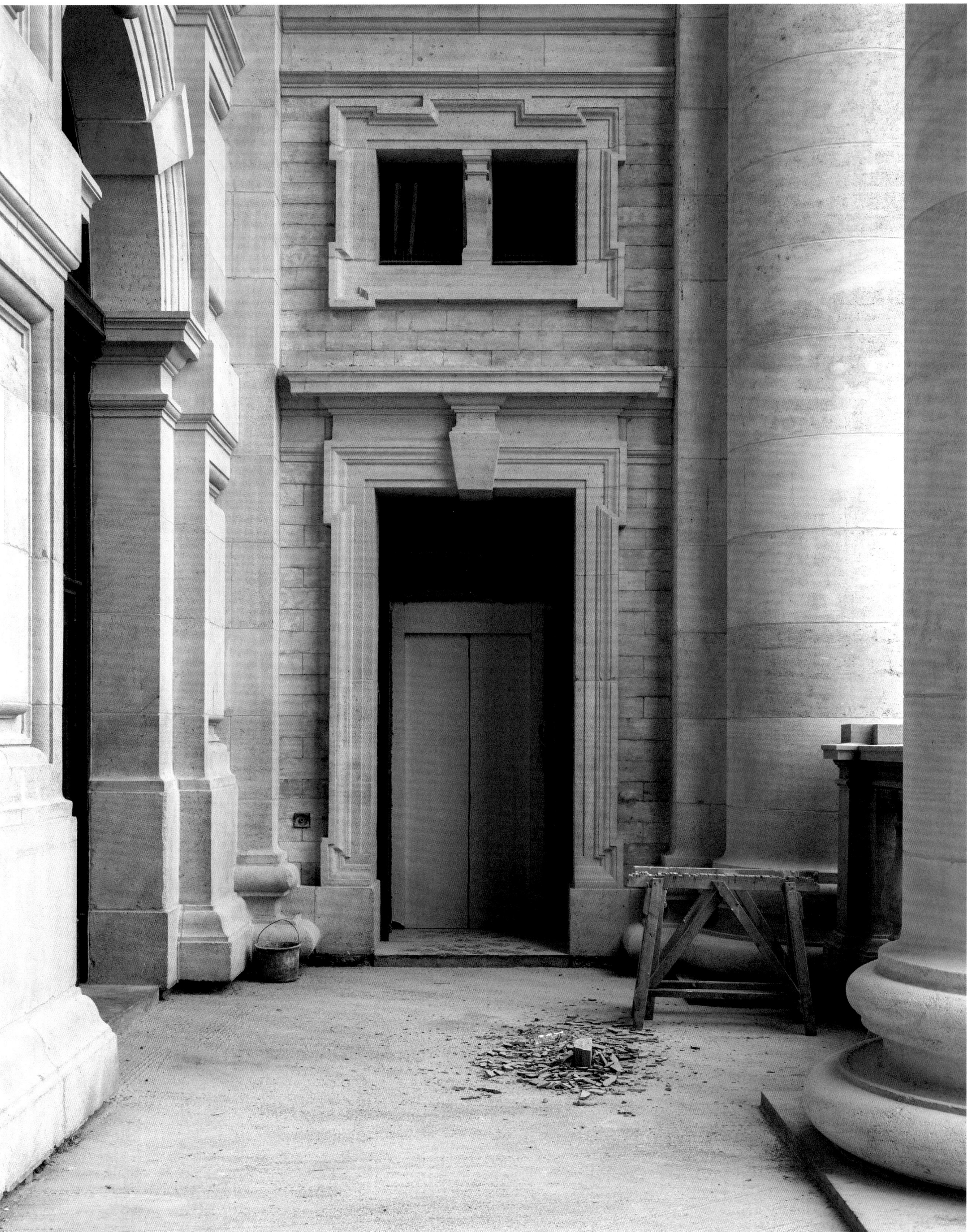

The story of the museum building

Drawing of the front façade by architects Winders and Van Dijk.

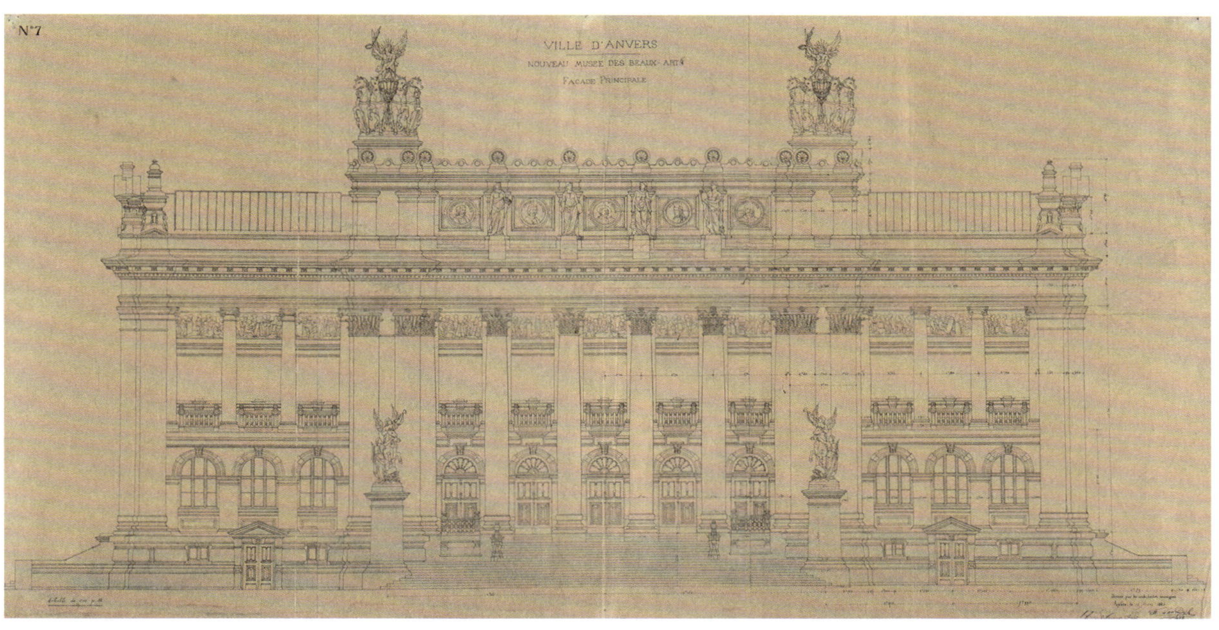

1810

Creation of the museum
On 5 May 1810, Napoleon I created the museum by imperial decree as an annex to the Academy. These institutions were both housed in the former Recollects Convent on Mutsaardstraat. The church and parts of the convent were transformed into exhibition galleries. The museum opened its doors to the public in 1816.

1877

A new museum in the South
Starting in the 1870s, Antwerp began to voice its dreams of a new museum for the fine arts. In 1875, the city decided to build the new museum in the South district, 't Zuid, on the site of the demolished Spanish citadel. The state also pledged its support. On 29 January 1877, the city organised a competition among Belgian architects. None of the 15 plans submitted was considered completely satisfactory.

In 1879, the six best candidates were invited to give it another shot. Jean-Jacques Winders won, with Frans Van Dijk a good second. Winders and Van Dijk were then commissioned to design the new museum together.

1883

Construction starts
In 1883, Antwerp city council gave Winders and Van Dijk the green light for their building plans. Construction started a year later. The architects designed the museum with the appearance of a classical temple, but their focus was not solely on the style of the building. Functionality and security were also important elements of their concept.

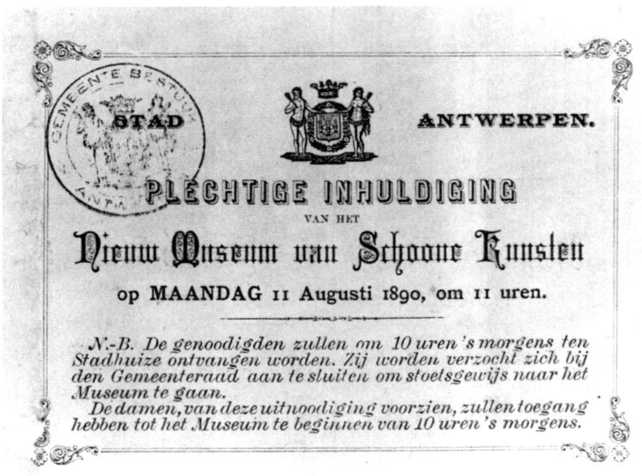

STAD ANTWERPEN.

PLECHTIGE INHULDIGING

VAN HET

Nieuw Museum van Schoone Kunsten

op MAANDAG 11 Augusti 1890, om 11 uren.

N.-B. De genoodigden zullen om 10 uren 's morgens ten Stadhuize ontvangen worden. Zij worden verzocht zich bij den Gemeenteraad aan te sluiten om stoetsgewijs naar het Museum te gaan.

De damen, van deze uitnoodiging voorzien, zullen toegang hebben tot het Museum te beginnen van 10 uren 's morgens.

Invitation to the grand opening of the museum in 1890.

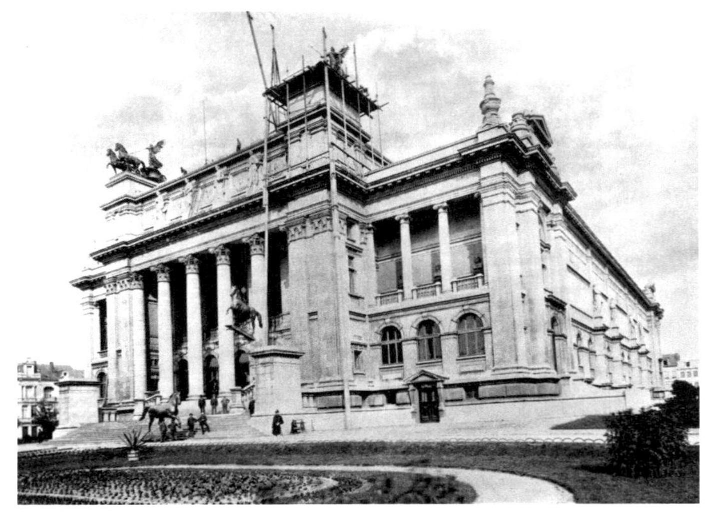

In 1905, the chariots designed by sculptor Thomas Vinçotte were lifted on to the roof.

1890

Grand opening
King Leopold II and Crown Prince Baudouin were given a private showing of the new museum on 25 July 1890. The real party kicked off on 11 August 1890, during the Antwerp funfair week. After a ceremonial reception at the city hall, the city council and the invited guests made their way to the museum for the official inauguration. They didn't walk alone. A colourful procession of 154 city societies accompanied the dignitaries. In the evening, the Cercle Artistique, Littéraire et Scientifique d'Anvers honoured the VIPs with a lavish banquet.

1891

An art-history lesson
At the time of the opening of the museum, the decorations for the façades were not yet finished. Only the sculptures on the front façade had been completed. This ambitious project engaged the talents of 22 artists: allegorical statues, medallions and busts brought to life the rich history of Western art and culture. The last of the façade statues was set in place in 1896.

1894

Exposition Internationale d'Anvers
In 1894, the city ventured to repeat the success of the International Exhibition of Antwerp in 1885. This time, the event also unfolded in the new city district in the South, surrounding the museum. Whereas the museum was still under construction in 1885, at the 1894 exhibition the brand-new building had become one of the attractions. With an additional marvel to behold on the ground floor: aquariums filled with tropical fish from around the world.

1905

Triumph of the Fine Arts
On 15 June 1905, contractor Godfried van Bergen and his workers hoisted into the sky two chariots, four horses and two winged female charioteers holding laurel wreaths aloft – all representing the triumph of the fine arts. From their elevated position on the roof, Thomas Vinçotte's sculptures became the perfect symbol of the museum.

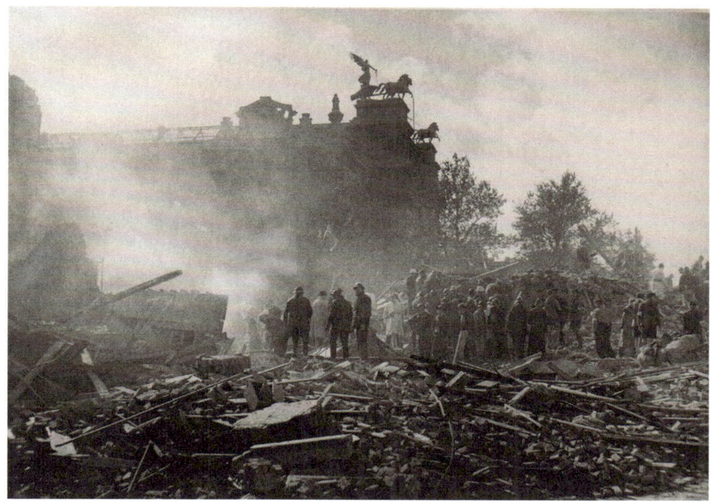

On 13 October 1944, a bomb fell on the corner of Schildersstraat and Karel Rogierstraat.

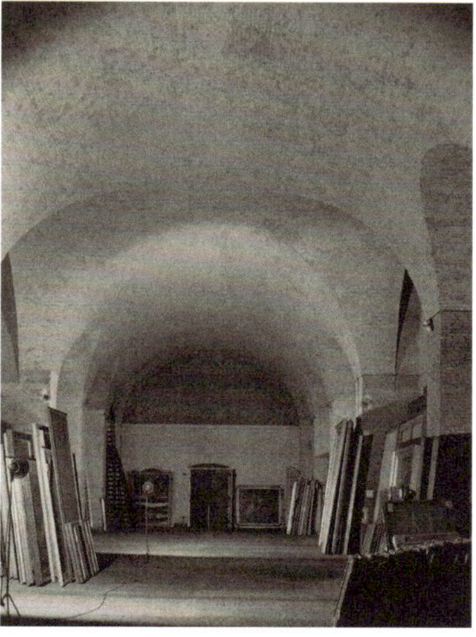

The bombproof shelter before the nuclear vault was built.

1925

First major expansion
The collection continued to grow, and the ensuing lack of space led to the first major rebuild. Architect Frans Van Dijk drafted the plans, which covered the four courtyards and converted them into large galleries. The windows on the side of the patios disappeared in this reconstruction. The long galleries were converted into smaller museum rooms. In the same period, the galleries on the top floor were given a makeover.

1927

Revamped museography
The new construction was completed on time for the 350th anniversary of Rubens' birth. From 28 May 1927, the public were able to enjoy an updated display of the collection, now meeting modern requirements. There were fewer works, all hung at eye level, and arranged in accordance with the prevailing art-historical and aesthetic criteria. For the first time, old and modern paintings were separated from each other and divided over two floors.

1944

War damage
On 13 October 1944, a German flying bomb landed on the corner of Schildersstraat and Karel Rogierstraat, just by the museum. The bomb killed 32 people and caused extensive material destruction. The museum was also severely damaged, with shattered domes, broken windows and ruined ceilings, cornices and artworks. It took until 1953 for the galleries to be restored and the building finally reopened to the public.

1952

Nuclear vault
In 1952, during the Cold War, the Ministry of the Interior had a nuclear vault built within the bombproof shelter of the museum. The robust concrete construction was engineered to protect the most treasured paintings in the collection from the force of an atomic bomb.

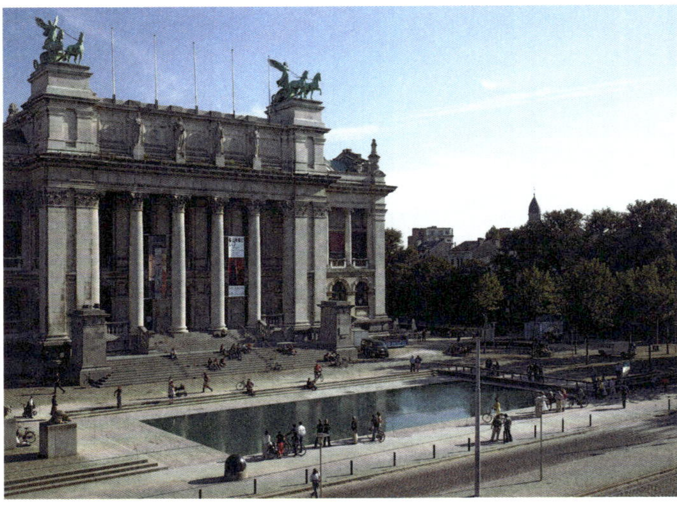

The grey weathered façade before the restoration.

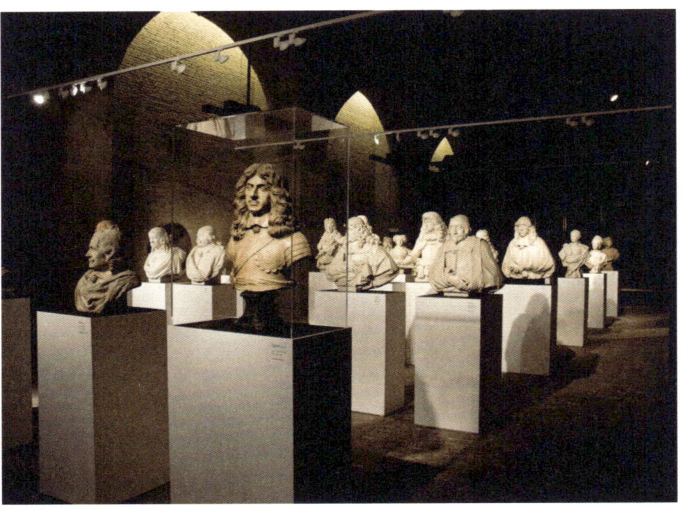

The bombproof cellar was converted into an exhibition space in 1997.

1976–1977

First major renovation
1977: Rubens year, Rubens madness. And a fabulous excuse for a thorough renovation. In the period leading up to this 400th anniversary year, the building was hidden behind scaffolding for a façade restoration. The roof was renovated and the museum finally installed the required technical equipment. The galleries were furnished with proper climate control, fire detection equipment and electric lighting. The museum decorated the exhibition rooms according to the latest fashions and also improved the public facilities.

1997

A new exhibition space
The museum proved once again to be too small. In the search for a new location for temporary exhibitions, it was decided to empty the old bomb shelter and nuclear vault and use this as exhibition space, following a design by architect Jan Thomaes.

1999

Old and worn out
A new top-class exhibition called for some much-needed modifications – this time to prepare for the *Van Dyck* exhibition of 1999. However, the engineers ran into all sorts of serious technical and structural defects. In order to turn the KMSKA into a beautiful, contemporary and well-appointed museum, a comprehensive approach was clearly needed. Architect Jan Thomaes was commissioned by the Flemish government to draw up an architectural programme of requirements for the KMSKA – a letter of intent for the creation of a masterplan.

2003

A museum for the 21st century
On 6 June 2003, Flemish master builder bOb Van Reeth issued an open call for a masterplan for the KMSKA, on the initiative of the Flemish government. The brief called for an update of the museum building to bring it into line with the needs of the 21st century. Out of the 95 entries, the committee selected five architectural firms, each of which was invited to present their masterplan vision in more detail: TOP OFFICE (Luc Deleu), Antwerp / B.A.S. (Dirk Jaspaert), Berchem; Driesen-Meersman-Thomaes, Antwerp; 51N4E Space Producers, Brussels; Claus en Kaan Architecten, Rotterdam; and Jeanne Dekkers Architectuur, Delft.

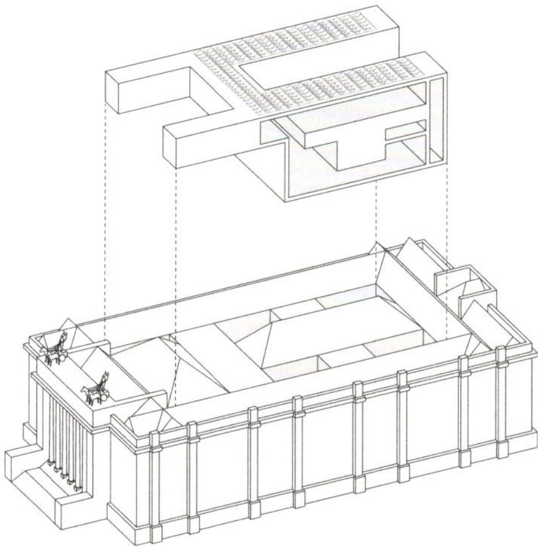

Model of the new museum based on the plans of KAAN Architecten.

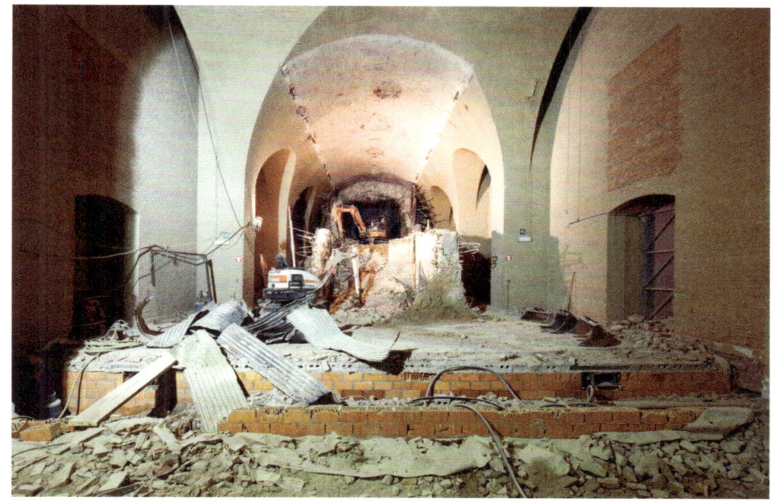

Two mini-diggers crushed the nuclear vault in the bombproof shelter with a pneumatic hammer.

2004–2006

The masterplan of KAAN Architecten
On 20 February 2004, the selection committee appointed the architectural firm of Claus en Kaan – now KAAN Architecten – to draw up a masterplan. On 12 January 2006, Minister of Culture Bert Anciaux, the Department of Culture, Youth and Media and KAAN Architecten signed the agreement for drawing up the masterplan. Ten months later, the architects presented their plan in full.

2010

Festive farewell
The KMSKA bid a festive adieu to its audience. From 24 April to 3 October 2010, visual artist Jan Vanriet designed a splendid route through the museum in which he measured his work against important objects from the collection. *Closing Time* was the aptly named final exhibition at the KMSKA before its closure. On Sunday 3 October 2010, the museum celebrated "the last day".

The museum was cleared out, although the exhibition of work by Anselm Kiefer was left in the empty lower rooms, in a collaboration with Musea Stad Antwerpen and M HKA.

2011

Closed for construction
After the international architecture exhibition *Museums in the 21st Century: Ideas Projects Buildings*, which was on display in the abandoned museum galleries from 29 January to 30 April 2011, the KMSKA closed its doors. The museum design by KAAN Architecten was given pride of place at the exhibition.

The moment had come for the most spectacular renovation in the museum's history. The first phase of the masterplan commenced. Between 1 December 2011 and 29 September 2015, contractor Artes Roegiers moved into the building. The team demolished, destroyed and dismantled obsolete structures, removed asbestos and old technical installations and, above all, built the new storage depot.

2012

Demolition of the nuclear vault
The first achievement of the masterplan was the construction of a hypermodern museum depot where the old bombproof 'cellar' used to be. Not an easy job, because the nuclear vault had to be dismantled first. For a period of three months, two mini diggers broke through, crushed and removed 1,350 tonnes of concrete and 81 tonnes of steel.

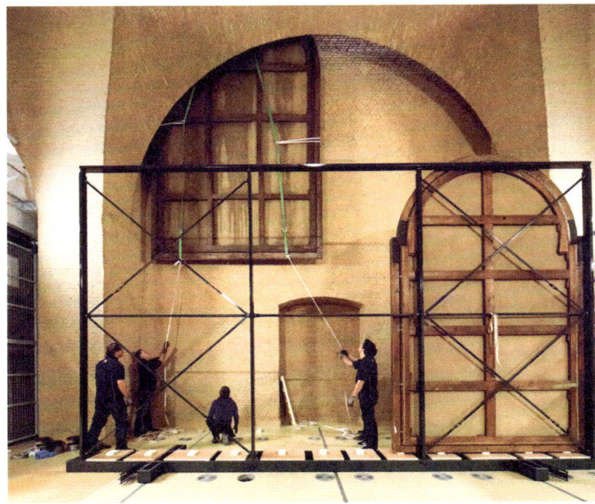

Monumental artworks are hoisted down
from the Rubens Gallery to the new storage depot.

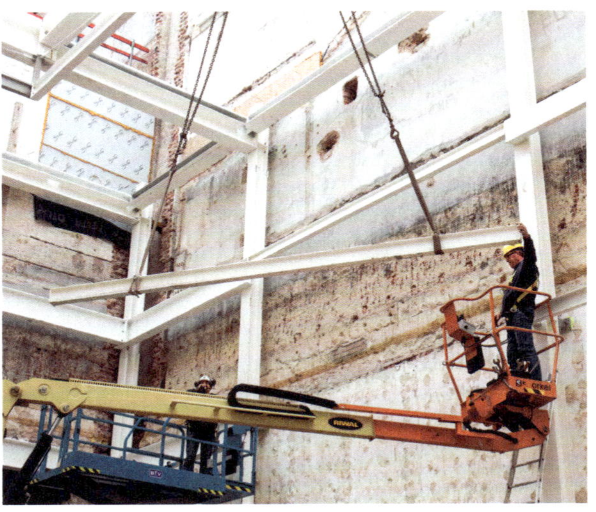

The patios are given a load-bearing
steel structure weighing a million kilos.

2013

The storage depot
The new art storage depot was completed in April 2013. It fully meets today's requirements in terms of security and climate control. It has 152 picture racks and can accommodate approximately 1,800 paintings. There is also room for climate-sensitive sculptures and works on paper.

2014

The great demolition
Things started moving forward on the building site. The first phase of the renovations – demolition mostly – was complete by autumn. Workmen had stripped the historic museum building and cleared space in the original patios. New museum galleries and two technology towers were destined to be built there, in steel and concrete. A comprehensive renovation programme was planned to restore the 19th-century galleries to their original grandeur. After removing false walls, the workmen discovered old decorative columns. They were kept. In this way, three old museum galleries regained their original aspect.

Phase 2 of the masterplan was complete. From December 2014 onwards, Artes Roegiers and Artes Woudenberg were jointly responsible for the works. These also encompassed the installation of a public area with a library, shop, café, cloakroom, sanitary facilities and reception, and the realisation of a conservation studio.

2015

Museum on columns
After three years of demolition, the time had come to rebuild. Instead of an extension outwards into the garden, KAAN Architecten opted for an extension inwards – a new museum volume housed within the 19th-century museum. This volume completely fills the former patios, but is separate from the original building. It's essential to drive in 147 piles to provide a proper foundation. Contractor Artes Roegiers built a structure of 1 million kilos of steel on top of the concrete foundation slabs.

2016

Hard as steel
The steel construction for the new building was completed in 2016. The architects deliberately didn't create a visual connection between the old and the new museum in their design. The finish of the new museum galleries will be given a finish that contrasts with that of the historic rooms. They are white and sleek and have a glossy, cast-resin floor. A passage cutting right through the 19th-century building connects the two parts of the new museum.

Directly under the museum lies Hernandez Bastion, one of the five bastions of the 16th-century Spanish citadel. A team of archaeologists uncovered remnants of the fortress during excavations in the patios and the garden. They are preserved in situ, but are not open to the public.

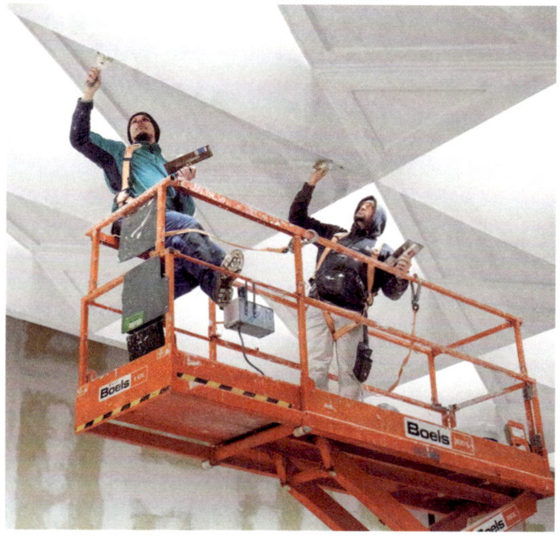

Interior finishing of the skylights.

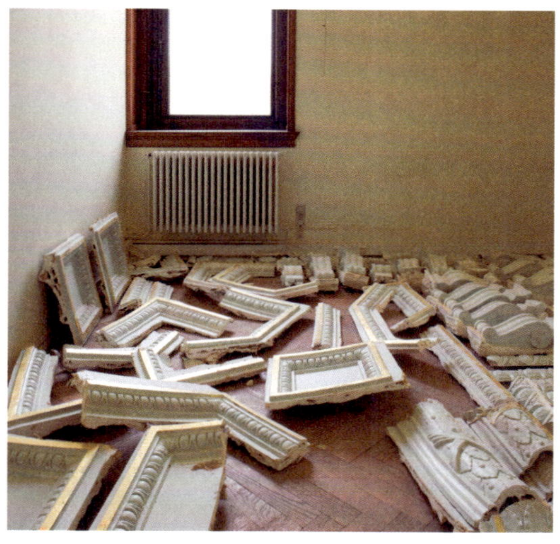

Ceiling mouldings were carefully stored and returned to their proper position later.

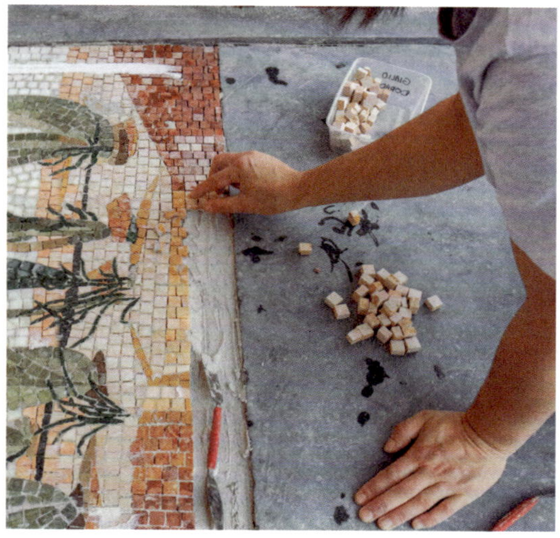

The Mosaico di Due studio team lays a new art mosaic in the portico, following a design by artist Marie Zolamian.

2017

Masterpieces
Light is of crucial importance to a museum. In the 19th-century building, which was designed as a daylight museum, sunlight entered the old halls through a *velum*, a glass ceiling. A blind regulated the strength of the light. The architects have extended the concept of the daylight museum to the new galleries. The roof of the new museum has 198 skylights that catch the daylight. All face north. Four large open spaces, 23 metres high, distribute the light over all the floors of the new museum.

Plenty of architectural triumphs can be found here. The staircases are veritable masterpieces. In the new museum, a 37-metre long staircase connects the lowest exhibition gallery with the top floor, while a winding staircase plays games with perspective. The striking spiral staircase In the reception hall was cast on site in one piece.

2018

Restored glory
After a thorough preliminary investigation, PERSPECTIV architects, together with contractor Artes Woudenberg, started on the restoration of the façades. Not only were they cleaned and restored, but the statues on the façade, the copper statues on the roof by Thomas Vinçotte, the exterior woodwork and the mosaic floors were also treated. The Mosaico di Due studio restored the historic floors and installed a new art mosaic, designed by Marie Zolamian, outside in the loggia.

2019

19th-century museum galleries
In the historic galleries, the workmen continued with their full restoration and renovation. For example, the air-conditioning system needed to be integrated into the ceilings. No sign of white is to be found here: the ceilings are dark brown, the walls Pompeiian red, antique red and olive green. Professionals also restored the old woodwork and the historic parquet floors. Where possible they made repairs, otherwise they restored the original timber with new wood.

2020

Climate-control test run
After another year of restoration, renovation and polishing, the contractor completed the second phase of the masterplan in December. The new KMSKA is finished.

The antiquated climate-control system had been one of the primary reasons for renovating the museum building. Royal HaskoningDHV designed a climate system tailormade for the museum in close collaboration with KAAN Architecten. To guarantee the perfect internal climate in every season, the new system had to undergo a long-term test period.

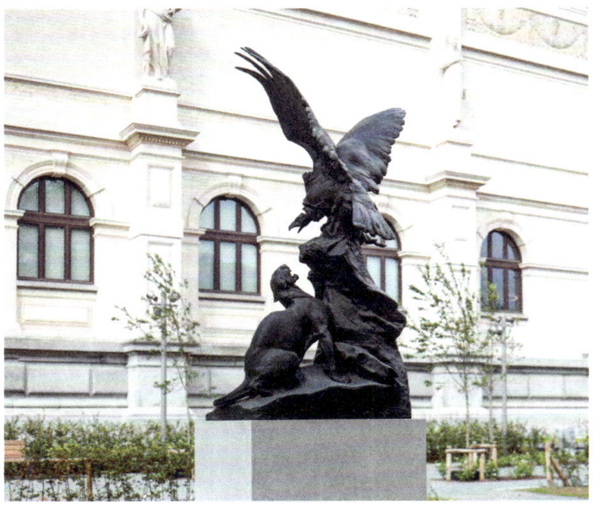

Vulture Protecting Its Prey, by Josuë Dupon, regains its place in the garden. The installation of the sculptures turns the garden into the first museum gallery.

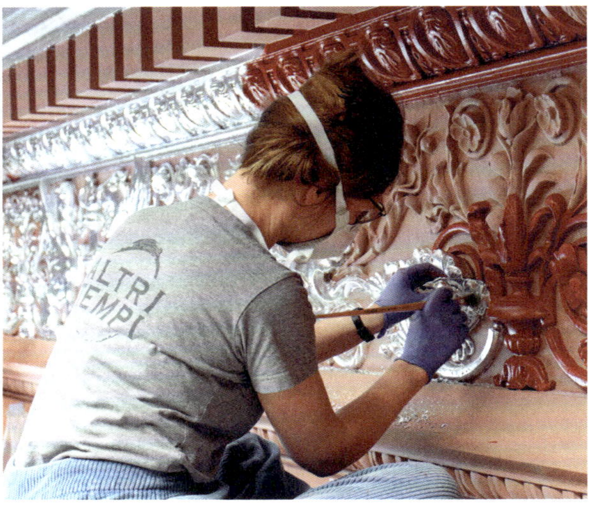

The honorary rooms of Rubens, Jordaens and Van Dyck are given back their gilded ornamental frames.

2021

The first museum gallery
The reconstruction of the museum garden started in March 2021. Team van Meer! looked to the historic garden designs from the late 19th century for inspiration. This led to an open design with a succession of parterre gardens providing pleasant spaces to socialise. Outdoor sculptures transformed the garden into the museum's 'first gallery'.

The honorary galleries of Rubens, Jordaens and Van Dyck were restored to their original lush richness. The decorative mouldings were gilded with a combination of aluminium foil and varnish with gold pigment.

On 17 June, the KMSKA and KAAN Architecten jointly won the European Award for Architectural Heritage – Intervention in the Built Heritage, for the renovation of the museum.

On 25 September, the museum announced the reopening of the new KMSKA: Saturday 24 September, 2022!

2022

The finishing touches
The last of the minor projects are being completed: the renovation of the office wing, the new roof for the De Keyserzaal, the installation of the loading platform for the delivery of large works of art. The final steps are to rehouse the artworks and the presentation of the collection in a scenography designed by Robbrecht en Daem architects & Aslı Çıçek, with multimedia productions by MoCHI and interventions by visual artist Christophe Coppens.

Saturday 24 September 2022. The Finest Moment has arrived. After all these years, the festive reopening of the KMSKA is about to happen. New visitors and familiar visitors, art lovers and other curious spirits are welcomed in to (re)discover the new KMSKA.

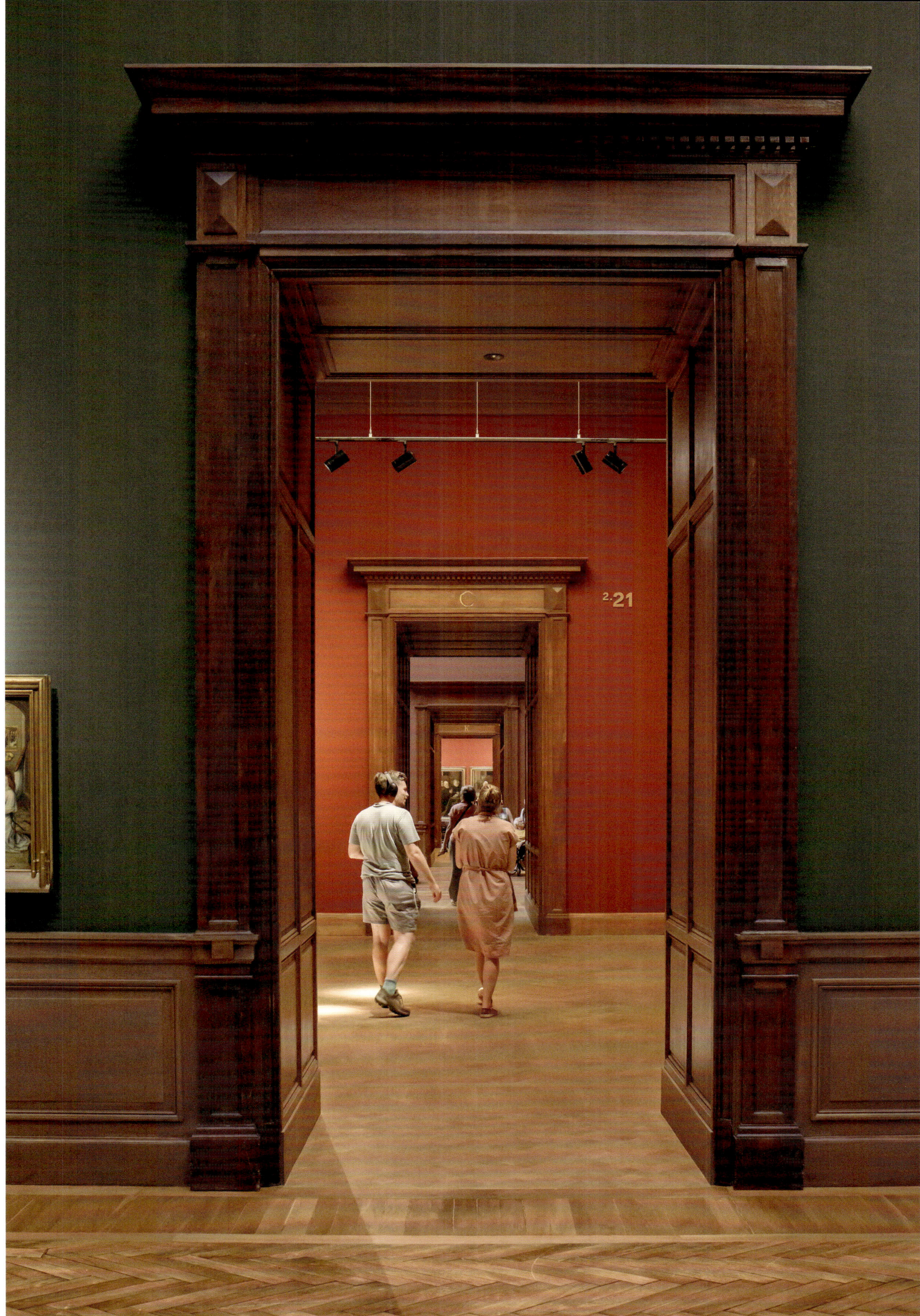
C
2·21

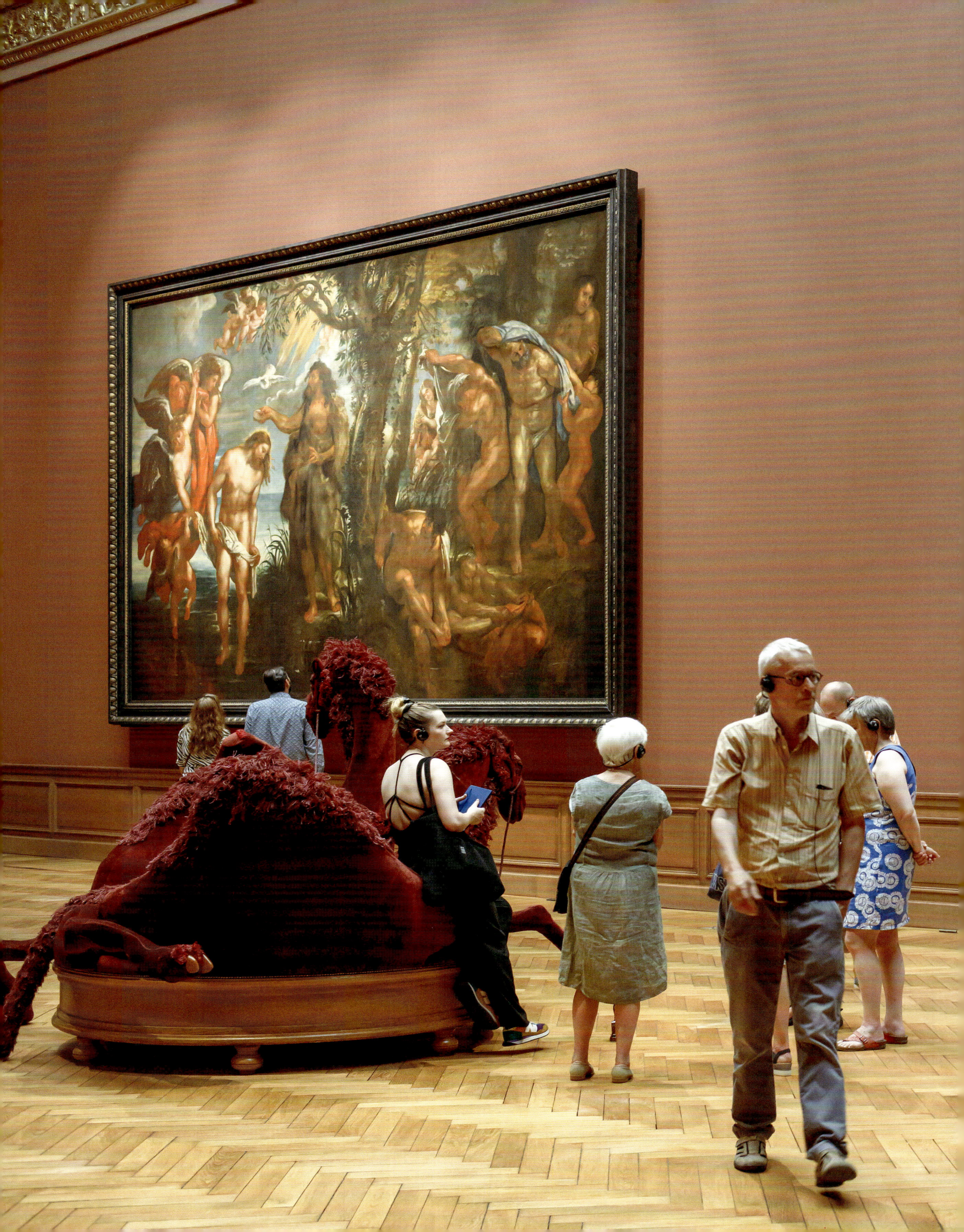

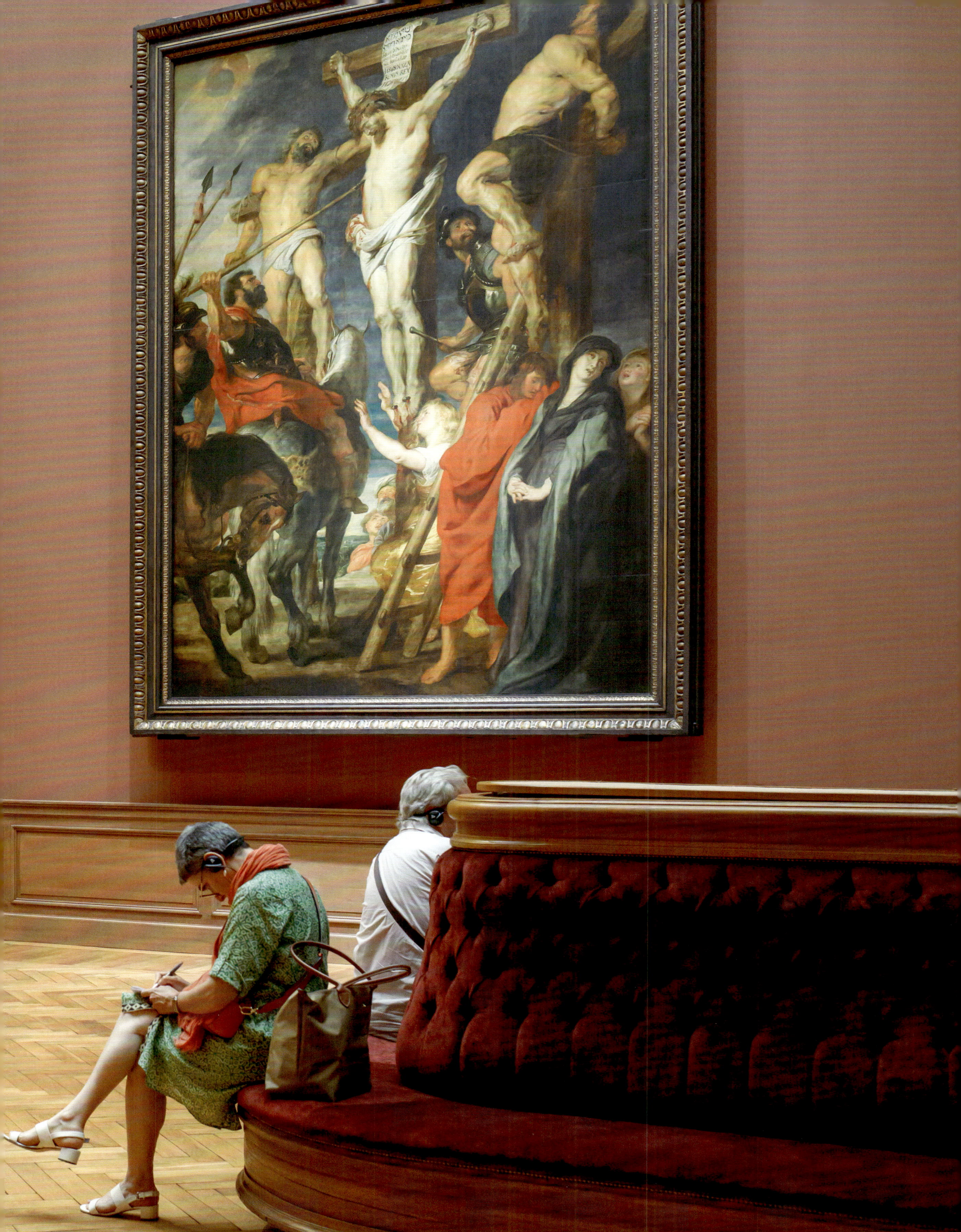

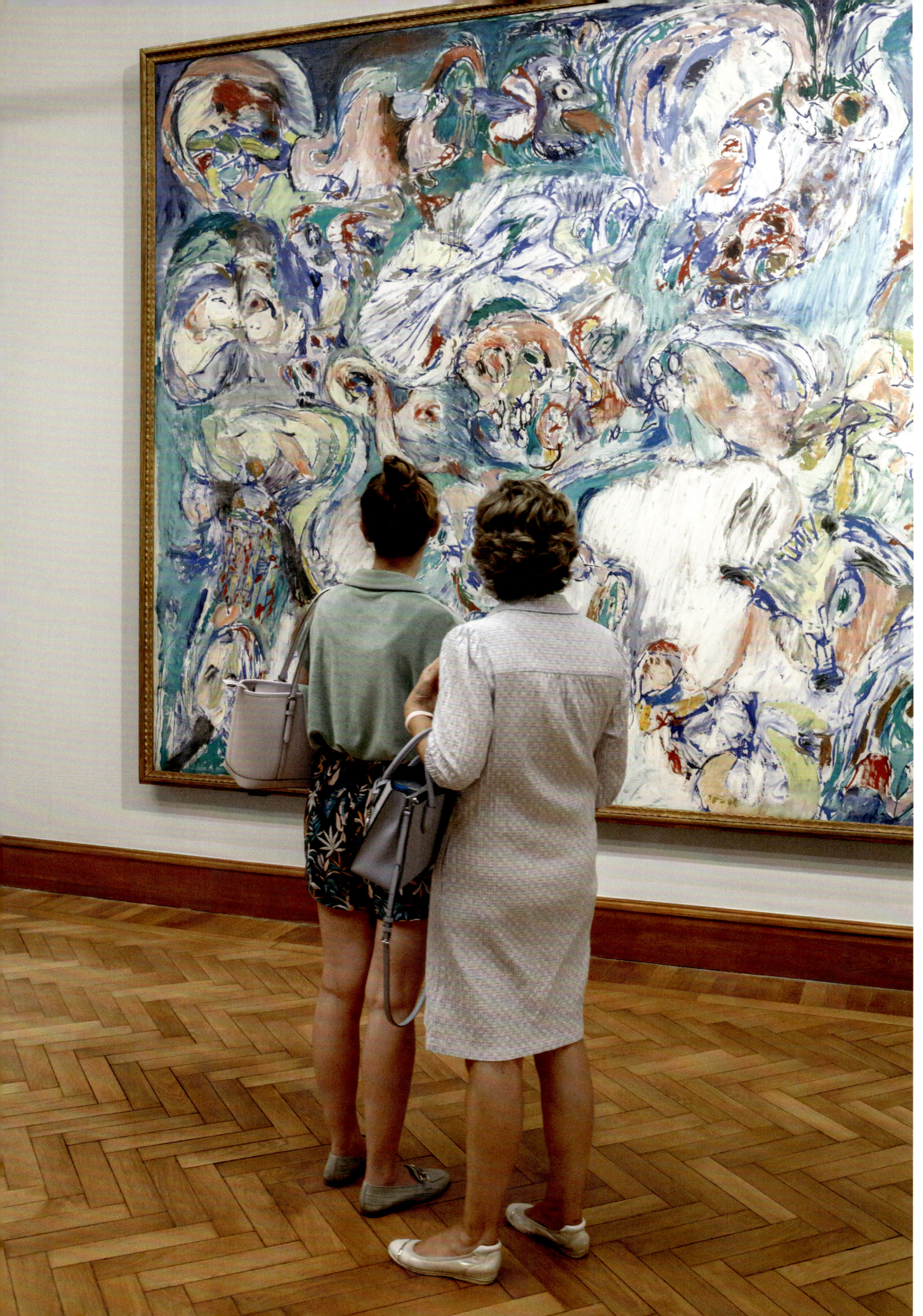

Alejandro Vergara
Prado, Madrid

"On one occasion, when trying to secure a commission, Rubens wrote the following: 'I confess that I am, by natural instinct, better suited to executing very large works than small curiosities... My talent is such that no undertaking, however vast in size or diversified in subject, has ever surpassed my courage.' It is not hyperbole to say that no museum space demonstrates the grand ambition of Rubens' art as well as the monumental Rubens Gallery at the KMSKA."

Ralph Gleis
Alte Nationalgalerie, Berlin

"I have been following the fortunes of the KMSKA with the greatest interest for a very long time. As a research fellow in 2007, I was able to see for myself the outstanding collection, the inspiring building and the wonderful team. Most recently, the Royal Museum was an important and reliable partner for *Decadence and Dark Dreams*, our exhibition on Belgian Symbolism. I wish the institution and its team a successful start in its fantastic new building, and am sure it will continue to occupy the high rank that it deserves in both Belgium and Europe."

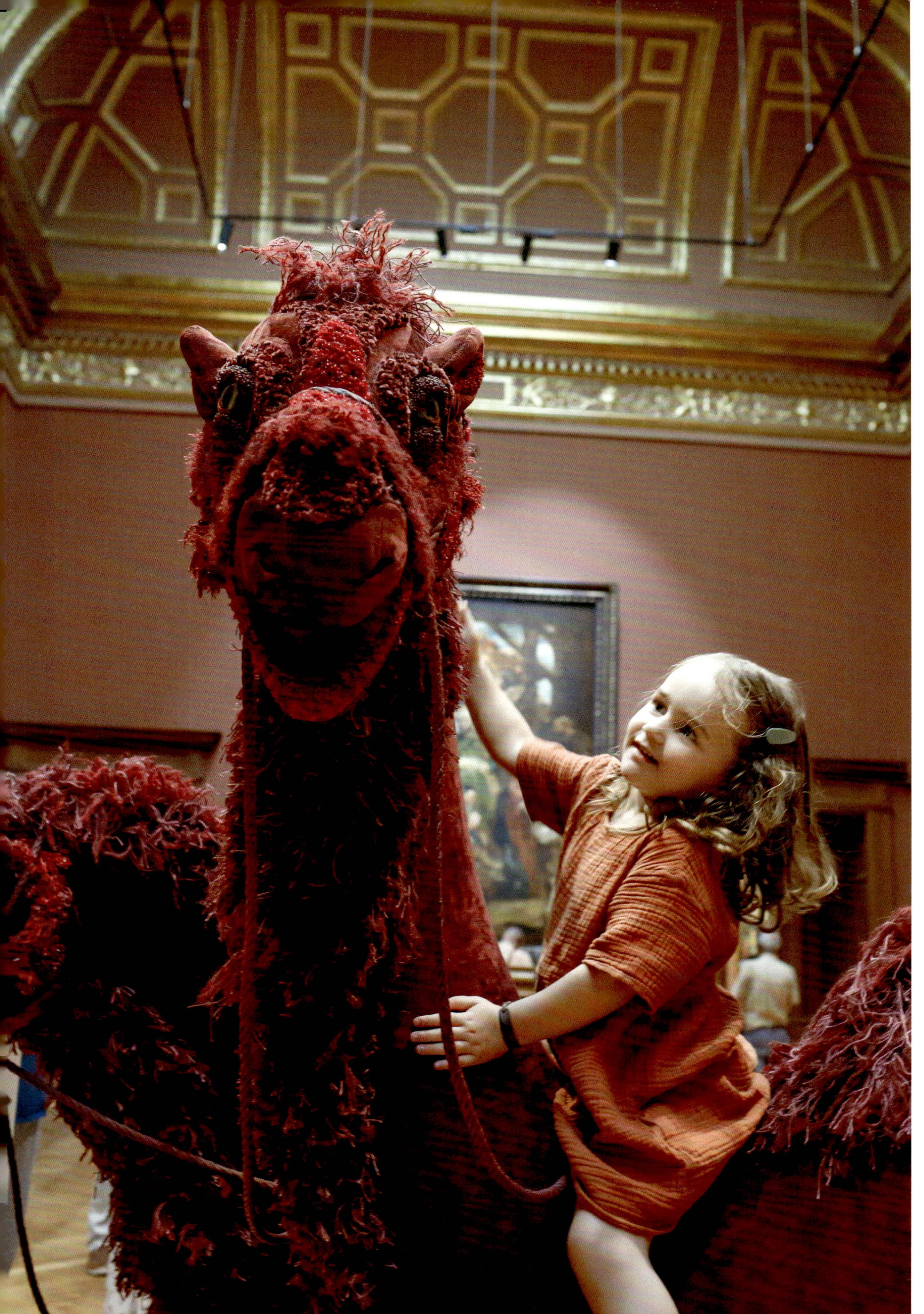

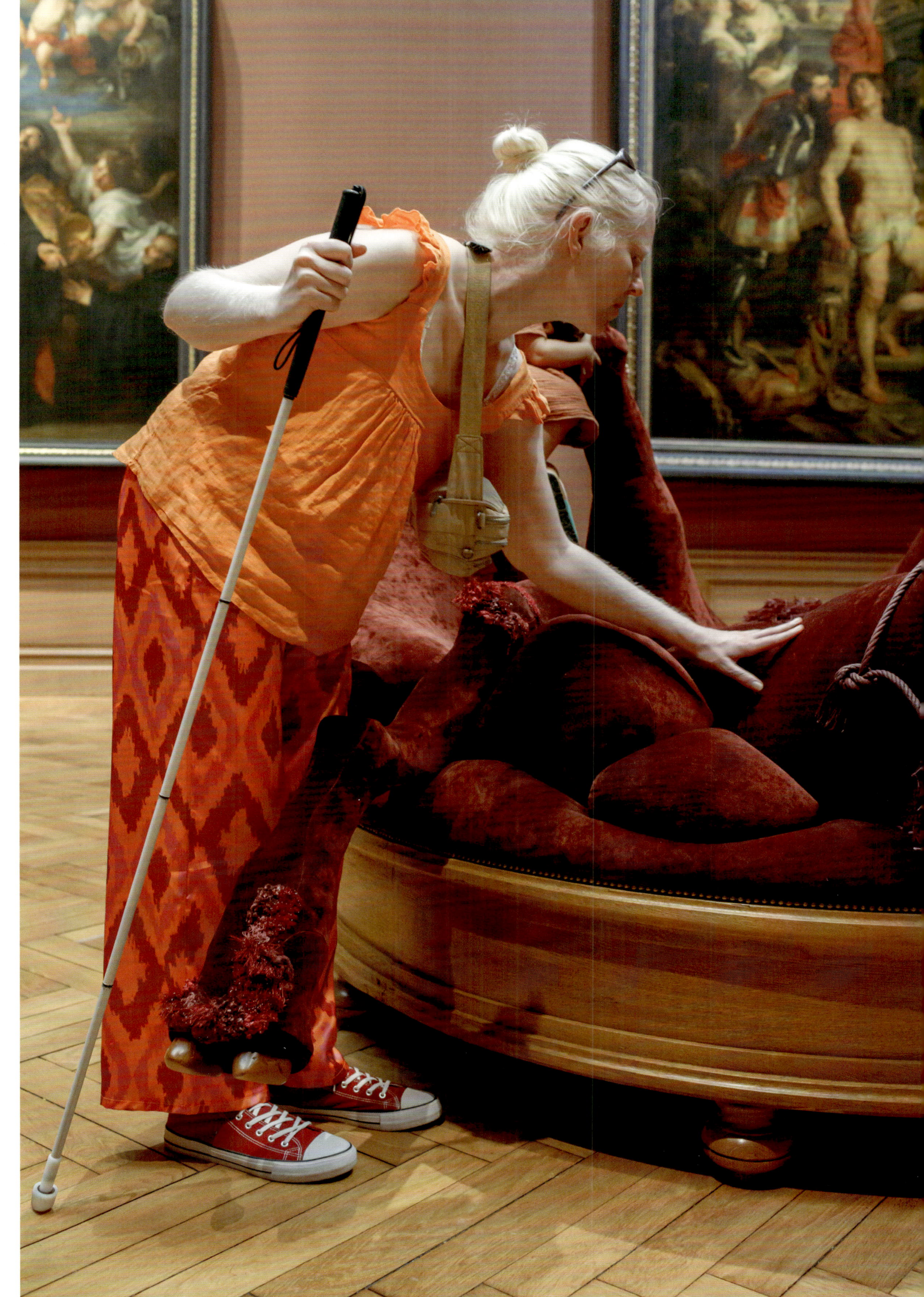

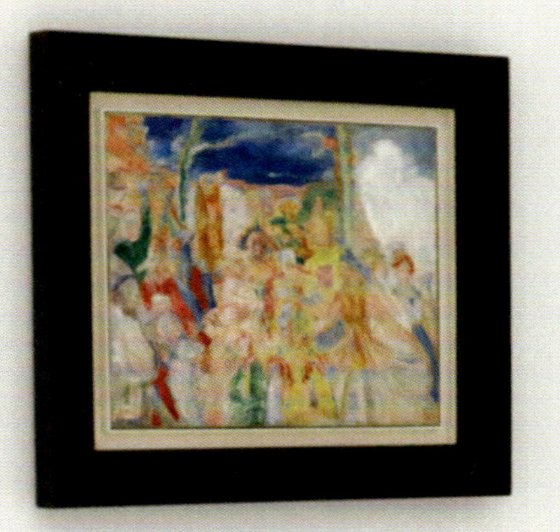

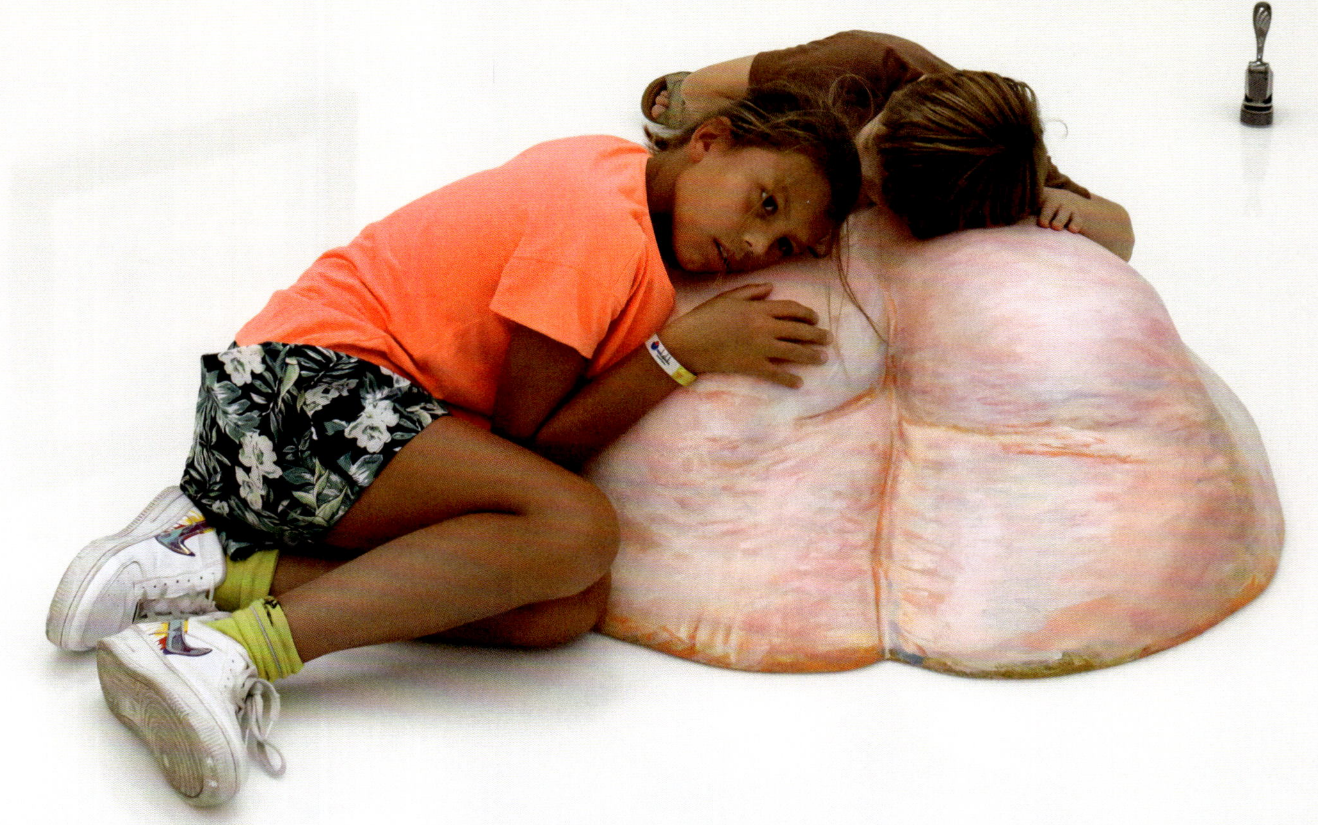

Jenny Reynaerts
Rijksmuseum, Amsterdam

"Some works of art travel with you throughout your life. As a young student, Memling's angels and Ingres' self-portrait made an indelible impression on me. And now that I can see them again after a long time, they are even dearer to me. In the reborn KMSKA, I rediscover not only them, but also a part of myself."

Gerlinde Gruber
Kunsthistorisches Museum, Vienna

"Rubens' *Venus Frigida* – the goddess of love with the most beautiful face is defenceless against hunger and cold. This is one of the most touching depictions of Venus that Rubens ever painted."

Bart De Baere
M HKA, Antwerp

"The centre of Antwerp is, for me, the central point in the composition of Rubens' *The Adoration of the Magi* in the KMSKA – the green-velvet belly of the black king. The KMSKA is the Borobudur of Flanders, our most important museum for the visual arts that are our world heritage."

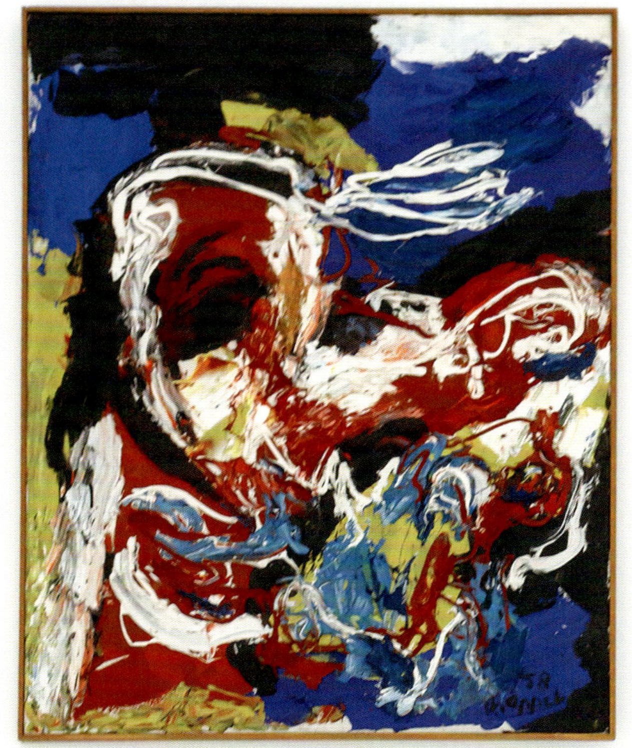
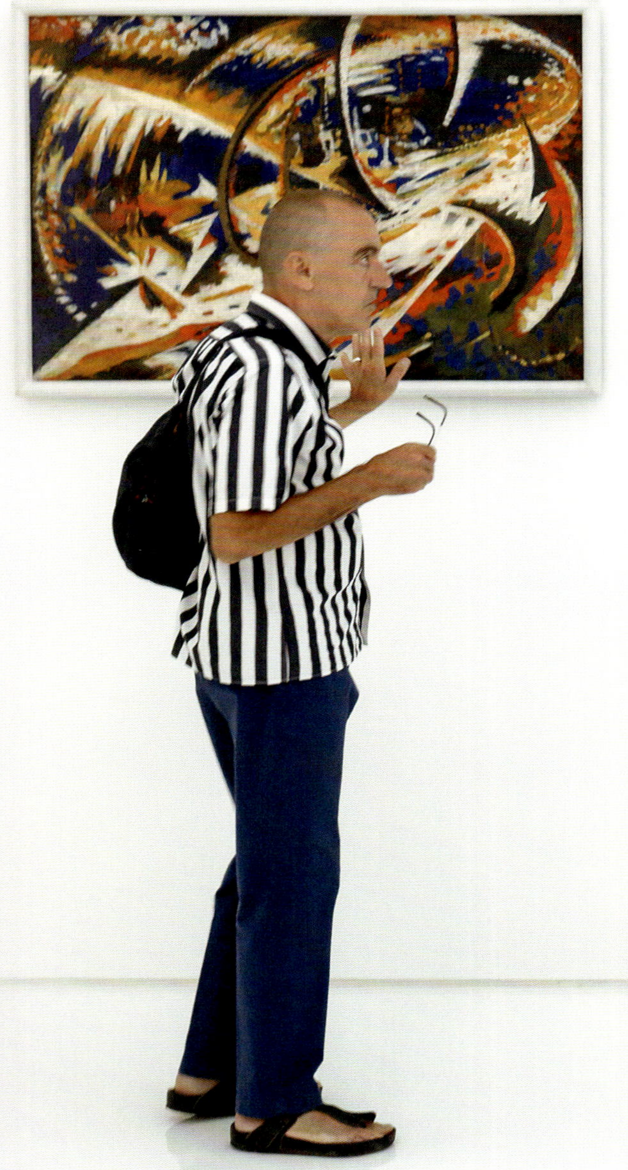
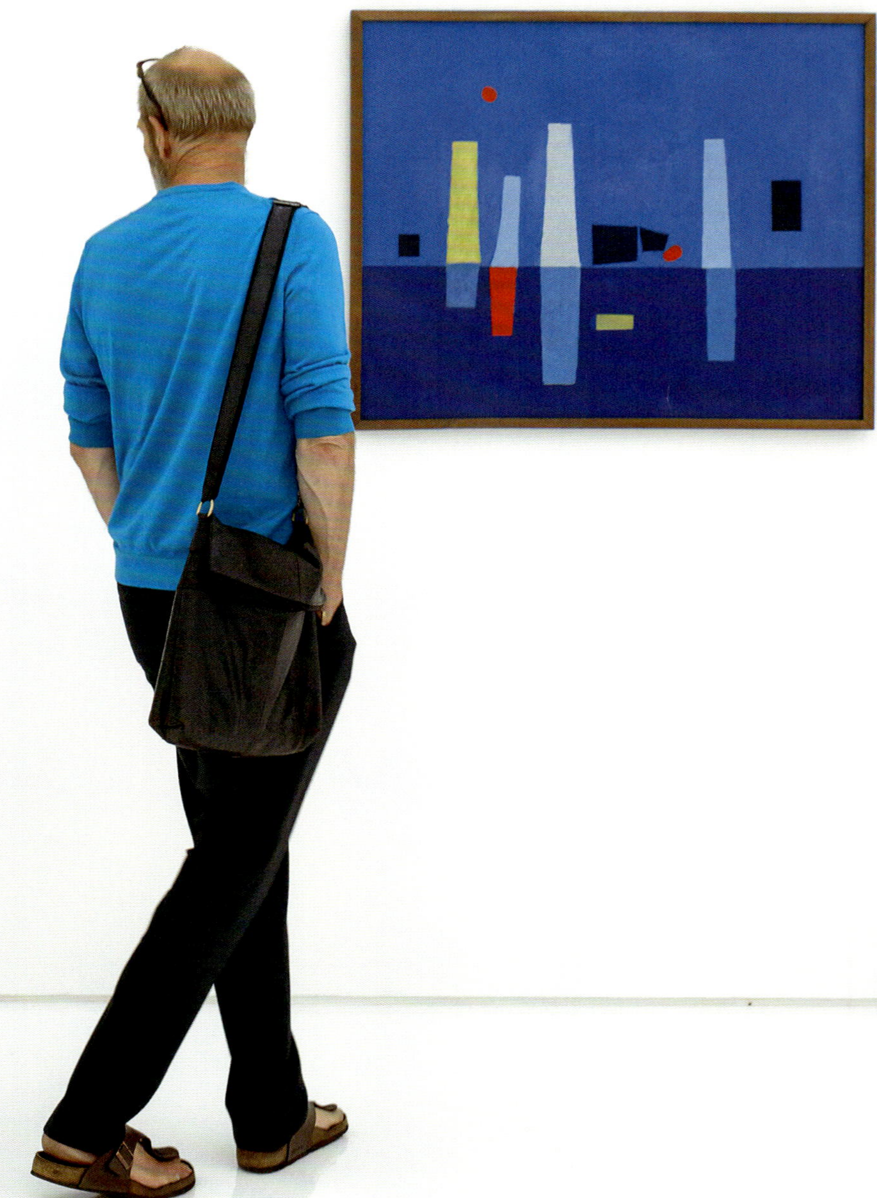

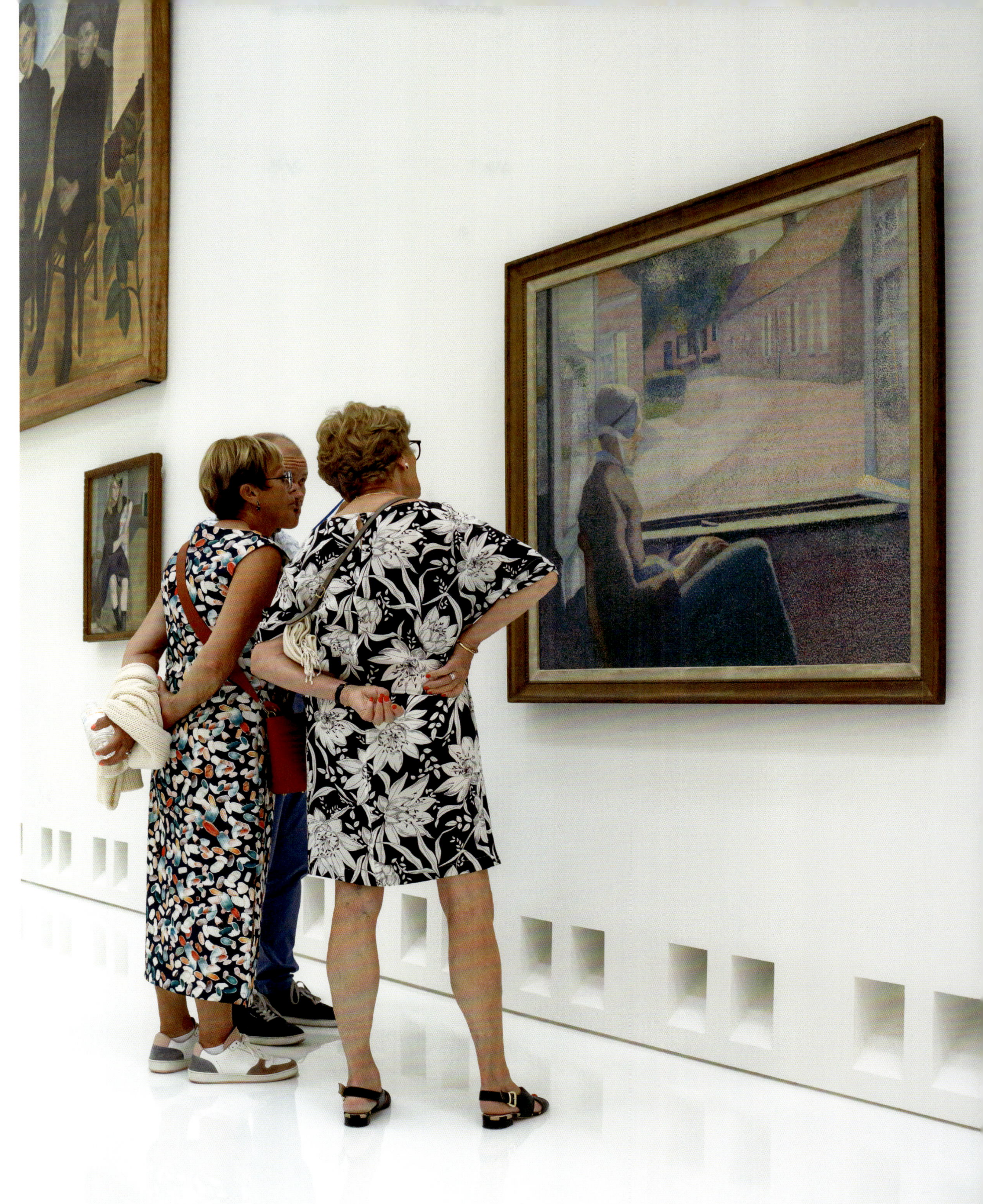

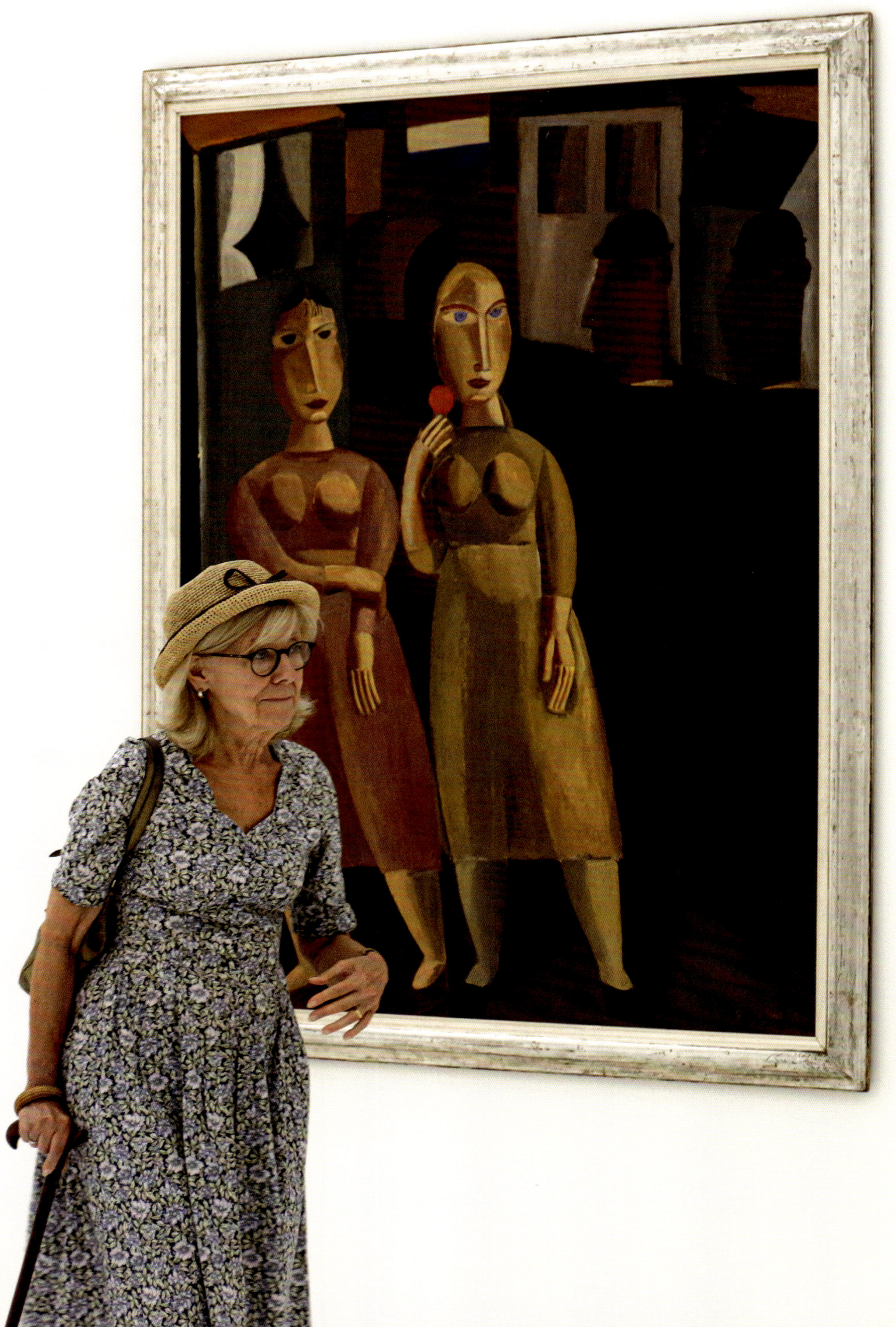

Doede Hardeman
Kunstmuseum, The Hague

"The beating heart of every museum is its collection. Along with the museum building, it determines the character and identity of the institution. It's the core elements that determine the quality of this wonderful collection. Where else in the world can you experience Rubens and Ensor, in all their variety, as beautifully as in Antwerp? The ensembles of international grand masters make the KMSKA a key link in the chain of European museums. My personal favourite: Rik Wouters! For me, the KMSKA is the museological pride of Belgium."

Véronique Carpiaux
Musée Félicien Rops, Namur

"'The artists of Antwerp have been most kind to me,' wrote Félicien Rops in 1894, after a visit to the beautiful city of Antwerp. Now, 150 years later, the paintings of the masters who had so warmly welcomed the Symbolist artist have appeared in our museum in Namur: Henri De Braekeleer, James Ensor, Rik Wouters, Virginie Breton and so on. It's with great joy that we're witnessing the reopening of the KMSKA, whose collection is one of the most exceptional in Belgium. We hope that the collaborations between our two institutions will continue to flourish and strengthen. We wish the KMSKA team every success!"

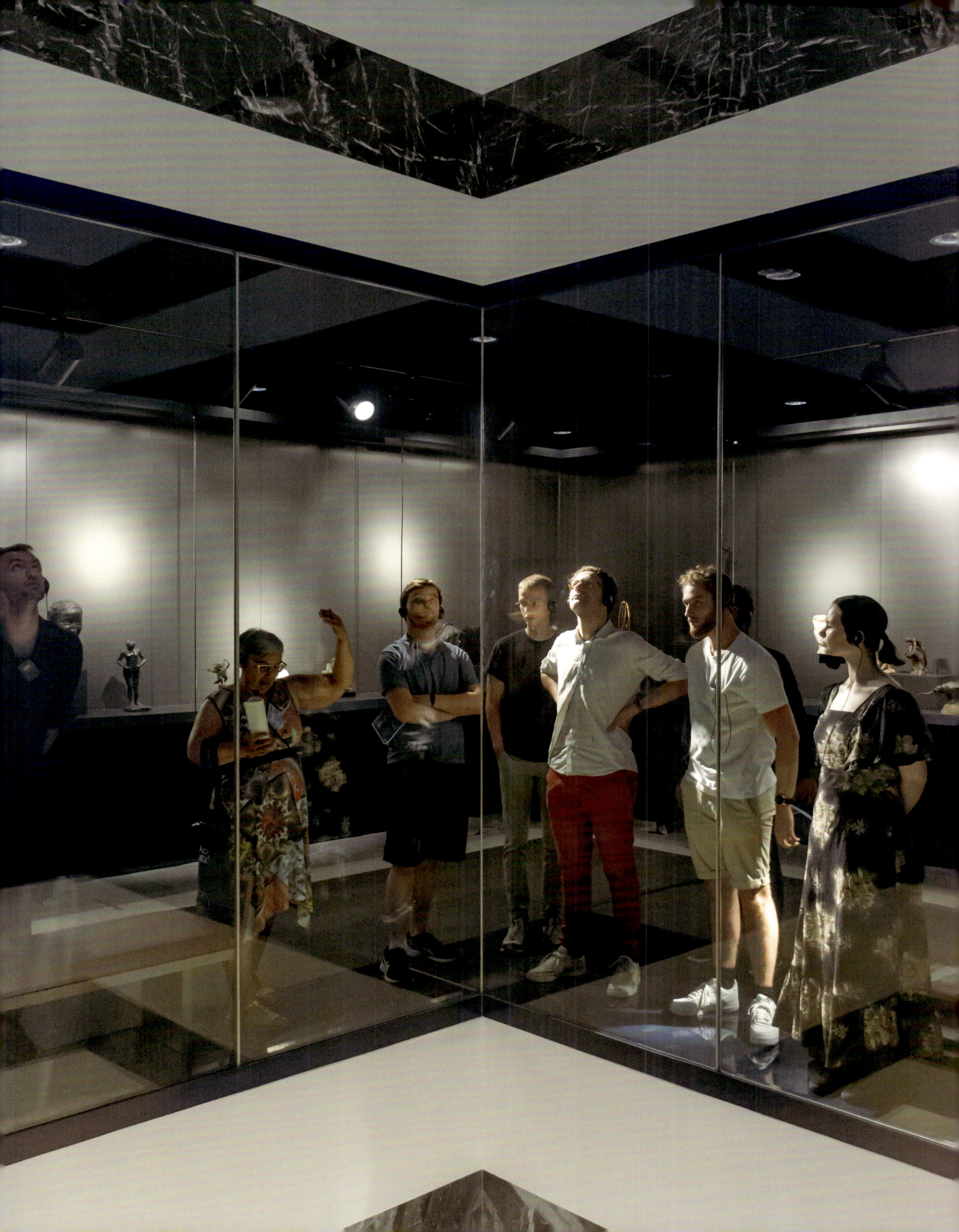

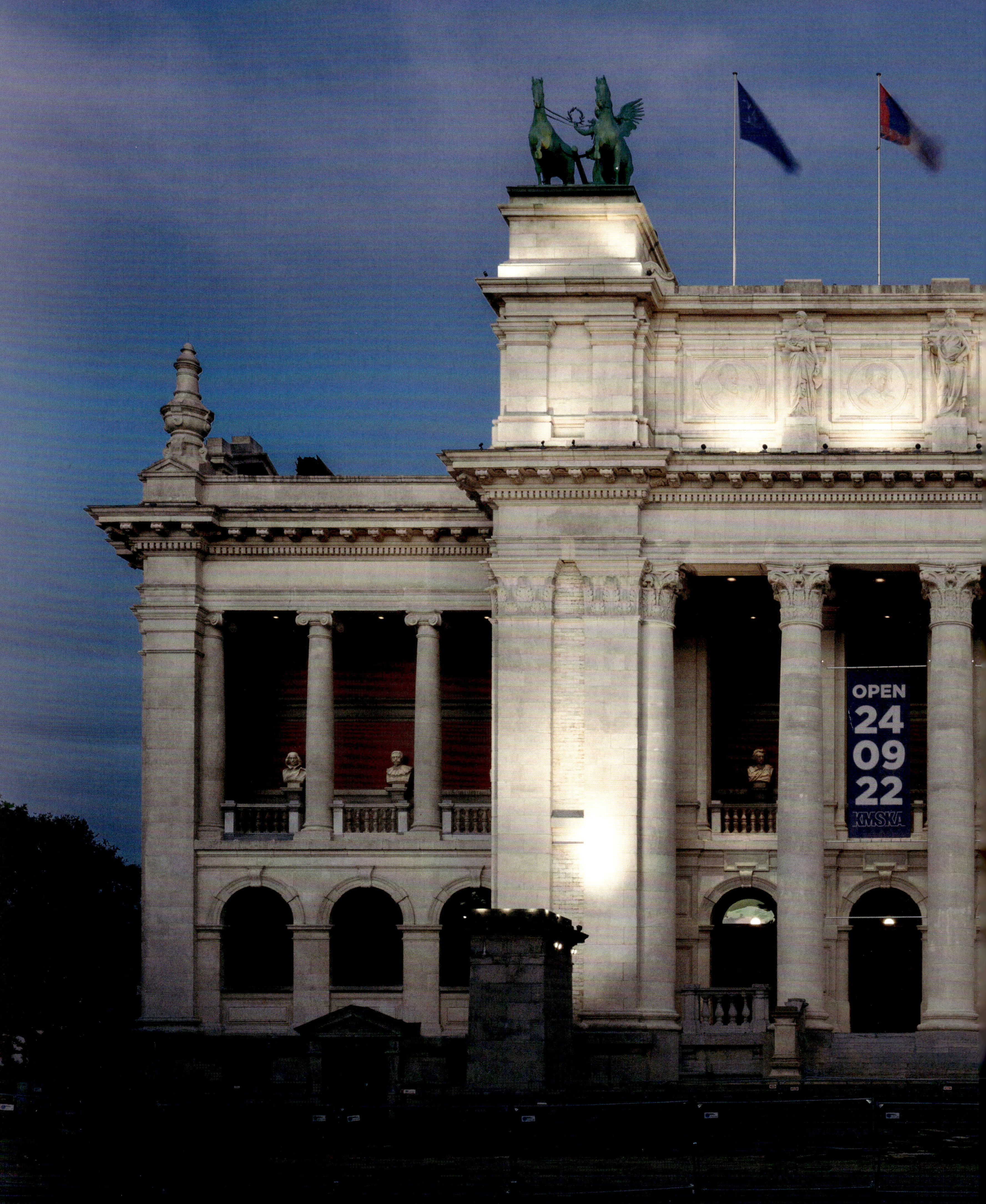
OPEN
24
09
22
KMSKA

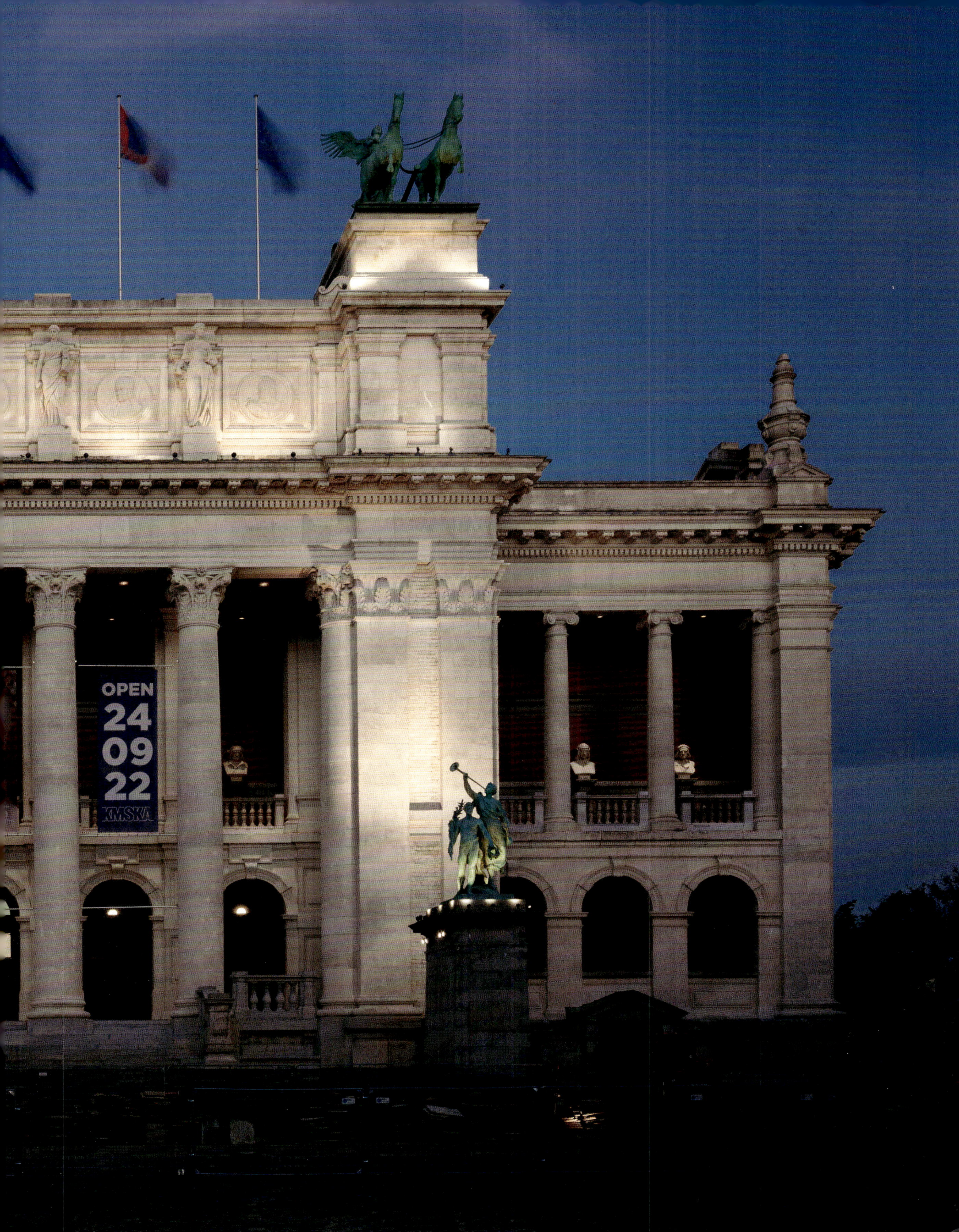
OPEN
24
09
22
KMSKA

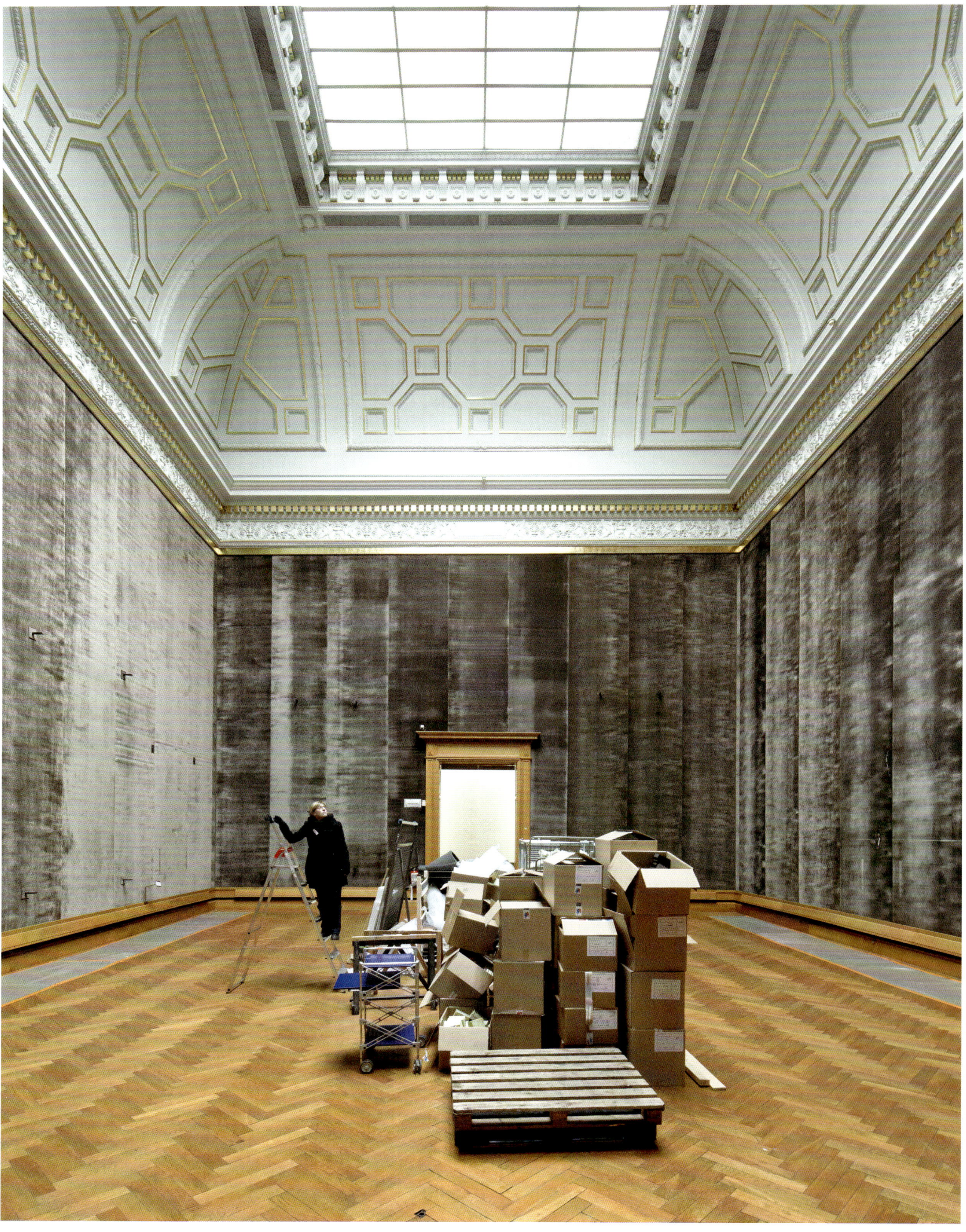

Karin Borghouts: "A photograph always serves as a record"

Karin Borghouts is the KMSKA construction site photographer. From start to finish, beginning in 2011 and ending in 2022, she has recorded the progress of the reconstruction, renovation and refurbishment works. She has registered the museum galleries at their most pure.

"In 2011, I was already deep into museum photography. I'd been allowed to take photos in the KMSKA once before, in between exhibitions. That was during my project *Interludium*, for which I was photographing art exhibitions in the process of being dismantled or assembled, all over Belgium. This is an expression of my affinity with spaces, interiors and buildings."

"It's always been a dream of mine to be able to photograph a majestic building such as the KMSKA. In a renovation on this scale you get to really experience the building itself and you can photograph things you'd never be able to in normal circumstances. Taking photographs here was a sometimes intensely physical experience."

"I generally don't photograph people, but now and then you can see a few people at work in these photos, because the images are also intended as records of the work being done. You can experience the scale of the building through the people too: the museum is phenomenally large, which really adds to the fascination."

"I take pictures with a painter's eye. Painting is also what I studied. Some situations remind me of paintings or other works of art: for example, a photo in one of the museum galleries with the wrapped Rubens panels looks a lot like an installation by Christo. I also have an eye for complementary colours: halls at the KMSKA that were painted red and green immediately caught my attention. Colours are so important to me, I could never be a black and white photographer."

Karin Borghouts (b. Kapellen, 1959) lives and works in Kalmthout. She studied painting and sculpture, worked as a graphic designer and later became a photographer. Her work can be found in the collections of the photography museums in Antwerp and Charleroi, the MAS, the STAM and in the art collections of the University of Antwerp, Delen Private Bank and Proximus. Her recent photography books are: 'Vincent was here' *(Ronny Van de Velde),* 'Paris Impasse' *(Snoeck Publishers),* 'The House' *(Snoeck Publishers).* 'A Painter's House' *(Snoeck Publishers) depicts the house of painter Marten Melsen (1870–1947).*

ACKNOWLEDGEMENTS

The texts in this book are composed to produce a mosaic of the various facets of the new KMSKA and its operations. It offers the reader an overview in word and image of everything undertaken in the renovation of and preparations for the new museum. The people involved in each element, and relevant experts, were invited to contribute their views. Here, we list the authors, staff members and other contributors. Patrick De Rynck edited the book from start to finish and any texts not included in the list below were written by him. The editor thanks Véronique Van Passel and Siska Beele for their invaluable support.

AN ENTERPRISING MUSEUM

Based on a conversation with Director Carmen Willems, spring 2022

1. A MASTERLY MASTERPLAN

Based on conversations with and texts by Dikkie Scipio, Nathalie Pauwels and Leen de Jong. Parts appeared previously in the KMSKA magazine *ZAAL Z*

FIRST-CLASS CRAFTSMANSHIP, DEVILISHLY HARD

Based on input from Thomas Musters and Tom Meirte van Artes

A EUROPEAN PRIZE

See eu-architecturalheritage.org

2. RECOVERED GRANDEUR: THE RENOVATION OF THE HISTORIC MUSEUM

The main text is based on a tour of the historic museum with Collection Researcher and Curator 19th Century Siska Beele, also curator of the *The Making Of* exhibition running from 24 September 2022 to 3 September 2023

RIP: THE BOMBPROOF CELLAR AND NUCLEAR VAULT

Based in part on: Wenke Mast, "Hoe krijg je een gewapende atoomkluis klein?", in: *ZAAL Z*, 2012, no. 2, pp. 39-42

NOT ALL THAT GLITTERS IS GOLD: THE GILDED DECORATION

Based on a text by Nathalie Pauwels and Maarten Bockstaele

3. THE GROWTH OF THE COLLECTION

GENEROUS BENEFACTORS

This text is based on the book *1818-2018. Schenkingen aan het Koninklijk Museum voor Schone Kunsten Antwerpen* by Leen de Jong with Nanny Schrijvers and Ulrike Müller, Lannoo, 2020

THE WONDROUS LIFE STORIES OF FIVE KMSKA ARTWORKS

Based on information from Collection Researchers and Curators of the KMSKA

PETER PAUL RUBENS IN DEPTH
Written by Head of Collection Research team Nico Van Hout

JAMES ENSOR: RESEARCH DOWN TO THE BONE
Based on a conversation between Eric Rinckhout, Herwig Todts and Annelies Rios-Casier

PAPER AND DIGITAL FOUNDATIONS: THE LIBRARY
Based on input from Ingrid De Pourcq

4. INTENSIVE CARE: THE CONSERVATION STUDIO

Based on the article “Het restauratieatelier als mini-universiteit” by Nathalie Pauwels, in: *ZAAL Z*, 2021–2022, no. 39, pp. 36–41

THE ART OF FRAMING
Based on: Siska Beele, “De kunst van het inlijsten”, in: *ZAAL Z*, 2021–2022, no. 39, pp. 30–35

5. THE INVISIBLE BASELINE: THE LIGHT AND CLIMATE OF THE MUSEUM

The main text is based on: Veerle De Meester, “Ingenieurs van klimaat en licht”, in: *ZAAL Z*, 2021–2022, no. 39, pp. 18–23

TRAVELLING GIANTS
Based on information supplied by the KMSKA

6. WHAT DO YOU SHOW, AND HOW? PRESENTATION AND SCENOGRAPHY

DYNAMIC AND DIVERSE: THE COLLECTION ON DISPLAY
Based on: Eric Rinckhout, “De collectie in het nieuw”, in: *ZAAL Z*, 2022, no. 40, pp. 37–45

ONE BIG FAMILY: THE SCENOGRAPHY
Based on: Aslı Çiçek and Lies De Rauw, “Lof van de ambachtelijkheid”, in: *ZAAL Z*, 2022, no. 40, pp. 32–36

SUPPORTING RUBENS
Text based on a conversation with Koen Mertens of Etoile Mécanique

7. A RENOVATED OPERATION

Based on a conversation with Birgit Pluvier, Head of Marketing, in spring 2022

YOU’RE THE GUEST AT MADONNA’S
Based on talking to Lorenz Lievens

THE SHOP: AN EXPERIENCE TAILORED TO THE MUSEUM
Based on a conversation between Eric Rinckhout and Kathleen Borms

8. REMOVING ALL BARRIERS: THE KMSKA OPENS UP

Based on: Patrick De Rynck, “Iedereen welkom”, in: *ZAAL Z*, 2022, no. 41, pp. 30–36

LOOK DIFFERENTLY, SEE MORE: RADIO BART
Based on: An Van Hertum, “Radio Bart. Anders kijken en meer zien”, in: *ZAAL Z*, 2022, no. 41, pp. 17–19

PLAYFUL AND EXCITING: THE TEN OF CHRISTOPHE COPPENS
Based on: Dennis Marien and An Van Hertum, “Oefening in nederigheid en verbeelding”, in: *ZAAL Z*, 2021–2022, no. 39, pp. 12–17

NEIGHBOURS SHARING WHAT THE KMSKA MEANS TO THEM
See Siska Beele, “Zes museumburen, zes museumverhalen”, in: *ZAAL Z*, 2022, no. 41, pp. 20–25 (slightly adapted)

9. THE FINEST FAÇADE: THE EXTERIOR

Based on: Leen de Jong, “Hoe ziet het museum er straks uit?”, in: *ZAAL Z*, 2018–2019, no. 27, pp. 22–27

HORSES IN THE SKY
Based on: Siska Beele and Véronique Van Passel, “Paarden op het dak”, in: *ZAAL Z*, 2014, no. 9, pp. 52–53

ROLLING OUT THE STONE CARPET
Based on: Wenke Mast, “Schilderen met steentjes”, in: *ZAAL Z*, 2020–2021, no. 35, pp. 4–9

10. THE FIRST MUSEUM GALLERY: THE GARDEN

Based on: Nathalie Pauwels, “Tuin in dienst van het museum”, in: *ZAAL Z*, 2021, no. 38, pp. 4–9

ART IN GREEN
Text based on input from Véronique Van Passel

THE STORY OF THE MUSEUM BUILDING
Siska Beele made the timeline for the *The Making Of* exhibition

KARIN BORGHOUTS: “A PHOTOGRAPH ALWAYS SERVES AS A RECORD”
Based on various interviews with Karin Borghouts

COLOPHON

This publication is issued on the occasion of the reopening of the KMSKA in September 2022.

KMSKA CHAIRMAN
Luk Lemmens

KMSKA MANAGING DIRECTOR
Carmen Willems

COORDINATION OF THIS PUBLICATION
Véronique Van Passel

KMSKA PUBLICATION MANAGER
Frédéric Jonckheere

TEXT
Patrick De Rynck

PHOTOGRAPHY
© Karin Borghouts, 2011–2022

TRANSLATION
Elise Reynolds

COPY-EDITING
Cath Phillips

PROJECT MANAGEMENT HANNIBAL BOOKS
Sofie Meert

ART DIRECTION HANNIBAL BOOKS
Natacha Hofman

DESIGN
Tim Bisschop

IMAGE RESEARCH
Eline Wellens [KMSKA],
Madeleine ter Kuile [KMSKA],
Séverine Lacante [Hannibal Books]

IMAGE EDITING
Karin Borghouts,
Wouter Bollaerts,
Tineke Deriemaeker,
Pascal Van den Abbeele,
Madeleine ter Kuile [KMSKA]

PRINTING
die Keure, Bruges

BINDING
Boekbinderij Abbringh, Groningen
die Keure, Bruges

PUBLISHER
Gautier Platteau

HARDCOVER
ISBN 978 94 6436 667 9
D/2022/11922/47
NUR 648

SOFTCOVER
ISBN 978 94 6436 668 6
D/2022/11922/48
NUR 648

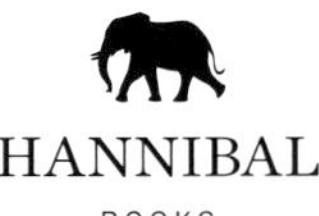

www.hannibalbooks.be
www.kmska.be

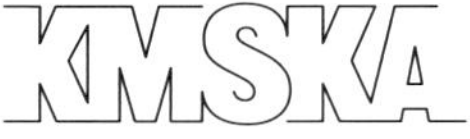

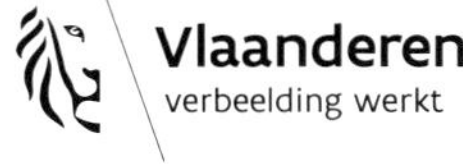

Cover image:
The renovated historical museum,
© Karin Borghouts.

Backcover image:
The winding staircase in the entrance hall,
© Karin Borghouts.

NOTE TO THE READER
All photographs in this book were taken before 5 August 2022.

PHOTO CREDITS

Archives Royal Museum of Fine Arts Antwerp (KMSKA) [pp. 33, 36, 127, 172, 200, 206, 225, 226, 227]

Wouter Bollaerts [pp. 40, 197, 212, 232 (right), 244, 247]

© Karin Borghouts [pp. 4–5, 10–11, 14–15, 16, 18, 19, 20, 21, 22, 23, 24, 25, 26, 27, 28, 29, 30, 31, 33, 37, 38–39, 41, 42–43, 44–45, 46, 47, 48, 49, 50, 51, 52–53, 54–55, 56–57, 58–59, 60, 61, 62–63, 64, 81, 82, 83, 84–85, 86–87, 88–89, 90–91, 92–93, 94–95, 96, 97, 98–99, 100, 101, 102–103, 104, 105, 106–107, 108, 109, 110–111, 112, 114, 120, 121, 123, 124–125, 126, 127, 128, 129, 130–131, 132–133, 134–135, 136, 137, 138–139, 140–141, 142, 143, 144, 145, 146, 147, 148–149, 150–151, 152, 153, 154–155, 157, 159, 160, 163, 164, 165, 166, 167, 168, 170–171, 173, 174, 175, 176, 177, 178–179, 180, 181, 183, 184, 185, 186–187, 188–189, 190–191, 192, 195, 201, 202–203, 204–205, 209, 210, 211, 213, 214–215, 216, 217, 218, 219, 220–221, 222, 223, 224, 229, 230, 231, 232, 233, 234–235, 236, 238, 239, 240, 242, 243, 245, 248–249, 250]

d/arch [p. 67]

Kristien Daem [p. 228]

Estate of George Grosz, Princeton, N.J. © SABAM Belgium 2022 [p. 77]

FelixArchief / City Archive Antwerp [pp. 34–35]

© Foundation Paul Delvaux, Sint Idesbald / SABAM Belgium 2022 [p. 115]

Rik Klein Gotink [pp. 68–69, 71, 76, 78, 79, 113, 115, 116, 117, 118, 119, 161]

© KAAN Architecten [pp. 17, 229]

Hugo Maertens [pp. 65, 66, 72–73, 74, 75, 77, 161, 163, 166]

Mu.ZEE, www.artinflanders.be, photo Kristien Daem / © SABAM Belgium 2022 [p. 162]

Dominique Provost [p. 162]

SABAM Belgium 2022 [67, 77, 116, 161, 162, 163]

Siska Vandecasteele [pp. 198–199]

© Succession René Magritte / SABAM Belgium 2022 [p. 162]

Cedric Verhelst [p. 196]

Wikimedia Commons [p. 32]